HUMAN MEMORY:
THEORY AND DATA

THE EXPERIMENTAL PSYCHOLOGY SERIES

Arthur W. Melton · Consulting Editor

HUMAN MEMORY:
THEORY AND DATA

BY BENNET B. MURDOCK, JR.
UNIVERSITY OF TORONTO

LEA **LAWRENCE ERLBAUM ASSOCIATES, PUBLISHERS**
1974 **POTOMAC, MARYLAND**

DISTRIBUTED BY THE HALSTED PRESS DIVISION OF
JOHN WILEY & SONS
New York **Toronto** **London** **Sydney**

Lawrence Erlbaum Associates, Publishers
12736 Lincolnshire Drive
Potomac, Maryland 20854

Distributed solely by Halsted Press Division
John Wiley & Sons, Inc., New York

Library of Congress Cataloging in Publication Data

Murdock, Bennet Bronson.
  Human memory: theory and data.

  (The Experimental psychology series)
  1. Memory. I. Title. II. Series.
[DNLM: 1. Memory. BF371 M974h 1974]
BF371.M77   153.1′2   74–888
ISBN 0–470–62525–2

Printed in the United States of America

CONTENTS

To my parents

PREFACE

My purpose in writing this book has been to document, consolidate, focus, and perhaps even extend the knowledge that we have gained about human memory over the past 15 years. From a rather modest beginning the field has mushroomed, and now it is growing rapidly. Perhaps the time has come to take stock and review what has been accomplished. In that way, further growth can build upon previous developments. So this book is intended for my colleagues in the field, past, present, and future.

I have attempted to survey and review the main theoretical and empirical developments in four different areas: item information, associations, serial ordering, and free recall. As it has turned out, this book is really two books in one. After an introductory chapter, the even-numbered chapters consider theory while the odd-numbered chapters consider data. Those readers who are more interested in the broad picture and the theoretical endeavors may prefer the former; the more empirically oriented readers may prefer the latter. The final chapter presents some of my own views on human memory.

To segregate theory and data is not a very satisfactory procedure. They should be thoroughly and carefully interrelated. However, we are not quite ready for that. On the one hand, none of the theories we now have explain in any depth and with great precision even an appreciable fraction of the relevant data. On the other hand, to consider data alone would be barren and uninteresting.

The first stage in the development of a science is the collection and documentation of empirical findings and relationships of reasonable reliability and generality (Wilson, 1971). We have certainly progressed that far in the study of human memory. The next stage is to construct theories and models from which the empirical relationships may be deduced. Considerable effort in this direction has been expended (e.g.,

Norman, 1970a), but no consensus is apparent. To focus the picture I have placed the theory chapters first and the data chapters second. There is not as much cross-referencing as I would like, but perhaps the reader can add some missing links.

What is there about the area of human memory that warrants a complete book devoted to this particular topic? Of course I am biased, but I think it is an interesting and significant area of research. Starting with the work of Broadbent (1958), Brown (1958), Miller (1956), and Peterson and Peterson (1959) the field of memory has taken on a new and different look. We have methods and techniques to study forgetting over short periods of time, we have many large and reliable empirical effects, and people are now beginning to theorize about and model internal information processes. What could be more important or more exciting than learning about how the human brain encodes, stores, and retrieves information?

Over the past 15 years I feel that the field of human memory really has undergone some profound changes. What they are, and what progress we have made, will be the subject matter of this book. At the end, I hope the reader will agree that a coverage this complete is warranted by our current state of knowledge.

It is a pleasure to acknowledge my many debts of gratitude. I thank Donald Broadbent and Con and Christopher Poulton for a delightful year in Cambridge; it served to broaden my outlook considerably. More recently Dick Atkinson and Gordon Bower were gracious hosts at Stanford. I owe a continuing debt of gratitude to members of the Ebbinghaus Empire here at Toronto for continued challenge, stimulation, and interaction. Elisabeth Wells has been most helpful in furthering (and correcting) my theoretical insights, and Rita Anderson has participated in some of the recent experimental work reported in the last chapter.

Gus Craik, Bob Lockhart, Endel Tulving, and Elisabeth Wells have been kind enough to read a first draft of the manuscript, and many improvements that were made are due to them. Endel Tulving has been a continuing source both of stimulation and frustration, and he has often made me see things in a different light. Finally, I owe a special debt of gratitude to a long-time mentor and friend, Art Melton. He has taken more than the usual editorial responsibility for this book. He methodically and painstakingly rewrote almost completely the first article I ever submitted to the *Journal of Experimental Psychology*. I can verify that his critical acumen has not declined over the intervening years.

BENNET B. MURDOCK, JR.

Toronto, Ontario, Canada
November, 1973

HUMAN MEMORY:
THEORY AND DATA

1
INTRODUCTION

This book deals with the study of human memory. Studies of learning and memory in lower organisms will not be included here. While the animal work is interesting and important, it deals with somewhat different issues than studies of human memory. Further, the very existence of human language seems to set the two fields apart. Perhaps when we better understand the biological basis of memory there will be a rapproachement, but at the present time the two fields seem to represent rather different areas of inquiry.

This book will also exclude much of the research on pattern recognition, speech perception, attention, understanding sentences, solving problems, forming concepts, and thinking. All these are specialized topics in their own right. Human memory is in a middle ground between the initial processing of external stimuli and the final manipulation or utilization of stored information. All three go to make up the cognitive processes, but here the emphasis is on memory.

Although the hope might be to cover all aspects of human memory, such a goal is too ambitious. As a consequence, some restriction is necessary. To restrict the scope of this book to manageable proportions, much of the emphasis will be on human short-term memory. By short-term memory I mean the memory system that people use when they encode, store, and retrieve information over brief periods of time. Whether or how it differs from long-term memory is a moot point. In my view, we simply do not know. The human memory system, considered in toto, seems incredibly complex. One has only to introspect and examine one's own capabilities to see what feats memory can perform. A few bars of music may be sufficient to identify a particular composition, its composer, or perhaps even the performing artist. We can watch an athlete in action and compare his performance with previous situations. A chance encounter with an old acquaintance that we have not seen for years still may lead to almost instant recognition and identification. Many other examples could be given, but the point is clear; human memory in everyday situations is so complex that any real understanding seems a goal beyond our present reach.

However, short-term memory is simpler and perhaps not so formidable. At least we can reduce the problem to manageable proportions. By the standard divide-and-conquer strategy of scientific investigation we can isolate systems and processes and bring them into the laboratory for experimental investigation. The risks are well known, but so are the alternatives. Studies of short-term memory are basically our first steps in tackling the problem of human memory. It would be wrong to claim that we have yet progressed very far, but at least we have made a beginning. Also, a further justification for the emphasis on short-term memory is that much of the recent research has centered on this topic.

ORGANIZATION

One way of organizing a book such as this is in terms of a temporal partitioning of memory. One starts with sensory stores, goes to short-term stores, then ends with long-term memory. These sections may be preceded by sections on pattern recognition and attention, or they may be followed by sections on learning and transfer. This general pattern has been followed by Broadbent (1971), Cermak (1972), Howe (1970), Kintsch (1970b), Neisser (1967), and Norman (1969a). That organization will not be followed here, for two reasons.

The first reason is that, singly and collectively, these books have said what there is to say. They have provided a new orientation and perspective on human memory, and they have done a fine job indeed. If one doubts that there have been any advances in the field, all one has to do is to compare these books with those available 15 years ago. The contrast is striking. While one could write a similar book, it seems unlikely that the result would be a sufficient advance to justify the effort.

The second reason is perhaps more important. I think that it is time to re-orient our thinking. I would like to suggest that memory is not divided into separate sensory, short-term, and long-term stores. Instead, it is continuous. We have memories of brief duration, memories that last a bit longer, and memories that are essentially permanent. One shades into another gradually, not abruptly.

Since a different organization will be used here, a brief introduction might be useful. There are three main types of information that, to date, have been identified as important in human memory. They are *item information, associative information,* and *serial-order information.* Item information enables us to remember objects and events, to recognize names, faces, pictures, musical compositions, tastes, smells, and much else that we encounter in our everyday life. Associative information, or associations, relate two things: names and faces, for instance, or words and meaning, or composers and compositions. Serial-order information refers to the memory for sequences of events or strings of items: the letters of the alphabet, the days of the week, or the spelling of words.

The basic question to consider is how this information is represented in memory— or, what is stored, how it changes over time, and how it is used at the time of test. That is, the basic questions pertain to the encoding, storage, and retrieval of these types of information. The position taken in this book is that these different types of information exist and that, at least for the time being, we should consider them separately. The answers to the encoding, storage, and retrieval questions may differ for item, associative, and serial-order information.

These topics comprise three of the four parts of the book. The fourth and final topic is free recall. Here the question is how do we recall objects or events when asked to name as many as we can. Everyday examples might be to name the countries of Western Europe, the teams of the Eastern Division of the National Hockey League, or all the major cities of the United States that you have visited. In experimental studies of free recall the subject is presented with a list of items to recall, and we want to know how the task is performed. It is not yet certain whether free recall is mediated by item information, associative information, or serial-order information.

In addition to characterizing separate types of information, this classification also provides a useful taxonomy for experimental paradigms in the field. We have recognition-memory procedures, paired-associate tasks, serial-order techniques, and single- and multitrial free recall. It is no accident; these various techniques have been developed to study these various processes. But it should be made clear that I am more interested in processes than paradigms. I feel this outline helps clarify human memory because it specifies the various processes involved; the fact that there are associated paradigms and procedures is simply an added benefit.

At the risk of being repetitive, let me say again that this book was not organized this way in order to take a paradigmatic approach. Human memory contains different kinds of information, and the main topics were selected to highlight this fact. I think that item, associative, and serial-order information is a reasonable classification for memorial information, and the main sections of the book will describe the theoretical and empirical knowledge we have gained about each.

It has recently come to my attention that conceptualizations of human memory from other disciplines make much the same distinctions. I have in mind the theoretical models of artificial intelligence which find it necessary to distinguish between knowledge of objects and events, relationships between them, and relations on relationships. This is true, for instance, of SIR, the semantic information retrieval program of Raphael (1968), of STUDENT, a set of computer programs designed by Bobrow (1968) to solve problems in algebra, and of the programming system Winograd (1971) designed to understand natural language. Their classification is directly comparable to what is here called item information, associative information, and serial-order information, though in each case the latter is a subset of the former. That is, I shall be considering primarily temporally-mediated associations, which is only one of many possible kinds of relationship; so too with serial-order effects. The interpretation of serial order effects may not become clear until Chapter 10.

The fact that such distinctions are represented in these computer programs does not, of course, prove that similar distinctions are valid for human memory. However, it does suggest that an analytic separation of this sort is logically useful and gives one confidence that one has made the right selection. Also, it emphasizes that there is no incompatibility between basic research on memory by psychologists and the broader aspects of human memory as studied by those interested in artificial intelligence. Psychologists are generally more interested in how the human memory system does work, while those interested in artificial intelligence are computer specialists who are developing and elaborating their ideas within the framework of computer programs.

The topics in this book are ordered from simple to complex. Item information is most basic, and it comes before associative information or serial ordering. We can recognize a particular individual as familiar but we do not remember his name. Associative information precedes serial ordering because associations involve a pairwise contingency, while seriation involves more than two. Free recall comes last because it provides a test of how adequately we understand simpler processes. Free recall is important because it provides a number of intriguing and challenging puzzles, but it is probably not a very analytic procedure for studying simpler processes.

As the development in this book proceeds from simple to complex, so too in the human organism. More complex processes may be built upon or subsume simpler ones. Thus, it is clear that utilization of associative information has as a prerequisite retrieval of item information; one must recognize the question before one can give an answer. Serial ordering can develop out of pairwise associations, though a simple chaining or linking of associations now seems unlikely. As we move from one level to another, the problems and issues existing at the simpler level may be ignored. I do this for ease of exposition, but there is a risk involved. We may be misled by overlooking certain factors or entertaining wrong assumptions. However, that is always the case so one can only note the danger, not escape it.

Within each topic a theory chapter precedes a data chapter. The reason for this order is as follows. The theory chapter states the issues and gives an overview. Then it reviews the various theoretical positions that have been taken. The data chapters review the evidence. Some of my colleagues might suggest that the purpose of theories is to explain the data, so that the ordering should be the other way around. I would disagree. It seems to me that it is the job of the theories to explain how human memory works, and that is of paramount importance. The data test the theories, but data need to be fitted into a theoretical framework if they are to have any lasting significance.

The coverage in each chapter will be selective. In the theory chapters, I have selected those theories and models that have seemed most promising. Some are better than others, of course, but each makes some contribution. For the data chapters, I have considered about seven main topics. They are related to the theories but not as directly as I would have liked. Generally, however, they are topics of some current interest and are under active investigation at present. In these selections, I have undoubtedly made errors of both types (omission and commission), but I hope not too many.

BIASES

Since my presentation may be partisan, it seems only fair to expose what biases underlie the selection of material for this book. One such bias is the restriction to replicable phenomena. No attempt will be made to explain anecdotal evidence. Questions such as how I am able to remember that the people who lived next to us in Missouri ten years ago were named Wilson, or why I can't remember the date of my parents' anniversary, are quite beyond the scope of this book. At the risk of sounding pompous, we extend our knowledge by the use of the scientific method, and unique events are beyond its pale. We should restrict our attention to events which are reliable and reproducible.

There will not be any consideration of the unusual or the exotic. I shall not consider the mnemonist, eidetikers, memory under hyponosis, repression, or the like. These topics are, of course, in a different category from anecdotes in that, at least in principle, they are quite capable of being studied in a rigorous and objective fashion. At the very least, one can always generalize to other situations with the same subject. The reason for these exclusions is quite simple. It is difficult enough understanding the memory of normal college students; it will be time to consider the abnormal cases after we can cope with the normal cases.

Where possible, simple explanations will be preferred to complex ones. Human memory is complex enough so that there is no need to make it more so. The value of a good theory is that it makes things easier to understand, not more difficult. After all, if one can adequately comprehend and encompass a given empirical phenomenon then there is no need for a theory or model, since the data would be understandable itself. I would rather be considered simple-minded and naive than propose erudite but recondite explanations for simple phenomena.

In defense of this view, a standard example is the computer. Computers can recognize patterns, solve problems, reason, and answer questions. These higher-order activities are the end result of cascading and concatenating very simple logical properties. Maybe the same is not true of human short-term memory, but I prefer to think that it is. At least I think we should proceed on that assumption for the time being.

I shall concentrate on reproductive rather than reconstructive memory. Reproductive memory is rote or verbatim, while reconstructive memory is more inferential. The two traditions stem from Ebbinghaus (1913) and from Bartlett (1932), respectively. (As noted by Ansbacher, 1973, many of Bartlett's ideas were anticipated by Bergson, 1913.) People are in fact capable of encoding, storing, and retrieving (with varying degrees of accuracy) whatever information we present to them. Given that the existence of reproductive memory is indisputable, it is simpler and more amenable to theoretical explanation.

Currently there seems to be considerable interest in the more complex phenomena of reconstructive memory. More and more studies on sentence memory and psycholinguistic approaches to memory are appearing in the literature. I certainly have no wish to deprecate this work; it is interesting and important in its own right. However, it will not be covered here, for the reason given above. After all, we still do not understand reproductive memory all that well, so perhaps we should not complicate the picture by introducing other cognitive processes which we understand even less well.

Similarly, I still believe that the understanding of short-term memory may come before the understanding of long-term memory. Fifteen years ago this view was iconoclastic; today it is anachronistic. At least some current thinking is that what we really need is a model of long-term memory, and then all the bits and pieces of short-term memory will fall into place. This view is surely fallacious. Deductions about short-term phenomena will only come at the cost of assumptions about long-term memory, and we know that empirical verification of assumptions about long-term memory is far more difficult than empirical verification of assumptions about short-term memory. Further, we are quite capable of studying short-term memory without knowing how long-term memory is organized. From the beginning we have taken pains to develop techniques to minimize its contribution. On the other hand, we do make use of long-term memory in short-term studies; we routinely assume that TWA is meaningful, that TAW is pronounceable, and that WTA is neither. One cannot deny the interplay of short-term and long-term features.

A more fruitful direction might be to look down, not up. Intensive work is now being conducted on biological mechanisms of storage, and some day we will have to relate our findings to the nature of the engram. On the one hand, as McGeoch (1932) argued forty years ago, the serial-position curve will not vanish once we know how RNA codes memory. On the other hand, something must underlie the verbal productions of our subjects, and it would be nice to know more about it. Unfortunately, little more than lip service will be paid to this principle here. Convinced though I am of the desirability and necessity of synthesizing biological and behavioral data, there is no real progress to report in this book.

A final bias—which will soon become apparent—is the value I place on explicit models. It matters not whether they are formal models, mathematical models, or computer-simulation models (and each have their advocates). The verbally-stated models that still predominate in our field are often vague, imprecise, and difficult to refute. Consequently, they are useful only in our early stages of comprehension. Also, what a theory or model predicts or does not predict seldom becomes clear until the model is developed explicitly.

Unfortunately, many of us have little training, competence, or interest in models. We have not learned to appreciate the beauty, the elegance, or the power of a good model. We can rationalize our distaste (or our lack of success) by claiming that such ventures are premature. And so they will be—until the right one comes along.

In this book I shall present some mathematical development, although not very much. There will be relatively more in the sections on item information and associations (because we know more about them) than in the sections on serial ordering and free recall. The interested reader is encouraged to work through the development where it is not obvious; little more than basic algebra and a smattering of calculus is needed. Others will have to take some statements on faith, but perhaps enough parallel processing is possible so that one can at least follow the gist of the argument.

PRETHEORETICAL ASSUMPTIONS

The following terms are used throughout the book. They are essentially pretheoretical assumptions.

Components

There are three components of memory: encoding, storage, and retrieval. Encoding is simply the representation of one thing by another. When a stimulus such as a word, a number, a picture, or a tone is presented to an individual, the stimulus *per se* consists of a pattern of radiant energy. It is a physical entity. This stimulus has some effect on the nervous system, and the memorial counterpart is some encoded representation of this stimulus. Thus, somehow, the nervous system has an internal code for physical objects and events.

Storage is the persistence of information over time. When one makes a tape recording of a musical composition, the iron oxide particles on the tape constitute the encoded representation of the sound; and when the tape is finished and placed on the shelf, the magnetic properties of the tape do not change (for all practical purposes). Or, a flip-flop in a computer memory retains its state until the next set pulse occurs. Human memory seldom approaches this degree of fidelity, but it does preserve at least a trace of prior experience. Loss of information over time, of course, is forgetting.

Retrieval is utilization of stored information. Persistence of information is no guarantee of its accessibility. Just as a misplaced book in the library may not turn up in a search, so in a sense stored information may be available but not accessible. As the terms are used, "availability" refers to the existence of stored information while "accessibility" refers to the ease with which it can be found. Like all such distinctions, cases can be found where the distinction becomes fuzzy and even misleading. But like other distinctions, there are more times when it is useful.

The terms encoding, storage, and retrieval have come into recent popularity, but the concepts certainly are not new. Melton (1963) used the terms trace formation, trace storage, and trace utilization. Before him, McGeoch and Irion (1952) talked about learning, retention, and remembering. In all probability even the Greeks recognized the existence of these three components.

Stages

Performance on any memory task involves two stages—memory and decision. The following processes are assumed to occur. In any memory test, some question must be asked. The question is "comprehended" and memory interrogated. The answer from the memory system is not necessarily offered as the answer to the ques-

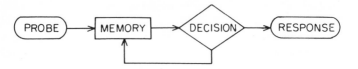

FIG. 1.1.   A simple flow chart to represent the memory and decision processes in answering a question.

tion. Instead, it undergoes some sort of internal editing. If acceptable, then it is given as the answer to the question. If the editing process suggests the answer may not be correct, then memory may be interrogated again. This process recycles until an acceptable answer is forthcoming or some stop rule is invoked; in the latter case, the person may simply say, "I don't know the answer to the question."

A schematic representation of the process is shown in Fig. 1.1. This flow chart is to be read from left to right. The probe stands for the question, and the arrow leading from it to the box labelled memory is intended to indicate that the question is comprehended and memory interrogated. The editing process is represented by the memory-decision-response loop. The diamond-shaped figure representing the decision stage is intended to indicate a choice point. Either the answer is acceptable, in which case the path leading from decision to response is followed, or the process recycles (the return loop to the memory system). The stop rule is not represented in this simple flow chart.

An early use of an information-flow diagram to represent mental processes can be found in the filter theory of Broadbent (1958), and a justification of such an application is given in a later paper (Broadbent, 1963). The diagrams come from computer programming, where they provide a convenient outline to sketch out the main components. Here they represent at a very global level the processes we have to consider to understand how the system works. Following standard convention, external or observable events (or, in computer terms, input and output) are represented by an oval while internal processes are box-like. A rectangle denotes a stage of processing and the diamond shape denotes a choice point. In general terms, the arrows depict the flow of information.

Why is it necessary to deal with decision processes in the understanding of memory? One might think they should be assigned to another area of psychology, so that we could more clearly focus upon and understand the memorial processes themselves. While many of us might wish we could, the system won't let us. Whether we like it or not, these decision processes intervene between memory and response, and to understand memory we must develop ways of understanding decision processes and memory separately.

By way of analogy, it has long been known that there is a difference between learning and performance. What an individual does is not necessarily equivalent to what he has learned. For instance, most students can report cases in which they simply could not think of the answer to a test question, even though they had learned the material and, perhaps, even remembered it shortly after the examination was over. Or, in more general terms, failure of performance on a memory test need not indicate forgetting. The information may not have been encoded properly in the first place, it may in fact have been forgotten, or it may have been momentarily inaccessible though still available.

To this list we must add that performance reflects the joint effect of memory and decision. The fact that a person says "I don't know the answer to the question" may reflect more the existence of a strict editing process than a memory failure *per se*. As another example, a long-standing issue in the study of recognition memory is how to correct for guessing on multiple-choice tests. The fact that the problem is generally recognized is tacit acceptance of this distinction. So, whether we like it or not, we must accept the presence of a stage of processing intervening between memory and response.

Associations

One of the basic elements of human memory is the association. We don't really know what an association is, and certainly no one has ever seen one. So how one chooses to conceptualize it is a matter of taste. At one time, people liked to think about associations in terms of conditioned responses, so it was likened to a connection between a conditionable stimulus and an unconditioned response that gradually developed through the repetitive procedures of classical (Pavlovian) conditioning. There was perhaps a time when some thought this view would provide the cornerstone on which to construct a complete theoretical edifice of human memory and learning.

Such a view has few adherents today, but the concept of an association is still alive and well (Anderson & Bower, 1973). Essentially an association is a rule or relationship between two stored memory traces that maps one into the other, or allows a cross-reference system to operate. In a library card index, you can find the title of a book if given the author's name; or, if you know a key word, you can use the subject index instead. In the same way you can picture the face of a good friend or, seeing the friend, you can remember his name. So we say there is an association between name and face, which means that there is communication between the two stored traces in the memory system.

Many other analogies could be given. A road connects two cities, or a river connects two parts of the country, so the road or the river would be the association. In computer programming, the address and content of a memory register are like an association in that a specific address provides access or leads to a specific content. In this same vein, indirect addressing in computer programming would seem to be a close parallel to the mediated generalization of stimulus-response psychology. Mathematically, f is the function mapping x into y in the expression $y = f(x)$, so f is an association. What analogy one likes is a matter of taste. Whatever it may be, the concept of association is essential to explaining many of the facts we have about the operation of human memory.

At a more general level, the associations we study in the laboratory may be a special case of the propositional structure discussed by those interested in semantic memory. As variously suggested (e.g., Anderson, 1972; Anderson & Bower, 1972a;

Kintsch, 1972b; Rumelhart, Lindsay, & Norman, 1972) one possible representation for information in human memory is in terms of labelled associations or propositions denoted by $\langle A\ B\ R \rangle$. A proposition consists of a function plus argument(s) and can be represented (in graph structure or linguistically) as a relationship R between two nodes A and B. A collie is a dog; "collie" and "dog" are the nodes and the relationship R is "is a class member." There are many possible relationships, and the one most extensively studied in the laboratory is temporal contiguity. I present the pair GALLANT–LEGEND to a subject but the relationship is as clear as in the sentence "A collie is a dog." The fact that laboratory studies have focused almost exclusively on temporal contiguity does not mean that those interested in such relationships necessarily reject application of their findings to other relationships.

Many theoretical discussions have developed over the relative merits of associationistic vs. an information-processing point of view. Associationism, of course, has a long history (Deese, 1965) and has provided the philosophical underpinnings of interference theory (Kintsch, 1970b). Those more enamoured of communication-theory and computer-based concepts find much to attack in interference theory, so there has come to be a feeling that information-processing concepts and the idea of associations are antithetical. Quite the opposite view is taken here. The information processed may be associative. Information processing is a general term that can denote the internal events occurring in the nervous system during the response to a probe or the answering of a question. That information which is processed may simply be a single association.

We have not yet defined the term "information." Technically it does have a specific definition and this definition has been of some considerable use in clarifying the nature of memory span and the concept of limited capacity. Here we can simply say that information is that which reduces uncertainty. The answer to a question reduces uncertainty, so it provides information. The more the initial uncertainty, the greater the possible reduction, and this initial uncertainty depends upon the probability distribution of the possible alternatives. For the purposes of this book a more formal definition is not necessary, but the interested reader may consult Abramson (1963).

The term "information processing" will be used frequently throughout the book. What does it mean? We know very well what it means with computers, but we don't know well at all what it means in human memory. In a computer, for instance, the machine is either operating in a fetch or execute mode, and this state is indicated by the major state generator. When a binary string is being interpreted it may be interpreted either as an instruction or as data. In either case there is a one-to-one correspondence between the binary digits and the outcome of the processing. When a DCA instruction is executed, the contents of the accumulator are deposited in a specified location and the accumulator is cleared. When an ISZ instruction is executed, a specific location is incremented and the next instruction is skipped if the contents of the specified location are then zero. Information is transferred in and out of core through the memory buffer, and the program counter holds the address of the next instruction. It is reasonable to suppose that something functionally equivalent to these computer processes is occurring in human information processing, but we certainly do not know exactly what. Perhaps the main justification for using these terms despite our current ignorance is that they may help us to ask the right questions, and this is generally acknowledged as an important part of any scientific enterprise.

In this vein, perhaps it should also be pointed out that there are various levels of understanding to which we could aspire. For instance, still in the computer case, suppose I want to understand how the computer processes the following FOCAL instructions:

$$7.5 \text{ FOR } I = 0, 47; \text{ DO } 8.5$$

$$8.5 \text{ SET SUM} = \text{SUM} + X(I)$$

At one level, I could understand that it adds 48 numbers to get a total. I could rewrite the instructions in assembly language using symbolic programming with eight or nine instructions setting up a loop, incrementing, stopping on an ISZ instruction, and storing the total in a given location. Or, I could write the program in machine language where I had to worry about the specific memory locations to be assigned. On a still more basic level, I could consider what was going on in the memory buffer or the program counter during the execution of the program, or I could worry about certain shift registers and flip-flops in the CPU, or I could even try to ascertain the changes in specified resistors and diodes as I single-stepped through the program. What do I have to do to "understand" the specified FOCAL instructions?

The point of this example is that one can understand computer programming at various levels, and so too in the case of memory. On the one hand, most of us are not content to restrict our understanding only to the most global level, namely, how the FOCAL instructions add numbers. On the other hand, as dry psychologists we are not trained to study what is going on at the lowest level (resistors and diodes). Our aim should be somewhat intermediate. As pointed out by Neisser (1967), we are software specialists not hardware specialists. Our skills and talents may explicate the workings of the program, but probably not the physical mechanisms by which it works.

Interference

Another issue of long standing is whether forgetting occurs through interference or decay. Interference implies an active process and decay implies a passive process. If I read you one name you can surely remember it; if I read you several perhaps you can remember them; but the more names I read you, the less likely you are to remember any but the last few. The latter names are said to interfere with the earlier ones. Decay, by comparison, is viewed as a more passive process. Were I to read you only one name and then allow some time to pass, a person taking a simple decay position would say the passage of time *per se* was sufficient to obliterate the trace.

By and large, the results from countless short-term memory studies show that what we have to worry about and explain theoretically is interference, not decay. That is not to say that decay does not occur. Perhaps it does; some evidence in its favor can be adduced. But even its staunchest advocates must admit that more forgetting is attributable to interference than to decay. Perhaps interference accounts for 85–98% of the variance and decay may account for the remainder.

There are two classical types of interference, retroactive and proactive. Retroactive interference is the interfering effect generated by items occurring after the presentation of the to-be-remembered (or target) item (hence they exert their effects retroactively, as it were). The second type of interference is proactive, where items presented before the target item generate the interference. This interference increases as the retention interval (the time between presentation of an item and its test) increases. The importance of proactive interference in list-learning experiments (which some might wish to call long-term memory) was convincingly and impressively documented by Underwood (1957).

As used here, the terms retroactive and proactive interference are descriptive terms, not theoretical concepts. As stated above, they simply refer to interference effects generated by prior and subsequent items. Interference theory also studies these phenomena, but no commitment to interference theory is implied by the use of these terms.

There are other dimensions along which to classify interference effects. For instance, Melton (1963) has suggested the idea of intraunit interference. Thus, 101 is easy to remember, 110110 is a bit harder, while 01101101000111 is a bit too much. Considering these binary digits as a 3-, a 6-, and a 14-item string, we can call this generally an n-gram string where the value of n denotes the number of items (here, digits) in the string. Melton suggested that interference effects work within the string, and the larger the value of n the more intraunit interference for memory.

Yet another way of classifying interference effects is in terms of the procedural contribution. One source of interference is in presenting additional items to study, either proactively or retroactively; the other is test interference. In test interference, the interference is generated by the attempted recall (or recognition) of other items in the list. Interference from studying other items may be called input interference, while interference from tests on other items may be called output interference.

Learning

The view espoused here is to assume that learning is increased resistance to forgetting. By learning, of course, we refer primarily to verbal learning, as the acquisition of skills and motor habits undoubtedly calls other processes into play. But in verbal learning, be it improved recognition, serial learning, paired-associate learning, or free recall, the improvement in performance that is characteristic of repetition is interpreted as increased resistance to forgetting.

The more traditional way of viewing learning is to conceive of repetition as strengthening associative connections. Or, for those who like finite-state models, transitions from an unlearned or guessing state to perhaps an intermediate state, followed by final absorption into a terminal or learned state. The distinction here is whether one conceives of repetition effects as being continuous or discrete. But in both cases the general view is that items start in some unlearned or low-strength state, then slowly and gradually move to some higher-level or stronger state as list presentation continues. An obvious parallel is to conditioned responses, which are infrequent and difficult to elicit early in the training session but gradually become quite predictable as the number of contiguous presentations of the conditioned and unconditioned stimulus increases.

Prestigious though this view may be, it is flatly contradicted by the recent work on short-term memory. For any method or procedure, the subject always knows what the last few items were. There is a recency effect. Thus, temporarily he can remember what these most recent items were, but as presentation continues—or as interference increases—he forgets. In the conventional list-learning procedure these short-term changes are masked by the randomization procedure used. Since these short-term effects are so marked, it seems reasonable to insist they be represented in any conceptual model.

However, the data show the case is even stronger than this. Figure 1.2 shows the results from a paired-associate experiment on short-term memory where a list was presented once, twice, or three times prior to test. The figure shows recall probability as a function of amount of input interference (number of subsequent pairs), and the three curves represent the three presentation conditions. These curves illustrate two very typical short-term memory effects: recency and asymptote. The recency effect refers to the initial forgetting represented by the steeply falling part of the curve at the left. The asymptote refers to the steady state achieved after the initial forgetting has stopped. Here the curves (all three, in fact) are level.

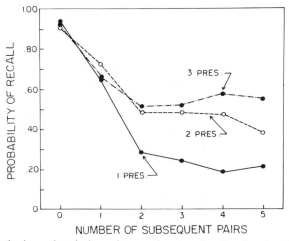

FIG. 1.2.   Forgetting in a probe paired-associate experiment as a function of number of presentations of the list. (Fig. 4 from Murdock, 1963d.)

The main point of Fig. 1.2 is that the asymptote is progressively higher as the number of presentations increase. Thus, probability of recall is perhaps .20 after one presentation, .45 after two presentations, and .55 after three presentations. Forgetting is still just as *rapid* after three presentations as after one, but the terminal level is higher. Repetitions increase the asymptote, so in this sense learning (as brought about through repetition) is increased resistance to forgetting.

Clearly, we are talking here about a very restricted type of learning. We are talking about the type of learning that occurs in verbal-learning experiments. Many other types of learning occur, both in and out of the laboratory. But this type of verbal-learning situation has greatly interested psychologists, and much experimentation and theoretical attention has been devoted to understanding it. The viewpoint here is that such learning is best understood as representing a gradual build-up of memory.

PREVIEW

Item information enables us to remember objects and events. It underlies the feeling of familiarity when we re-encounter a previous experience. Since objects and events are a bit unmanageable for laboratory study, we tend to work experimentally with simpler things, like words or pictures. The term "item" is simply a generic term that encompasses all these instances. The important issues are (a) what information is encoded, (b) how it changes over time, and (c) what processes occur at retrieval.

At a general level, three possibilities have been suggested for encoding. At the time of presentation some long-term memory representation could be incremented, marked, or tagged; or, a memory trace could be laid down, which would be characterized in terms of its strength; or, the representation could be in terms of a collection (bundle or vector) of attributes. For tags, the trace would be all or none; for strength, it would be graded; for attributes, it would be multidimensional. The changes over time could either be loss through decay or loss through interference. What is lost depends upon what is assumed to be encoded initially. Retrieval is either by direct access or search. With direct access, the relevant memory location is interrogated directly, as in a content-addressable or associative memory. Search implies a process wherein many registers, or memory locations, must be examined to find the target item. The search could be serial (one at a time) or parallel (more than one at a time).

These three dimensions are orthogonal, so any combination of encoding, forgetting, and retrieval assumptions would be possible. The three theories to be discussed in Chapter 2 are threshold theories, strength theory, and attribute theories. They are distinguished primarily on the basis of their encoding assumption. The format of store they assume are tags, strength, and attributes, respectively. Actually, to associate threshold theory with the concept of memory tags is my interpretation. I suggest it here to make a threshold model of memory more reasonable, as a threshold model does seem to be what a tagging model would be like if explicated formally.

Theories of associative information deal with associations. The experimental material is paired associates, again often of a verbal nature. For encoding, associations are either graded or discrete. The former, of course, is a strength view while the latter is an all-or-none view. With discrete states there may be two or more than two states. Changes over time can be gradual or abrupt, but these are not orthogonal. Gradual forgetting goes with graded acquisition, while all-or-none learning goes with all-or-none forgetting. However, with finite-state models, the forgetting can be permanent or reversable. As for retrieval, a generate and edit, or search and decision, process is generally assumed.

The theories to be covered are interference theory, stimulus-sampling and multistate Markov models, and a two-state fluctuation model. Interference theory assumes graded acquisition and forgetting while others do not. Interference theory and the stimulus-sampling models are more oriented toward list-learning data and long-term memory, while the multistate and the fluctuation models describe short-term memory. These latter models do not assume that forgetting is permanent, but differ in how they characterize the changes that do occur.

Theories of serial ordering propose various possibilities for the format of storage. One possibility is arrays or bins; one has a set of ordered locations that are filled much as incoming mail may be filed in mailboxes at the time it arrives. Another possibility is to assume a chaining mechanism wherein serial ordering takes place much as links form a chain. A third possibility is some sort of hierarchical structure, and it can be pyramidal or nested. With a pyramid structure a superordinate representational scheme is envisaged, while nesting is a horizontal arrangement. However, the two are closely related.

Two different types of forgetting are assumed, and they differ in importance. Serial strings include both item and order formation. The item is the content (which *letter* is in the mailbox), and the order is the address (which *mailbox*). The forgetting of item and order information can be either independent or dependent. If the latter, one can be primary and the other secondary or derivative. That is, loss of order information can result because the items are forgotten, or loss of items can result because the order has been forgotten. Retrieval is generally assumed to be simply a direct readout of the contents of memory, but other alternatives may deserve consideration.

In free recall the emphasis is on the retrieval process. Some of the models discussed there do indeed make assumptions about encoding and storage of information. The assignment of models to sections is more the other way around. The models and theories of item information, associative information, and serial-order information generally have little or nothing to say about free recall. Models of free recall obviously do; they may or may not be quite specific about other processes as well.

One main possibility for retrieval in free recall is a generate and edit, or search and decision, process. In some way the contents of the appropriate memory store are examined and the acceptable items reported. Random sampling is another possibility, while following tagged associative pathways is still a third. Another question at a more general level is the nature of the retrieval cues in free recall. One can theorize about the cues used in the retrieval process without commitment to the particular process itself.

TABLE 1.1

Terms Used to Characterize the Encoding, Storage, and Retrieval
of Item, Associative, and Serial-Order Information

Types of information	Memory	Experimental paradigm	Encoding	Storage (Forgetting)	Retrieval
Item	Objects Events Experiences	Recognition memory	Tags Strength Attributes Representational	Decay Interference	Direct access Search Serial Parallel
Associative	Relationships Temporal Categorical Logical	Paired associates	Graded Discrete Two states More than two	Gradual Sudden Permanent Reversible	Generate and edit
Serial-order	Strings of objects Sequences of events	Memory span	Bins or arrays Linked chains Hierarchies Pyramidal Nested	Item Order	Direct readout Unpacking

In following chapters, then, we shall be concerned with the encoding, storage, and retrieval of information from human memory. These issues will be examined successively for item information, associative information, serial-order information, and free recall. By way of summary, some of the main terms and concepts to be used are presented in outline form in Table 1.1. A few of the terms will be explained more fully in Chapter 10.

2
THEORIES OF ITEM INFORMATION

Theories of item information attempt to specify the nature of item information, how it changes over time, and how it is used in retrieval. These theories take their data from studies of recognition memory. A typical experimental paradigm for the study of item recognition memory is as follows. The subject is presented with a list of items, and each item is shown one at a time. After the study phase has ended, the test phase begins. One by one, additional items are presented, some old and some new. An old item is one that had been presented in the study phase, while a new item is a lure. It is an item not previously encountered which must be included in the test phase to make it a real test. In this procedure the subject is expected to respond to each item. In one version, to each item he either says, ''Yes, this item was in the list,'' or ''No, this item was not in the list.'' The more accurate his memory, the more often he will say ''yes'' to old items and ''no'' to the new items or lures. The ''items'' are at the discretion of the experimenter: words, pictures, sentences, or whatever.

As studied experimentally, then, item recognition does not investigate whether the subject has ever encountered the test items before. Since the stimulus materials typically are such things as words or pictures, clearly in this sense they are familiar to the subject. Instead, what is being tested is whether the subject remembers the occurrence of a particular item in a particular context. This context is generally the list he has just seen. Or, perhaps, it could be a list shown a few lists back or on a previous day. But in any event the judgment of ''yes'' or ''no'' refers to whether or not the subject remembers the item in the designated laboratory setting.

In this chapter three main theories of item recognition will be considered. They are threshold theories, strength theories, and attribute theories. Threshold theories are a legacy from psychophysics, and it seems that many of our intuitive assumptions about recognition memory have been more formally stated and developed in connection with work on sensory thresholds. Implications from threshold theories have been tested and found wanting, but in the process they have increased our understanding of recognition memory. Strength theory is an alternative to a threshold theory and is not only more popular in the psychophysical area today, but also much more in accord with experimental data on item recognition. Some of the basic assumptions of strength theory have a long history as well. Finally, recent problems with strength theory have suggested a rather different line of theorizing, and this approach is embodied in the current attribute theories. They will be discussed in turn.

THRESHOLD THEORY

This theory has been discussed more by its detractors than by its proponents. In fact, it is not clear who really has supported it, at least recently. It could be what people have in mind when they talk about memory tags, although this concept is seldom made explicit. So we shall cloak it with anonymity and refer to it simply as a traditional point of view. Even though it clearly seems to be wrong, it will serve as a useful vehicle to introduce some important concepts. Further, we generally learn quite a lot from seeing just where and how a particular theory fails.

According to threshold theory, then, let us imagine the following. In the test situation described above, the subject recognizes some proportion of the old items as familiar. He does not recognize any of the new items as familiar. He could simply say "yes" to those items that seemed familiar and "no" to the remainder. For whatever reason, he chooses to guess. For some proportion of the unfamiliar items he also says "yes." Thus, there are two cases; "yes" responses to old items that were familiar plus guessed "yes" responses to unfamiliar items that may have been old or may have been new.

The above describes a threshold theory in the psychophysical sense. That is, when an observer is attempting to detect the presence of a weak stimulus, the experimenter insures that the energy level of the presented stimuli brackets his sensory "threshold." So too in the memory case. Stimuli whose familiarity exceeds this threshold seem familiar, while those below it do not. The threshold concept, at least in this crude form, is not fashionable in psychophysics today either, but this parallel at least suggests its historical antecedents.

This viewpoint was clearly stated, tested, and proven false by Egan (1958) in a technical report frequently cited but never published. From its preface, apparently it was considered little more than an exercise. However, because of its subsequent importance we shall summarize the argument here, though in a somewhat different way.

How can this threshold view be tested? One can conduct the experiment as described above (i.e., present a list of items, then observe the frequency of "yes" and "no" responses to old and new items). Hypothetical (though not atypical) results are shown in Table 2.1, where the outcome is presented in the form of a 2 × 2

TABLE 2.1

Hypothetical Data to Show Frequencies of "Yes" and
"No" Response to Old and New Test Items

Test	Responses		
items	"Yes"	"No"	Total
Old	65	15	80
New	8	72	80
Total	73	87	160

table. There were 80 old items, of which 65 were so identified, and there were also 80 new items, or lures, of which 8 were mistakenly described as old. A standard terminology for describing such data has developed, which we explain next.

Terminology

Test items are old or new, and the probability that any given item is old is the *a priori,* or prior, probability. In this case it happens to be .5, but it need not be. Further, it is of some general concern whether or not the subject is informed prior to the test of the item's probability. (Unless there is some reason to the contrary, the subject should be informed.) Of the old items, the proportion of items receiving a "yes" response is the hit rate. The hit rate is a conditional probability, the probability of a "yes" response being given to an old item. In this case its value is 65/80, or .81. The complement of the hit rate is the miss rate, or misses. Here its value is .19. The false-alarm rate is also a conditional probability, the probability of a "yes" (or "old") response being given to a new item—here .10. Its complement, for the fourth time a conditional probability, is the correct rejection rate, in this case, .90. Clearly, hits and misses are redundant in that, knowing one, the other is determined (merely the complement). So too with false alarms and correct rejections. However, the descriptive labels are useful in that, at various times, it is more convenient to be able to denote one rather than the other.

So far we have been conditionalizing horizontally. However, one can conditionalize vertically, which has some uses too. The *a posteriori* probability, or simply posterior probability, is the probability that the test item was old given a particular response. Since there are two responses ("yes" and "no"), there are two posterior probabilities. Numerically, they are 65/73 or .89 for "yes" responses, and 15/87 or .17 for "no" responses. Another way of representing much the same information is the likelihood ratio, but we shall postpone that until later. Finally, just as there is an unconditional *a priori* probability that can be assigned to a stimulus, so response bias can be represented by the probability of a "yes" response. Here the noes outnumber the yesses, so there was a slight bias to be conservative in the data.

These then are the basic terms and concepts to characterize performance in a recognition-memory task. Most of it seems fairly obvious and straightforward, except for the *a posteriori* probabilities. In fact, *a posteriori* probabilities are not basically different from hit rates and false alarms in that both are simply conditional probabilities. In one case, one is conditionalizing on the stimulus (i.e., whether it was old or new), then asking what proportion of this subset were, say, "yes" responses. In the *a posteriori* case, one simply conditionalizes on the response and asks what proportion of this subset were old stimuli. While the redundant complements are not named in the latter case but are in the former case, that is simply because a standard convention about determining *a posteriori* probabilities has been followed. *A priori* probabilities are looking forward in a sense that, given the stimulus, one asks about the response. *A posteriori* probabilities are looking backward in that, given the response, one asks about the stimulus. While the theoretical controversies are not trivial (see discussions of Bayes's theorem in books on probability theory) at least at this simple computational level they are comparable (or, if you wish, symmetric) concepts.

What does such an analysis tell us about the adequacy of threshold theory? Nothing. The reason it tells us nothing is that such data could have come about in several ways. Some ways would be consistent with threshold theory and hence would support it; others would be antithetical to it. We must refine this simple yes-no testing situation to test threshold theory, but first we must understand why as it stands it is no test. As a prelude to discussing a proper test, let us consider two models which could explain such data. These models are two particular versions of a more general threshold theory.

These models make assumptions about the underlying distributions. Both models say we have old and new items which differ in their familiarity. Everyone appreciates that this statement means that, on the average, old items are more familiar than new ones. To be more precise, there is a distribution of familiarity for the old items and a distribution of familiarity for the new items, and the mean of the old-item distribution is greater than the mean of the new-item distribution. If you are not comfortable with the notion of distribution and statements about them, refer to any textbook on statistics or probability theory.

What do distributions of familiarity values have to do with recognition memory? There must be a distribution involved, because all items surely are not equally familiar. In fact, many sets of data on recognition memory can easily show that the assumption of a point distribution (i.e., that all items are equally familiar) is untenable. So the questions must be: What are these distributions and how do they differ for old and new items? The models we shall be discussing are at least explicit as to the form of the old-item and the new-item distribution. They do not always state what the x-axis variable is, but generally it can be considered "familiarity." As they will be explained here, these models may not seem to have much face validity. However, a formally equivalent version of these models was quite generally accepted before (and, sad to say, for some while after) Egan's pioneering technical report.

Models

The first model is shown in Fig. 2.1. Both new and old item distributions are shown as uniform (or rectangular) distributions. The new item distribution is $f_n(x) =$

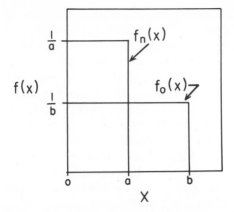

FIG. 2.1. Old and new item distributions for one version of a threshold theory.

$1/a$, $0 < x < a$, while the old item distribution is $f_o(x) = 1/b$, $0 < x < b$. That is, both distributions are rectangular in shape, $f_o(x)$ long and low, and $f_n(x)$ tall and narrow. They are aligned at their lower limit, 0. These are both probability density functions, which means their area must be unity. Multiplying their length by their width will verify that such is the case. The variable x is simply the familiarity dimension, a variable which we cannot observe directly. As will be seen shortly, deductions from this model make it quite testable.

The second model (see Fig. 2.2) is only slightly different. Here $f_o(x)$ is $f_n(x)$ displaced to the right, so it is located above $f_n(x)$. As before, both are probability density functions with unit areas.

Less formally, these models both say that all possible familiarity values are equally likely. This assumption may be a bit hard to accept at first because it is somewhat uncommon. It is as if you were picking numbers out of a hat, and all num-

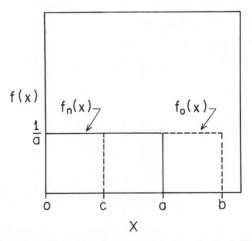

FIG. 2.2. Old and new item distributions for a second version of a threshold theory.

bers were equally possible. To carry the analogy one step further, the first model says that if the numbers in the hat varied, say, from 0–4 for the new items, then the numbers in the hat might vary from 0–9 for the old items. The second model says that if the numbers for the new items varied from 0–9, then the numbers for the old items might vary from 5–14. In each case, however, all permissible numbers would be equally frequent. Both models say that there are some old items that are more familiar (or higher on the number scale) than any new items. Only the second model says that there are also some new items that are less familiar (lower on the number scale) than any old items.

How can these models be tested? The distributions characterize the distribution of familiarity of the old and new items. It is assumed that when an item is presented for recognition it gives rise to a feeling of familiarity. The strength of this feeling is represented by some point on the x axis. However, the subject has to respond with a simple binary response. To do so, assume that the subject has adopted a cutoff point or criterion on the familiarity scale. If the strength of the feeling evoked by the test item is greater than this criterion, then the subject will say, "Yes, that is familiar." If the strength is less than this criterion, the subject will say, "No, that is not familiar." Thus, even though the sense of familiarity varies continuously along the x axis, only discrete responses are allowed, and the continuum is mapped into a dichotomy according to whether the familiarity of the item in question does or does not exceed the criterion.

We can now use this graphic representation to describe the concepts introduced in connection with Table 2.1. In Fig. 2.3 we have drawn the criterion for Fig. 2.1 as a vertical line which intersects the abscissa (or has the value of) x_c. All observations falling to the right of x_c lead to a "yes" response. The term "observation" means the following: As each test word is presented, the subject somehow compares it to his memory or assesses its familiarity; thus the observation is simply the familiarity of each test word. Since this theory is a threshold theory, all observations falling to

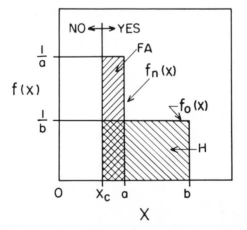

FIG. 2.3. Hits (H) and false alarms (FA) for one version of a threshold theory.

the left of x_c lead to a "no" response. Since the criterion x_c dichotomizes both distributions, there are both hits and misses for $f_o(x)$ and both false alarms and correct rejections for $f_n(x)$. (Remember, these four terms denote conditional probabilities.)

The hit rate is given by the area of $f_o(x)$ falling to the right of x_c, which is cross-hatched down to the right. The false-alarm rate is given by the area of $f_n(x)$ falling to the right of x_c, which is cross-hatched down to the left. The old and new item distributions are probability density functions; their area is unity. For a probability density function, probabilities are given by areas under the curve. The entire curve has an area of unity. Therefore, the probability of any particular observation (sample from the population, if you prefer) exceeding a particular cutoff point is the area under the curve to the right of a vertical line partitioning the distribution at this particular point. Thus, for the case in question, the hit rate and the false-alarm rate shown in Fig. 2.3 are (or can be made) numerically equal to the values reported in Table 2.1. There is an isomorphism between the tabular presentation in Table 2.1 and the graphic presentation in Fig. 2.3.

It may not be immediately apparent how one could juggle the variables to make the numbers come out the same. One might think that certain entries could be found for Table 2.1 that could not possibly be represented graphically. As long as the false-alarm rate does not exceed the hit rate (and in practice it never does) then one can always construct a graphical equivalent of any data. There are two degrees of freedom. First, one can (indeed, must) place x_c properly to give the appropriate hit and false-alarm rate. Second, one parameter of the distribution must be free to vary. The standard convention is to take the new item distribution as fixed or given and let the old item distribution vary. That is, the overall familiarity of items in memory will clearly vary with characteristics of the task. A slow presentation rate with a short retention interval and vivid, meaningful words will be relatively memorable, so such words should be remembered much better (i.e., be more familiar) than nonsense syllables presented at a fast presentation rate with a long retention interval. Clearly the model must have some way of representing such variation in the familiarity of items. Otherwise it would not even be worth discussing. Nor is such variation contradictory to a threshold notion either. The threshold notion does not deny stimulus variability; all it says is that there is some area of non-overlap.

To accommodate variations in average familiarity, this model would have one free parameter; namely, the value of b. The closer b is to a, the lower the average familiarity of old items; the further b is from a, the higher the average familiarity of old items. Perhaps you can also appreciate the fact that there will be a parallel change in the variability or variance of old items too, but this aspect will be considered later. It might also be worth pointing out that the areas under the curve will remain at unity despite variations in the location of a, since compensatory changes in the ordinate follow movements along the abscissa.

Here we begin to see what is intended in Fig. 1.1, the separation of memory and decision. Even in this very simple high-threshold model, there are two parameters—one to characterize the operation of the memory system, and one to characterize the operation of the decision system. The former is b; the latter is x_c. They are independent in the sense that one can vary without the other varying. Experimental separation is possible, and has been attempted (though not for this particular model). Experimental separation means that one can find at least one independent variable that affects b and not x_c and a second independent variable that affects x_c and not b.

Since we have the two parameters of the model, we can fit perfectly any data from a 2×2 table that does not violate convention (i.e., the convention prohibiting a false-alarm rate greater than the hit rate). To convince a skeptical reader, take any value you wish for hit rate (HR) and false-alarm rate (FA). Let $a = 1$, let $x_c = 1 - FA$, and let $b = x_c/(1\text{-}HR)$. Use these values of a, b, and x_c and, by simple geometry, compute the predicted values for hits and false alarms. You will finish with the empirical values with which you started.

For the curious reader, the given equations involve only the simplest of integral calculus and the solution of two simultaneous equations. From consideration of definitions it follows that

$$HR = \int_{x_c}^{b} f_o(x)\, dx = \frac{b - x_c}{b} \tag{2.1}$$

$$FA = \int_{x_c}^{a} f_n(x)\, dx = \frac{a - x_c}{a}. \tag{2.2}$$

The expressions for x_c and b are obtained simply by solving Eqs. 2.1 and 2.2. Parenthetically, it might be noted that a is not a free parameter of the model. It is set equal to 1 for convenience but, unlike b and x_c, it is quite independent of the data.

We have now considered this model in some detail, and for two reasons. First, being as simple as it is, it is easy to understand and work through in order to comprehend basic concepts of recognition memory. Second, a consideration of how it can be disproved leads to newer and better models. So, let us see how it can be disproved. What happens when x_c varies? Qualitatively, it is probably clear that, for any given value of b, as x_c moves from right to left both hits and false alarms increase. That is not enough. It is *how* they increase that is important, and it leads to the way that we reject the model. The answer, first stated then derived, is that the model predicts hits to be a linear function of false alarms.

Psychology has a long tradition of plotting graphs in one particular way, namely, a dependent variable (some measure of behavior) as a function of an independent variable (some experimental manipulation). Here we have another technique, one in which two dependent variables are plotted against each other. It is necessary to plot the hit rate as a function of the false-alarm rate. The name for this type of function is the ROC curve, and the acronym stands for receiver operating characteristic. The historical background for this development comes from signal-detection theory, and for a detailed treatment of its application to psychophysics the interested reader should consult Green and Swets (1966).

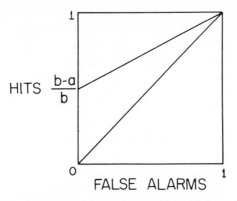

FIG. 2.4. Receiver operating characteristic (ROC) curve for model shown in Fig. 2.1.

It may be obvious by inspection that the ROC curve for the high-threshold model depicted in Fig. 2.3 is a straight line. Whether or not it is obvious, it is instructive to show how it can be obtained analytically, for this technique is standard. In general, one sets up expressions for the hit rate and false alarms, integrates them, solves for x_c and equates. The result is an expression for the ROC curve. Here, from Eqs. (2.1) and (2.2) (still with $a = 1$) $x_c = b(1 - HR) = 1 - FA$. The solution is simply $HR = 1 - (1/b)(1 - FA)$; a straight line with a slope inversely proportional to the value of b. The ROC plot is shown in Fig. 2.4. The diagonal line (running from 0,0 to 1,1) is the chance line that would result if the two distributions $f_o(x)$ and $f_n(x)$ were identical.

So far the discussion of ROC curves has been limited to one particular version of a high-threshold model, that of Fig. 2.1. The ROC curve for the other version (Fig. 2.2) is not greatly different. It is shown in Fig. 2.5. Like the ROC curve of Fig. 2.4, it too is linear, but the hit rate reaches unity before false alarms do. As an exercise, it might be useful for the reader to work out the expressions for hits and

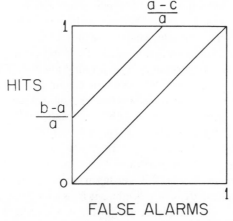

FIG. 2.5. Receiver operating characteristic (ROC) curve for model shown in Fig. 2.2.

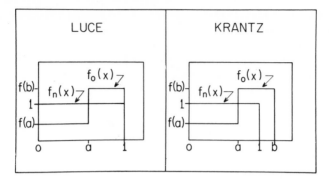

FIG. 2.6. Old and new item distributions for models of Luce (1963) and Krantz (1969).

false alarms, then obtain an explicit expression for the ROC function of Fig. 2.5. One can easily determine the effect of variations in the parameters a and c.

It may seem to the reader that we are wasting our time discussing such simple models. In rebuttal, it takes only rather small changes in the assumptions about the nature of the old-item distribution $f_o(x)$ to make these theories quite respectable. Two such cases are shown in Fig. 2.6. The left panel shows what the Luce two-state low-threshold model might look like (Luce, 1963), while the right panel shows what the Krantz low-high threshold model might look like (Krantz, 1969). One can derive the expressions for the ROC function analytically or by geometric construction. ROC functions obtained from studies of recognition memory do not differ greatly from what these models predict, and it is neither a simple nor a trivial matter to disprove these models.

Model Tests

To conclude this section, we now consider how these simple high-threshold models can be tested. If the criterion varies, the predictions made by these models are unambiguous. What is needed is a way of manipulating the criterion, or, what is equivalent, obtaining different hit rates and false-alarm rates so one can plot an ROC curve on the basis of a subject's performance. The simplest way of doing this is to use a confidence-judgment procedure. It is a rating method. The subject not only gives a "yes" or "no" response, but rates how certain or confident he is that he is correct. A three-point scale is common where the subject labels each response as certain, probable, or guess. Combined with "yes" and "no" responses, one has a six-point scale: + + + (sure old), + + (probably old), + (guess old), − (guess new), − − (probably new), and − − − (sure new).

With a confidence-judgment procedure, there are assumed to be many criteria rather than one criterion. In Fig. 2.3, for instance, the dichotomy is between yes and no. In a confidence-judgment procedure it is assumed that the subject sets up one criterion cut for each confidence judgment, + + + near the right and − − − near the left. When the test item is presented it gives rise to some feeling of familiarity, and when the subject responds with the appropriate degree of confidence he is in effect telling us where that observation arose. That is, he is locating approximately its position on the x axis. So, by saying, for instance, that he is fairly sure it is an old item, he is saying he is more than guessing but less than certain.

We are really only making an ordinal assumption—that $+++$ is to the right of $++$; $++$, to the right of $+$; etc. Since

$$HR = \int_{x_c}^{b} f_o(x)\, dx \text{ and } FA = \int_{x_c}^{a} f_n(x)\, dx,$$

with six confidence judgments we have five usable values of x_c (if $x_c = 0$ then hits and false alarms must both be unity). Therefore, even though we don't know directly the familiarity values of the criterion values, by cumulating we can obtain five different points from a confidence-judgment matrix to plot an ROC curve. So, we test the model by plotting an ROC curve from data obtained with a confidence-judgment procedure.

Representative data from a single subject from a recent experiment by Murdock and Dufty (1972) are shown in Table 2.2. The confidence-judgment matrix shows the relative frequencies with which each rating was used. They are partitioned (by the experimenter) into old and new items. Briefly, the experimental details were as follows: Each study list consisted of the presentation of 15 common English words randomly sampled from 1024 words. The presentation rate was 0.8 sec/word, and after the study part, 30 items were tested, 15 old and 15 new. To each the subject responded on this six-point scale ($---$ to $+++$). Subjects were tested individually; there was one practice session followed by six test sessions. Each session consisted of 32 study-test lists. Everything was randomized; the sample of words from the pool, the order in which the items were tested, and, for each item, the lag between its presentation and test.

Both raw frequencies and proportions are shown in Table 2.2. The proportions were obtained by cumulating from right to left, as is conventional. These proportions

TABLE 2.2

Absolute Frequencies and Cumulative Proportions of Confidence Judgments to Old and New Test Items (Data of One S from Murdock & Dufty, 1972)

Item type	Confidence judgments					
	$---$	$--$	$-$	$+$	$++$	$+++$
	Frequencies					
Old items	42	111	472	701	465	1089
New items	1137	925	628	161	18	11
	Proportions					
Old items	1.00	.985	.947	.783	.540	.378
New items	1.00	.605	.284	.066	.010	.004

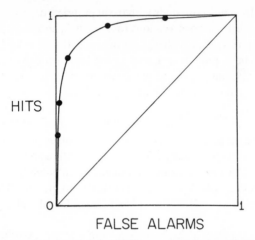

1

HITS

0

FALSE ALARMS

⌈ FIG. 2.7.⌉ Receiver operating characteristic (ROC) curve for data shown in Table 2.2.

then give us five plottable (free) points for an ROC curve, which is shown in Fig. 2.7. Clearly, the obtained curve is not like the curve predicted from either version of the high-threshold model. Such results were obtained by Egan in 1958, and it is reasonable to state that results such as shown in Fig. 2.7 are typical. It is on the basis of such data, then, that high-threshold models have been rejected. The *a posteriori* probability functions discredit them as well; they will be discussed further in the next section.

STRENGTH THEORY

Strength theory is a formal model of recognition developed in a series of theoretical and experimental papers by Norman and Wickelgren (Norman & Wickelgren, 1969; Wickelgren & Norman, 1966; Wickelgren, 1970a). In its simplest form, it (*a*) replaces the rectangular distributions of threshold theory with normal distributions, (*b*) uses a decision rule taken over from the theory of signal detection, (*c*) suggests how memory trace strength varies with lag, and (*d*) tries to incorporate latency measures as well as confidence judgments into the model. Lag is the number of items intervening between presentation of an item and its test.

Memory and Decision

Let us start with the concept of memory trace strength. In discussing the threshold models in the previous section I used the term ''familiarity'' quite freely. It seemed the easiest way to talk about the models. Strength theory substitutes the notion of memory trace strength for the notion of familiarity, if there is a difference. The probability distributions, then, are defined on a strength dimension.

The concept of memory trace strength is certainly not new. In fact, it has much in common with Hullian notions of habit strength, and in one of his unpublished mimeographed memoranda Hull discussed the concept of memory trace strength within the context of his general behavior theory. Many others have used the term, and it certainly does not violate common sense to imagine that there are memory traces of varying degrees of strength. In fact, people might easily characterize strong traces as readily accessible and highly resistant to forgetting. These have their counterparts in two of Hull's measures of reaction potential, latency of response and resistance to extinction (Hull, 1943).

As in threshold theory, new items vary in strength (for whatever reason), only this distribution is presumed to be normal, not rectangular. Presentation of an item (during the study part of an experiment, for instance) boosts the strength of an item from its resting or "noise" level to some higher level. As interference (study or test) builds up, forgetting occurs. The strength of the item in question gradually drops back to its initial resting level. Assessing the strength of an item at different lags will permit us to trace out a forgetting curve. But we must plot the forgetting curve in terms of the proper unit.

If we hold lag constant, then we simply have a new-item distribution $f_n(x)$ which can most easily be considered a unit normal curve with $\mu = 0$ and $\sigma = 1$ and an old-item distribution $f_o(x)$ with $\mu = d'$ and $\sigma = 1$. Since we do not know and will not be able to measure directly the parameters of either distribution, the measures are relative; so it is for reasons of convenience that $f_n(x)$ is considered a unit normal curve. The measure d' of memory trace strength is taken over from signal-detection theory, and simply specifies the mean value of $f_o(x)$. There is no way that the variance of $f_o(x)$ can be less than the variance of $f_n(x)$, but there are many ways that it can be greater. In fact, the ratio of the two variances or, equivalently, the variance of $f_o(x)$ is a useful parameter of the strength-theory model.

As in threshold theory, there is a criterion which dichotomizes "yes" and "no" responses. The reasoning is exactly the same, and those observations from both distributions that exceed criterion receive a "yes" response (so becoming hits and false alarms); those which do not, become misses and correct rejections. The presumed relationships are shown in Fig. 2.8.

The next point to consider is how the criterion is set. As noted above, strength theory follows signal-detection theory in this regard. The subject is assumed to try

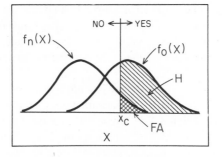

Fɪɢ. 2.8. Old and new item distributions according to strength theory.

to maximize expected value where he is rewarded (by pennies, nickels, or a feeling of satisfaction) for correct responses (hits, correct rejections) but punished for incorrect responses (misses, false alarms). A more rigorous development is given in the next two paragraphs. The reader who is not interested in the derivation should skip ahead.

Assume the subject has a gain of $+1$ for each correct response but a loss of -1 for each incorrect response. Let the hit rate be $p(y|o)$, the false alarm rate be $p(y|n)$, and the *a priori* probability be q. Then one can write the following expression for *EV,* the expected value:

$$EV = [p(y|o)]q - [1 - p(y|o)]q - [p(y|n)](1 - q) + [1 - p(y|n)](1 - q). \tag{2.3}$$

Expand, collect terms, and one has

$$EV = 2[p(y|o)]q + 2[p(y|n)]q - 2q - 2[p(y|n)] + 1. \tag{2.4}$$

Next, it is necessary to differentiate the expression with respect to the criterion. This requires differentiating an integral with respect to its lower limit of integration. If $v = \int_a^\infty f(x)\,dx$ then $dv/da = -f(a)$. Consequently, taking the derivative and setting it equal to zero we have

$$- 2qf_o(c) - 2qf_n(c) + 2f_n(c) = 0. \tag{2.5}$$

Solving, we have

$$f_o(c)/f_n(c) = (1 - q)/q = \beta. \tag{2.6}$$

Thus, to maximize the expected value, the criterion should be set equal to the odds against the occurrence of an old item. For values of q of .2, .5, and .8, the maximum-likelihood values of β are 4, 1, and .25, respectively. The Greek letter β is commonly used to describe the criterion, and it is $f_o(c)/f_n(c)$, that is, the ratio of the ordinates of the two distributions at the cutoff point.

The above derivation is nonparametric in the sense that it does not depend upon assumptions about the underlying distribution. Thus, it is not only for the normal-normal model that the maximum-likelihood rule holds. It does assume a symmetric payoff matrix, but even this assumption can be relaxed somewhat without perturbing the conclusion. Since there has been little or no explicit manipulation of payoff matrices in recognition-memory studies, the symmetric assumption will be made throughout.

The above account of strength theory has blurred a few distinctions in order to facilitate exposition. In the interests of accuracy they should be cleared up here. In the initial account (Wickelgren & Norman, 1966) noise was attributed solely to the decision process, and with criterion variability there should be equal variability for old and new items, resulting in ROC plots with unit slopes. Subsequently Norman and Wickelgren (1969) permit noise in either the trace strength or the location of the criterion, which then makes the slope a free parameter. Also, originally the criterion was defined on a strength continuum and nothing was said about its placement. Later (Norman, 1969a; Norman & Wickelgren, 1969; Wickelgren, 1970a) they seem to espouse the maximum-likelihood decision rule of signal-detection theory, thus presumably making the criterion placement sensitive to the standard variables (*a priori* probability and the payoff matrix).

Model Tests

We have, then, a rationale for the memory and decision components of short-term memory and a measure (d' and β) for each. We are now in a position to make contact with data. We have two options. The first is to see how these measures vary with experimental manipulation. The second is to see how appropriate such measures really are.

Here, the proper first step might be to attempt a fairly complete quantitative description of the phenomena in question. Then, one might start to manipulate independent variables. If one has a proper description with which to begin, then at least one can hope to find out how the parameters of the distributions change with experimental conditions. In this vein, we shall confine our attention in this chapter to examining the adequacy of strength theory to describe data from recognition-memory experiments, and postpone the rest to the next chapter.

How can one test the descriptive power of strength theory with data? There is one standard method, which is really not very good at all. That is to plot an ROC curve on double-normal probability paper (or convert the proportions to standard scores and plot an ROC curve on arithmetic graph paper) then test, if only by inspection, for linearity. One constructs an ROC function in exactly the same way as described

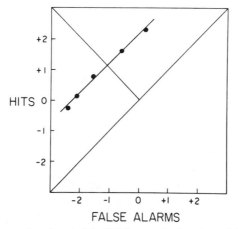

Fig. 2.9. Receiver operating characteristic (ROC) curve for data shown in Table 2.2.

for the threshold model. The data from Table 2.2 are plotted in the appropriate fashion in Fig. 2.9 and, as can be seen, the fit is very respectable. As strength theory says it should be, the data points fall close to the line of best fit. Whether the slope is unity is generally of secondary importance providing, of course, it is not greater than one; technically it is a measure of the variance ratios of the two distributions.

Why then is this a poor measure? Because many other cases result in predictions which are virtually indistinguishable from the double-normal model. If the assumed distributions were Poisson or gamma distributions such a result would not be surprising, since in the limit both cases approach the normal distribution. However, consider the case shown in Fig. 2.10. Clearly the ramp and rectangular distributions are far from being normal, but the data points clearly fall very close to a straight line.

A better test is to evaluate goodness of fit by a standard statistical test, such as χ^2. Here one needs some optimization procedure to guarantee that one does indeed have the best fit possible. Ogilvie and Creelman (1968) have developed a maximum-likelihood estimation procedure for the confidence-rating ROC that is based on a close approximation to the normal distribution, the logistic distribution. For this particular set of data, the maximum-likelihood estimates were $d' = 2.40$ and slope $= 0.836$ with $\chi^2(3) = 18.79$. (If one remembers that the expected value of χ^2 is equal to the number of degrees of freedom, this fit is not all that good. Actually, it was about average for the subjects of this experiment.)

With a $2 \times k$ confidence-judgment matrix there are $k - 1$ degrees of freedom. The row totals are fixed, and in addition you lose two degrees of freedom for the slope and d' parameter, and also $k - 1$ degrees of freedom for the confidence judgments.

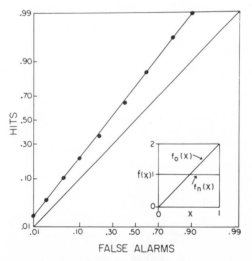

FIG. 2.10. Receiver operating characteristic (ROC) curve for rectangular and ramp distributions. (Fig. 2 from Lockhart and Murdock, 1970.)

It might be thought that only two free parameters are needed to characterize the data with a strength model. That is correct for a yes-no procedure but not for a confidence-judgment procedure. There are in fact $k + 1$ free parameters in this model, which is an important point to keep in mind in its evaluation.

Another way to look at the data is to plot the *a posteriori* probabilities as a function of confidence judgment. An example is shown in Fig. 2.11 where these probabilities are plotted for the data of Table 2.2. What is shown there is commonly found (at least with prior probabilities around .5 and reasonable values of d'), and there are two main points to note. The first and more important point is that the extreme confidence judgments ($- - -$ and $+ + +$) show *a posteriori* probabilities very near 0 and 1. In fact, in this particular case they are .036 and .990, respectively. The second point is that they are monotonic, with *a posteriori* probabilities increasing without exception from left to right. This second point is less important because of the differential reliability of these points in the data. Under certain conditions (practiced subjects, slow presentation rate, repeated lists, etc.) one or more of the middle confidence judgments may be rarely used. Consequently, the middle points may be less (or much less) reliable than the extremes, so the odd inversion is bound to occur.

These *a posteriori* probability functions are not so much a test of strength theory as they are a tribute to the subject's ability to make accurate discriminations about memory traces in his head. Strength theory does indeed require the monotonicity, but so do most other theories that one could envisage. Since the location of the confidence judgments are free parameters in the fitting, little significance one way or the other can be attached to this result. However, the accuracy of discrimination is impressive, especially when one remembers that these extremes may be based on a thousand or so observations each. When one is correct 975–995 times in 1000, one comes to feel that one can believe the subject when he is confident.

FIG. 2.11. *A posteriori* probability as a function of confidence judgment for the data of Table 2.2.

In addition to their intrinsic interest, these *a posteriori* probability functions have some theoretical value. The use of ROC curves to test models has been variously discussed (e.g., Larkin, 1965; Broadbent, 1966a) and problems noted. A more satisfactory way has been proposed by Krantz (1969) who suggests as a viable candidate a three-state low- and high-threshold model (see also the right-hand panel of Fig. 2.6). He concludes that the most promising way to reject such a theory would be to show that the *a posteriori* probability can approach zero for moderate signal strengths. Whether memory traces can be characterized as of moderate strength is a moot point, but at first glance such a three-state model would be applicable here, given the very low *a posteriori* probability for a "sure no" response.

Also, *a posteriori* probability functions can be useful in testing whether subjects set their criterion in accord with a maximum-likelihood principle, as strength theory now seems to say they should. In an unpublished doctoral dissertation Donaldson (1967) tried to test this point directly. In two conditions of his experiment, the *a priori* probability of an old item was either .5 or .2. (He used a continuous procedure, which will be more fully discussed in the next chapter, and also three-digit numbers rather than words, but these changes probably are not crucial.) If subjects followed a maximum-likelihood principle, they should have changed their criterion from 1.0 to 4.0 as the *a priori* probability symbolized by q in Eq. (2.6) changed from .5 to .2. They did not; in fact, a more accurate description of the subject's response to this experimental manipulation (of which, of course, they were informed) was that they used exactly the same cut-off points on the strength dimension under the two conditions. Such a decision rule can be inferred from consideration of the *a posteriori* probability functions. This point is discussed at greater length and illustrated elsewhere (Murdock, 1972).

However, one would be rash to reject completely the maximum-likelihood principle on the basis of this particular finding. For one thing, it is only one experiment and additional verification is needed. Secondly, a psychological theory is not like a principle of logic, where one single exception is sufficient to reject it. Any theory that we have can be contradicted by some data somewhere, so one must assess the pros and cons rather than adopt an unrealistically high criterion. Most important, a decent theory is never terminated by negative findings; it is replaced by more adequate theories. So a reasonable approach might be to make a mental footnote about this problem of strength theory, not reject it out of hand.

However, the fact remains that some experimental separation of the parameters of strength theory would be desirable. As noted above, one would like to find one manipulation to affect d' and another to affect β. Donaldson tried and was unsuccessful. Looking for something else, an unpublished experiment conducted at Toronto by Elisabeth Wells succeeded. In her experiment, the stimulus items were either CVC (consonant-vowel-consonant) or CCC (consonant-consonant-consonant) combinations and (testing only a single item after each study list of 12 items) the *a priori* probabilities were either .60 or .86. Her results are shown in Table 2.3, and it is abundantly clear that the type of material affects d' but not β, while the *a priori* probability affects β but not d'. The cause of the discrepancy between the Donald-

TABLE 2.3

Effects of Type of Material and *a Priori* Probability
on d' and β
(Elisabeth Wells, unpublished)

A *priori* probability	d'		β	
	CVC	CCC	CVC	CCC
.60	1.04	0.57	1.09	1.04
.86	1.01	0.43	0.72	0.79

son results and the Wells results is certainly not clear, but we could suggest several possible reasons. The more important point is that experimental separation of strength-theory parameters is possible. Perhaps it should be mentioned that the .86 condition followed the .60 condition and that judgments of recency were added in the former as well. One cannot be sure that these factors did not play a role in the results. Although the above analyses are based on pooled data, when d' and β are computed separately for each subject the analyses of variance provide statistical documentation. The type of stimulus material had a significant effect on d' but not on β, while *a priori* probability had a significant effect on β but not on d'.

Evaluation

What, then, is our current assessment of strength theory? Clearly it has strengths and weaknesses. In regard to its strengths, we have found that it consistently does an excellent job in describing the data from relatively simple recognition-memory experiments. The ROC curves are quite reasonable, and the *a posteriori* probability functions are well-behaved. Experimental separation of its two parameters (d' and β) is possible. Whether or not subjects really do follow a maximum-likelihood principle is probably not all that important; if (or when) they do not, this aspect of the theory can be changed without otherwise changing the model. More important is the fact that explicit predictions about the criterion can be obtained from the theory.

There is another important advantage that has not yet been mentioned. From strength theory it is possible to make predictions about performance in an *m*-alternative forced-choice (*m*-AFC) procedure. So far we have referred to yes-no and confidence-judgment procedures. Yet a third procedure is one in which, on each test trial, *m* alternatives are presented, of which one is an old item and $m - 1$ are lures (new items). If for a given subject under a certain set of conditions we know the value of d', then it is possible to predict the probability of a correct response under an *m*-AFC procedure for any value of *m*. This is a powerful way of testing the theory, as it could provide evidence for trans-situational invariance.

Such a prediction can only be obtained if one is willing to make assumptions about the processes involved in the forced-choice task. The general assumptions commonly made are that there are m normal distributions, $m - 1$ of them the unit-normal distributions previously used to characterize $f_n(x)$, and the one old-item distribution $f_o(x)$ with $\mu = d'$ and unit variance. The predicted probability of a correct response is then the probability that one observation drawn at random from $f_o(x)$ exceeds all observations drawn (one each) from the $m - 1$ new-item distributions. As far as I know, no analytic solution has been found, but the problem can be solved by numerical methods and tables for such solutions exist (see Appendix 1 in Swets, 1964). Experimental work on this problem and tests of the strength-theory prediction have been reported by Green and Moses (1966) and by Kintsch (1968a). In both cases the results were positive. Further, Murdock and Dufty (1972) have shown that d' values from yes-no and confidence-judgment procedures are consistent with each other. Thus, so far all the evidence suggests that the three procedures (yes-no, confidence-judgment, and m-AFC) give interchangeable results, and this finding provides very strong support indeed for strength theory.

One final point before turning to criticisms of the theory. Strength theory also has some things to say about encoding and about forgetting. In particular, it has been suggested that

$$p(i) = \alpha\phi^i \tag{2.7}$$

where $p(i)$ is the strength of the memory trace of the item at lag i (measured in terms of d'), α is the encoding parameter, and ϕ is the forgetting parameter (Norman, 1969a, p. 151). This particular formulation predicts that forgetting (decrease in d' with lag) should be exponential. There is abundant evidence that it is (e.g., Wickelgren, 1970b). This empirical finding is more a testimony to the reliability of data than a credit to the theory. The exponential-forgetting assumption (Wickelgren & Norman, 1966) was selected because it was said to be most in accord with the available data.

On the negative side, two main criticisms may be advanced. The first criticism of the theory concerns its sufficiency. While it may do very well in the highly structured situation of recognition-memory experiments, extension to more complex situations may reveal strength theory to be lacking. Such criticisms have recently been advanced by Anderson and Bower (1972a). Their criticisms basically revolve around the question of discriminability. Strength theory seems to make no provision for such an ability. Thus, subjects remember much more than just the strength of an item. They can report many of its attributes. Perhaps more telling, non-list items which may be similar to presented items and which subjects have encountered (e.g., in mnemonic constructions to help remember the list, or in the instructions intervening between presentation and test) seldom occur as intrusions in recall or, presumably, as false alarms in recognition tests. If all that characterized the memory trace of an item was some unidimensional trace strength, then there is no provision for discrimination.

The second criticism is the lack of fruitfulness of strength theory. Somehow, it just does not seem too useful to say that items are represented in memory by some strength value, that the distributions are normal, and that the important processes can be captured and represented by the parameters d', β, α, and ϕ. Somehow there is more to memory than that. Just what will become clearer in the next section.

So, useful though it is within a particular sphere of applicability, strength theory is less useful in the more general case. Its proponents could (indeed, may) modify it accordingly. Indeed, any theory can be modified and improved, but then it is a different theory. Rather than await such modification or attempt it ourself, let us turn to versions of an attribute theory which have been constructed with exactly such problems in mind.

ATTRIBUTE THEORIES

The general view here is that the memory trace is not unitary; instead, it is a collection of attributes. These attributes may refer to physical properties of the stimulus or associative properties of the response. Just as a tangerine is round, yellowish-orange, divided into sections, and has string-like fibers on the surface, so it is a class of objects that is edible, a fruit with a rather bland taste, slightly acidic, and certainly more similar to oranges than to bananas. The attributes, of course, are in the encoded representation of the stimulus object.

These then are possible attributes of one particular object, although they are certainly neither exhaustive nor universal. Imagine a recognition-memory experiment with such stimuli. Perhaps when the tangerine is presented nothing corresponding to tangerine *per se* is encoded; instead, some subset of its possible attributes are. Over time some of these attributes may be forgotten. At the time of test, whether or not the subject remembers having seen a tangerine in the test list depends upon how many of the encoded attributes are still intact.

Background

Such a view was clearly stated and thoroughly developed in the influential multi-component paper of Bower (1967b). He suggested that the memory trace be considered a vector of attributes. The elements of the vector were the particular attributes encoded. The input to the memory system was the output from the pattern recognition system. That is, one must recognize what an object is before it can be entered into memory, so there must be separate systems or stages of processing—one for recognition and one for memory. Some mechanism is also needed on the output side. Bower suggested distinguishing between a primary code and a secondary code. The primary code is the vector of attributes; the secondary code is, perhaps, a verbal label. More generally, it is something that enables the person to name what he has just seen.

Even at the time of Bower's paper, attribute representation of stimuli was not new. A distinctive-features representation of speech sounds had been suggested by Jakobsen and Halle (1956), with some impressive experimental confirmation by Miller and Nicely (1955). In vision, Eleanor Gibson (1965) had suggested an analogous feature system for letters, and she has more recently used it as a basis for studying perceptual development and reading (Gibson, 1969). Even in linguistics, the notion of semantic markers had been suggested (Katz & Fodor, 1963) wherein an attribute (marker) system was used to characterize meaning. And in the computer simulation field the EPAM (Elementary Perceiver and Memorizer) model of Feigenbaum and Simon (1963) and the SAL (Stimulus and Association Learner) model of Hintzman (1968) used a sorting tree based on features that would recognize stimuli. (For a far more extensive treatment of work in pattern recognition than can be given here see Kolers, 1968; Lindgren, 1965a, 1965b, 1965c; Neisser, 1967; and F. Smith, 1971.) However, Bower was the first to make a thorough and detailed application of pattern recognition to human memory.

A later attempt to do much the same was a paper by Norman and Rumelhart (1970) in a book edited by Norman (1970a). In the Norman and Rumelhart paper, on the perceptual side they considered the extraction of relevant features from the sensory image and the identification with a previously learned structure. On the memory side, they considered the distinction between short- and long-term traces, the transfer mechanism from short- to long-term memory, and the retrieval cues used by subjects in answering questions. It was, perhaps, on Norman's part an attempt to improve strength theory by embedding it within a larger framework, thereby vitiating some of the criticisms of strength theory made at the end of the previous section. As in the Bower paper, there was considerable mathematical development, and in both cases what seems to have caught on and become popular is the general viewpoint rather than the detailed model *per se*.

The most recent version of such a theory is given in a paper by Bower (1972b) entitled "Stimulus-sampling theory of encoding variability." It modifies and, presumably, supersedes the multicomponent paper. It draws heavily on the stimulus-sampling theory of Estes (see Neimark & Estes, 1967). Since the concepts of stimulus-sampling theory are so directly and immediately applicable to an attribute model of memory, let us start with a simple introduction.

Stimulus-Sampling Theory

Stimulus-sampling theory provides for representation of stimuli, responses, associations, and reinforcement. Let a stimulus be represented by a population of stimulus elements:

$$S = \{s_1, s_2, s_3, \dots, s_N\} \tag{2.8}$$

These are hypothetical constructs, and stimulus-sampling theory never becomes very definite as to what they are. However, the tangerine example given previously might be illustrative, where S stands for the stimulus object itself and $s_1, s_2, \dots, s_N$ are its various attributes. However, note that these attributes are to be considered internal not external events, that is, perceptual or psychological events rather than physical ones (in the sense of radiant energy impinging upon the organism).

The responses are mutually exclusive and exhaustive; they can be represented as $A_1, A_2, \dots, A^*$ where A^* is a wastebasket category to represent everything else. In many cases, only two responses are considered. Thus, in a yes-no recognition-memory procedure A_1 might be the response "no" and A_2 the response "yes." If the subject was forced to make a response every time (i.e., omissions or saying "I don't know" were not permitted) then this enumeration would be exhaustive.

For reinforcement, if there are response classes A_1, A_2, A_3, . . . , A_K, then it is necessary to define $K + 1$ reinforcing events E_1, E_2, . . . , K_K, E_o. The last of these, E_o, is no reinforcement. If E_i follows A_i then all elements in S which were sampled on that trial become conditioned or associated to A_i. If E_j or E_o follows A_i then the sampled elements do not become conditioned. On any given trial, the system starts in some state. The stimuli are sampled, a response occurs, it is followed by an outcome, and then a particular E_i. A new state is formed, which characterizes the system at the start of the next trial.

This formulation is deliberately made very general so that stimulus-sampling theory can be applied to a variety of situations. These have included classical conditioning, T-maze performance by animals, probability learning, paired-associate learning, and, most recently, encoding variability. One of the most readable general accounts is found in Hilgard and Bower (1966, pp. 338–375). But let us turn directly to the Bower (1972b) model.

Bower Attribute Model

It is assumed that each nominal stimulus in the experiment can give rise to N possible elements, or attributes. When a nominal stimulus is presented, s of the N elements are sampled. For example, one may think of certain aspects or attributes of the stimulus, but not others. This makes for two sets, the active set of size s and the inactive set of size $N - s$. Then, during the retention interval, fluctuation takes place. Performance on a recognition test depends upon how much the response to the probe resembles the degraded vector of the original response.

The concept of fluctuation is very important in stimulus-sampling theory in general and in the encoding-variability model of Bower in particular. Fluctuation is essentially a change in state from one moment to another. Here, a conditioned element may move from the active set to the inactive set. The process is symmetric, so there is a compensatory change in the other direction. To maintain equilibrium, a conditioned element that moves from the active to the inactive set is replaced by an (unconditioned) element that moves from the inactive to the active set. A hypothetical example is shown in Fig. 2.12 where the active set starts with three conditioned elements (attributes) and the inactive set starts with four unconditioned elements. The middle panel indicates the change about to take place, and the right-hand panel shows the state of affairs after the exchange has occurred.

Clearly, this fluctuation is a simple process, but it has a number of very considerable conceptual advantages. First, such an elemantaristic viewpoint suggests an overall way of conceptualizing such processes as learning, forgetting, extinction, and spontaneous recovery. Secondly, it is mathematically tractable, as the process can be represented by a very simple Markov process that has explicit solutions that are easy to derive. Third, it produces a geometric or exponential forgetting function, which roughly agrees not only with our intuitions but also with much of our data. Not

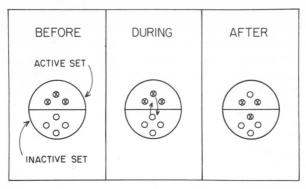

FIG. 2.12. Illustration of fluctuation in the encoding-variability model of Bower (1972b).

that there is any such thing as *the* forgetting function, but if we had to pick one, it would be exponential.

Fluctuation is assumed to occur over time as a Poisson process. That is, in each small unit of time there is a constant probability of an interchange. (This is a very common assumption for such models.) In the Bower model c is the probability of an interchange in any given unit of time. The probability that an element will move from the active set to the inactive set is the probability that it will be selected, (which is $1/s$) times the probability c that, if selected, it will interchange. (Think of marbles in an urn; there are red marbles in Urn I and green marbles in Urn II. At any point in time there is a constant probability of an interchange, which means a red marble going to Urn I and being replaced by a green marble from Urn II. For a particular red marble to transfer it must be both selected and moved.) Correspondingly, the probability that an element from the inactive set moves to the active set is $c/(N - s)$. We can then write the transition matrix T, which is

$$T = \begin{array}{c} \\ A_t \\ \bar{A}_t \end{array} \begin{array}{cc} A_{t+1} & \bar{A}_{t+1} \\ \left[\begin{array}{cc} 1 - c/s & c/s \\ c/(N - s) & 1 - c/(N - s) \end{array} \right]. \end{array} \qquad (2.9)$$

In a transition matrix such as this, the rows specify the states of the system at one point in time, and the columns specify the states of the system at the next point in time. Here the states of the system are A (the active set) and $\bar{A}$ (the inactive set), and the subscripts t and $t + 1$ represent one point in time and the next point in time. The entries in the matrix are the transition probabilities. There is one probability (c/s) for fluctuation from A to $\bar{A}$ (and its complement, $1 - c/s$, for no fluctuation). There is another (different) probability for fluctuation from $\bar{A}$ to A (and again its complement for no fluctuation). The transition probabilities for fluctuation in the two directions will be equal only if the size of the active set is the same as the size of the inactive set.

From such a transition matrix, there are various ways in which one can arrive at an explicit equation to characterize the forgetting process. For solutions see Goldberg (1961, pp. 221–228) or Levine and Burke (1972, pp. 150–152). The solution can be represented as

$$a_t = J - (J - a_0)h^t \qquad (2.10)$$

where $J = s/N$ and h is the rate constant (a function of c, s, and N). In this equation a_0 is the starting state (active or inactive) and a_t is the state at time t. At $t = 0$, $a_t = a_0$ by definition; as t approaches infinity, a_t approaches the asymptote J and at an exponential rate determined by the value of the parameter h.

The application of this model to recognition memory is now quite straightforward. New items have not previously been presented, so one might think they would have zero conditioned elements. Were such the case, there would be no false alarms, which is patently false from examination of the data. So it is necessary to assume (as all other models do too, one way or another) that some rather small number of their attributes in the active set will have been activated or conditioned by prior presentation of other items. Assuming independence, then the distribution of active elements across new items will be the binomial $B(x; p, s)$. That is, it will be a binomial distribution in x where p is the probability of any particular element having been conditioned earlier, and s is simply the size of the active set.

For the old item distribution, there are two components that determine performance. One is the residual fluctuation state. That is, the more conditioned elements that are still in the active set at the time of test, the higher the probability of a "yes" response. The second component is the "false recognition" component. If a small number of elements from new items can have become conditioned, such must also be the case for old items as well. Thus, one has two sources of active elements to comprise the old-item distribution.

The decision rule is straightforward. At the time of test the subject assesses the number of conditioned elements in the active set and responds accordingly. One simply has two binomial distributions, where $f_n(x) = B(x;p,s)$, and $f_o(x) = B(x;r,s)$ where r is a probability reflecting the joint contribution of the two ways the elements can be conditioned for the old-item distribution. If the count exceeds the criterion, then the subject says "yes"; otherwise, "no". The extension to the confidence-judgment procedure is like that in strength theory, so the ROC curve is deducible from the model in exactly the same way. The fact that the distributions are assumed to be binomial means that, for moderate values of (the product of) the parameters, the binomial is indistinguishable from the normal distribution. Strength theory falls out as a special case of the Bower model. For extreme values quite different-looking distributions result.

The model can handle much more than performance in a simple recognition-memory situation. In his paper, Bower extends it to the 2-AFC situation, lag effects in repetition, learning effects, absolute and relative judgments of recency, and list differentiation. This latter application requires some further concepts and provides a link to free recall.

What evaluation of the Bower model can be given? On the favorable side, it seems to be the best general model for item recognition that we have; in fact, it may with some justification be thought of as the only general model for item recognition. Threshold theory is clearly wrong, the encoding-variability model subsumes the strength model as a special case and covers much more, so what else is there? Fanciful and counter-intuitive as some of the stimulus-sampling theory notions may seem upon first exposure, they have turned out to be very general and very powerful in their application. And in a sense we are really talking about models. We are talking about ways of characterizing the system. We would like to know, of course, how the mind really does work. But we are so far from that goal that for the present we should be satisfied with the next best thing—how it might work. The strength and significance of a model such as stimulus-sampling theory in general, or the encoding-variability model in particular, is that it provides a conceptual framework to integrate a number of otherwise disparate phenemona and, with its precision and potential rigor, provides within it a basis for its eventual demise. Stated otherwise, it is capable of disproof. As has been stated before and will be stated again, that is the only way we are going to progress—by testing current theories, finding out exactly where and how they are wrong, and replacing them with better theories.

What is wrong with the Bower model? First, the model simply makes very general predictions of an ordinal variety. No parameter estimation is presented in the paper, and no indices of goodness of fit. More important, there is no evidence of transsituational invariance, that is, parameters estimated from data in one situation holding constant when applied to another situation. There is, of course, no reason why this omission could not be rectified, and the previous successes of stimulus-sampling models auger well in this regard.

However, there is one fairly important point where the model is contradicted by the data. In strength-theory terms, the d' value will be determined by the distance between the mean of the two distributions, which in turn will reflect the number of conditioned elements in the active set for old and new items. As the model is stated, the more items that have been presented, the greater the number of conditioned elements in the new-item set. Consequently, in a continuous task there should be a decrease in d' over the course of the session. It is well-known that false alarms in a continuous recognition-memory task increase throughout the course of the list (Shepard & Teghtsoonian, 1961). However, a study by Donaldson and Murdock (1968) showed that this change was basically a criterion change rather than a change in d'. This finding seems contrary to what the Bower model would predict.

To conclude this section, let us consider another attribute model, one proposed by Robert Lockhart at a summer conference on mathematical models held at Massachusetts Institute of Technology in 1969. In many ways it is similar to the Bower model, but two differences justify its inclusion here. First, it is not a legacy of stimulus-sampling theory, hence it can be said to be a realistic competitor to the encoding-variability model of Bower. Secondly, it is slightly more elegant in that several special cases fall out quite unexpectedly.

Lockhart Attribute Model

The Lockhart model starts off very much like the Bower model. Assume there is a set of activated elements that are the encoded representation of a stimulus item. Each item has its own set of elements, and each element is in one of two states, activated (A) or not (N). The basic unknown is the number of activated elements. For encoding, during presentation over each small instant of time there is a constant probability p that any particular element will be activated. By a perfectly standard development (e.g., Feller, 1968, pp. 156–159) it then follows that the distribution of activated elements will be Poisson; specifically,

$$P(x = k) = \frac{e^{-\phi}\phi^k}{k!} \tag{2.11}$$

where $\phi = pt$ and $E(x) = \phi$. Thus, the distribution of activated elements is here represented as Poisson, not binomial as in Bower's model; also, the effect of presentation time on initial encoding is immediately represented.

For storage, the Estes fluctuation process is assumed, as in the Bower model. Let α be the probability that an activated element will move from State A to State N (become de-activated), and let β be the probability an inactive element will move from State N to State A (become activated). Then the transition matrix T is

$$T = \begin{array}{c} \\ A_t \\ N_t \end{array} \begin{array}{cc} A_{t+1} & N_{t+1} \\ \left[\begin{array}{cc} 1 - \alpha & \alpha \\ \beta & 1 - \beta \end{array} \right]. \end{array} \tag{2.12}$$

With this transition matrix, P_t, the probability that an element is activated at time t, is

$$P_t = \frac{\beta}{\alpha + \beta} + \left(1 - \frac{\beta}{\alpha + \beta}\right)(1 - \alpha - \beta)^t \tag{2.13}$$

which is, of course, the exact counterpart of Eq. (2.10) in Bower's model.

Next, assume that attributes fluctuate independently. Then the conditional distribution is binomial; specifically, $P(Y_t = j \mid x = k) = B(j; P_t, k)$.   That is, Y_t is the number of activated elements at time t which is what we want, since that will provide the basis for response in the recognition-memory test. It is conditional on the starting state; if the number of activated elements at the time of presentation were, for instance, five, how many are still activated at time t? It turns out that the marginal distribution is simply

$$P(Y_t = j) = \frac{e^{-\phi P_t}(\phi P_t)^j}{j!} \tag{2.14}$$

That is, the distribution of activated elements at time t is also Poisson, now with parameter ϕP_t. This is a nice result, and the interested reader is encouraged to work through the proof himself. All one needs to do is set up the bivariate distribution with a Poisson marginal and a binomial conditional distribution, multiply terms, factor out the right quantity in each expression, and one then arrives at the other marginal (unconditional) distribution which is shown in Eq. (2.14).

We have, then, an encoding process, a forgetting assumption, and a distribution to characterize the system at the time of the test. A retrieval assumption can be incorporated to make statements about recall. We turn now to some of the special cases that fall out of this model.

First, at asymptote let $s = \beta/(\alpha + \beta)$. Then the distribution of activated elements is Poisson with parameter ϕs. If $\beta = o$, then

$$P(Y_t = j) = \frac{e^{-\phi(1 - \alpha)^t}\left[\phi(1 - \alpha)^t\right]^j}{j!} \tag{2.15}$$

and $E(Y_t) = \phi (1 - \alpha)^t$. That is, forgetting should be exponential, and it is the expectation of a random variable. This relationship, then, is predictable from the model and is not simply assumed *ad hoc*. If $\beta \neq 0$ then $E(Y_t) = \phi(s + (1 - s)b^t)$ where $b = 1 - \alpha - \beta$. This exponential function has been found by Wickelgren and Norman (1966).

Suppose the components function as a pattern (in the Estes sense) and so are all or none. Then

$$P_t = \frac{\beta}{\alpha + \beta} + \left(1 - \frac{\beta}{\alpha + \beta}\right)(1 - \alpha - \beta)^t \tag{2.16}$$

since there is only one element to consider. This formulation has provided the cornerstone for a finite-state decision model suggested by Murdock (1967b, 1970, 1972) for paired associates. This model will be discussed further in Chapter 4.

Finally, and perhaps most surprising, suppose recall is possible if at least one activated element exists at the time of attempted retrieval. Then if $\beta = 0$

$$P(Y_t \geq h) = 1 - \sum_{j = 0}^{n - 1} \frac{e^{-\phi P_t}(\phi P_t)^j}{j!} = 1 - e^{-\phi(1 - \alpha)^t}. \tag{2.17}$$

This equation is a Gompertz double-exponential, which has long been known to characterize the serial-position effect of single-trial free recall (Murdock, 1962a, 1972). Thus, as special cases we have the exponential-forgetting function characteristic of studies of item recognition, we have the fluctuation model for paired associates, and we have the Gompertz double-exponential function for single-trial free recall.

The Lockhart attribute model, then, would seem to provide a very useful conceptual framework for looking at item recognition. Like the Bower model it is untested, as no serious parameter estimates have been made. Consequently, no invariance relationships have been found, nor do we know whether they will be. Further, I have made a few preliminary attempts to reconcile the Gompertz Eq. (2.17) with one known to describe serial-position effects (see Murdock, 1962a, p. 484) but have not been too successful in the attempt to match them. However, the Lockhart model has sufficient scope and explanatory power to warrant further investigation.

SUMMARY

Item information is studied experimentally by means of recognition-memory procedures. These procedures test whether the subject remembers the occurrence of a particular item in a particular context (e.g., the most recent list). Theories of item information attempt to characterize the encoding, storage, and retrieval processes.

Threshold theories are relatively formal and precise models of intuitive ideas about item information and may be the appropriate characterization of the view that list presentation simply tags some long-term memory representation of the item. A simple threshold model says that there are separate memory-trace distributions for old and new items, and these distributions may be characterized as rectangular. Criterion cuts partition the responses into four types: hits, false alarms, correct rejections, and misses. Variations in the location of these criterion cuts make it possible to generate ROC curves, and threshold models predict that such curves should be composed of linear segments when hits are plotted as a function of false alarms on arithmetical coordinates. The ROC curves obtained from recognition-memory experiments are generally curvilinear instead. Confidence-judgment procedures make it possible to plot *a posteriori* probability functions. Threshold theories predict they should be step-like or discrete (two- or three-valued), but they are generally graded or continuous over the confidence judgments used.

Strength theory assumes underlying normal, rather than rectangular, distributions defined on a dimension of memory-trace strength. Trace strength is assumed to decay exponentially with lag, and the decision rule is based on the maximum-likelihood principle of signal-detection theory. Many of the findings from studies of recognition memory (e.g., the ROC curves, the *a posteriori* probability functions, forced-choice predictions, and the retention curves) are in good agreement with strength-theory predictions. However, subjects seem able to make discriminations between memory traces on bases other than strength; also, they seem to remember many of the attributes of items.

Attribute theories take a different view of memory. The memory trace is considered to be a collection or vector of attributes, and these define the item. Attributes are lost over time, but some characteristics endure longer than others. Attribute models have a natural representation in the stimulus-sampling theory of Estes.

One attribute theory is the encoding-variability model of Bower, which is directly in the stimulus-sampling tradition. Some number of attributes of an item are conditioned at the time of presentation, and these attributes fluctuate over time. Recognition responses and confidence judgments are based on the number of activated elements at the time of test. New items are also assumed to have some low number of conditioned elements, and these produce the false positives in the experimental data. The encoding-variability model can account for many findings from recognition-memory experiments.

The Lockhart attribute model assumes the initial encoding to be a time-dependent process; the distribution of encoded attributes is Poisson, not binomial as in the Bower model. The same fluctuation process is assumed, but at any retention interval the distribution of encoded attributes is still Poisson. Exponential decay, the all-or-none pattern case, and a Gompertz double-exponential all fall out as special cases of the model.

3
DATA ON ITEM INFORMATION

In this chapter we shall present some of the important experimental data from studies of memory for item information. The particular topics to be considered are the nature of the forgetting function, confidence judgments and latency, variations in stimulus material, the number and nature of the test alternatives, recall-recognition comparisons, judgments of recency and frequency, and retrieval processes in recognition memory.

FORGETTING FUNCTIONS

How does familiarity decrease over time? The best general answer is to say that d', the strength-theory measure of memory, decreases exponentially with lag. Lag is defined as the number of items intervening between the presentation of an item and its test. Sometimes the term decay is used in this context, but no theoretical commitments to decay theory are intended. The causal factor is presumed to be the interference generated by the intervening items, so it is an interference conception, not temporal decay. Equation (2.7) is a particular formulation of this forgetting function, and illustrative data are given in Figure 3.1.

In this figure the data are plotted in two ways. The upper panel shows probability of recognition as a function of lag with the false-alarm rate shown below. The lower panel shows the data converted to a d' measure as discussed in the last chapter. It is d', not probability of recognition, that decreases exponentially with lag. To test, simply take logarithms of both sides of Eq. (2.7) and one has

$$\ln P(i) = i \ln \phi + \ln \alpha. \qquad (3.1)$$

That is, memory strength on a log scale will be a linear function of i, the amount of

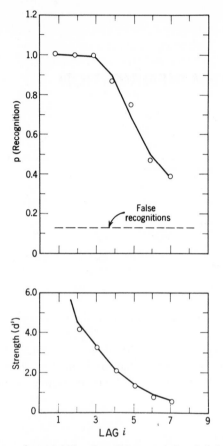

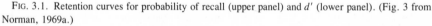

FIG. 3.1. Retention curves for probability of recall (upper panel) and d' (lower panel). (Fig. 3 from Norman, 1969a.)

interference, with slope of ln ϕ and intercept of ln α. With experimental data there are a variety of methods to obtain estimates of the parameters α and ϕ. The simplest perhaps is graphical; see Murdock and Cook (1960). More powerful methods exist, if the data warrant their use.

Even though this function is espoused by strength theory, it is an empirical not a theoretical function. Initially it was chosen because it described data (Wickelgren & Norman, 1966); it was not deduced as a consequence of any underlying assumptions. However, it is useful theoretically in that it can, in principle, separate encoding and forgetting; also, it provides a way of detecting differences in the rate of forgetting as a function of various experimental conditions. However, the evidence to date is meager. In one experiment, Wickelgren (1970b) presented lists of 9 or 15 letters at rates of 1, 2, or 4 letters per second and found the expected exponential forgetting. However, decay rates were not constant as measured either in terms of elapsed time or number of intervening items. In a study of an amnesic patient, Wickelgren (1968) found the same short-term decay rates for single digits, digit triples, and the pitch of pure tones, and the rate constant was within the range of normal variation. Also, Norman and Waugh (1968) compared study and test interference effects. In the former case interference is due to the presentation of additional items, while in the latter case interference is due to the testing of old items. Unfortunately, the two experiments reported were discrepant. In the first experiment, study and test interference were equal; in the second experiment, each test item produced interference equivalent to two study items.

In studies of this kind one can either use a discrete-trials procedure (as above) or a continuous recognition-memory paradigm (to be discussed). In the former, study and test trials are clearly separate (generally they alternate); in the latter, study and test trials are intermixed. With a discrete-trials procedure one can test anywhere from one to all items in the list. The former would be a probe test, and if more than a single item is tested the problem of output interference arises. As noted above, the data here are discrepant; also, there is a problem as to the proper false-alarm rate. That is, new items by definition have no lag, so one must use a common false-alarm rate to estimate d' for all old items. Analysis of the data of Murdock and Dufty (1972) showed that the distribution of confidence judgments to new items changed appreciably over the course of testing. The solution is not clear, but the problem should be recognized.

In an old experiment by Strong (1912), either 5, 10, 25, 50, 100, or 150 magazine advertisements were presented at a rate of one item per second followed by a yes-no recognition test. The results are shown in Table 3.1, and a semilog plot of these data are, except for the 50-item list, well fit by a straight line. Averaging over lag may introduce a bias; still, the data from discrete-trials procedures do seem to show that d' does generally decrease exponentially with lag.

In a continuous recognition memory task with a yes-no procedure Shepard and Teghtsoonian (1961) found that hit rate falls off sharply with lag, and their data are shown in Fig. 3.2. Comparable results for a forced-choice procedure were found by Shepard and Chang (1963). These effects have been replicated in a number of studies, both published and unpublished, and there is little doubt as to their relia-

TABLE 3.1

Hit Rate, False Alarms, and d' for Recognition Memory
for Advertisements (Strong, 1912)

Length	Mean lag	Hit rate	False alarms	d'
5	7.5	.822	.008	3.32
10	15	.815	.010	3.22
25	37.5	.729	.012	2.87
50	75	.616	.034	2.11
100	150	.564	.045	1.87
150	225	.404	.038	1.53

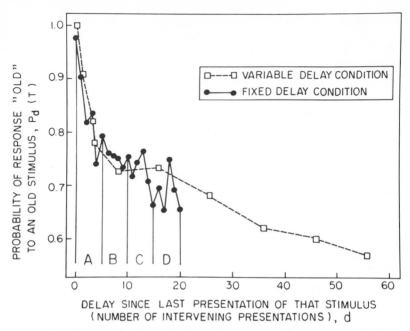

FIG. 3.2. Forgetting as a function of lag in a continuous recognition-memory experiment. (Fig. 1 from Shepard & Teghtsoonian, 1961.)

bility. An interpretive problem arises in the increasing number of false alarms over trial blocks but, as noted in the last chapter, this effect seems to be due more to criterion than to loss of discrimination *per se*.

Although no studies have systematically traced out retention curves as a function of number of presentations, there is evidence (Kintsch, 1965a) that errors decrease with repetition. In a further study using a shift design (Kintsch, 1966) it was found that items repeated at a short lag fared badly when shifted to a long lag, but the converse was not true. The theoretical interpretation was elaborated in a later paper (Kintsch, 1967) where a synthesis between a finite-state Markov model and a continuous familiarity dimension was suggested. This position and a review of the literature has most recently been given in Kintsch (1970a).

As has been noted, the exponential forgetting found with the discrete-trials procedure is consistent with an attribute model for item recognition. In the Lockhart model, for instance, the relevant equations were given in the last chapter. Intuitively, it can be understood at a very simple level. If memory consists of a bundle of attributes, and if the attributes are independent, all-or-none, and forgotten with a constant probability, then forgetting must be exponential, because the loss of attribute information with each item of interference is proportional to the number of attributes yet to be lost. If recovery is allowed, as in the fluctuation assumption, then an asymptote is introduced but the forgetting is still exponential.

CONFIDENCE JUDGMENTS AND LATENCY

In the last few years investigators have started to supplement the conventional accuracy measures with two additional measures, confidence judgments and latency. You will remember that in a confidence-judgment procedure the subject not only identifies an item as old or new, but assigns a rating to indicate his degree of confidence. The latency measure is simply the time elapsed between the onset of the probe and the execution of the response. One can either time a simple binary yes-no response and let the confidence judgment follow, or one can combine the yes-no response and the confidence judgment into a 6- to 10-point scale and measure the reaction time for this single response. The latter procedure is generally followed, though without any particular theoretical rationale.

Confidence Judgments

As discussed in the previous chapter, this rating method was first used for the study of item recognition by Egan (1958). Since then it has been used by a number of investigators (e.g., Bernbach, 1967a; Donaldson & Murdock, 1968; Kintsch, 1967; Murdock & Dufty, 1972; Norman & Wickelgren, 1965), and the results are quite consistent. The ROC curves are generally linear on a double-normal plot (see Fig. 2.9), and the *a posteriori* probability functions are generally monotonic (see Fig. 2.11). Further, it is quite clear that d', the strength-theory parameter, varies as expected with changes in the retention interval (lag) and with number of repetitions (e.g., see Banks, 1970, or Grasha, 1970).

What do these results mean? At a very general level they are consistent with a view suggested a number of years ago by Brown (1959). His position was that memory traces were stored with considerable redundancy and that forgetting could be conceptualized in terms of a decrease in the signal-to-noise ratio. Although not stated in signal-detection terms, the ideas and concepts are rather similar.

More specifically, these data suggest that there are in fact two underlying distributions (i.e., for old items and for new items) and that these distributions overlap. Therefore, regardless of where the subject sets his criterion, there will be errors of both types (i.e., false alarms and misses), though the frequency of each will vary with the cutoff point. One hesitates to make the flat statement that the *a posteriori* probability data rule out any possible two-state model (Krantz, 1969) but, given not only the monotonicity but also the extreme range covered by these judgments, any simple two-state model would require considerable embellishment to account for these data. So, the problem is to explain what these distributions represent.

How does the subject decide where to set his criterion? I have suggested elsewhere (Murdock, 1972) that the decision is not based on a likelihood ratio, since the data of Donaldson (1967) did not show the expected effect when prior probability (of an old item) was varied. In terms of either the Bower or the Lockhart attribute model, each item in memory can be represented by a set of attributes. When presented with a test item, the subject simply assesses the number of activated attributes or elements and responds accordingly. If the number is small, the response is "no"; if it is large, the response is "yes"; and the intermediate cases give rise to responses with low confidence judgments. The way the information is preserved in memory differs somewhat in these two models, but the decision process is much the same. The difference between them is that, in the Bower model, $f_o(x)$ and $f_n(x)$ are assumed to be binomial distributions differing only in the parameter p, but in the Lockhart model they are assumed to be Poisson distributions.

A somewhat different alternative has been suggested by Parks (1966). The suggestion is that subjects probability-match; that is, set their criterion in such a way as to make the relative frequency of an old response equal to the probability of an old item. Thus, in the Donaldson (1967) study where *a priori* probability was either .2 or .5, to probability-match subjects should make 20% and 50% of their responses "yes" in the two conditions. By now, there is a fair amount of data in support of a probability-matching hypothesis, and it seems preferable to a maximum-likelihood rule (Thomas & Legge, 1970). However, it is descriptive in the sense that all it tells is the outcome to be expected; it says nothing about the mechanism by which the decision system functions. Also, it does not explain confidence judgments.

While there are still some contentious issues and problems yet to be resolved, confidence-judgment methods do seem to be useful in testing the theories and models. However, we have reached the point where this work should be considered more than just an application of signal-detection theory to the area of human short-term memory. What we need are theories of memory that will predict the data, not just a routine computation of the d' and β statistics. That, of course, is just what strength theory and the attribute theories attempt to do.

Latency

Norman and Wickelgren (1969) have suggested a possible relationship between memory trace strength and response latency. A representation of the presumed relationship is shown in Fig. 3.3. The decision axis s is trace strength, the criterion is represented by the vertical line as s_c, and the latency is shown below the decision axis and is portrayed as decreasing on either side of the criterion. Thus, the slowest responses would be those whose strength was nearest the criterion. The most extreme observations (i.e., very weak and very strong traces) would give rise to the fastest responses ("no" and "yes," respectively). The function mapping strength into latency is shown here as exponential, but strength theorists have not made this particular assumption.

Murdock and Dufty (1972) have found that, as assumed by strength theory, latency of response is directly released to distance from the yes-no criterion. Data from this study are shown in Fig. 3.4, where latency is plotted as a function of confidence judgment. The most extreme judgments ("no-3" and "yes-3") were the fastest, and each step down in confidence (i.e., from 3 to 2, or from 2 to 1) increased the time to respond by approximately 250 msec. A further test of strength theory was less favorable. As documented in their article, strength theory should also predict that the variability in the latency of incorrect responses (misses or false alarms) should be less

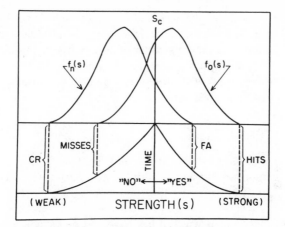

FIG. 3.3. The relationship between trace strength and latency from a strength-theory point of view.

than the variability in the latency of correct responses (correct rejections or hits). Perhaps this prediction can be appreciated intuitively from a study of Fig. 3.3. In any case, the prediction failed; correct responses were not only faster but also less variable than incorrect responses.

The Bower attribute model simply says that, from what is known from statistical decision theory, the more extreme the evidence, the faster the responses should occur. So these data are consistent with the model. The Lockhart model does not make any specific predictions about latency.

It might not be inappropriate to conclude this section with a caveat. If responses in short-term memory experiments are a function of memory and decision, so presum-

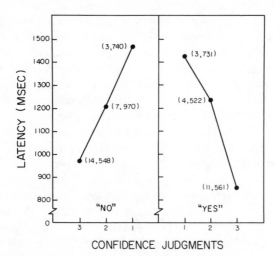

FIG. 3.4. The relationship between confidence judgment and latency in a short-term recognition-memory study. (Fig. 2 from Murdock & Dufty, 1972.)

ably are their latencies. Thus, the measured reaction time has two components, one for the memory stage and one for the decision stage. In an additive model, the observed latency distribution is the convolution of these two components. If such a two-stage model is really appropriate, then there is ample evidence (e.g., Christie & Luce, 1956; Luce & Green, 1972) that separation may be difficult. We should be careful about too glib an explanation.

STIMULUS MATERIAL

In this section we shall consider two main topics, the effect of type of stimulus material on recognition memory and the current experimental evidence for attributes.

Type of Material

The nature of the stimulus material has large and predictable effects on recognition memory. An example would be the meaningfulness of the material (Martin & Melton, 1970). Experimental manipulations such as meaningfulness provide one way of investigating the Höffding problem (Höffding, 1891; Rock, 1962). The Höffding problem was originally formulated in terms of associations. Before an association can be elicited, the probe or external stimulus must somehow make contact with its stored representation. If an association is represented as a–b, then the stimulus A must first elicit its memorial counterpart, a, before the trace of A can elicit the associated component b. The Höffding problem is obviously not restricted to associations, so in a very general sense it is coextensive with the whole issue of item recognition. Varying the stimulus material then has been one of the traditional ways to approach this problem.

A recent elaboration has been suggested in the encoding-variability hypothesis (Martin, 1968). Martin has suggested that there will be different encodings of the same nominal stimulus A so that on its first presentation it might be encoded as a_1, whereas on its second presentation it might be encoded as a_2. The differences between a_1 and a_2 will vary as a function of meaningfulness and play an important role in transfer and retroaction paradigms. The general view suggested by Martin is a current formulation in the tradition that probably started with the concept of the pure stimulus act of Hull (1930) and evolved through the generalization and differentiation model of Gibson (1940), the acquired distinctiveness of cues concept of Dollard and Miller (1950), the experimental work on transfer and mediated generalization in the 1950's, to culminate in the theoretical papers by Lawrence (1963) on the stimulus-as-coded and by Underwood (1963) on stimulus selection.

In terms of the encoding-variability hypothesis of Martin, variability should be greater for low-meaningful trigrams than for high-meaningful trigrams. Also, in the comparison of consonant-vowel-consonant (CVC) trigrams with consonant-consonant-consonant (CCC) trigrams, the latter should be more fragmentary or subject to intraunit interference (Melton, 1963) than the former. In an experimental test Martin and Melton (1970) examined the retention of low-, medium-, and high-meaningful CVC and CCC trigrams in a Shepard and Teghtsoonian paradigm. The pooled false-positive rates were .394, .375, and .220 for low-, medium-, and high-meaningful CCCs, and .417, .294, and .186 for low-, medium-, and high-meaningful CVCs. The corresponding hit rates (pooled over lag) were .792, .824, and .903 for CCCs and .874, .924, and .958 for CVCs. These are the corrected or conditional hit rates, namely, conditional on a new response at the first presentation.

It is an easy matter to convert these values into d' scores, and a plot of d' based on these data is shown in Fig. 3.5. Clearly the results are in general agreement with an encoding-variability hypothesis. There is a difference between CVCs and CCCs, and this difference decreases with meaningfulness. However, it is not clear whether a chunking interpretation is supported. It could be argued that a CVC trigram is a single unit and a CCC trigram is three units. Predictions based on such a view would have to be developed with some care in order to be tested by these data.

In quite a different vein, interesting comparisons have been made among the retention of words, pictures, and sentences. In perhaps the best-known study, Shepard (1967) reported very high accuracy when subjects had to remember a large number of such stimuli. They had to look through an inspection series of about 600 single stimuli which, for different groups, were either single words (half common and half rare), short sentences (e.g., "A dead dog is no use for hunting ducks"), or colored pictures (selected for high saliency and low confusability). The inspection series was followed by a two-alternative forced-choice test of about 60–70 pairs. In the forced-choice test the subject was simply to pick out the old item.

The impressive aspect of the data is the high level of performance demonstrated by the subjects despite the very heavy memory load. The accuracy level (percent of times the old item was correctly selected in the two-alternative forced-choice situation) was approximately 90% for the words and sentences and even higher (96.7%) for the pictures. That subjects could remember even more is suggested by Haber (1970) who reported showing 2,560 photographic slides at a rate of one every 10 seconds (which apparently required two four-hour sessions on successive days). One

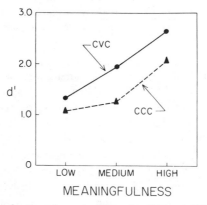

FIG. 3.5. Plot of d' as a function of meaningfulness for CVC and CCC trigrams. (Based on data from Martin & Melton, 1970.)

hour after the end of the inspection series a two-alternative forced-choice test on 280 pairs was given, and Haber reports 85–95% accuracy.

Experimental evidence on the role of eye fixations and their role in recognition memory for pictures has recently been reported by Loftus (1972). He presented pairs of pictures with a predetermined point scale. The subject would be given 1, 5, or 9 points for each picture remembered, and the value of each picture was indicated at the time of presentation. All combinations of 1, 5, and 9 points for both pictures of a pair were used, and eye fixations were recorded. As might be expected, the higher the value of a picture, the more time was spent observing it, and the better it was remembered. However, when the viewing time was decomposed into number of fixations and time per fixation it turned out that the number of fixations was far more important. What mattered in terms of memory was how many fixations a picture received, not the amount of time per fixation. There are other studies (e.g., Potter & Levy, 1969; Shaffer & Shiffrin, 1972) showing temporal variables to be important, but they did not record eye movements. Presumably there is no contradiction.

Much of the evidence about memory for pictures is consonant with what we know about verbal memory (see also Dallett, Wilcox, & D'Andrea, 1968). An exception may be rehearsal time, which Shaffer and Shiffrin (1972) found not to affect picture memory. However, to make the work on picture memory articulate with attribute theory will require further effort. A promising line of further development might be to pursue the eye-movements recording. Given the current state of the art, there seems to be no reason to speculate about what subjects are looking at when it can be directly measured and observed.

There is much evidence to suggest that memory for pictures is better than memory for words (e.g., Paivio, 1969). However, simple comparisons of this sort are difficult to interpret because of the many differences that exist between these types of material. On the one hand, one can attribute such differences to different memory codes or, perhaps, even to hemispheric differences which might underlie them. On the other hand, there may be a more prosaic explanation in terms of characteristics such as the number or salience of the attributes themselves. In an experimental study, Wells (1972) used recognition memory and found no difference between verbal and pictorial stimuli when they were equated for the number of attributes.

Evidence for Attributes

Acoustic or articulatory attributes are quite salient in studies of short-term memory. In a classic study Conrad (1964) showed that, in a memory-span task, when one item in a visually-presented list was incorrectly reproduced, it was quite likely to be an item that was acoustically confusable with the correct item on a listening test. An analysis of these acoustic confusion data by Murdock (1967a) gave some evidence that these acoustic (or articulatory) attributes were independent. As shown in Fig. 3.6, the intrusion is most likely to differ from the correct response on only one distinctive feature (Miller & Nicely, 1955), and the geometric distribution found would be expected on the assumption of independence. The term Hamming distance comes

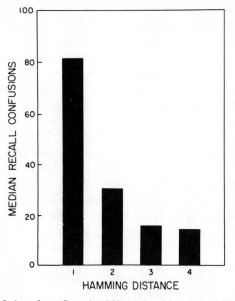

HAMMING DISTANCE

FIG. 3.6. Recall confusions from Conrad (1964) analyzed in terms of Haming distance. (Fig. 7 from Murdock, 1967a.)

from coding theory (e.g., Abramson, 1963) and is simply a measure for representing similarity (distance) between two binary-coded numbers.

A cued-recall study by Bregman (1968) tested for target items with contiguity, phonetic, graphic, and semantic cues. The retention curve for each attribute separately was quite sharp (perhaps exponential, or perhaps more like the Shepard and Teghtsoonian curve shown in Fig. 3.2), and in general the data seemed quite consistent with an attribute interpretation. There is further evidence for forgetting at the level of item attributes in studies by Bregman and Chambers (1966) and Wickelgren (1965c). More recently, the extensive work of Wickens and his colleagues (Wickens, 1970, 1972) on release from proactive inhibition is consistent with an attribute interpretation, but discussion of this work will be deferred until Chapter 7.

A recent study by Shulman (1970) tested to see whether subjects could remember whether a word in the list was similar in sound or in meaning to the test item. Both accuracy of recognition and the speed with which the subject responded to the probe decreased as interference increased, and the functions varied somewhat with presentation rate. Synonyms gave poorer performance than homonyms for both measures (accuracy and latency), but homonyms were as accurately recognized as old items (i.e., probes that were words from the list). However, homonym-synonym comparisons are difficult to make because of commensurability problems.

Underwood (1969a) has also suggested that memory is composed of a number of attributes, and he has discussed evidence for temporal, spatial, frequency, modality, orthographic, and associative attributes. Further, Underwood and his colleagues (e.g., Ekstrand, Wallace, & Underwood, 1966) have suggested that the frequency attribute is particularly important in recognition studies in general and verbal discrimination studies in particular. In a verbal discrimination study, the subject is shown pairs of words and must learn which item of the pair the experimenter has arbitrarily designated as correct. They (e.g., Underwood & Freund, 1970a) have amassed considerable evidence to support their hypothesis that the frequency attribute mediates verbal discrimination. It should be noted that an attribute conception of frequency or repetition implies some sort of counting mechanism; this is the direct antithesis of strength theory, which says that repetition gradually increases the strength of a trace.

In a different vein, the work of Posner on visual and name codes is consistent with the idea of attribute representation of information in memory (Posner, 1969). There is a difference in the time to recognize the letter identity of lower-case and upper-case letters one-half second after presentation, but this difference disappears at intervals of one to two seconds. That is, at short intervals letter-identity matches take longer when the letters differ orthographically than when they do not. One interpretation of these findings is that the subject makes the match on the basis of a visual code at the short intervals of time, but this visual code is superseded by a name code subsequently. Not only can name codes be generated from visual presentation, but also there is evidence to suggest that appropriate visual codes can be generated by the subject, though such generation takes a second or so judging by the reaction-time data. By and large, effects such as those reported by Posner and his colleagues have generally been studied only over short retention intervals (i.e., a second or two).

However, a different interpretation might be possible. Consider the results of Posner, Boies, Eichelman, and Taylor (1969). They reported that subjects can more rapidly decide whether two successive letters have the same name if they are physically identical than if they are not. That is, reactions to A and A or to a and a will be faster than reactions to A and a or to a and A. Perhaps in both cases there is a name match, but it is faster in the A–A or a–a case because of the well-known repetition effect (Bertelson, 1963). That is, both the first letter and the second letter evoke a name, but the evoked response is faster when the second stimulus is physically identical to the first. Were this a readout from an iconic store, the effect might dissipate over the brief interstimulus intervals used. Some supporting evidence for this possibility may be found in Eichelman (1970).

In the last five years considerable evidence has accrued on modality effects in human short-term memory. There seem to be different (separate?) representations in memory for visually and auditorily presented information. Obviously this would be true if the comparison was between words and pictures, say, but it also holds true for visual and auditory presentation of verbal material (digits, letters, words). Much of this work has involved recall rather than recognition, but there is at least some evidence that the effects also hold for recognition (Murdock, 1968a; Walker, 1967; though see also Donaldson, 1971a). By one line of reasoning, this result would localize the effect in encoding or storage processes.

In addition to modality differences, there is the question of the duration of the persistence of modality-specific attributes. It has been assumed (e.g., Crowder & Morton, 1969) that modality-specific attributes persist only for a second or two after presentation. It now seems that they may last somewhat longer. For instance, in a four-channel study (simultaneous presentation of two visual and two auditory words) Murdock (1971a) found evidence that auditory and visual attributes of verbal stimuli persisted for at least 5 seconds. Phillips and Baddeley (1971) used dots in a 5 × 5 matrix and found evidence for visual persistence as long as 9 seconds. With verbal material, Kroll, Parks, Parkinson, Bieber, & Johnson (1970) have shown visual persistence for as long as 25 seconds. They used a shadowing task where the subject simply repeated letters of the alphabet that were spoken at a fairly rapid rate (120 letters per minute). A single to-be-remembered letter would be presented while the shadowing task was in progress, and even 25 seconds later a visually presented letter was recalled correctly about 70% of the time. Perhaps more impressive is a recent finding by Parkinson (1972) that eight letters resulted in a serial-position effect at 20 seconds that was only about twenty percentage points below the serial-position curve obtained at 1 second. These data will be shown later (Fig. 7.9). In general, then, it seems quite clear that, even with verbal stimuli, modality-specific attributes persist well beyond the millisecond range generally allowed for iconic and echoic memory.

When attributes are binary (i.e., auditory or visual, male or female voice, upper-case or lower-case type, left or right side of the screen) asking the subject to identify the attribute of a presented stimulus can be considered recognition, even though the instructions may ask the subject to "recall" this information. Madigan and Doherty (1972) found that even though there were no differences in recall accuracy, considerable information about the original modality of presentation (auditory or visual) was retained over an appreciable retention interval. Bray and Batchelder (1972) and Mann (1970) report a high level of accuracy in the identification of presentation modality in a free-recall situation. In the four-channel study, Murdock (1971a) found approximately 90% accuracy in the attribute report (i.e., whether a probe word had been presented in a male or female voice, or in lower- or upper-case type). These effects were obtained over a retention interval of about 5 seconds, in which the subject was prevented from rehearsing by being required to recall the four words that had just been presented (two visually and two auditorily).

Finally, some recent work by Kirsner has extended these findings somewhat. He used a continuous recognition-memory paradigm, tested directly for attribute information, and collected latency data as well. In one study (Kirsner, 1973a) an orthographic attribute (upper-case printing versus lower-case printing) was investigated, while in another study (Kirsner, 1973b) the attribute was modality of presentation (auditory or visual). In both studies there was evidence suggesting at least some representational persistence for as long as 90 seconds. A similar conclusion was drawn about modality effects by Hintzman, Block, and Inskeep (1972).

The general implication of all this work is that some form of representational memory does persist, even with verbal material. An immediate translation into a linguistic code with no memory for the format of presentation simply does not occur. Such a view was popular a while back, but recent studies such as those mentioned above show that such a position is no longer tenable. However, whether the format of storage is solely in terms of attributes is another issue.

TEST ALTERNATIVES

The number and nature of the alternatives used as lures in any recognition-memory test has a predictable effect on performance. The general effects are clear and well documented. As the number of alternatives increases, the proportion of correct responses decreases. As the similarity between the incorrect alternatives or lures and the correct item increases, again the proportion of correct responses decreases.

Number of Alternatives

The first effect, decrease in performance with number of alternatives, is completely consistent with the strength-theory view outlined in the previous chapter. Thus, as shown there, in an m-AFC situation the subject's performance can be described as if he were drawing one sample from $f_o(x)$ with a certain mean and variance, and $m - 1$ samples from $f_n(x)$. The probability correct is simply the probability that the former will exceed any one of the latter. For item recognition, studies by Green and Moses (1966) and by Kintsch (1968a) have provided experimental confirmation of this view.

In the Green and Moses study, a list of 90 CVC nonsense syllables was shown to the subjects once, then half the items were tested by a yes-no confidence-judgment procedure and half by a forced-choice procedure. In the former the *a priori* probability of an old item was .5; in the latter $m = 2$ so each old item was shown with one lure. The data from the rating procedure gave the parameters necessary to predict percent correct in the 2-AFC situation for each subject. The main findings from this study are reproduced here as Fig. 3.7, and the obtained and predicted results agree reasonably well. Each subject on both sessions is within two standard deviations (represented by the vertical bars) of the predicted value.

In the Kintsch study, five 4-consonant strings (CCCC) were shown to the subject, followed by a subtraction task, then a test. As in the Green and Moses study, items were either single (CCCC) stimuli which were old or new, or multiple choice with 1, 3, or 7 lures on the test card. Four subjects were tested intensively, and the consistency across test methods determined for each subject. Such a comparison requires a theoretical rationale, and Kintsch concluded that (what is here called) a strength-theory interpretation was probably best. However, alternate interpretations were also reasonable. One of these was a cross-out rule suggested by Murdock (1963b); this rule will be discussed in connection with paired associates. Also there was a prediction derived from the Bower (1967b) multicomponent paper, and still a third derived from the choice theory of Luce (1959). All three seemed reasonably consistent with the data.

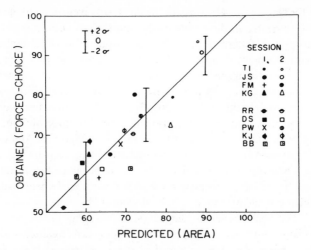

FIG. 3.7. Comparison of predicted and obtained results in predicting forced-choices results from confidence-judgment procedure. (Fig. 3 from Green & Moses, 1966.)

The effect of number of alternatives was also demonstrated by Davis, Sutherland, and Judd (1961) who found that the number of correct recognitions decreased as the recognition test went from 30 items to 90 items. [In looking at their data I computed hits and false alarms for the three conditions, and was somewhat surprised to find that, both for letters and for numbers, d' stayed essentially constant across conditions (number of alternatives) but β increased by a factor of two.] In any case, their main point was demonstrating the difficulty of comparing recognition and recall, since recall may involve searching through some very large ensemble. From an information-theory point of view, one must then consider the number-of-alternatives factor to be a confounding variable in recall-recognition comparisons. Follow-up studies of the Davis et al. design have been reported by Field and Lachman (1966) and Slamecka (1967a). An interpretation of the phenomenon in terms of performance rather than learning has been suggested for the multitrial situation by Teghtsoonian and Teghtsoonian (1970).

Nature of Alternatives

Dale and Baddeley (1962, 1966) experimentally questioned one of the assumptions of an information-theoretic view, namely, that all alternatives are equally probable. They presented their test items first for recall and noted what extra-list intrusions occurred. Then to a different group of subjects they gave two versions of a recognition test, one with common intrusions as lures and another with rare intrusions as lures. As they predicted, the number of correct responses was less when the lures were those responses commonly intruded in recall. Similar results have also been reported by McNulty (1966). This finding does not, of course, vitiate the main point of the Davis *et al.* (1961) paper; it does, however, point to the importance of the similarity variable in the nature of the alternatives used.

The similarity of the alternatives leads to a consideration of false alarms. There are two noteworthy aspects of false alarms in studies of memory for item information. One is the fact that false alarms (or false positives) become more numerous during the course of an experimental session when the continuous recognition-memory procedure of Shepard and Teghtsoonian (1961) is used. This effect has been replicated in several studies (e.g., Donaldson & Murdock, 1968; Martin & Melton, 1970), and it can be very large indeed (see for instance Fig. 1 of Martin & Melton, p. 130). While a study by Olson (1969) found a much smaller effect (see his Fig. 3, p. 383), it may be due to the fact that he pooled data over rather large blocks (50 trials to a block). The interpretation of the false-positive rise has already been mentioned. As shown by Donaldson and Murdock (1968), it seems to be more a criterion shift than a change in d'. For whatever reason, subjects seem to change the basis on which they make their decisions as they proceed through a continuous recognition-memory task.

The second aspect of the false-alarm data that is of interest is the effect of associative relationships upon false positives. To illustrate, if the word DOG is presented in the list and then later one of the test items is CAT, the subject is more likely to call CAT an old item (even though in fact it is new) than a control item. In this case there are two possible controls. One would use each item as its own control, so the comparison would be between CAT preceded by DOG compared to CAT not preceded by DOG. The other would be to use different pairs for control, so CAT preceded by DOG would be compared to DAY not preceded by NIGHT. (Counterbalancing of associatively-related pairs across subjects would, of course, be necessary in both cases). Which control one uses depends at least partly on the theoretical mechanism presumed to underlie the effect.

This false-recognition effect was first noted by Underwood (1965). He had four types of relationships, antonyms (BOTTOM and TOP, GIVE and TAKE), converging associations (BUTTER, CRUMB to BREAD; BED, DREAM to SLEEP) superordinates (MAPLE, OAK, ELM, BIRCH to TREE), and sense impressions (BARREL, DOUGHNUT, DOME, GLOBE, SPOOL to ROUND). There was no false-recognition effect (experimental versus control difference) for sense impressions, but the other three types of relationship did show more false positives than the control items. (Actually, there were two subsets of antonyms and they differed, but it seems safe to conclude that overall there was an effect.)

This study illustrates the importance of controlling the location of experimental and control items. As shown in the original article (Fig. 1, p. 126) the false-alarm rate to control items increased over trial blocks. Of necessity the experimental items must be tested rather late in the sequence, since they must have been preceded by their associately-related mates, and there is generally a long lag between the two. Because of the false-positive drift the comparison must be made at comparable trial blocks, and Fig. 1 in the Underwood article makes clear the requisite comparison.

The interpretation suggested by Underwood was in terms of implicit associative responses. It was assumed that when a word such as DOG was presented to a subject, not only did he say it to himself but also he might well think about related words, especially CAT. Since these are internal responses, no one wants to be very specific about just what they are—whether it is literally some sort of subvocalization process, or just a thought, is not clear. But whatever representational response (along with its memorial counterpart) is assumed to occur when an item is presented, so some similar associative response is assumed (with some probability) to occur and persist. Then, since the subject has already laid down some sort of memory trace for the item, calling the new word "old" on the later test is understandable. Basically, it would seem to be a failure to discriminate between what the experimenter had presented to the subject and what the subject thought of himself.

A different interpretation was suggested by Anisfeld and Knapp (1968). They argued for a distinctive features interpretation. In their view, a word consists of a unique and distinguishing constellation of features, which may be semantic, syntactic, phonological, and orthographic. The encoding of a word would be the activation of its feature set, and the false recognition would be attributable to feature overlap. That is, new items might share some features in common with words which had already been presented, and this overlap could mediate the false alarms.

The evidence presented by Anisfeld and Knapp was twofold. First, they showed that synonyms (e.g., BABY and INFANT; CARPET and RUG) could produce the false-recognition effect. Second, by manipulating forward and backward associations they suggested that the features had to be activated at the time of presentation. Some associations (e.g., KING and QUEEN, BOY and GIRL) are bidirectional in that each elicits the other. Others (e.g., BITTER and SWEET, FINGERS and HAND) are not, according to the norms. So, presenting say FINGERS could induce a subsequent false recognition of HAND, but presenting HAND would not prime FINGERS. In quite a different vein, Tulving and Osler (1968) have suggested that a retrieval cue is effective for subsequent recall if and only if it is stored at the time of presentation.

As pointed out by Fillenbaum (1969), although the data of Anisfeld and Knapp are consistent with a feature interpretation, they do not demand it. Since synonyms are generally of the same concept class, feature analysis would not be required to produce the effects reported by Anisfeld and Knapp. Overlap of concepts rather than features *per se* could be involved. In an attempt to tighten the argument, Fillenbaum compared the false recognition for antonyms as well as synonyms. From a feature view, two words that were antonyms would have the same marking on all features but one. Fillenbaum found a comparable false-recognition effect for antonyms and for synonyms and concluded that his data supported a feature-type model. Similar studies have been reported by Anisfeld (1970) and by Grossman and Eagle (1970).

These latter studies, then, document the false recognition effect but provide an alternative explanation to that suggested originally by Underwood. Also, a difficulty with the Underwood interpretation exists in data discussed by Anderson and Bower (1972a). These authors claim that in fact subjects are very good at discriminating between self-generated responses and those stimulus events presented by the experimenter. If such were the case, then it is difficult to see how implicit associative responses could underlie the false-recognition effect. Perhaps subjects are good but not perfect at this discrimination. Then one might rationalize the two views and say there should be some false positives but not too many. Perhaps this is what the data show.

While the interpretations of Anisfeld and Fillenbaum are clearly in accord with the attribute view espoused earlier, there may be a problem. Some recent experiments by Donald Thomson, reported to me informally, suggest that the false-recognition effect may not vary with lag. Acceptance of TABLE as an old item may be as frequent immediately after CHAIR has been presented as at, say, lag 30. It seems unlikely that any current theory of false positives in recognition memory would predict the absence of a lag effect. However, there does seem to be a lag effect when the test alternative is orthographically or acoustically similar to the target item (Raser, 1972a).

RECALL-RECOGNITION COMPARISONS

In this section we shall consider word-frequency effects and the effects of organization on recognition. Both topics have significance for the nature of the difference between recall and recognition. This recall-recognition issue will be introduced in the context of word-frequency effects.

Word-Frequency Effects

The main finding in studies of the effects of word frequency on item recognition is that rare words are generally more memorable than common words. Word frequency is generally determined from tables such as those contained in the extensive word count by Thorndike and Lorge (1944), that is, how often each word occurs in a large sample of English text. If lists are constructed with common words such as MORNING, PEOPLE, DOLLAR, HOW, THEIR, and DROP, they will be less accurately identified on a subsequent recognition-memory test than rare words such as SOBRIQUET, AMYLOPSIN, CHARWOMAN, METEMPSYCHOSIS, EQUERRY, and NABOB. Such effects have been reported, for instance, by Gorman (1961), McCormack & Swenson (1972), and Shepard (1967).

The basic study on word frequency effects is that of Shepard (1967) who clearly demonstrated that low-frequency words are more likely to be recognized than high-frequency words. On theoretical grounds Underwood and Freund (1970b) were bothered by such results, and they compared recognition accuracy of low- and high-frequency words when pitted against low- and high-frequency lures. The recognition test was a two-alternative forced choice in which the subject had to pick the old item from a pair consisting of one old item and one lure. As is generally found, low-frequency words were more accurately identified than high-frequency words when compared to lures of the same type, but there was a crossover in the mixed condition. High-frequency words with low-frequency lures were more accurately recognized than low-frequency words with high-frequency lures (see Underwood & Freund, 1970b, Fig. 1, p. 347). However, this finding is difficult to interpret since a between-subjects design was used. Since any given subject had only one type of test, it would seem as if in the mixed conditions subjects could select old words on the basis of judged word frequency, even if their memory for the presented items was nil. (Contrary opinions are expressed by the authors; see their pp. 347–348).

In retrospect, word-frequency effects may not seem to be surprising since rare words seem more vivid and memorable than common words. However, in another sense they are quite surprising and have posed something of a puzzle. There is a reasonable amount of evidence (e.g., Hall, 1954; Murdock, 1960b; Sumby, 1963) that common words are more often recalled in free recall than rare words. A common view has been that recall and recognition involve common processes, but recall is more difficult than recognition because of a difference in threshold. If recall and recognition involve common processes, how can an experimental variable (in the present case, word frequency) have one effect on recognition but the opposite effect on recall?

This traditional position is illustrated in Fig. 3.8 which shows, on the left, two distributions, $f_L(x)$ for low-frequency words, and $f_H(x)$ for high-frequency words. In addition, two cutoffs or thresholds are shown with the recall threshold above the recognition threshold. The cross-hatched area to the right of the recall cutoff is smaller than the cross-hatched area to the right of the recognition cutoff. Consequently, the expected results should show that an increase in an independent variable such as word frequency should have a facilitative effect on both recall and recognition. Given this point of view, the obtained crossover effect in the experimental literature is directly contrary to the model.

Word frequency is not unique in having a differential effect on recall and recognition; more examples are given in Anderson & Bower (1972a), Kintsch (1970a), and McCormack (1972). The common resolution seems to be to modify the original hypothesis about the nature of recall and recognition. Today there are probably few people who would subscribe to the interpretation suggested by the left panel of Fig. 3.8. Instead, recall and recognition are generally presumed to involve different pro-

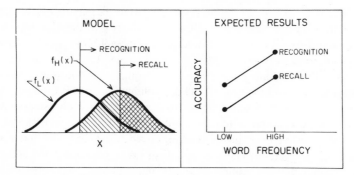

FIG. 3.8. Traditional explanation of recall-recognition comparisons with expected outcome for word frequency effects.

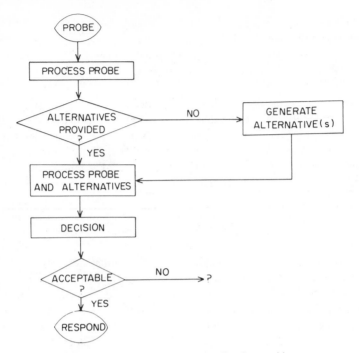

Fɪɢ. 3.9. Flow chart to illustrate difference between recall and recognition.

cesses. Exactly what these different processes are depends upon one's theoretical position, but at least in very general terms this is how one is reconciled with the fact that there are independent variables that have differential effects on recall and recognition.

One current view of recall and recognition is that recall involves some processes in common with recognition but one (or more) additional process as well. A likely candidate for the latter is a search process. As variously suggested (e.g. Bahrick, 1970; Bower, Clark, Lesgold, & Winzenz, 1969; Kintsch, 1970a; Lachman & Tuttle, 1965; McCormack, 1972; Murdock, 1968a) recall may involve a metaphorical search through memory which is by-passed in any recognition test in which the correct alternative is directly presented to the subject. One possible representation of this difference is shown in the flow chart of Fig. 3.9. When the alternatives are not provided the subject must generate them, and herein lies the difference between recall and recognition (e.g., Field & Lachman, 1966). The subject does not have to search memory to generate the alternatives in a recognition test. Although this flow chart is more appropriate to describe the retrieval of associative information, it is introduced here to portray current thinking on recall-recognition differences.

To return to the word-frequency effect, there are two ways it could come about. One can speculate that recognition judgments could be mediated either by positive certainty or by negative certainty. As used here, by positive certainty I mean certainty that the probe is in fact an old item, one presented in the list. By negative certainty I mean certainty that the probe is a new item, i.e., that it had not been presented in the list. Differences in level of performance could be due to either or both of these two processes. With low word frequency, one could more often experience positive certainty for old items, or one could more often experience negative certainty for new items.

An experiment performed in our laboratory some years ago by Madge Grace suggests that it may actually be more negative than positive certainty that is involved. This experiment used a standard Shepard and Teghtsoonian (1961) procedure with a deck of 160 cards, each having a single word on it. Eighty different words were used, each occurring twice. The subject would go through a deck at his own rate and identify each item as old or new (i.e., as second or first presentation, respectively). One deck consisted of common words (randomly selected from the 1,000 most common words in the Thorndike-Lorge count) while another consisted of rare words (randomly selected from words occurring at least once per four million words, but less than once per one million words). The words given in the second paragraph of this section came from this experiment. The lag (number of items intervening between presentation and test) was approximately equally distributed over the range 0–9, but in some cases trailed out to 15.

Positive certainty can be measured by the hit rate and negative certainty by false alarms. The corrected hit rate was .910 for common words and .924 for rare words, which did not differ significantly by a sign test. (The corrected hit rate deletes all items that were incorrectly identified as old on their first presentation, since item-specific effects may be involved; see Melton, Sameroff, & Schubot, 1967.) However, there were exactly twice as many false alarms for common words as for rare words, and the difference was significant by a sign test at the .05 level. The actual false-alarm rates were .025 and .050 for rare and common words, respectively.

This experiment, then, provides at least suggestive evidence that the word-frequency effect is due more to differences in negative certainty than differences in positive certainty. Such a view is not inconsistent with an attribute model of recognition memory. In order to account for any false positives at all, there must be some provision for conditioning or tagging the elements of the not-yet-presented items. The extent to which this happens will reflect overlap among the items. After the fact, it is not unreasonable to imagine that there is more overlap among common items than among rare items, whether this overlap is seen as overlap in associations, overlap in meaning, or whatever. On the other hand, if there is no difference in positive certainty then the implication would be that, once presented, loss of the conditioned attributes occurs at the same rate for common and rare words.

Organization and Recognition

This section deals with the question of whether organization facilitates recognition. The term "organization" refers to some sort of structure either provided by the experimenter in the construction of the list or generated by the subject in the process of learning the list. Typically it is manifest in some sort of grouping of the responses, which can show up either in stereotypy of order of report (e.g., Bousfield & Bousfield, 1966; Bower, 1972a; Tulving, 1962, 1968) or in interresponse times (e.g., Patterson, Meltzer, & Mandler, 1971; Pollio, Kasschau, & DeNise, 1968). There is ample evidence (e.g., Mandler, 1967; Tulving, 1968) to suggest that organization facilitates free recall. The question here is whether it also affects recognition.

The forerunner of later studies on organization and recognition was a study by Dale (1967). He used the names of English counties as the items in a single-trial free-recall experiment. The 40 county names varied appreciably in accessibility from high (Hampshire, Yorkshire, Berkshire) to low (Westmoreland, Huntingdonshire, Monmouthshire), where accessibility was measured by the frequency with which a separate group of subjects was able to name them when simply asked to list as many as they could. Recall was facilitated by accessibility, but recognition was not. The results were interpreted in support of a two-process theory. When the subjects could readily generate the alternatives (e.g., Hampshire, Yorkshire, Berkshire) providing them in the recognition test was of no benefit, but for items such as Westmorland, Huntingtonshire, and Monmouthshire they might well fail to generate them in recall yet identify them as old on the recognition test.

Kintsch (1968b) studied the effect of structure on recall and recognition. In the first of two experiments, high- and low-structure lists were constructed from the Connecticut norms of Cohen, Bousfield, and Whitmarsh (1957), which consisted of the most dominant and the least dominant members of common categories. Examples of the former might be hammer, saw, screwdriver, nail, and chisel; examples of the latter might be mitre box, wood drill, shears, planer, and nut; both groups are from the category of carpenter's tools. In the second experiment there were high- and low-structure nonsense syllables, where the structure was determined by the sequential constraints within the syllables. In both experiments, the dominant category members or the high-structure nonsense syllables were better recalled than their counterparts, but recognition was equally good for both. This result was replicated and extended by Bruce & Fagan (1970).

Bower et al. (1969) reported a series of studies with material that could be formed into a hierarchical structure. An example is the minerals category shown in Fig. 3.10. In the first experiment, recall was shown to be much higher in the blocked condition than in the random condition. In the blocked condition the organization such as shown in Fig. 3.10 was preserved, but in the random condition it was not; the arrangement of the words had no such taxonomic structure. In the second experiment, the difference between blocked and random structure was attenuated (though not eliminated) under a recognition procedure. Although the authors interpret these results as being consistent with the studies by Dale and by Kintsch discussed above, they do point out a problem. If differences as a function of some experimental manipulation (such as blocking) decrease but do not disappear in recognition memory, it is difficult to make rigorous comparisons without some theoretical view of the processes involved. Because recall and recognition operate at different base levels, it is difficult to claim even that differences decrease going from one experimental condition to another. As they say, there is no atheoretical way to interpret such findings.

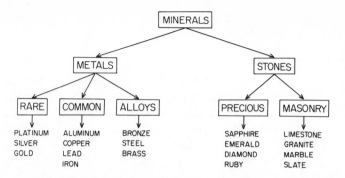

FIG. 3.10. The Minerals conceptual hierarchy. (Fig. 1 from Bower *et al.*, 1969.)

Mandler, Pearlstone, and Koopmans (1969) examined the effect of the number of categories subjects used in a sorting task on subsequent recognition. In previous work, Mandler (1967) had found that the number of words recalled increased directly as a function of the number of categories subjects used when first asked to sort words into categories. In the recognition study the number of categories also had the same effect, namely, the more categories the better the recognition. To explain their results they suggested the idea of a post-recognition retrieval check. In the event that the subject was uncertain about the familiarity of a test item he might check to see whether it was capable of being retrieved by whatever processes are involved in free recall. The recognition decision would then be based on the outcome of this retrieval check. This postrecognition retrieval check is one possible explanation of what the question mark in Fig. 3.9 might be.

A theoretical discussion reviewing this work is given in Mandler (1972). In disagreement with others, his position is that organization does affect recognition, at least when class recognition is allowed to operate. He seems to espouse a two-factor theory. Occurrence tags can mediate recognition but, if they are unreliable, the postrecognition retrieval check would be used. Since the efficacy of the latter would clearly depend upon the degree of organization, so should accuracy of recognition. More generally, Mandler feels that his data are not consistent with the conventional wisdom that states that recall involves search and decision, but that recognition involves only decision.

JUDGMENTS OF RECENCY AND FREQUENCY

In the last few years studies using judgments of recency and frequency have become an effective tool to test theories of item recognition. In either a discrete-trials procedure or a continuous task, when presented with a probe the subject is asked to report how recently he has seen the item (what its lag is) or how often he has seen the item (its frequency) in some designated time period (generally since the beginning of the list). Clearly one is testing more than simple memory for item information, but strength theory and attribute theories make some simple and direct predictions of what should (or should not) occur.

Judgments of Recency

Yntema and Trask (1963) first studied judgments of recency in a continuous-task procedure using two-alternative forced choice. On the test card, there were two items and the subject merely had to select the item that had occurred more recently. The more recent the newer item, or the greater the separation between the two items, the more accurate the selection; and performance seemed better than chance even at long lags (one hundred or so items). They suggested the term "time tag," which has since become popular. It is as though information in memory about the presentation of an item also includes something that may be called a time tag, which makes possible judgments of recency.

Time tags are simply a descriptive label to point out the fact that people can make recency judgments, but they do nothing to clarify the process involved. As pointed out by Lockhart (1969a), it is by no means obvious how the nervous system encodes time as a dimension compared, say, to frequency or intensity. Whatever the mechanism, one way that 2-AFC judgments could come about would be if subjects made absolute judgments about each member of the pair separately, then picked the one with the lower estimate. Lockhart tested this hypothesis, and the data supported it. Thus, the comparison process envisaged by strength theory for m-AFC seems also to characterize judgments of recency.

One prediction that a strength theory would make is that when two events of unequal strength have been presented sequentially, then the subject should be more often correct in reporting their relative order when the stronger followed the weaker. That is, if memory-trace strength contributes to judgments of recency, then in one case true recency and judged recency should summate; but in the other case, should tend to work against each other. Confirmation of this prediction for high- and low-meaningful nonsense syllables has been reported by Wolff (1966), and for pictures and nouns by Fozard (1970), both using a 2-AFC procedure. However, neither study measured memory for the items *per se*, and an alternative interpretation of such results could be that, in those cases where a subject had forgotten the occurrence of the weaker item, he used this information to mediate his selection in the two-alternative case. In another study Fozard and Weinert (1972) asked for absolute judgments of recency for words and pictures at various lags and did find, at least at the shortest lag used, that pictures were judged more recent than nouns. Also, Morton (1968) found that performance (in 2-AFC) was worse when the first item was repeated than when it was not.

One unexpected result that has turned up is a crossover effect, where short lags are overestimated and long lags underestimated. An example is shown in Fig. 3.11 (from a study by Hinrichs, 1970) where three groups were given different instructions about the maximum possible lag. The true lags were always the same and, while a nice family of curves resulted, each group separately overestimated short lags and underestimated long lags. The crossover point shifted with instructions.

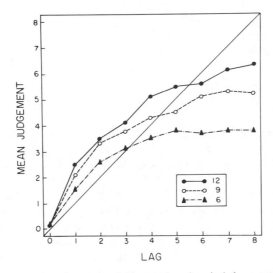

FIG. 3.11. Overshoot at short lags and undershoot at long lags in judgments of recency. (Fig. 3 from Hinrichs, 1970.)

not supported

One interpretation is that judgments of recency are based on trace strength. When presented with a probe, the subject directly assesses the strength of this trace and converts strength into a recency dimension. This interpretation was tested by Peterson (1967) who expected to find two presentations of an item judged more recent than one. In fact he did not, but a second attempt (Peterson, Johnson, & Coatney, 1969) was more successful. Hinrichs (1970) compared several decay and decision models, and the best was exponential decay with the assumption of variable criteria. It might be noted that the predictions differ according to whether a unitary trace is assumed, or multiple traces each with its own strength are assumed.

Qualitatively, almost any memory-and-decision model would predict a crossover effect in judgments of recency. As pointed out to me by Robert Lockhart, if a subject either remembers and makes a veridical judgment or forgets and guesses the mean lag, then the interaction will be found. A slightly more elegant finite-state model was suggested by Murdock (1972) where all-or-none retention of item information was assumed. It was suggested that the subject executed a backward serial scan to find the item. If found, he would count the number of intervening available items and give that as his recency judgment. If not found, he would guess the mean lag. Qualitatively, this model is capable of giving results like those shown in Fig. 3.11. Also, it has considerably fewer free parameters than the strength model suggested by Hinrichs. This model will be discussed further in Chapter 10.

Judgments of Frequency

As for judgments of frequency, a series of recent studies has been reported by Hintzman (Hintzman, 1969b, 1970; Hintzman & Block, 1970, 1971). Judgments of frequency increase with number of presentations, but not in linear fashion; judgments of frequency are essentially not affected by duration, so a temporal summation (or total-time) hypothesis is not indicated; and (as would be expected from studies of distributed practice) spaced presentations result in larger judgments of frequency than massed presentations. In another vein, Underwood, Zimmerman, and Freund (1971) have studied the forgetting of frequency information over time and conclude that their data support the view that frequency discrimination is basic in item recognition.

Two repetition mechanisms have been suggested. A strength-theory adherent might say that there is only one memory trace, but each presentation adds to its strength. A multiplex view would suggest that a separate trace might be laid down with each presentation. One way of testing these two alternatives is to vary the location of the repetition within parts of the list. A second way is to vary the number of presentations between and within lists, and then ask for judgments of frequency. Hintzman and Block (1971) reported some evidence more consistent with a multiplex version than a trace-strength version when they found that subjects could, with reasonable accuracy, report the number of presentations of items presented 0, 2, or 5 times in each of two different lists. Perhaps even more impressive was their finding from the within-list design (Exp. II; see Table 1, p. 301) that subjects could accurately discriminate between different loci of repetition. That is, items were presented in any two of four "zones" of a 50-item list, and both first-position and second-position judgments were consistent and essentially independent of the other.

A recent unpublished study by Elisabeth Wells at Toronto produced further difficulties for a strength-theory interpretation. She presented lists of 12 items that were either CVCs or CCCs, then asked for judgments of recency in a probe test. Her main finding was that CCCs were judged older than CVCs at short lags, but CVCs were judged older than CCCs at long lags.

The assumptions needed by strength theory to explain these data are shown in Fig. 3.12. In the left panel, decay functions are shown with CCCs having the larger rate constant. The middle panel shows the necessary mapping function, the relationship between strength and recency. These functions must differ in both slope and range to account for the results. The steeper slope for CVCs means that, at long lags, they will be judged older than CCCs, even though their strength is greater. At short lags the strength difference is sufficient to put judgments of recency for CCCs over CVCs. If the same or parallel mapping functions were used, then the interaction would not be predicted. It seems a bit unlikely that the mapping functions should be as depicted in the middle panel of Fig. 3.12.

Although a multiplex model is better, it too has problems. As will be discussed in connection with the lag effect in Chapter 9, repeated items are better remembered the greater the separation (lag) between repetitions. A simple multiplex model cannot explain this phenomenon. If one suggests that a second presentation does not lay down a new trace if the old one is intact, then the problem to explain is why twice-presented items are better remembered than once-presented items when the repetition is detected.

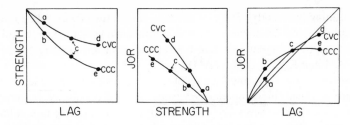

Fig. 3.12. Interrelationships between strength, lag, and judgments of recency (JOR) necessary to explain data of Wells (unpublished).

Finally, a second study by Wells (also unpublished) suggests that any simple theory relating judgments of frequency and item recognition is not going to work. In a continuous recognition task, words were presented once, twice massed, or twice spaced. On test, subjects had to give a three-point judgment of frequency (new; old, once-presented; or old, twice-presented), and a wide range of lags was covered. The critical result is the probability that an item is recognized as a repetition (i.e., judged as old, twice-presented) as a function of the probability that it is recognized as old (which was controlled by the lag manipulation). A strength theory that postulated two criterion cuts to generate the three-point judgment-of-frequency scale would (assuming equal variances) predict a single function with points for once-presented and twice-presented items interspersed. A multiplex model would predict two different functions but no difference between massed and spaced presentations. Since in fact there were three different functions, neither model in this simple form was supported by the data.

RETRIEVAL PROCESSES

The final topic in this chapter is the evidence for and the nature of retrieval processes in recognition memory. Two main topics will be considered, context effects and high-speed scanning. The context studies have been used as evidence to document the position that retrieval processes are involved in recognition. The scanning studies are intended to tell us something of the nature of these retrieval processes.

Context Effects

Light and Carter-Sobell (1970) compiled lists of adjective-noun phrases, which were embedded in sentences. The sentences comprised the study part of the experiment while the adjective-noun phrases were shown alone on the test part. The semantic interpretation of the noun was biased by the sentence and the adjective, and could be different at presentation and test (e.g., STRAWBERRY JAM and TRAFFIC JAM; SUGAR CUBES and GEOMETRICAL CUBES; SPIKED PUNCH and HEFTY PUNCH). When the adjectives on the study and test part were the same, hits were higher and false alarms lower than when the adjectives were changed to bias the meaning differently. The magnitude of these effects was quite large. Having a condition with no adjective resulted in intermediate performance, as did having a condition with a different adjective biasing the same meaning (e.g., STRAWBERRY JAM and RASPBERRY JAM).

The conclusion that Light and Carter-Sobell came to was that a model for the recognition process needs to incorporate considerations of accessibility. If nothing else, some mechanism seems necessary to provide for *which* memory representation is accessed, say, in the case of noncued recall. Which JAM was it, for instance. A somewhat stronger position on this issue was taken by Tulving and Thomson (1971). They presented a long list of words in which some words were presented singly, others with weak associates (e.g., ART and GIRL), and still others with strong associates (e.g., HATE and LOVE). In the doublet conditions each word was both a to-be-remembered item and a context for its mate. Words were subsequently tested either singly, with, or without their original mate present. Their findings can be subsumed under the generalization that the closer the context at the time of test matched that at the time of presentation, the more accurate the recognition. They conclude that context does affect recognition, that it is unlikely that there is anything inherently different about recall and recognition, and that recall-recognition comparisons presumably cannot be very useful in separating availability and accessibility (or storage and retrieval effects). Further experiments in a similar vein are reported by Thomson (1972) and by Winograd and Conn (1971).

These studies demonstrate in convincing fashion that changes in context affect performance. Whether they lower accuracy is a moot point, since obviously OFFICIAL SEAL and PERFORMING SEAL are not the same "seal." Perhaps the subject should have been scored correct when he responded "no" to a changed item. That context does affect recognition is hardly newsworthy (one may not recognize a familiar face in an unfamiliar setting), but these experiments provide a useful experimental technique to study the problem further.

Whether these experiments demonstrate the existence of a retrieval process in recognition memory is less clear. It depends on the definition of "retrieval," and the term is often used quite loosely. It is probably not too fruitful to debate the issue of whether or not a retrieval process is involved in recognition memory. A more fruitful approach might be to try to specify just what the nature of these retrieval processes are.

A further demonstration by Tulving shows some very impressive evidence for context effects in recognition memory. In some tests of the encoding-specificity principle Tulving and Thomson (1973) report a situation in which subjects could apparently recall specific items when they could not recognize them. A list of 24 items was presented in the manner of Tulving and Osler (1968) with weak cues accompanying to-be-remembered items. This was followed by three tests—the first with strong cues, the second a matching test, and the third a recall test with the weak cues that had been presented at input. The matching test was novel: Subjects were given a word-association test with the strong cues, asked to associate, and their responses then used in an m-AFC situation. The subjects were even told that some of their generated associates were to-be-remembered items, and all they had to do was pick them out. Typical results would be 30% recall under strong cue, 30% correct performance on 4-alternative forced-choice recognition, but 50–60% recall with weak cues. If this effect turns out to be genuine, it would indicate that it is possible to reverse the usual recall-recognition finding. With appropriate retrieval cues, subjects can recall more than they can recognize when the recognition test is given in the absence of these retrieval cues.

High-Speed Scanning

Sternberg (1966, 1969a) has used reaction time to study the effect of number of alternatives on response latency in subspan lists. The general finding, confirmed many times in many different laboratories, is that reaction time increases as a linear function of set size (number of alternatives) with parallel functions for positive and negative probes. A positive probe is an old item, one shown in the list; a negative probe is a new item or lure, one not included in the list. Typical results for this task are shown in Fig. 3.13.

The original interpretation of these results (e.g., Sternberg, 1969b) was in terms of stages of processing. The probe was encoded, a comparison process ensued, a

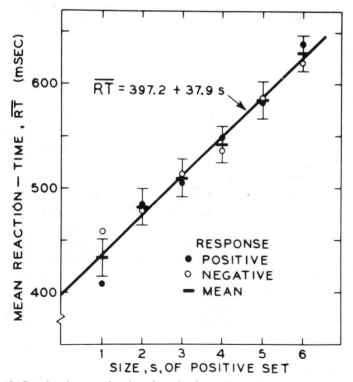

FIG. 3.13. Reaction time as a function of set size for positive and negative probes. (Fig. 4 from Sternberg, 1969a.)

decision was reached, and a response executed. The general argument for stages of processing was additivity in that, if the stages were actually separate and independent, then separate manipulation of two variables presumed to affect different stages would result in main effects but no interaction in analysis of variance. In the reaction-time tradition such studies have been reported by Biederman and Kaplan (1970), Hohle (1965), Palef (1973), and Taylor (1966); for a review see Laming (1968). In the recognition-memory area, supporting results have been found by Sternberg (1966, 1969b) and many others.

The recognition-memory set-size effects were originally explained in terms of a serial exhaustive scanning process during the comparison stage. As suggested by Sternberg (1966), if all items in the memory set were examined one by one and no response was made until all items had been examined, then the resulting functions would be not only parallel but linear, and the slope (generally on the order of about 35 msec per item) would be a measure of the time required to examine each item in memory. Extended practice speeds up the scanning process, but there is disagreement as to whether it changes its basic nature (Briggs & Blaha, 1969; Burrows & Murdock, 1969; Simpson, 1972).

One of the main problems for an exhaustive scanning model is the existence of serial-position effects in the reaction-time data. As noted by many (e.g., Burrows & Okada, 1971; Clifton & Birenbaum, 1970; Wingfield, 1973) the reaction times are not independent of the serial position of the probed item. Middle items have the longest latencies, and both primacy and recency effects are generally found. Usually the latter predominate; recency effects both span a larger range and are greater in magnitude than primacy effects.

Another problem for an exhaustive scanning model is the question of whether set size affects only the comparison stage. Studying naming-latency facilitation, Kirsner (1972) and Kirsner and Craik (1971) have suggested that set size may affect the encoding stage as well. If so, then the usual figure of 35 msec per item as the scanning rate would be an overestimate. Evidence for a rather faster scanning rate comes from a study by Colotla (1969), who used a different type of paradigm. Short lists of digits were presented for numerical recall (682749 would be recalled 246789), and the lowest digit in the list was either 0, 1, 2, or 3. When reaction times to initiate recall were plotted as a function of lowest digit, linear functions were found with slopes of approximately 15 msec per item both for auditory and visual presentation. Since there were no serial-position effects, the data suggest that subjects scanned the list exhaustively first for 0, then 1, then 2, etc. This method of numerical recall may be one way of avoiding possible artifacts due to naming-latency facilitation in the standard Sternberg paradigm.

If the serial scanning interpretation were correct, it would have considerable implications for retrieval processes in recognition memory. It would rule out any direct-access model and give us clear guidelines as to the nature of the retrieval process. Unfortunately, however, other theoretical interpretations seem to apply as well, if not better, to these data. Theios, Smith, Haviland, Traupmann, and Moy (1973) have argued for a probabalistically-ordered memory stack with self-terminating search. Baddeley and Ecob (1970) and Corballis, Kirby, and Miller (1972) suggest a strength-theory interpretation, and Okada (1971) has tested some implications of a trace-strength model in a continuous recognition-memory paradigm. Finite-state models that postulate two different comparison times for old items depending upon the state of the memory trace at the time of testing can predict both linear reaction-time functions and serial-position effects (Aubé & Murdock, 1974; Burrows & Okada, 1971; Forrin & Cunningham, 1973). Atkinson, Holmgren, and Juola (1969) have suggested a parallel-processing approach that can accommodate the usual linearity effects. Murdock (1971b) reported a parallel-processing model which accommodated not only parallel linear functions but serial-position effects as well. Townsend (1971) has even questioned the identifiability of parallel and serial models. All in all, while the data are very consistent and clear, their theoretical interpretation now seems rather uncertain. We cannot yet be sure how item recognition occurs even in very simple situations.

REVIEW

Let me close this chapter with a final consideration of theory and data. First, there is little doubt that a simple high-threshold or tagging model that says that a subject either remembers an item perfectly or not at all is inadequate. The main reason is the *a posteriori* probability functions. There are data demonstrating that these functions are monotonic over at least a six-point confidence-judgment scale with *a posteriori* probabilities running from .05 at the low end to .98 at the high end. If it could explain such data, a high-threshold model would still need considerable elaboration before it could even begin to explain in any serious fashion such findings as ROC functions, retention of attributes, latency, and judgments of recency and frequency.

Strength theory is perhaps intuitively more attractive but it too has its problems. There are all the objections noted in the Anderson and Bower (1972a) paper, the main point being that memory is capable of much finer discriminations than strength theory would seem to allow. Also, strength theory has no obvious way of accommodating similarity effects. Finally, data discussed in the section on judgments of recency and judgments of frequency show that, when strength theory is taken seriously and pushed to some stringent tests, it does not fare too well.

The most promising approach at this point may be an attribute model such as suggested by Bower or Lockhart. On the one hand, it reduces to a strength-type theory in certain situations and so has the natural appeal and advantages of strength theory in these situations; yet on the other hand it has greater explanatory power and avoids some of the obvious pitfalls of a simple strength interpretation. Thus, when a subject has to make a confidence judgment (or a judgment of recency or a judgment of frequency) presumably he can simply count the tagged attributes, set up one or several criteria, and respond exactly as strength theory says he does. Thus, all the signal-detection-like properties of the data fall out from the model.

Still, there are some real problems with an attribute model which should not be disregarded. Perhaps the main problem is that, in accounting for the parts, it forgets about the whole. Thus, the stimulus is not encoded or represented in memory;

only its components are. It seems likely that any conceivable feature experimental ingenuity is likely to conjure up can be tested and found present in a short-term memory task. Thus, one could ask if there was a word in the list with two vowels separated by a consonant, or if there was a letter T with a horizontal bar colored violet. Assuming the subject remembers, does that mean we have feature detectors and attributes for VCV combinations and for violet cross-bars?

To answer such questions with the reply that the subject has encoded the ortho-graphic or the chromatic attributes of the stimulus and generated a representation from them is not completely satisfactory. The list of encoded attributes gets longer and longer as the number of challenges increases, so one begins to wonder whether it might not be easier—and more parsimonious—simply to assume that the stimulus *qua* stimulus is encoded and its memorial representation gradually becomes de-graded or impoverished over time. The further defense of an attribute theory (name-ly, that there is a very transitory representational memory which mediates perfor-mance over the very short term) can probably be countered with data which show that the time intervals are in fact surprisingly long.

Such a viewpoint has not been explicitly developed and so, at this point, can not be considered a serious alternative to an attribute model. On the other hand, it is surprising to discover the complete absence of any serious tests of an attribute model. As far as I could tell, despite widespread allegiance to this general viewpoint the only article in this whole area that made parameter estimates and reported χ^2 values for goodness of fit was the Hinrichs (1970) paper—and that was testing strength theory. It is all very well and good at the beginning to work at the level of ordinal predictions, but sometimes theories and models do not seem quite so attrac-tive after they have been subjected to quantitative goodness-of-fit tests.

Let us briefly consider how the Bower model might handle an attribute probe test. Suppose in a continuous recognition-memory test words were presented in either upper- or lower-case type. On a subsequent retention test the subject is asked, first if the item is old, and second, if old, whether the type case on the second presenta-tion is the same as on the first. If you accept the Bower model, there are encoding operators and the yes-no judgment will be based on the number of active operators elicited by the probe. If the operator that encoded type case is a member of the active set, then the subject can tell whether the probe was in upper- or lower-case type. But there does not seem to be any way he could tell about the first presentation.

Perhaps it is worth pointing out more explicitly the difference between the multi-component view of Bower (1967b) and the encoding-variability view of Bower (1972b). In the former, there were two vectors, one for the first presentation and one for the second. A point-by-point comparison of the two would allow same-different judgments to be made, contingent on the attribute in question still being intact. In the latter, there are simply different operators or stimulus-analyzing mechanisms operative under the two presentations, and all the subject can tell is the number and identity of encoded attributes and what responses (list tags and associations) are con-ditioned to them. There is no forgetting in the sense of loss of information or degra-dation of the trace at all. There is simply a drift over time in the contents of the active set, so the observed decrements in performance seem wholely due to changes in context.

In understanding and interpreting these data on recognition memory, one or two general points should be made in closing. It is by no means clear that the many studies of item recognition that have been conducted in the laboratory are representative of what goes on in everyday situations. Intuitively it seems just the opposite. In everyday life our experiences are rich and elaborate, then our recollection is reinstated by some fragmentary cue. This effect is well known and goes under the name "redintegration." The laboratory studies by contrast use an impoverished situation (say lists of unrelated words) and a probe that is as rich as (and sometimes richer than) the original event. So if this analysis is correct such studies may not be telling us too much about what happens in everyday life. This comment, of course, is not intended to be critical. There are good and sufficient reasons for laboratory experiments, and there is no requirement that they should capture the flavor of our normal existence. But when they clearly do not, at least the fact should not pass without mention.

Related to this comment is the familiar experience one has of immediate and automatic recognition (or so it would seem) of objects and events even in the most unexpected of circumstances. Clearly we do not go about in everyday life primed to give "yes" and "no" responses, yet we do seem to experience a sense of familiarity even though we were not expecting to encounter the situation at all. How such "testing for familarity" comes about is neither represented in our theories or in our data.

SUMMARY

The most characteristic forgetting curve for item information shows d' to decrease exponentially with lag, at least in a discrete-trials procedure. With a continuous recognition-memory task the curve is probably steeper. An exponential function is quite consistent with an attribute model.

Confidence judgments and latencies can supplement accuracy measures in recognition-memory experiments. The ROC curves from a confidence-judgment procedure are generally those predicted by strength theory, though this is not a strong test. The *a posteriori* probability functions, along with the shape of the ROC curves, seem to rule out any simple all-or-none model. Latencies show a nonmonotonic U-shaped function, being slowest for the least certain responses. High-confident "yes" and high-confident "no" responses are appreciably faster, and the relative variability of correct responses and errors runs counter to what strength theory would predict.

Variations in the type of stimulus material (e.g., its meaningfulness) have an appreciable effect on recognition memory. A theoretical interpretation of some of the experimental results is provided by the encoding-variability hypothesis of Martin. Pictures seem more memorable than words, though the comparison is difficult to interpret because of various confoundings. Acoustic or articulatory effects can be quite pronounced and lend support to a view of phonemic encoding in short-term memory. However, evidence for other attributes (associative, semantic, orthographic) is not lacking. Modality differences also occur, and the persistence of representational information seems to outlast that of iconic or echoic memory.

Recognition accuracy in a forced-choice procedure declines as the number of alternatives increases. Strength-theory predictions from a yes-no procedure to an m-AFC procedure have been found to be quite satisfactory. The nature of the alternatives also affects recognition accuracy, with similar lures lowering performance. False positives increase over the course of a continuous recognition-memory task, and false alarms are also more common to semantically, associatively, or categorically related words. While this finding is one of the main lines of support for an attribute model, the exact explanation is not yet established.

Word-frequency effects and the effect of organization on recognition memory are two ways of testing the conventional views on the difference between recall and recognition. Rare words are more memorable than common words, and there is at least some evidence to suggest that organization affects (free) recall but not recognition. A one-process view which assumes a higher cutoff or threshold for recall than recognition is rendered doubtful by such findings. An alternative interpretation suggests that recall involves one or more additional processes than recognition, and a common suggestion is that it might be a search or retrieval process that is unnecessary in recognition.

Experiments utilizing judgments of recency require the subject to indicate when an item occurred; with judgments of frequency, they must indicate how often it occurred. Such experiments are useful to separate a strength model from a multiplex model. One possible strength model says there is only a single trace that is strengthened by repetition and that underlies judgments of frequency and recency. The experimental data are negative. While they are more in accord with a multiplex view that suggests separate traces, this multiplex model has difficulties in explaining lag effects.

Context has a clear effect on recognition performance. Embedding a particular word in a different context at presentation and test reduces the frequency with which it is identified as an old item. These results have been interpreted as demonstrating a retrieval process in recognition. The nature of the retrieval process has been investigated in studies of high-speed scanning. Reaction times increase in linear fashion as the number of alternatives increases, at least for the small set sizes investigated. The functions for positive and negative probes are generally parallel with slopes near 35 msec per item. One interpretation, as suggested by Sternberg, is a serial exhaustive high-speed scan where the comparison process is separate from the other stages. Serial-position effects and naming-latency facilitation pose problems for this model, and a variety of other interpretations have been suggested.

4
THEORIES OF ASSOCIATION

This chapter will cover theories of association. How do we remember that *port* is left and that *starboard* is right, that the French word *fenetre* means window, or that the name of the person in the corner is John Wilkinson? The formation and retention of associations has been studied experimentally by the method of paired associates. In paired associates the two items (e.g., FENETRE and WINDOW) are explicitly designated by the experimenter, and they may be words, pictures, nonsense syllables, letters, digits, or whatever. As in recognition, the term "item" is simply a generic name for a class of stimuli. Also, in this context an item sometimes denotes the pair itself (e.g., FENETRE–WINDOW).

Although short-term memory for single paired associates has been studied with a distractor technique (e.g., Peterson & Peterson, 1962), the more general method is to use a probe technique. A list of items (i.e., paired associates) is presented one by one, then one of them is singled out for testing. If an individual pair or item is designated A--B, then we can test for specific associative information by probing for B with A or by probing for A with B. This probe technique was used by Murdock (1961b) to trace out a retention curve for single associations, and very rapid forgetting was found.

A probe technique such as this has the advantage of eliminating output interference (the interference generated by attempted or successful recall of other paired associates). The technique can be extended to include both input and output interference if one wishes, where input interference is generated by presenting other pairs to study and output interference is generated by testing other pairs for recall. In a discrete-trials procedure, study and test periods are alternated, while in a continuous-task procedure they are intermixed. In the single-trial situation each pair is only presented once; in the multitrial situation, each pair is presented many times.

In the latter, a discrete-trials procedure is generally used; study and test trials regularly alternate. This method, of course, is one of the two standard paired-associate learning methods used in research on verbal learning. The other is the method of anticipation. Here the retention of each pair is first tested. Then, re-presentation of each pair follows immediately. Until recently the anticipation method was the method of choice, but now the study-test method seems more popular.

In this chapter, four main theories of association will be discussed. The first is interference theory, the classical position which has developed out of association theory as stated, e.g., by Carr (1931) and Robinson (1932). The second theory is the one-element model, a special case of stimulus-sampling theory which has been applied to paired-associate learning. The third are various multistate models which have been developed in an attempt to remedy some of the failings of the one-element model. Finally, we shall close with a fluctuation model that was designed expressly to account for some of the short-term memory effects discovered with the probe technique.

INTERFERENCE THEORY

Historically, interference theory goes back at least as far as McGeoch (1932), and reviews may be found in Adams (1967), Anderson and Bower (1973), Hall (1971), Jung (1968), Kintsch (1970b), or Postman and Underwood (1973). In his early paper McGeoch pointed out the inadequacies of decay theory and the importance of interference effects. In very general terms, he suggested that the reason we forget an association that we have previously learned is that interference from other associations occurs. Further, the less similarity between the members of the competing associations, the greater the interference, and so the more the forgetting. If I have learned one association a–b and then I learn a second association a–d, the more similar b and d are to each other the more likely I am to remember a–b. (The convention used here is to let capital letters denote external stimuli and responses and to let small letters denote their memorial representations.)

A two-factor theory was suggested by Melton and Irwin (1940) when they found that the amount of measured interference did not account for the total obtained interference. One of the two factors was response competition. If you know a–b and a–d and are presented only A, then b and d may compete with each other when you try to respond. The second factor they labelled Factor X, and suggested it might be unlearning. If you know a–b and then must learn a–d, perhaps in the process of forming a stable a–d association there is some weakening or extinction of the a–b association. The two factors together (response competition and unlearning) would summate to produce the total amount of interference.

A modified free-recall method was used by Briggs (1954) to minimize response competition, and an improved or modified modified [sic] free-recall (MMFR) procedure was used by Barnes and Underwood (1959). In the latter, which is now a fairly standard procedure, the A term is shown the subject who is asked to give both

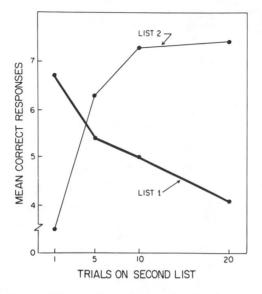

FIG. 4.1. Mean correct recall from Lists 1 and 2 as a function of amount of practice on List 2. (Fig. 1 from Barnes & Underwood, 1959.)

the B and D terms to which it is associated. By asking for both responses and allowing ample time to respond, response competition (hopefully) is minimized.

Direct evidence for the existence of unlearning was reported in the Barnes and Underwood data, here shown as Fig. 4.1. Subjects were given either 1, 5, 10, or 20 trials on a list containing 8 A–D pairs after they had learned a list containing 8 A–B pairs to a criterion of one perfect trial. Retention was tested by an MMFR procedure and, as can be seen, the better learned the a–d associations, the less well recalled the a–b associations. It is this decrement in List-1 recall that was given as evidence for the unlearning hypothesis. (For a different interpretation see Banks, 1969.)

The line of theorizing discussed so far has been concerned with retroactive inhibition—the decrement in recall produced in the experimental group by learning an interpolated list, compared to a control group that does not have an interpolated list (Underwood, 1966, p. 554). Thus, if you have learned a–b, your subsequent recall will suffer if you have to learn a–d in the interim. (To control for nonspecific effects, the control group may learn c–d rather than nothing.) Another main type of interference is proactive inhibition, the decrement in recall produced by prior learning. Thus, the experimental group learns a–b, then learns a–d, then after a suitable retention interval tries to recall a–d. Retention will be poorer than in a control group which has only learned a–d (Underwood, 1966, p. 564).

Although the emphasis of interference theory had long been on retroactive inhibition, Underwood (1957) made a convincing case for the importance of proactive

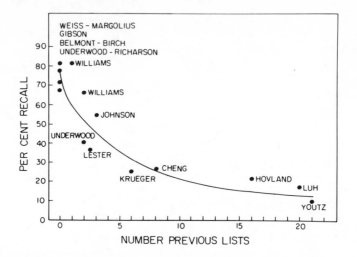

FIG. 4.2. Recall of a single list after a one-day retention interval as a function of the number of lists previously learned and recalled. (Fig. 3 from Underwood, 1957.)

inhibition in forgetting. He analyzed the data of many previous investigators and found that the more previous lists the subjects had learned, the less well they remembered the most recent list. These data are shown here as Fig. 4.2. After a 24-hour retention interval, subjects who had learned no previous lists recalled with 75% accuracy; those who had learned, say, 10 previous lists recalled with only 25% accuracy. This effect is robust and reliable. I tried it once with three volunteer college students who, for 10 successive days, learned a 24-item list to criterion and then recalled it 22 hours later. Just as these data show, for each subject their first-day recall was about 75%, but their tenth day recall was about 25%. It might be noted that these studies used serial lists, not paired associates.

A two-factor interference theory says that the forgetting obtained in a retroactive inhibition paradigm occurs because of unlearning the a–b associations during the learning of a–d and response competition between b and d at the time of test. Why does forgetting occur in a proactive-inhibition paradigm? As before, when learning a–d there is unlearning of the a–b associations. So, if the test is immediate, there is no decrement in the recall of the a–d list. But, says the theory, over time there is spontaneous recovery of the a–b associations. The more time, the more the recovery, with greater possibility for response competition at the time of recall and interference with the second-list associations. Thus, the forgetting in a proactive-inhibition paradigm results from spontaneous recovery. One prediction that immediately follows from this analysis is that proactive but not retroactive inhibition should increase over time. This prediction was confirmed in an early study by Underwood (1948).

These two themes, retroactive inhibition and proactive inhibition, come together in a paper on extraexperimental sources of interference in forgetting (Underwood & Postman, 1960). The subject is not a *tabula rasa* when he comes in for an experiment. His prior language habits are strongly established. To learn a list his prior associative repertoire must be modified, and the ease with which this can happen will be reflected both in speed of acquisition and amount of forgetting to be expected. With very low-meaningful material (e.g., low-association value CCCs) prior letter-sequence habits will have to be unlearned. Once the list is learned, it should be highly vulnerable to spontaneous recovery. Thus, such lists should be hard to learn and hard to remember. At the other end, highly meaningful words will be juxtaposed in bizarre sequences, so prior unit-sequence (word) habits will conflict. Thus, for the same reasons, lists of highly meaningful words arranged in a random sequence should be hard to learn and hard to remember. Intermediate lists composed of high-association value nonsense syllables should be easy to learn and remember. Since these nonsense syllables are high in association value, the letter-sequence interference should be at a minimum. Since they are nonwords, the unit-sequence interference should be at a minimum. Since these two sources of interference are presumed to summate, so also the combined interference should be minimal.

Tests of the hypothesis of extraexperimental interference have been consistently negative. There seems to be no unlearning of prior experimental habits (Slamecka, 1966), and a number of attempts have failed to show the expected variation in recall with meaningfulness (Underwood & Ekstrand, 1966). One possibility is that language habits are too ingrained to be modified by a brief laboratory experience. Extraexperimental interference might show up when more malleable associations are employed. A recent test showed that recall of a categorized list improved the more tightly the structure conformed to pre-existing normative categories (Underwood & Zimmerman, 1973). However, while it may be possible to explain away the experimental failures with strong language habits, the fact remains (to be explained) that single lists of words and nonsense syllables are forgotten.

The classical version of interference theory has postulated three types of associations: forward associations (from a to b), backward associations (from b to a), and context associations (from the experimental situation to the b response terms). A study by McGovern (1964) showed that a simple additive model would result in correct ordinal predictions about the amount of transfer expected in various experimental paradigms. Consequently, it was quite disconcerting to find that when recognition rather than recall was used, the forgetting pattern was quite different. Specifically, Postman and Stark (1969) found that there was no significant retroactive inhibition when memory was tested by a recognition (multiple choice) procedure in the traditional A–B, A–D paradigm. This result has served to cast doubt on another basic interference theory precept, namely, the unlearning of specific a–b associations. In its place, the concept of generalized response competition (Newton & Wickens, 1956) or response-set suppression (Postman & Stark, 1969; Postman, Stark & Fraser, 1968) has been suggested. That is, first-list responses as a whole become less accessible as a consequence of second-list learning. Thus, in an A–B, A–D paradigm a memory deficit in recall would show up because the first-list responses as a whole are less accessible. However, since recognition minimizes or eliminates the retrieval problem, the effect would not be apparent when memory was tested by forced-choice recognition.

Supporting evidence comes from a rather different type of study reported by Tulving and Psotka (1971). Subjects learned either 1,2,3,4,5, or 6 successive free-recall lists, then attempted to recall the whole lot. Each list contained 24 words, six categories with four words per category. The main results are shown here in Fig. 4.3. The lower two curves show the number of words recalled and the number of categories recalled from the first list as a function of the number of interpolated lists. They show a typical inhibition effect, decreasing from left to right. The upper curve shows a ratio; it is simply the number of words recalled per category. This top curve fell off little if at all, so the retroactive inhibition affected the number of categories accessed, but not the categorized information *per se*. Further, in a cued recall test, category names were presented to the subjects who then attempted to recall all instances. By and large there was little difference in cued recall as a function of amount of interpolation. The conclusion from these findings was that retroactive inhibition serves to reduce the accessibility of mnemonic information but not its availability. Essentially the same finding in a more traditional paradigm has also been reported by Ceraso (1967). In an A–B, A–D paradigm he found little loss over 24 hours on an associative matching test but considerable loss in an MMFR procedure. Thus, again retroactive inhibition seems to be more a loss of accessibility than a weakening of the association *per se*. However, evidence that associative interference is not completely lacking has recently been reported by Cofer, Faile, and Horton (1971).

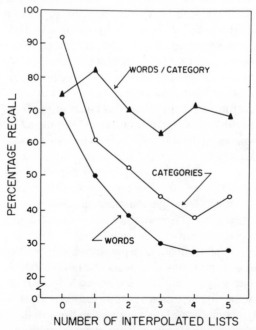

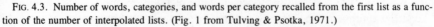

FIG. 4.3. Number of words, categories, and words per category recalled from the first list as a function of the number of interpolated lists. (Fig. 1 from Tulving & Psotka, 1971.)

A somewhat different interpretation of retroactive-inhibition effects was offered by Slamecka (1969a). There is some reason to believe that the total time required to learn a list of paired associates does not depend upon how this time is allocated between presentation time (time per trial) and number of presentations (trials). The total time to master a list will be about the same as long as the product of these two is fixed. This constant (multiplicative) relationship has been dubbed the total-time hypothesis (Cooper & Pantle, 1967). Extending this notion to the two-list situation characteristic of experiments in retroactive inhibition, Slamecka has suggested that total recall will depend upon both absolute and proportional time. The more practice with (time spent learning) the first list or the second list, the greater the total recall (sum of first-list and second-list items). Also, the more the practice on one of the two lists, the greater its proportional recall. As an example, consider the Barnes and Underwood data shown in Fig. 4.1. Each group (i.e., those with 1, 5, 10, or 20 trials on the second list) recalls about 12 words in all, but the relative preponderance of first-list and second-list items changes systematically with the amount of interpolation. There is much more evidence of this sort reviewed in the Slamecka article.

Finally, the encoding-variability interpretation has been applied here by Martin (1971). Unwilling to give up the idea of item-specific associations, he argues that the same nominal stimulus A in first-list learning is not the same functional stimulus A in second-list learning. The encoding of A_2 will differ from the encoding of A_1. Then, following a model of Greeno (1970) it is suggested that learning is a two-stage process where the first stage is forming a memorial representation of the pair (taken as a unit) and the second stage is forming a retrieval route that will guarantee recall. We shall discuss this theory further in the third main section of this chapter, but for the time being one additional point should be noted. This point concerns the independence of the specific first-list and second-list associations.

Item dependence has long been assumed (e.g., Postman, 1961), almost as a matter of course. Is this point not obvious from data such as Barnes and Underwood, since as one curve goes up the other goes down? As it happens, no. A more critical test is to look at the items pair by pair. For each A member of the list there is a first-list B member that is or is not recalled and a second-list D member that is or is not recalled. The direct test is to construct a 2 × 2 contingency table, do a frequency count of the four possible combinations, and then test for independence by some appropriate measure. The evidence, surprisingly enough, indicates that in fact the first-list and the second-list associations are independent (Martin, 1971; Wichawut & Martin, 1971). Although the statistical analysis is not quite as simple as described here (Hintzman, 1972a) the data still seem to be quite clear in their support of independence (Martin & Greeno, 1972).

Where does this leave us? Clearly divergent views are emerging. A defense of the traditional two-factor theory and an answer to its critics has recently been offered by Postman and Underwood (1973), and response-set suppression still seems important as a supplementary concept. Martin and Greeno seem to feel that retrieval factors are more likely to provide an understanding of retroactive-inhibition effects.

Finally, Slamecka has introduced quite a new conception, that of total time spent learning and a trade-off between memory for first- and second-list associations.

In summary, what can be said about interference theory by way of evaluation? Despite what its detractors may say, it does have some explanatory power and it has certainly generated a very large amount of research. In a general sense, it can explain why memory improves with degree of original learning, why memory is worse with interpolated learning, why retroactive and proactive inhibition occur, why different transfer paradigms yield the ordering they do, and why similarity effects operate as they do. On the other hand, the theory is only capable of making predictions at an ordinal level. It has not succeeded in coping with extraexperimental interference. It really does not explain in any very deep sense why proactive inhibition occurs at all; if the MMFR procedure does in fact eliminate response competition, and if prior language habits are largely isolated from experimental learning, where does the interference come from? Despite what has been claimed (e.g., Postman, 1971) interference theory really has not had much to say about organizational effects, and clearly it has not emphasized the importance of retrieval processes as much as some might wish.

In my opinion, it has not come to grips with detailed mechanisms and processes involved in memory. It continues to treat the list as the unit of analysis. It is reluctant to look at the microstructure of learning and memory—what is happening to individual pairs of items over short retention intervals. If you wish, it has neglected short-term memory. It has outlined and organized a number of empirical findings and suggested some possible mechanisms that could be operative. But to take a reductionistic view, these can be explained or described at a more molecular level of analysis, and that is what the subsequent models in this chapter attempt to do.

ONE-ELEMENT MODEL

Interference theory assumes that associations vary in strength. They become stronger with repetition, they become weaker with unlearning, or they may regain some strength with spontaneous recovery. In this regard, interference theory is like the strength theory of Norman and Wickelgren discussed in Chapter 2. Interference theory does not use the statistical machinery of signal-detection theory. Also, it is more concerned with acquisition, transfer, and retention over relatively long intervals, while strength theory is more concerned with immediate memory effects and decay parameters of forgetting functions. However, the underlying premise—that memory traces vary in a continuous fashion along a dimension we can call strength— is the same in both theories.

The contrary point of view is a finite-state model. It would say that the gradations are discrete, not continuous. Physically, an analogy would be the difference between a ramp and a staircase. Finite-state models vary in the number of states (or steps) they postulate. The simplest and most extreme view would be to suggest that there were only two states. An association between a and b either exists or it does not exist. It is all or none. An all-or-none model, then, says that associations are two-valued, not finely graded or continuous.

A learning model that embodied such a view was Bower's one-element model (Bower, 1961, 1962). It was a special case of the more general stimulus-sampling theory of Estes. Consider the representation of a stimulus in terms of elements as shown in Eq. (2.8); then assume there is only one element in the set. If one such stimulus element characterizes each paired associate in a list, then each pair can be in one of two states. In stimulus-sampling terms, the element is either conditioned or unconditioned; in terms of associations, there is an association or there is not an association. Thus, each pairwise association is all or none.

Consider a standard paired-associate learning situation. There is a list of pairs that are shown one by one on the study trial; then (in a different random order) each pair is tested. The A member of each pair is shown and the subject tries to respond with the appropriate B member. Then another study trial is given, then all pairs tested a second time, and so on. Study and test trials alternate, and both presentation and testing order are randomized to a greater or lesser degree. The one-element model assumes that, with each presentation, there is a certain probability that a given pair is learned. Denote this probability as c. This parameter c is constant over pairs and constant over trials. That is, all pairs are equally likely (or unlikely) to be learned on a particular trial, and the probability c does not change over trials. Thus, no matter how many previous (unsuccessful) presentations, there is still the same probability that an unlearned pair will go from the unlearned to the learned state on the next presentation. Clearly, such a view is the direct antithesis of strength theory, which would say that memory-trace strength gradually builds up with repetition.

The learned state was considered to be "absorbing." Once a pair had been learned it stayed in the conditioned or learned state for the duration of the experiment. Let us characterize the learned state by the letter A (for associated) and the unlearned state by $\bar{A}$ (for not associated). Subscripts to the states denote trial number. Then the transition matrix

$$
T = \begin{array}{c} \\ A_n \\ \bar{A}_n \end{array}
\begin{array}{cc} A_{n+1} & \bar{A}_{n+1} \\ \left[\begin{array}{cc} 1 & 0 \\ c & 1-c \end{array}\right] \end{array}
\tag{4.1}
$$

characterizes the effect of each study trial on each individual pair. On study trial $n + 1$, with probability c an unlearned pair becomes learned, but with probability $1 - c$ it does not. With probability 1 a learned pair stays learned, so there is zero probability that it moves from A to $\bar{A}$.

To characterize performance, it is necessary to specify a vector for the starting state and a vector for the response rule. Both are simple. It is assumed that all pairs start in the unlearned state. For the response rule, it is assumed that a pair in the

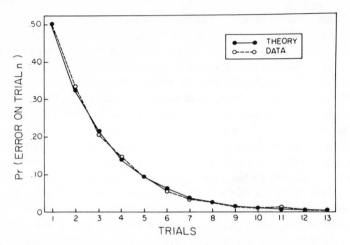

FIG. 4.4. Expected and obtained number of incorrect responses during paired associate learning for the one-element model. (Fig. 1 from Bower, 1961.)

learned state will be correct with probability 1, but a pair in the unlearned state will be correct with probability g. This latter probability is a guessing parameter. In terms of the model, if a pair is in the unlearned state all a subject can do on a test trial is guess, and if he guesses he will be correct with probability g.

Simple though this model is, a number of detailed predictions may be derived from it. They include such measures as the expected number of errors over trials, the distribution of the total number of errors per item, the distribution of the number of errors before the first success, the distribution of the number of errors before the kth success, and the distribution of the trial number of the last error. The experimental situation Bower chose to test the model was paired-associate learning with binary responses. The fit of the model was extremely good. Only one example is shown here, the mean learning curve. This is shown in Fig. 4.4, and the agreement between theory and data could not be much better. But many other predictions were substantiated in equally impressive fashion (e.g., Bower, 1961).

In order to make the quantitative estimates it was only necessary to estimate the value of the learning-rate parameter c. Since there were only two responses, $g = .5$. The derivations are not shown here; the interested reader can consult the original articles. Also, many of the derivations are given in Atkinson, Bower, and Crothers (1965) and Levine and Burke (1972).

The Bower one-element model has many problems, and in fact one could probably even say that in some aspects it is clearly wrong. But before considering what these problems are, let us briefly consider its virtues. First, it demonstrated in clear and compelling fashion that a simple quantitative model for paired-associate learning could do what any adequate scientific theory must do: postulate the basic principles involved, derive predictions, and accurately and extensively describe the data obtained in an experimental task. Second, it provided a viable alternative to a strength theory of memory. By taking a finite-state approach, it showed that the traditional explanations of verbal learning and memory phenomena were not the only possible ones. Third, it showed the utility of simple stochastic models to characterize change in performance over trials. Earlier, Miller (1952) had suggested that Markov models could be a useful tool for the understanding of learning processes, and the one-element model of Bower is a clear confirmation of this view.

As for the difficulties, the main empirical problem seems to be that it only works for binary responses. That is, if there are only two possible responses for each A term then the model works quite nicely. But if there are more than two—in the extreme case, if the B terms are nonsense syllables or random words, where the ensemble size is large—then the fit of the model to the data becomes worse. The main way it worsens is in terms of stationarity. It has already been stated that, in the one-element model, the conditioning probability c is constant over trials. Thus, the probability of a correct response prior to learning should be constant, or stationary, over time. Evidence that it is not was provided by Suppes and Ginsberg (1963). Further evidence is shown in Fig. 4.5. The solid curve shows the probability of the first correct anticipation of a pair on Trial n as a function of n. The B members of the pairs were common words, so the guessing probability was essentially zero. Were stationarity to obtain, the curve would be flat. Clearly it is not; these results contradict stationarity. The dotted curve is the result of a simulation of a particular model, and it will be explained later.

Other data incompatible with the one-element model come from studies using a second-guess procedure or a ranking procedure (Bower, 1967a; Brown, 1965; Murdock, 1963b). Suppose a subject gives a response that is wrong. Provided there are more than two possible responses he can try again. If learning is all-or-none then the second guess should be at chance. In actuality, it is generally above chance. Or, in a multiple-choice recognition test the subject can rank the possible alterna-

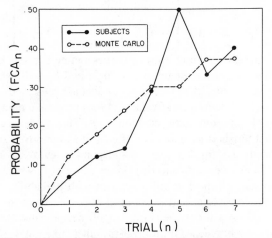

FIG. 4.5. Probability that the first correct anticipation (recall) of a pair occurs on trial n, as a function of n. The solid curve shows experimental data, the dotted curve a Monte Carlo simulation. (Fig. 13 from Murdock, 1972.)

tives from most likely to least likely. According to the model, if the first choice is wrong the distribution of correct selections across rankings should be uniform; in general it is not. The correct response is more likely to be given second than third, and perhaps even more likely to be given third than further down in the ranking.

Theoretically, I think that the main problem with the one-element model is that it starts with learning, not with memory. As stated before, the belief here is that learning is the increased resistance to forgetting. To say that the only thing that happens to a pair during paired-associate study and test trials is that, at some unknown point, it moves from the unlearned to the learned state quite overlooks the short-term memory effects that occur immediately after presentation. This is the point illustrated in Fig. 1.2. Also, to characterize the learned state as "absorbing" probably is unrealistic. The probability of a correct recall may approach unity, but it seems unlikely that it ever becomes unity.

MULTISTATE MODELS

In an attempt to remedy the deficiencies of the one-element model, a number of multistate models for paired associates have been proposed. Suppes and Ginsberg (1963) suggested a two-element model where there are three states rather than two. Call the states $A0$ where neither element is conditioned, $A1$ where one element is conditioned, and $A2$ where both are conditioned. The probability of a correct response is g, g', and 1 for states $A0$, $A1$, and $A2$, respectively. The transition matrix can be represented as

$$T = \begin{array}{c} \\ A2_n \\ A1_n \\ A0_n \end{array} \begin{array}{ccc} A2_{n+1} & A1_{n+1} & A0_{n+1} \\ \begin{bmatrix} 1 & 0 & 0 \\ b & 1-b & 0 \\ 0 & a & 1-a \end{bmatrix} \end{array} \qquad (4.2)$$

The authors say that the resulting learning curves can be either concave or convex upwards, depending upon the relative values of a and b, and that nonstationarity is predicted. However, no fits of the model to data are presented.

In a different vein, Atkinson and Crothers (1964) propose a model with assumptions about a short- and long-term retention state. This model was explicitly developed to account for short-term memory effects. It assumes four states. Pairs start in state U (uncoded) and, for them, subjects respond by guessing at random. Once the A member of a pair becomes encoded (in the sense of Lawrence, 1963) it goes into a short-term state S where it will be correct with probability 1. However, as other pairs are presented or tested, it can drop back to a forgotten state F where, though still encoded, it will only be correct by chance. Finally the learned state L is absorbing, and it can be reached from any of the other three states, U, F, or S.

This model has three parameters. One parameter is c, the probability that encoding will occur on any given presentation. A second parameter is a, the probability that it will be forgotten and so drop back from state S to state F. In the paper, the designation of this model is LS-3, standing for long and short (the two memory states) and 3 for the number of parameters to be estimated from the data. A reduced version is LS-2 where c was set to 1; there were only two parameters to be estimated from the data. To say $c = 1$ simply means that encoding occurs on the first presentation of a pair. If we consider LS-2, then the theory can be characterized by the transition matrix

$$T = \begin{array}{c} \\ L_n \\ S_n \\ G_n \end{array} \begin{array}{ccc} L_{n+1} & S_{n+1} & G_{n+1} \\ \left[\begin{array}{ccc} 1 & 0 & 0 \\ a & (1-a)(1-f) & (1-a)f \\ a & (1-a)(1-f) & (1-a)f \end{array} \right] \end{array} \quad (4.3)$$

Here states F and U have been combined into a guessing state G.

In their paper, the authors show that the two models LS-3 and LS-2 do a better job of accounting for data from several paired-associate experiments than the one-element model of Bower, a single-operator model suggested by Bush and Mosteller (1955) where each presentation results in a constant increase in the probability of a correct response, several variations of a linear model proposed by M. F. Norman (1964), and the two-element model of Suppes and Ginsburg. Two features of the LS-2 model are that the transition probabilities are the same in states S and G, and items can enter the learned state L from either S or G.

A modification of the Atkinson and Crothers model was suggested by Bernbach (1965), and the analogous transition matrix was

$$T = \begin{array}{c} \\ L_n \\ S_n \\ G_n \end{array} \begin{array}{ccc} L_{n+1} & S_{n+1} & G_{n+1} \\ \left[\begin{array}{ccc} 1 & 0 & 0 \\ a & (1-a)(1-f) & (1-a)f \\ 0 & 1-f & f \end{array} \right] \end{array} \quad (4.4)$$

In this model, items must pass through the short-term state S to go from the unlearned state G to the absorbing state L. Thus, the main difference between the models represented in Eqs. (4.3) and (4.4) are the probabilities associated with state G.

Yet a further variation was suggested by Greeno (1967).

$$T = \begin{array}{c} \\ L_n \\ S_n \\ G_n \end{array} \begin{array}{ccc} L_{n+1} & S_{n+1} & G_{n+1} \\ \left[\begin{array}{ccc} 1 & 0 & 0 \\ 0 & 1-c & c \\ a & (1-a)(1-b) & (1-a)b \end{array} \right] \end{array} \quad (4.5)$$

Here, the main feature is that items cannot go from the short-term state to the long-term state. Instead, they must be forgotten first, and so they can reach state L only from state G. The main reason for this feature is the lag effect. In previous studies (Greeno, 1964; Peterson, Saltzman, Hillner, & Land, 1962) it had been found that retention at long intervals was poorer if two earlier presentations had been massed rather than spaced. The model of Greeno shown in Eq. (4.5) would predict this effect, since a pair in state S is actually at a disadvantage compared to one in state G. Evidence for the futility of massed presentation has been reported by Calfee (1968).

This same article by Greeno pointed out one disturbing consideration. When the models represented by Eqs. (4.2), (4.3), and (4.4) are compared, there are parameter values that will make them indistinguishable. That is, all models could make the same predictions. If that is the case, then clearly there is no point whatever in trying to make comparative experimental tests.

Some characteristics of three-state models in general, and the Long-Short model of Atkinson and Crothers in particular, were discussed by Bower (1967a). Among other things, he pointed out that there is still a problem with the second-guess data. Even though correct performance can come from either of two states, in each the association is all or none. As a direction for further investigation he suggested that perhaps a more fruitful way to proceed would be to base a multistate model on differences between storage and retrieval. Such a view seems represented in the current thinking of Greeno and his associates. This last model we shall consider is not only the most recent but also the only one that makes real contact with the same data base used by other theories of association. In particular, it concerns itself with the same phenomena of transfer and retroactive inhibition that interference theory attempts to explain.

This model (Greeno, 1970; Greeno, James, & DaPolito, 1971) suggests that there are two different stages in the process of learning associations. The first stage is learning to store a pair, and the second stage is learning to retrieve it. It is assumed that, in the first stage, the A–B pair is stored as a unit much as Gestaltists (e.g., Asch, 1969) have suggested. To do this, some sort of relational property is necessary to form the link or connection between the two members of the pair. The second stage requires finding or developing a retrieval cue which will be effective in eliciting the association (the stored pair) on presentation of the probe. This view contrasts somewhat with an interference-theory position that the two main stages of paired-associate learning are response learning and the learning of an associative hookup (Underwood & Schulz, 1960).

If the states are denoted G, S, and R for guessing, storage, and retrieval, then the transition matrix is

$$T = \begin{array}{c} \\ R_n \\ S_n \\ G_n \end{array} \begin{array}{ccc} R_{n+1} & S_{n+1} & G_{n+1} \\ \left[\begin{array}{ccc} 1 & 0 & 0 \\ c & 1-c & 0 \\ ab & a(1-b) & 1-a \end{array}\right]. \end{array} \qquad (4.6)$$

Thus, a pair could be stored and a retrieval cue generated in a single presentation, if the subject could find an effective cue for a pair that had been stored. No regressions occur; neither encodings nor retrieval cues are forgotten.

For transfer of training predictions, if a subject had learned A–B, the first stage of second-list learning should be easier if he next had to learn C–D than if he next had to learn either A–D or C–B. This difference would reflect storage interference which would be attributed to persistent encoding. As for the second stage, learning C–D or C–B should be easier than learning A–C or A–B$_r$ (the first-list items repaired) since learning to retrieve is, according to the model, primarily dependent upon the first term of the pair. Supporting data for these predictions are presented in Greeno *et al.* (1971). Stage duration is assessed by standard parameter estimation techniques (for details, see Humphreys and Greeno, 1970).

It is perhaps too early to make any strong pronouncements about the strengths and weaknesses of this model; it is not clear just what it can and cannot do. For instance, it would not seem able to handle the Postman and Stark (1969) transfer data too well, though perhaps I am wrong. More surely it would seem to fall into the same difficulty as the Bower one-element model in terms of complete disregard of all short-term memory effects. While it meshes nicely with much transfer and retroaction data, it is neither as broad in coverage as interference theory nor as detailed in analysis as the fluctuation model considered next.

FLUCTUATION MODEL

All of the models considered so far are designed basically to account for list-learning effects. Memorial effects, as it were, are an afterthought. Suppose we turn it around and start with a model designed expressly to accommodate short-term memory effects. Then perhaps we can extend it to account for list-learning effects as well. We shall consider recall first, then recognition.

Recall

The fluctuation model I have suggested (Murdock, 1967b, 1970, 1972) goes as follows. Let us assume that there are only two states, and let us call them A and N. When an association is in state A it is available, so if it is tested at that particular moment in time, correct recall will occur. That is, if the subject is probed with the A member of the pair he will be able to respond with the appropriate B member of the pair. If the association is in state N then it is not available and he will have to guess. In all probability he will not be correct.

When an A–B pair is presented to a subject it starts in state A with a certain probability; call this probability p_0. With probability $1 - p_0$ it does not start in state A; that is, it starts in state N. Generally p_0 is close to 1, and sometimes it can simply be assumed to be 1, but there are other cases where it seems to be lower. In any event, we have a starting vector

$$s = (p_0 \quad 1 - p_0) \tag{4.7}$$

which describes the initial effect of presentation.

This model is an interference model, not a decay model. Something happens to an association when other events occur, not merely through the passage of time *per se*. In particular, a change in state can occur under either of two different conditions. One is when an additional paired associate is presented for study. The other is when another association is tested for recall. In either case (and they are henceforth considered equivalent) an association in state A can change to state N, or an association in state N can change to state A. The transition matrix is

$$
T = \begin{array}{c} \\ A_n \\ N_n \end{array}
\begin{array}{c} A_{n+1} \qquad N_{n+1} \end{array}
\left[\begin{array}{cc} 1 - \alpha & \alpha \\ \beta & 1 - \beta \end{array} \right] \tag{4.8}
$$

One can use the terms forgetting and recovery to characterize these changes. When an association changes from state A to state N it is forgotten, since the correct response to a probe is no longer available. On the other hand, when an association changes from state N to state A we have recovery; a previously unavailable association now is available. The transition probabilities are simply α and β. That is, α is the probability that an association will be forgotten when another pair is studied or tested, while β is the probability that an association will recover when another pair is studied or tested. This is a fluctuation model in that transitions in either direction are possible.

With these assumptions it is a relatively easy matter to develop an equation for the retention curve. It is

$$
P_A(i) = \frac{\beta}{\alpha + \beta} + \left(p_0 - \frac{\beta}{\alpha + \beta} \right)(1 - \alpha - \beta)^i \tag{4.9}
$$

where $P_A(i)$ is the probability that an association will be in state A after i units of interference. Several features of this equation are worthy of comment. First, at $i = 0$ then $P_A(i) = p_0$, as it must. Second, the asymptotic value is $\beta/(\alpha + \beta)$, a ratio involving the two parameters α and β. Third, the forgetting curve is a decreasing geometric function stepping down from p_0 to asymptote with a rate constant determined by $1 - \alpha - \beta$.

At first glance such a model may seem too simple and unrealistic. Surely it would seem that associations can vary in strength, as we have strong and weak associations. If an association is forgotten and is no longer available, how can it possibly recover? Even worse, how can an association that does not start in state A later become available? And, finally, are we not completely disregarding the retrieval problem, since surely information can be available but not accessible?

By way of a preliminary answer, one should not judge a model or a theory in terms of intuition. Although it may well violate notions of common sense, one can argue that common sense is simply the residue of prejudices and misconceptions that have accumulated over centuries of ignorance and have yet to be clarified and corrected by scientific progress. Instead, one should judge a model in terms of its explanatory power and predictive potential. So the reader is urged to keep an open mind about the value of this simple fluctuation model until he sees what it can and cannot explain.

To fit the fluctuation model to data one needs estimates of the numerical values of the three parameters p_0, α, and β. They can be obtained by a simple graphical method (Murdock, 1970) or by more powerful estimation techniques (Murdock, 1972); neither method is very difficult. An illustration of the model is shown in Fig. 4.6, where the staircase shows the predicted values of $P_A(i)$ as a function of i for parameters .9, .39, and .13 for p_0, α, and β, respectively. The data points are represented by vertical bars, which show means and standard deviations across subjects.

The first point to note is that, with these parameter values, the model predicts a steep and very abbreviated recency effect. Only the last two or three pairs would be much above asymptote. One of the very consistent findings from countless probe studies of short-term memory for paired associates using a discrete-trials procedure is that the recency effect only spans the last few serial positions, so in this respect the fluctuation model is clearly in accord with the data. However, one small discrepancy might be noted. Since the forgetting is geometric, the difference in the number of items recalled between $i = 0$ and $i = 1$ should be greater than the difference in number recalled between $i = 1$ and $i = 2$. Generally our data show it to be the other way around, though by a small amount. This discrepancy could be caused by guessing. For the next-to-last serial position in particular, it would not take much to inflate the observed figure on proportion correct.

The second point to note is the asymptote. The curve flattens out so one can say that forgetting stops. Although not shown in Fig. 4.6, if the number of subsequent

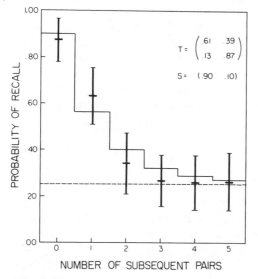

FIG. 4.6. Theory and data for fluctuation model. (Fig. 9 from Murdock, 1972.)

pairs were taken beyond 5, the measured performance should not drop. Actually, the dotted line in the figure is the asymptote; and with parameter values of .39 and .13 for α and β, the forgetting curve asymptotes at a value of .25. Thus, one of every four pairs should be correctly recalled no matter how much interference there was.

Why is forgetting not complete? Simply because the fluctuation process results in a steady state. Transitions in either direction are possible, and eventually a level is reached such that the changes in each direction exactly balance. The probability of a downward change is higher, but the pool is larger. Consequently the number of pairs fluctuating in either direction is the same. As an example, the genetic make-up of a population can change over time and, though offspring may differ from parents, at some point stability is reached as a consequence of balance in dominant and recessive genes.

The third point to note is that no primacy effect is predicted. Unlike single-trial free recall, probe paired-associate studies generally do not find greater recall for pairs at the beginning of the list. Actually, a change from primacy to recency does seem to occur over the very first few trials with a naive subject (Murdock, 1964). Thus, there may then be a primacy effect with concomitant reduced recency. As is generally true of such effects, they are very transitory. However, the fluctuation model as it stands only characterizes the performance of practiced subjects.

One of the assumptions of the model (and other models like it) is that items are independent. Also, probability values are assumed to be constant across pairs and across subjects, and no provision is made for idiosyncratic variation (subject-item interactions). While these assumptions are only approximations, it might be thought that the approximations would be quite poor. As it happens, these assumptions are not as unreasonable as one might think. A statistical test is possible (Grams & van Belle, 1972; Murdock & Ogilvie, 1968) and, for the sets of data analyzed, these assumptions do not seem to be contradicted by the data.

Three more findings which the fluctuation model can explain will be noted next. First, as shown in Fig. 4.7, the recency effect disappears but the asymptote is un-changed if some interpolated activity intervenes between the end of list presentation and presentation of the probe. In this experiment, subjects shadowed numbers for 0, 5, or 10 seconds before the probe was presented. In terms of the model, shadowing would simply increase the value of i for the last pairs in the list and so drive them to the same base level as early pairs. Further, in an unpublished experiment much the same effect was manifest when an unfilled retention interval preceded the probe, though the recency effect was not completely eliminated by 10 seconds of silence.

A second finding relates to the effect of variation in the interval between two test trials. If a pair is tested twice without an intervening presentation then, within limits, the longer this interval the more frequently there should be instances where the first recall is wrong and the second correct. Data reported by Arbuckle (1964) show this to be the case. Actually, it should also be the case that, with a long enough retention interval, performance on the second test should be independent of performance on the first test. Also, repeated tests should eventually yield a correct re-

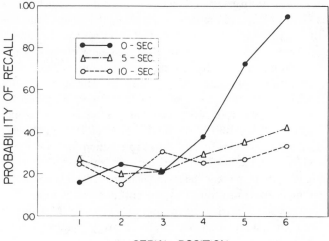

SERIAL POSITION

Fɪɢ. 4.7. Data of probe paired-associate experiment where 0, 5, or 10 seconds of shadowing (repeating) two-digit numbers preceded the probe. (Fig. 4 from Murdock, 1967c.)

sponse, at least with probability p_0. It seems unlikely that either of these effects occur.

The third finding is perhaps the most stringent test yet. To say that the asymptote of the short-term-memory function with a probe test is .25 means that there is 1 chance in 4 that the probed pair will be correctly recalled. If a number of pairs are presented and all are tested then the chance should still be 1 in 4 that any one would be correctly recalled. From this it follows that if the number of presented pairs is systematically varied, then a plot of the number of pairs recalled as a function of number of pairs presented should be a linear function with a slope of 0.25. Supporting data are shown in Fig. 4.8. Two subjects were given lists ranging (in square

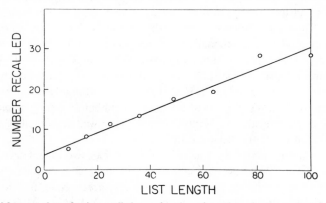

LIST LENGTH

Fɪɢ. 4.8. Mean number of pairs recalled as a function of number of pairs presented (list length). (Fig. 2 from Murdock, 1967b.)

root steps) from 9 to 100 pairs, and they had to learn the complete list. Only first-trial recall is shown here, and the data points show the mean number of pairs recalled. The linear fit is not unreasonable, and the least-squares slope was .267. Thus, perhaps the asymptote is not completely a figment of our imagination.

Parenthetically it might be mentioned that this study was originally designed to test the length-difficulty formulation proposed by Thurstone (1930a, 1930b). Originally it was thought that the number of trials to criterion should vary as a linear function of the square root of list length, and the data clearly supported such a model (see also Carroll and Burke, 1965). However, an error in the derivation has been pointed out by Bogartz (1968), so the linear prediction does not hold. The correct prediction is given as Equation 21 in the Bogartz paper.

Before one can do much more with this fluctuation model it is necessary to specify what variables might affect its parameters, and how they might do so. On the basis of current information, the following suggestions may be made. Modality of presentation affects encoding, presentation time affects recovery, and number of correct recalls affects forgetting.

The forgetting curve shown in Fig. 4.6 has an intercept, a slope, and an asymptote. Its intercept is p_0, its slope is a function of $1 - \alpha - \beta$, and its asymptote is $\beta/(\alpha + \beta)$. To say that the modality of presentation affects encoding means that the rate and terminal level of forgetting should be the same regardless of whether the presentation is visual or auditory. As far as we know, they are. However, the intercept or starting value is higher if presentation is auditory rather than visual (Murdock, 1972). I have no very good idea as to why this occurs, nor would I try to pretend that somehow this identification explains the modality effect in question. All it does is suggest that we try to explain modality effects in terms of encoding processes, not look for differences in rate of forgetting or in long-term memory. It should be noted that a comparable effect for a continuous paired-associate task has been reported by Brelsford and Atkinson (1968).

The effect of presentation rate is depicted in Fig. 4.9, showing the results of an experiment where four different rates were used. Parameter estimation, both for pooled data and individual subjects, suggested that the differences were more in β than in α. This conclusion is not necessarily obvious by inspection, since slope and asymptote in the fluctuation model are not independent. Both are affected by α and β. However, for the group data the estimated values of β were .000, .065, .225, and .259 for presentation times of 1, 2, 3, and 4 seconds per pair. For α, the corresponding estimates were .345, .295, .301, and .271. Roughly, then, presentation time seemed to affect recovery as measured by β but not forgetting as measured by α. The role of prior recalls in forgetting is not yet too well documented (though see Izawa, 1971); it is briefly discussed in Murdock (1972).

Before turning to recognition, let us briefly consider two other aspects of recall performance, namely, latency and confidence judgments. It is quite clear that, in this type of experiment, the curve for latency of correct recall as a function of i follows very closely the accuracy curve (Madigan & McCabe, 1971; Murdock, 1968b; Waugh, 1969). Also, confidence judgments show that here, as in item

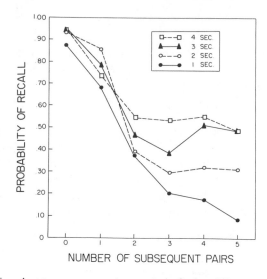

FIG. 4.9. Recall in a short-term memory probe experiment for four different presentation times. (Fig. 10 from Murdock, 1972.)

recognition, *a posteriori* probabilities can be graded (see, for instance, Fig. 4 in Murdock, 1970). If associations are really all or none, as the fluctuation model suggests, how can these gradations occur?

For latencies, one possibility is that reaction time measures how much time the subject chooses to use before emitting a response, not how much time he must use. In other words, it could reflect criterion factors rather than some characteristic of the trace *per se*. Since in addition there is evidence (Murdock, 1966a) that the criterion changes markedly over serial position, the increased latency could reflect a stricter criterion. This line of reasoning, plus some not-too-compelling data, have been presented elsewhere (Murdock, 1968b).

A simple strength-theory view of associations would say that latency and accuracy were, if not interchangeable, at least highly correlated. High probability of response would be associated with short latencies, and vice versa. Evidence that this interpretation is wrong comes from a recent study by Arbak (1972). In a continuous paired-associate task he tested pairs twice and recorded latencies. The question of interest was the relationship between recall accuracy on the second test and recall latency on the first test (conditional upon a correct response). In two experiments, neither case supported a strength-theory interpretation. Strength theory would predict that the faster the latency on the first test, the stronger the response; consequently, the higher its recall probability should be on the second test. In fact, in the first experiment it went the other way (the longer the latency on the first test, the higher the recall probability on the second test). In the second experiment there was essentially no relationship; probability of recall on the second test was not a function of recall latency on the first test. While these data do not compel an interpretation of latency in terms of decision factors, at least they seem to show clearly that a simple strength-theory interpretation is inappropriate.

As for confidence judgments, several processes which could yield graded posterior probability functions in the context of an all-or-none model have already been suggested (Murdock, 1970). To recapitulate, one possibility would be that the confidence judgment reflects the number of attributes which characterize each pair. The association could be all or none but the attributes could be graded in number. Another possibility would be that the confidence judgments reflect the number of copies of the association, in the spirit of Bernbach's replica model (Bernbach, 1969, 1970). Finally, confidence judgments could reflect the number of searches required to find a match. Although these possibilities are all very speculative, the point is that neither the graded latencies nor the graded posterior probability functions necessarily refute an all-or-none model for associations.

Recognition

How can the fluctuation model handle recognition? The rest of this section will be devoted to this question. Three possibilities will be considered. The first is a three-state Markov model which is the short-term memory analog of a popular three-state learning model. The second is an access-time model, in which the time to gain access to a memory trace determines its familiarity and, hence, recognition. The third is a cross-reference model with forward and backward associations, as suggested by Wolford (1971).

Three-state model. A general three-state model for learning has been discussed by a number of authors (e.g., Bower & Theios, 1964; Estes & DaPolito, 1967; Evans & Dallenbach, 1965; Kintsch & Morris, 1965). The general idea is that items start in a null state, then move to an intermediate recognition state where they can be recognized but not recalled, and then proceed to an absorbing learned state where they can be both recalled and recognized. Estes and DaPolito, for instance, use this model to explain why there is little difference between incidental and intentional learning on a recognition test but a considerable difference (favoring the intentional group) on a paired-associate recall test. The general argument is simply that the transition parameter to the intermediate state is the same for incidental and intentional instructions but not to the higher recall state.

Suppose we simply turn this model around and make it suitable for short-term memory. Upon presentation all pairs start in state RR where they can be both recognized and recalled. Then they drop down to state R where they can be recognized but not recalled. They are available but not accessible, if you will. Then there is the lowest state, state N, where they can be neither recalled nor recognized. The transition matrix

$$T = \begin{array}{c} \\ RR_n \\ R_n \\ N_n \end{array} \begin{array}{ccc} RR_{n+1} & R_{n+1} & N_{n+1} \\ \left[\begin{array}{ccc} 1-a & a & 0 \\ c(1-b) & (1-b)(1-c) & b \\ 0 & d & 1-d \end{array} \right] \end{array} \quad (4.10)$$

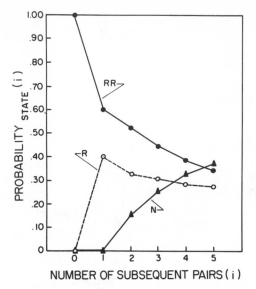

FIG. 4.10. Three-state short-term memory model for parameter values $a = .4$, $b = .4$, $c = .67$, and $d = .2$.

would result in an asymptote both for recall and recognition, since state N is not absorbing and recovery from state R is possible. A graph showing state changes for a particular set of parameter values is presented in Fig. 4.10.

Two implications of the model are that (a) recognition should asymptote later than recall and (b) recognition conditional on recall failure should be nonmonotonic, increasing then decreasing. Note that the only way one can track state R is by a conditional analysis, since simple recognition performance is not sufficient to discriminate between state R and state RR. These deductions from the model are a bit slippery, because they are not parameter independent. That is, the particular functions shown in Fig. 4.10 will vary somewhat with the particular numerical values of the parameters. I have done a small grid search over the parameter space to get some feeling for the range of variation to be expected. Although the above implications are generally true, there are exceptions.

In any case, two experiments will be briefly reported, both of which cast doubt on the model. The first experiment was a recall-recognition comparison with three conditions. In all cases six-pair lists were used, followed by a probe. In one condition, subjects had to recall the B term when probed with A. Under the recognition-same condition one A term was presented and the alternatives were the six B terms from the same list. Thus, it was a 6-alternative forced-choice procedure with one target and five lures. Under the recognition-different condition, four of the five lures were from different lists (the two prior lists). It was a within-subjects between-lists design in which each subject had all three conditions in an unpredictable sequence. The pairs consisted of common English words paired at random, sampled without replacement from a large pool, and the presentation time was 2 seconds per

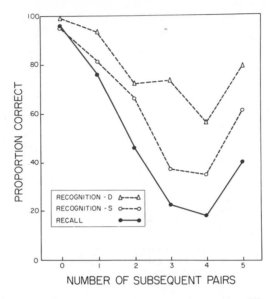

FIG. 4.11. Retention curves for recall, recognition-same, and recognition-different conditions of experiment comparing recall and recognition.

pair. There were 48 subjects, tested individually on 54 lists, so there were 18 trials per subject per condition.

The main results of this experiment are shown in Fig. 4.11 where proportion correct is plotted as a function of number of subsequent pairs. At all but the first point recognition-different is better than recognition-same, which in turn is better than recall. Although the data are a bit noisy, the conclusion that I would draw from them is that recognition and recall asymptote at the same point horizontally (not vertically). That is, all three curves would be characterized by the same rate constant. Thus, contrary to a three-state model, recognition does not asymptote later than recall. (The obvious primacy effect here is exceptional, and it is probably attributable to a minor procedural point.)

The second experiment used a conditional 2-alternative forced-choice recognition test. If the subject failed to recall the correct B term for the probe he was given two alternatives for recognition—one, the correct alternative, and the other (wherever possible), the B term from an adjacent serial position. The lure was never the response given by the subject in recall. In a replication each of the six serial positions was probed once; there were 36 subjects with 7 replications per subject. The main results are shown in Table 4.1. The conditional probability (probability of a correct recognition given incorrect recall) could not be much flatter across serial position.

Thus, not only does recognition seem not to asymptote later than recall, but there is little sign of nonmonotonicity in the conditional recognition function. Another problem is that the grid search already mentioned suggests that it would be hard or impossible to find parameter values that fitted both the recall and the conditional

TABLE 4.1

Number of Incorrect Recalls, Correct Recognitions, and Probability of a Correct
Recognition Given a Recall Failure for Experiment on Conditional Recognition

	Number of Subsequent Pairs					
	0	1	2	3	4	5
Number of Incorrect Recalls	2	63	172	185	203	210
Number of Correct Recognitions	1	40	113	119	127	130
Conditional Probability	—	.63	.66	.64	.63	.62

recognition functions quantitatively. It is not clear how the model could handle
different kinds of lures. Nor is it particularly parsimonious in terms of the number
of free parameters. All in all, the three-state memory model does not look very
promising.

Access-time model. A second possible model for recognition is one based on
the amount of time that it takes to gain access to a memory trace. As Kintsch
(1970b, p. 276) has noted, a long-standing suggestion is that speed of retrieval be
used as the basis for familiarity, hence recognition. Let us formalize this view somewhat, as it leads to an interesting model. Suppose on a recognition test the time to
find the association in memory has a waiting-time distribution. There are two such
distributions, one for old pairs and one for new pairs. (What we are here calling old
and new pairs were previously designated A–B and A–X in Murdock, 1965a.)
Let the old-item distribution be $f_o(t) = \lambda e^{-\lambda t}$ and the new-item distribution be $f_n(t)$
$= e^{-(t - t_d)}$ where λ is the rate constant for $f_o(t)$ and t_d is the displacement of the
origin of $f_n(t)$ along the time dimension. This view is similar to the exponential model
discussed in Green and Swets (1966).

Assume that rapid access leads to positive certainty and slow access leads to negative certainty. Then we can write the expression for hit rate *HR* as

$$HR = \int_0^{t_c} f_o(t)\, dt \tag{4.11}$$

and the expression for the false alarm rate *FA* as

$$FA = \int_{t_d}^{t_c} f_n(t)\, dt \ . \tag{4.12}$$

That is, the hit rate and the false-alarm rate are simply the areas under the curve
to the left of t_c, the criterion cut. These relationships are illustrated in Fig. 4.12.

Given the above, it is an easy matter to obtain an explicit equation for the ROC
curve. All that is necessary is to solve Eq. (4.11) and (4.12) for t_c and equate. The
resulting expression for the ROC curve is

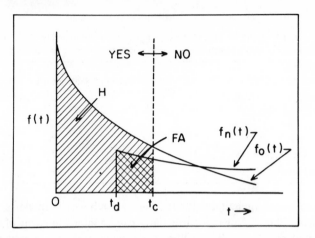

FIG. 4.12. Waiting-time distributions for old and new items. It is assumed that observations to the left of t_c (the criterion) lead to "yes" responses which are hits (H) and false alarms (FA) for the old and new distributions, respectively.

$$\ln (1 - HR) = \lambda \ln (1 - FA) - \lambda t_d. \tag{4.13}$$

Thus, a plot of misses $(1 - HR)$ as a function of correct rejections $(1 - FA)$ on log-log coordinates should be linear with a slope of λ and an intercept of λt_d. Since a straight line fitted to a set of data points has two free parameters (slope and intercept) the values of λ and t_d can easily be obtained.

Also, one can derive an expression for the probability of a correct response on an m-alternative forced-choice recognition test. With the standard assumption that it is the probability that one observation drawn at random from $f_o(t)$ exceeds all $m - 1$ observations drawn at random from $f_n(t)$ then

$$PC(m) = \int_0^{t_d} f_o(k)\, dk + \int_{t_d}^{\infty} f_o(k) \left[\int_k^{\infty} f_n(t)\, dt \right]^{m-1} dk \tag{4.14}$$

where $PC(m)$ is the desired probability. The resulting expression is not very tidy, but at least it exists; it is

$$PC(n) = 1 - e^{-\lambda t_d} + \frac{\lambda e^{-(\lambda + n)t_d}}{\lambda + n} \tag{4.15}$$

where $n = m - 1$, the number of lures in a multiple-choice situation. If $t_d = 0$, then $PC(n) = \lambda/(\lambda + n)$.

I would like to report three tests of this access-time model for paired-associates recognition data. First, ROC curves were examined for each of the 24 subjects in a previous study where a confidence-judgment procedure was used (Murdock, 1965a). The fits varied across subjects from very good to spectacular. Thus encouraged, Elisabeth Wells developed a maximum-likelihood estimation procedure called LOGROC which is comparable to EPCROC, a maximum-likelihood estimation procedure of Ogilvie and Creelman (1968) for the signal-detection model. Maximum-likelihood estimates for each subject were obtained by LOGROC for the access-time model and by EPCROC for the double-normal model. Goodness of fit was evaluated by χ^2, and in 22 of the 23 cases where a solution was possible, the access-time model fitted better than the double-normal model. The total χ^2 values were 169.9 for EPCROC and 87.9 for LOGROC. Since the expected value of χ^2 equals its degrees of freedom, which here were 80, not only does the access-time model fit better than the double-normal model, but also the deviations are well within the chance range.

The second test involves latency measures. Measured reaction time will be the sum of two components—that taken by the memory system and that taken by the decision system. The access-time model specifies what the former should be, as the time taken to find the trace in memory provides the input on which the decision system operates. To make latency predictions, it is necessary to make some assumption about the time taken in decision. To be consistent with what was said about item recognition, assume that the length of time taken by the decision system is inversely proportional to the distance from t_c, the yes-no criterion. This assumption is depicted in Fig. 3.3. Then, without knowing the numerical values of the parameters of the decision component, the only unambiguous prediction that emerges is that the latency of hits should be less than the latency of correct rejections.

We have recently been running a series of computer-controlled experiments on paired associates where both confidence judgments and latencies are obtained. One experiment used a yes-no procedure which otherwise was essentially a replication of a confidence-judgment study reported earlier (Murdock, 1965a). There were eight subjects, each given 80 lists on each of five sessions. There was absolutely no difference, individually or collectively, in the latencies of hits and correct rejections. However, eight more subjects were run under a confidence-judgment procedure where our usual six-point scale running from sure-no to sure-yes was used. When one looks only at the high-confident "yes" and "no" responses, all eight subjects were faster on hits than correct rejections, and the mean difference was 980 msec. It is not at all clear why the latency prediction should be confirmed with a confidence-judgment procedure but not with a yes-no procedure.

The third test used an m-alternative forced-choice procedure. After each list, the probe and either 2, 3, 4, or 6 alternatives were presented. If the probe was an A member from the first four pairs, the alternatives were B members randomly selected from the first four positions as well (except for the 6-alternative case, where all B terms had to be used). If the probe was from one of the last two pairs, one lure was from the last two pairs as well. Since stimulus presentation as well as response recording was under computer control, everything was randomized: what words appeared in what list, what pair was tested (with a 4:1 bias in favor of pairs from the first four serial positions), what the lures were (subject to the above constraint), etc. Of the eight subjects who had been tested in the confidence-judgment experiment, four returned to go through five additional sessions on the m-alternative forced-choice procedure.

First, for each subject separately we used LOGROC to obtain maximum-likelihood estimates of λ and t_d. Then, using Eq. (4.15) we found predicted values of $PC(n)$ for each of the four conditions (2, 3, 4, and 6 alternatives) of the m-alternative forced-choice experiment. When obtained and predicted values were evaluated by χ^2, it was found that two of the four subjects gave results that departed significantly from the predicted values, and the total value of χ^2 (summed over the four subjects) was 41.9. With a total of 16 degrees of freedom that is not very good. On the other hand, the test was rather severe. Since the parameters λ and t_d were obtained from the confidence-judgment experiment, there were no free parameters used in predicting percent correct in the forced-choice experiment itself.

On balance, the evaluation of the access-time model is a bit mixed. It seems like a relatively interesting model; it is simple and easy to work with, and lends itself to the development of explicit expressions. Experimentally, the ROC curves strongly support it, as data from a confidence-judgment procedure are linear on a log-log plot. The latency prediction works very nicely for, but only for, a confidence-judgment procedure; a yes-no procedure obliterated the differences. Finally, prediction from confidence judgments to forced choice, while not impossible, certainly was not very reassuring.

Cross-reference model. The third possible model to account for recognition memory is a cross-reference model based on forward and backward associations. Although a number of people have made suggestions along these lines, the most detailed and explicit are those of Wolford (1971). Following him, assume that there are two associations, one from a to b and one from b to a. These two associations are independent and all-or-none. In a yes-no procedure, if tested with an old (A–B) pair the subject says "yes" if either the association a to b or a from b is intact; otherwise he guesses. If tested with a new (A–D) pair, the subject says "no" if either the association a to b or c from d is intact; otherwise he guesses. Recall occurs if the relevant association is intact, and recognition is better than recall, because either of two possible associations can support it.

A number of aspects of the data already reported are consistent with this model. For a yes-no procedure,

$$PC_o = 2p - p^2 + (1 - 2p + p^2)g = PC_n \qquad (4.16)$$

where PC_o and PC_n are probability correct for old and new pairs, p is the probability that a single association is intact, and g is the guessing probability which, with a yes-no procedure, would be .5. If we assume from typical recall data (e.g., Fig. 4.6) that $p = .25$, then $PC_o = .719 = PC_n$. The obtained value from a representative experiment (Murdock, 1965a) was .740, which is surely close enough. Also, it was approximately the case that $PC_o = PC_n$; the actual values were .755 and .724 respectively (see Murdock, 1965a, Table 1, p. 445).

If we assume that, in a confidence-judgment procedure, subjects assign their confidence judgments on the basis of number of associations then, however they do

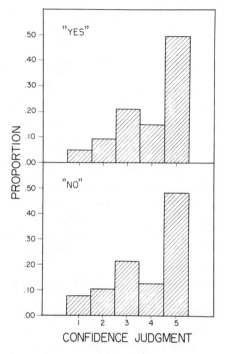

FIG. 4.13. Distribution of confidence judgments for "yes" and "no" responses, pooled over new and old pairs. (Data from Table 1 of Murdock, 1965a.)

it, there should be symmetry of positive and negative certainty. That is, the distribution of confidence judgments for "yes" responses should be the same as the distribution of confidence judgments for "no" responses. The distributions from these same data are shown in Fig. 4.13, and the symmetry certainly seems to hold. (These distributions are pooled over old and new pairs, a partitioning known to the experimenter, but not to the subjects.)

All of the above assume associative symmetry. That is, the model assumes that the probability that a forward association is intact is the same as the probability that a backward association is intact. Such need not be the case, and with different classes of stimulus material probably will not be. However, in the experiments under discussion both the A and B members were unselected common words. Under these conditions, there already is abundant evidence for associative symmetry. In several attempts (e.g., Murdock, 1966b) we have consistently found that forward and backward associations are equally strong.

In his article Wolford presents some very impressive evidence that this model will encompass recall, yes-no, and forced-choice recognition (see particularly his Table 4, p. 311). To develop the forced-choice prediction, assume that the subject will be correct if either the association a to b or a from b is intact. If it is not, he will eliminate all alternatives for which the backward association (from d to c) is intact, then guess randomly from the remainder. Then

$$PC(n) = 2p - p^2 + (1 - p)^2 \sum_{k=0}^{n} \frac{B(k;n,p)}{n + 1 - k} \qquad (4.17)$$

where $B(k;n,p)$ is binomial in k with parameters n and p, PC and n are as defined in Eq. (4.15), and p is as defined in Eq. (4.16).

To test this model with our data, we took those four subjects who had been tested with the m-alternative forced-choice procedure described a few paragraphs back. Using the simplex method of function minimization suggested by Nelder and Mead (1965) we found minimum χ^2 values for each subject, with p the parameter to be estimated. Only one of the four subjects gave a significant χ^2, and the total χ^2 value was 12.64 for 12 degrees of freedom. This result could not be much better.

Some years ago I suggested a very simple cross-out rule for an m-alternative forced-choice procedure, saying simply that subjects eliminated as many incorrect alternatives as possible, then guessed randomly among those left (Murdock, 1963b). When the same estimation procedure is used with this model the fit is much worse. The χ^2 value goes up from 12.64 to 26.03 with the same number of degrees of freedom. Consequently, a cross-out rule that says the subject uses his associative repertoire rationally before resorting to random guessing is, for these data at least, clearly superior to a model that says nothing about the elimination of incorrect alternatives, except that they are binomially distributed.

It would seem, then, that in terms of data currently available that a cross-reference model based on forward and backward associations may be more promising than either a three-state Markov model or an access-time model. The single most important factor in its favor is that it can readily account for recall, yes-no recognition, and forced-choice recognition, all with the same parameter values. The model makes quantitative predictions which are confirmed in very impressive fashion by the data. It is also consistent with the symmetry of positive and negative certainty, a finding that is not immediately obvious in terms of the access-time model.

This model does not have anything to say as yet about latency data, though presumably such development would not be impossible. What does still seem puzzling, however, is the log-log ROC plots. They do provide such convincing support for an access-time model that it is hard to believe that they are fortuitous. On the other hand, one could easily embellish a cross-reference model to handle confidence-judgment data by saying that confidence judgments were directly related to the number of intact associations. Somewhat to my surprise, a cursory simulation of such a model yielded results which, for not unreasonable parameter values, gave reasonably linear ROC plots on log-log coordinates.

All in all, a fluctuation model augmented by the idea of forward and backward associations seems able to account qualitatively, where not quantitatively, for a large number of findings. To enumerate, they are the short-term forgetting function with its recency, asymptote, and no primacy; pairwise independence and binomial variability; the elimination of recency with interpolation; the effect of intertest interval;

the function relating single-trial recall to list length; modality effects; effects of presentation rate; short-term recognition functions; recall-recognition comparisons; conditional recognition data; associative symmetry; symmetry of positive and negative certainty; comparisons among recall, yes-no, and forced-choice recognition; and perhaps even confidence judgments and ROC functions. Pedestrian though it may seem, this model appears to work.

In conclusion, then, are we to infer that interference theory is wrong and that an embellished fluctuation or cross-reference model is correct? No, this position is too extreme. These two theories are really concerned with two different domains. The fluctuation model deals with short-term memory effects: recency and the asymptote, rates of forgetting, confidence and latency, recall and recognition. Interference theory deals with list-learning effects, transfer of training, and proactive and retroactive inhibition. If these two domains are to be considered separate and distinct, then we must have two different theories. If you wish, we must have one for short-term memory and one for long-term memory.

In fact, that seems to be the current state of the field, but hopefully it is only a temporary state of affairs. I think that most researchers and theorists would agree that some unification is desirable. They differ on how to proceed. The interference theorist (e.g., Keppel & Underwood, 1962) would like to be able to say that short-term memory effects are basically no different from long-term memory effects and that the principles of the latter will explain the former. For my part (e.g., Murdock, 1963a) I would prefer to think that the phenomena of long-term memory (list-learning effects, transfer, retroaction and proaction) will be explicable in terms of short-term memory. I would rather start from the bottom and work up than start from the top and work down. In particular, the fluctuation model can be extended to multiple presentations of an item, and work is currently in progress along these lines. However, it is too early to say much about it yet.

It might be noted that the concepts of interference theory and the concepts of the fluctuation or cross-reference model are not all that different. Interference theory has assigned an important role to specific forward and backward associations; for instance, see the McGovern (1964) analysis of transfer and retroaction. Unlearning and spontaneous recovery have their counterpart in the forgetting and the recovery of the fluctuation model. Interference theory has been a strength theory (e.g., Underwood & Keppel, 1962), whereas the fluctuation model assumes that associations are all-or-none. However, the transition probabilities are graded so perhaps the distinction becomes blurred.

In this chapter we have not considered the all-or-none issue *per se*. This issue is whether associations are formed suddenly in one trial, or gradually and it was the focus of considerable interest some years back (e.g., Estes, 1960; Postman, 1963; Rock, 1957; Underwood & Keppel, 1962). However, the *coup de grâce* was given by Restle (1965) who pointed out that any particular all-or-none result could not be decisive for any extant theory. One should not infer that whether associations are all-or-none or graded is unimportant. Rather, it is whether experimental data on this question discriminate between theories, and Restle suggests that they do not.

SUMMARY

Temporal contiguity is the relationship most often investigated in experimental studies of association. The probe technique is useful to track the state of an association over brief periods of time.

Interference theory assumes that associations vary in strength; they become stronger with repetition and weaker with unlearning. A two-factor position explains retroactive inhibition in terms of unlearning and response competition. Proactive inhibition necessitates the concepts of spontaneous recovery and extraexperimental interference. Analyses of transfer and retroaction suggest the existence of specific forward, backward, and context associations, but recent results using recognition-memory procedures are not consistent with the theory. The concepts of nonspecific associations and response-set suppression are becoming more important in explaining the various empirical effects, but different views seem to be developing out of the interference-theory tradition.

The one-element model of Bower assumes that associations are all or none and that repetition does not increase the probability of a transition from an unlearned to a learned state. While the model can predict in great detail a number of the experimental findings from paired-associate learning with binary responses, it does less well when there are more than two responses. Two particular problems are nonstationarity, where the probability of a first correct response increases with repetition, and second-guess performance, which is generally above chance.

Multistate models assume more than two states, and various possibilities have been suggested. In general there is an unlearned state, an intermediate state, and a final learned or absorbing state. The models differ primarily in terms of the possible transitions from one state to another. Perhaps the Greeno three-state model is most consistent with short-term memory concepts; the first stage requires finding or forming a relationship to store the pair, and the second stage requires finding or developing a workable retrieval cue.

A fluctuation or cross-reference model has been developed to explain the short-term memory data directly. There is initial encoding, forgetting, and recovery, but no absorbing state is assumed. The transition probabilities are sensitive to experimental manipulations such as presentation time or number of presentations. No accessibility problems are envisaged for recall; if the probe can be recognized (the Höffding problem) the correct response will occur if the association is available. Several models for recognition are possible; the best seems to be one based on separate and independent forward and backward associations. Combined with a reasonable guessing assumption, such a model can relate the data from recall, confidence-judgment, and forced-choice procedures with the same set of parameter values.

5
DATA ON ASSOCIATIONS

In this chapter we shall present some of the important experimental data on memory for associations. The particular topics to be considered are the nature of the forgetting functions, confidence judgments, repetition effects, test-trial effects, associative symmetry, mediation and imagery, and optimization of the learning process.

FORGETTING FUNCTIONS

As noted in the previous chapter, the forgetting curves for single paired-associates show a brief but precipitous recency effect, then a stable asymptote or steady state. In general there is no primacy effect. Typical examples of such curves are shown in Figs. 4.6 and 4.9. For other examples see, for instance, McConkie (1969) or Madigan and McCabe (1971).

A primacy effect does show up with serial ordering. That is, if the first member of each pair is its ordinal position (e.g., 1—GALLANT, 2—LEGEND, 3—INSPIRE, . . .) then the first pair or two will be better remembered than the middle pairs (Tulving & Arbuckle, 1963). However, the difference between the serial result (primacy) and the paired-associate result (no primacy) is not necessarily a result of the presentation format *per se*. Palmer and Ornstein (1971) found that the appropriate result would occur depending on whether the subjects rehearsed a serially-presented list in serial or associative fashion. (The associative rehearsal was in overlapping pairs (A, aB, bC, cD, . . .) which is not the standard pair-by-pair arrangement. The effect of this variation is not known.)

For concrete nouns the probe paired-associate forgetting curve seems to be much the same regardless of whether the subjects are given imagery instructions or repetition instructions (Smith, Barresi, & Gross, 1971). They found that the asymptote was appreciably higher under imagery than under repetition conditions. They also found that the recency effect went the other way, but there was a concomitant spoken-written variation as well. This latter variation could operate like a modality effect. The function that results when latency of response rather than probability of response is plotted as a function of serial position (or input interference) seems to mirror perfectly the accuracy curve (Madigan & McCabe, 1971; Murdock, 1968b; Waugh, 1969). Of course, latency goes up as response probability goes down, but both the extent of the recency effect and the existence of the asymptote seem much the same.

In single-trial situations, similarity manipulations seem to have little effect. Baddeley and Dale (1966) varied the semantic similarity between the A member of two adjacent pairs in lists with either 2, 3, 4, or 6 pairs. They suggested that it could be considered a miniature retroactive-inhibition paradigm if the first of the yoked pairs was tested, but a miniature proactive-inhibition paradigm if the second of the yoked pairs was tested. In neither case did semantic similarity have a significant effect. Bruce and Murdock (1968) did much the same with acoustic similarity, and while there was no decrement in the retroactive case there was some effect, though not too large, in the proactive case. That is, memory for a probed pair was worse if its predecessor had an acoustically similar first term (e.g., PHRASE and PRAISE, LAMP and RAMP, MEND and BEND, or TRESS and DRESS) than if they were unrelated. Baddeley and Levy (1971) obtained a big effect when they covaried pairwise semantic compatability and similarity, but the compatability variation seemed to account for more of the effect than the similarity variation. In the multitrial situation, similarity may affect stimulus recognition more than associative retrieval (Nelson & Borden, 1973).

Varying the presentation rate or increasing the number of presentations before the test affects primarily the asymptote but not the recency effect (Murdock, 1963a). As would be expected from knowledge of list-learning effects, the more presentations or the slower the presentation rate, the higher the asymptote. Apparently one can trade off the two such that, if the total presentation time is constant, performance is essentially invariant as a limited-capacity hypothesis would predict (Murdock, 1965b). By contrast, modality of presentation affects recency but not the asymptote (Murdock, 1966d, 1967e). The last pair or two in a list is better remembered if the presentation is auditory than if it is visual, but any difference is limited to these last two pairs (Murdock, 1972).

All of the above effects apply to an immediate recall test. Apparently quite different results obtain if a so-called final recall test is given. This innovation was first reported by Craik (1970) in a free-recall situation. There, ten lists were given one at a time with immediate recall for each. At the end, subjects were asked for final free recall, that is, to recall as many words as they could remember from all ten lists. A comparable procedure has been used by Madigan and McCabe (1971) and McCabe and Madigan (1971) with a short-term paired-associate probe technique.

In these latter studies, after each list of 5 A–B pairs had been presented, A was given as the probe for B. Then, after 40–50 lists had been presented and probed, a final recall test was given; selected pairs from these lists were probed (again, A as the probe for B) without any additional study trials. The results from their first study are shown here as Fig. 5.1. The immediate test (T1) gives a typical forgetting function, but the delayed test (T2) is quite different. Not only is there no positive recency effect, there is actually a negative recency effect. The last few pairs in the list were less well remembered on the final recall test than the early pairs. This negative recency effect applied both to pairs that were and were not tested on immediate recall (Madigan & McCabe, 1971). The negative recency effect also holds when the components of the pairs are tested separately on a final item-recognition test for the A and B members (McCabe & Madigan, 1971).

One explanation for the negative recency effect is in terms of two-store models of memory. These models and more data on negative recency will be discussed in the chapters on free recall. However, it might be noted that the Madigan and McCabe results do not necessarily localize the effect as one of associations *per se*. As noted, they find a comparable negative recency effect for item recognition as well. By now there is some evidence that associations are unavailable or inaccessible if the A member of the pair is not recognized (Asch, 1969; Bernbach, 1967b; Martin, 1967a, 1967b). Consequently, the negative recency in final recall with paired associates could be a stimulus recognition loss rather than an associative deficit *per se*.

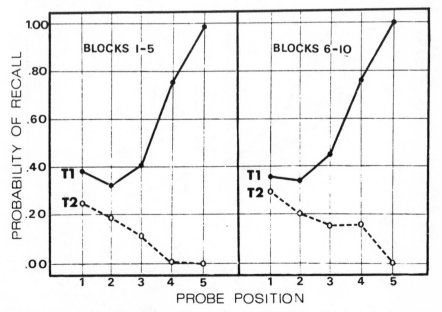

FIG. 5.1. Immediate (T1) and final (T2) test of selected paired associates in a negative recency study. (Fig. 1 from Madigan & McCabe, 1971.)

Continuous paired-associate tasks have been used by a variety of investigators. In the keeping-track studies (Yntema & Mueser, 1960; Yntema, 1963) the subject must remember the most recent state of each variable (e.g., FOOD could be melon, toast, jello, or peas; WEATHER could be stormy, cloudy, fair, or unsettled). The states kept changing; presentation of new information and tests of old information were interspersed unpredictably. Accuracy decreased sharply with lag (number of questions and messages intervening between presentation and test) though the recency effect was more extensive than, say, the data shown in Fig. 5.1. Compared to a completely scrambled condition, performance was better when the possible states of different variables were segregated (Yntema & Schulman, 1967). The authors attribute this result to the discriminant rule of Stowe, Harris, and Hampton (1963).

In a continuous memory task, the greater the average storage load the poorer the retention (Lloyd, Reid, & Feallock, 1960). The authors varied the number of items per category the subject had to remember, and subsequently the load reduction as well (Reid, Lloyd, Brackett, & Hawkins, 1961). In a more analytic experiment Elmes (1969a) showed that storage load had a large effect on retention even when retroactive and proactive interference effects were held constant. In general these studies have not traced out forgetting functions but have been content to demonstrate the importance of the variables under investigation. One reassuring point is

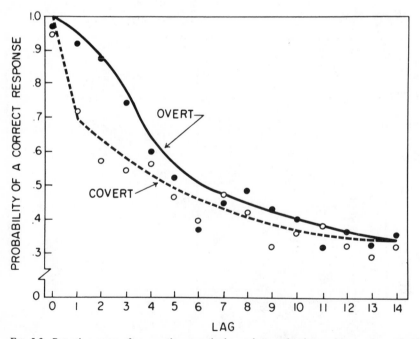

FIG. 5.2. Retention curves for a continuous paired-associates task where subjects rehearsed either overtly (filled circles) or covertly (open circles). (Fig. 18 from Atkinson & Shiffrin, 1968.)

that discrete tasks and continuous tasks seem to yield very similar proactive-inhibition effects with paired associates (Elmes, 1969b).

Atkinson and his colleagues have made extensive use of a continuous paired-associate procedure using a computer-based laboratory with the attendant advantages of randomization and response recording. In their typical procedure (e.g., Atkinson & Shiffrin, 1968), a pair was presented once, later tested, then immediately re-paired. A limited set of A members was used for a given subject on a given session; they were two-digit numbers chosen from the set 00–99. The B terms were letters of the alphabet, randomly chosen hence randomly paired. A trial was defined as the test of an old pair followed by the re-pairing of that number with a new letter. The lag was the number of trials intervening between the study and the test of a pair. A sample retention function (see Fig. 5.2) shows the difference between an overt and a covert rehearsal procedure.

The difference between overt and covert rehearsal is whether the subject says the pair aloud or studies it silently, and when visual presentation is used the difference is analogous to that between auditory and visual presentation. On the one hand, there is a greater recency effect for the overt procedure, as we should expect from discrete trials procedures. On the other hand, the retention functions do not look much like those, say, of Fig. 5.1 (or Figs. 1.2, 4.6, or 4.9 either, for that matter). The recency effect is much more extensive, and in general the type of retention functions obtained with a continuous task seems quite different. One possible reason for the difference is that essentially the Atkinson procedure uses an A–B, A–D paradigm which, with different lags, makes the contribution of proactive-inhibition effects much more pronounced than it generally is with paired associates. However, this explanation is speculative since there seem to have been no experimental attempts to unravel the differences between a discrete and a continuous task procedure.

As will be discussed in Chapter 7, one of the striking characteristics of forgetting in a Brown-Peterson distractor technique is the marked build-up of proactive inhibition over the first few trials. What seems to happen with paired associates is that retention of the first pair in a short list deteriorates over trials, while retention of the end pairs (particularly the next-to-last pair) improves. Overall the change from primacy to recency seems to balance out quite nicely, so there is no proactive inhibition in the sense of decreased overall performance (Murdock, 1963d, 1964). These studies used different words in each list, but a comparable absence of proactive inhibition with an A–B$_r$ paradigm has been reported by Campos and Siojo (1969). They used six A terms and six B terms which were simply re-paired on each trial. Despite the fact that this is a well-known negative-transfer paradigm, there was little deterioration over the course of six trials.

CONFIDENCE JUDGMENTS

Confidence judgments can supplement accuracy data either with a recognition or with a recall procedure. With the resulting data one can construct either posterior probability functions or ROC curves. These curves may be considered Type I or stimulus conditional, if based on recognition, but Type II or response conditional if based on recall (Lockhart & Murdock, 1970). Type I is stimulus conditional because the *a priori* probability is determined by the relative frequencies with which the experimenter presents old and new items on the test trials. Type II is response conditional because the *a priori* probability is determined by the relative frequency with which the recall is correct. Thus, in Type II the subject first gives a forced response (recall attempt), then evaluates this response by giving a confidence judgment to indicate how sure he is that this response is correct.

Examples of posterior probability functions are shown in Figs. 5.3 and 5.4 for recognition and recall, respectively. The recognition experiment used a ten-point confidence judgment scale going from "sure no" ($- - - - -$) to "sure yes" ($+ + + + +$), and the data are pooled over all 24 subjects and serial positions 1–4. The recall experiment used a six-point confidence-judgment scale going from $- - -$ to $+ + +$, and the lists were only five pairs long. A comparison of these two curves suggests that a response-conditional procedure leads to finer discrimination than a stimulus-conditional procedure, but there are also other differences between these two experiments.

Perhaps it should be specifically mentioned that by recognition we mean here recognition of associative information. It is different from recognition of item information. In item recognition, one presents a single item and asks the subject to report whether it is old or new. In associative recognition one presents the two words of a pair and asks the subject to report whether the *pairing* is old or new. These are quite different, both experimentally and theoretically.

In a very general sense, such posterior probability functions derived from confidence judgments provide eloquent evidence for the discriminability of memory

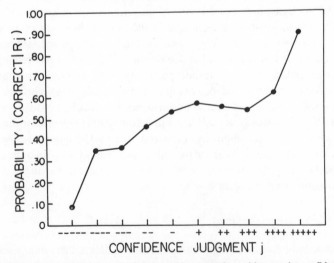

FIG. 5.3. Posterior probability function for recognition procedure with ten-point confidence-judgment scale. (Data from Table 1 of Murdock, 1965a.)

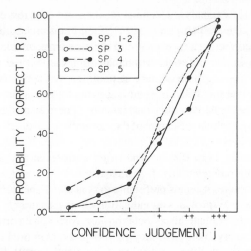

FIG. 5.4. Posterior probability function for recall procedure with six-point confidence judgment scale. (Fig. 2 from Murdock, 1966a.)

traces. In those cases where the subject says that he is sure, then he is correct most of the time. (Correct in his evaluation, that is.) To say much more requires some sort of a theoretical commitment. What such data mean, in any deeper sense, depends upon one's theoretical orientation. This view would apply not only to Type II procedures, but to Type I as well (Lockhart & Murdock, 1970). In terms of the views expressed in the last chapter, one possibility would be to assume that confidence judgments are based on the number of intact associations at the time of the test. However, specification of the guessing rule is necessary if one is to attempt any type of quantitative assessment.

Use of confidence judgments leads to a consideration of the separation of memory and decision processes in general, and criterion factors in particular. In a Type I procedure, one can assume that the subject simply sets several cuts in the decision axis (whatever it is) and then bases his confidence judgment on where a particular observation falls relative to these cuts. In a Type II procedure, two criteria are involved, and they should be distinguished. One criterion presumably affects response evocation, and it will determine whether a subject responds to the probe or says instead, "I don't know." If he responds, then he still must give a confidence judgment, and a second criterion is involved here. There is a function mapping some characteristic of the response into a confidence judgment, and the nature of this function is affected by this second type of criterion. Presumably different experimental manipulations could separate these two types of criterion.

Several studies have reported that Type II d' stays constant over serial position in a single-trial situation or over repetition in a multitrial situation (Bernbach, 1967a, 1971b; Donaldson & Glathe, 1970; Murdock, 1966a). While probability correct certainly increases over trials, the d' measure itself does not, and this finding has significance for the finite-state decision model of Bernbach (1967a). However,

Hintzman (1972b) has reanalyzed some of the data on which this conclusion is based and showed that there are item differences. When items are segregated on the basis of the number of correct recalls, each group of items when analyzed separately does show an increase in d' over trials. Hintzman suggests that the previous invariant relationship may have been an artifact of pooling over items. In reply, Bernbach (1972) points out that the differences among items in their location on the decision axis seems to be systematic rather than random. There seems to be a rather basic point of disagreement about the nature of the variation in the distribution of new items on the decision scale.

The possibility that Type II d' may not vary with serial position or repetition at least suggests caution in regarding d' as a measure of memory trace "strength." As I have suggested before, it seems preferable to consider Type II d' a measure of discriminability. That is, it provides an indication of how accurately (or with what precision) a subject can evaluate his associations as correct or incorrect. Just as people can judge, say, sensory quality, so they can judge the memorial evidence on which their responses are based. When probability correct and Type II d' measures go their separate ways, then we have an indication that we are dealing with different processes.

As further evidence, Lockhart (1969c) found that noun cuing of adjective-noun pairs resulted in a higher probability correct but a lower Type II d' than adjective cuing. Murdock (1969) found that, in an auditory-visual study, accuracy of response to a position probe was higher for auditory presentation but the Type II d' was higher for the visual presentation. Perhaps most surprising, Banks (1969) found that, in an A–B, A–D paradigm, recall probability in an MMFR procedure was much lower following 20 interpolated trials than 2 interpolated trials, but Type II d' was essentially the same in the two cases.

There now seems to be a fair amount of evidence to show that criterion shifts can occur in short-term recall (Banks, 1969; Bernbach & Bower, 1970; Murdock, 1966a). As the *a priori* probability (probability of a correct recall) decreases the criterion becomes more strict, as a maximum-likelihood principle says it should. In this situation there are various ways to measure the criterion. One is the classical signal-detection measure, simply the ratio of the two ordinates at the cut-off point. Other possible measures would be a standard score or the proportion of acceptances. Healy and Jones (1973) discuss various measures of a Type II criterion, and their paper points up the importance of a psychological definition that is tied to theoretical constructs.

Use of Type II measures in paired associates is still somewhat contentious, and all the issues certainly have not been resolved (e.g., Banks, 1971; Bernbach, 1971b). Some strength theorists would prefer not to use Type II measures at all, and Bernbach (1971a) reports that several versions of a strength theory cannot predict the Type II invariance which is generally obtained. However, two early papers using confidence judgments and recall (Suboski, Pappas, & Murray, 1966a, 1966b) suggested that useful information could be obtained thereby, and elsewhere I have argued likewise (Murdock, 1970). We are getting to the point where we may be able to achieve a theoretical integration of recall, confidence-judgment procedures, and forced-choice procedures. The next step will be to attempt to interrelate Type I and Type II data, and when we can do that at a quantitative level then perhaps we can begin to feel that we are making real progress.

REPETITION EFFECTS

The traditional methods for studying the effect of repeated presentation on memory for paired associates are the anticipation method and the study-test method of verbal learning. The study-test procedure is an RTRT procedure as reinforcement (study) and test trials alternate. It is well known that retention improves with repetition, even past the point at which the list has been mastered (e.g., Krueger, 1929). An illustration of how performance improves with practice is given in Fig. 5.5, which shows some data of subjects learning a list of 20 pairs in a study-test procedure. The solid curve is the data of real subjects; the dotted line is a Monte Carlo simulation which will be mentioned later in this section. In general, acquisition curves for paired associates are not exponential as they are for multitrial free recall (compare Figs. 5.5 and 8.1).

Latency data are not as readily available or quite so consistent as accuracy data. Millward (1964) reported a study with binary responses (two buttons to depress) in which he aligned all pairs at the trial of the last error. Before the last error, latencies were essentially constant; after the last error, they declined fairly regularly for at least 10 trials (see his Fig. 4, p. 313). Similar results for a GSR measure were found in Experiment I of Kintsch (1965). In a study with three response alternatives Suppes, Groen, and Schlag-Rey (1966) found that, in general, latencies

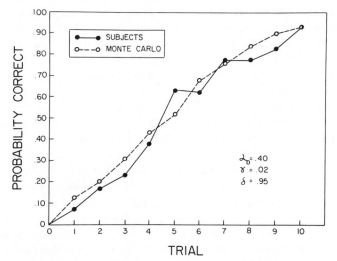

FIG. 5.5 Data from human subjects (solid line) and Monte Carlo simulation (dotted line) for 10 study-test trials on a list of 20 paired associates. (Fig. 12 from Murdock, 1972.)

decreased over trials, but there was an unexpected peak on the trial of the last error. They had intended to fit the latency data by the three-state model of Suppes and Ginsberg (1963) described in the previous chapter, but this last finding was sufficiently disquieting so they did not.

With a very small number of possible responses (e.g., 2 or 3) it is difficult to interpret latency data without a specific model, because of the guessing problem. On the other hand, the specific models do not work so well when applied to latency data, so the situation is not too good. I once collected some latency data to replicate an early study by Postman and Kaplan (1947) and used, as did they, common words to eliminate the guessing problem. Postman and Kaplan found a monotonic decrease in latencies over the first five trials. I aligned pairs on the basis of the ith correct recall for $i = 1,2,3,4,$ and 5 and also found a monotonic decrease, very much like that reported by Millward. Using common words again, Waugh (1969) found that repeated retrievals became faster and faster, apparently approaching as a limit simply the time to copy an item. So perhaps there is a communality across small and large response ensembles after all.

To return to accuracy measures, we may need more analytic procedures and models if we are to further our understanding of repetition effects on memory. One alternative to an RTRT procedure is an RTT procedure where one administers several test trials for each study or reinforcement trial. This procedure was suggested by Estes (1960) for studying one-trial learning, and it has been useful in separating study and test-trial effects. In particular, it now seems very clear that successive tests are not independent. If the subject is correct on T_1 (the first test) he is much more likely to be correct on T_2 (the second test) than if his first response was wrong. This typical finding would seem to lend credence to the suggestion by Eimas and Zeaman (1963) of subjective reinforcement. Somehow the subject knows when he is correct, and there is an attendant decrease in latency on the next test trial. Such a view of course is consistent with *a posteriori* probability data from confidence-judgment studies. Test trials also have a substantial reinforcement effect on long-term (i.e., 24-hour) retention (Allen, Mahler, & Estes, 1969).

The complement to an RTT paradigm is an RRT paradigm where one presents the pair for some designated number of study trials before the first test. The data are quite consistent with the simplest possible independence model; if p is the probability of a correct recall after a single presentation, then the predicted probability of a correct recall after n study trials in an RRT paradigm would be $1 - (1 - p)^n$. This is the multiplex model; each presentation lays down a separate and independent trace, and recall succeeds if the subject can retrieve at least one of them. At least as a first approximation, data from RRT studies agree with an independence model (e.g., Estes, 1964; Postman, 1963). In an unpublished study I did some years ago, stimuli consisting of 9 Gibson squiggles (Gibson & Gibson, 1955) paired with single digits were presented for 1, 2, 4, or 8 trials before a test trial. Presentation rate was 6 sec/pair, and the intertrial interval was about 10 sec. Recall probability was .212, .318, .518, and .664, which again is at least reasonably consistent with a multiplex model.

One of the main problems with a simple multiplex model is the Peterson Paradox, or lag effect. As discussed in the previous chapter, the massing of two presentations (in an RRT paradigm) has an adverse effect on subsequent recall. In studies by Greeno (1964) and Calfee (1968), a massed presentation was little better than a single presentation, and this effect was considered sufficiently important so that, in the Greeno model shown in Eq. (4.5), items cannot enter the long-term state from the short-term state. The lag effect is paradoxical in the following sense. The greater the lag between two presentations, the less likely the initial presentation will be remembered when the second presentation occurs. Yet (provided the retention interval following the second presentation is not too short) the longer the initial lag, the better the performance on the eventual test. Consequently, the more that is forgotten (after the first presentation) the more that is remembered (after the second presentation). This is the Peterson Paradox, so named because it was first reported by Peterson and his colleagues (Peterson, Hillner, & Saltzman, 1962; Peterson, Wampler, Kirkpatrick, & Saltzman, 1963).

Such a result is clearly not what a multiplex model would predict. If the second presentation simply laid down a second (independent) trace, then the interval between the two presentations should not matter. One might be tempted to think that an encoding principle could extract a multiplex model from this difficulty. It might be argued that formation of the second trace was optional not obligatory; if the subject could remember the first association then a second association would not be laid down. Especially when combined with a fluctuation model such an explanation seems attractive. Because successive study and test trials are not independent, one should probably have separate conditions to test the multiplex explanation: one condition to trace out the retention function for the $R_1 - R_2$ lag, and another to assess T_1 performance as a function of this lag. More detailed analysis of these problems and relevant data can be found in Bjork (1966, 1970a), Potts (1972), and Rumelhart (1967).

We would like to be able to describe and explain the vast amount of data on repetition effects that already can be found in the literature on paired-associate learning. One approach is to try to use such analytic procedures as the RTT and the RRT paradigm to untangle experimentally some of the relevant factors. The other approach is to try theoretically to represent the processes involved in an RTRT procedure. Elsewhere (Murdock, 1972) I have suggested that each presentation of a pair in a study-test procedure increments β, the recovery parameter of the fluctuation model. On the test part, each correct retrieval decreases the forgetting parameter α. The dotted curves in Figs. 4.5 and 5.5 show the result of a Monte Carlo simulation based on these assumptions; it was reasonably in accord with the data. More recently, with the help of Elisabeth Wells we have been able to formulate the model as a nonhomogeneous Markov process and to estimate parameters directly rather than depend upon simulation. Early results look promising, and attempts are in progress to compare this model with others. Clearly our understanding of repetition effects will come slowly, but perhaps a judicious combination of analytic procedures and theoretical formulations is the best way to proceed.

TESTING EFFECTS

Memory is affected not only by what happens on study trials but also by what happens on test trials. It would be nice to think that, during presentation, the experimenter's manipulation has some effect on the memory system which is then measured but not modified on the test; in this way the experimenter could systematically track the effect of his manipulation to find out how the memory trace was changing. Unfortunately it is not quite this simple. As a general scientific principle we know that the act of measurement has an effect on that which is measured, and memory is no exception.

One illustration is the conditional-probability data obtained in an RTT paradigm that was discussed in the previous section. With paired associates, the probability of a correct recall on the second test given that the first test is correct is generally quite high, on the order of .70 or above (e.g., Estes, 1960). Of course, as noted by many (e.g., Jones, 1962) the conditional-probability data may reflect artifacts of item and subject selection as much as all-or-none learning. That is, partitioning data on the basis of T_1 may simply serve to place more easy items or good subjects in one subset and more hard items or poor subjects in the other subset. To demonstrate unequivocally that the conditional-probability results show test trial inter-dependence, it would probably be necessary to run a control condition with comparable subjects (and comparable items) who were given T_2 without having had T_1. Then the question would be whether or not the RT data could be generated by pooling the two conditional probabilities from the RTT group.

Perhaps the most direct evidence for testing effects comes from the test-trial potentiation effect (Izawa, 1967, 1969, 1971). In a multitrial RTTT paradigm where the number of test trials is systematically varied, the additional test trials seem to have the effect of reducing the amount of forgetting which would otherwise follow the next study trial. The extent of this effect is impressive; in one study Izawa (1970) reports that the benefits increase to a maximum at seven (i.e., RTTTTTTT). Thereafter they decrease, though slightly. In terms of efficiency, test trials are not as effective as study trials for later performance. Izawa interprets this potentiation effect in terms of the stimulus-sampling model of Estes (1955a, 1955b), suggesting initially that the function of test trials was to decrease sampling variability. To account for the fact that test trials can have both forgetting-prevention effects and potentiation effects in a way stimulus-sampling theory would not predict, Izawa (1971) has suggested that the interchange of unconditioned elements proceeds more rapidly during test trials. Since the interchange is faster, there will be more conditioning on the next study trial; the fluctuation will go to asymptote more rapidly, hence the forgetting-prevention effects.

Despite considerable experimental work, there is still much that we do not know about test-trial potentiation effects. One question is whether there is a differential potentiation for items which are correctly recalled on these test trials. If there is, then another question would be whether it is systematically related to the latency of the correct recall. The effect of time spent retrieving has been largely neglected to date, but some fragmentary data are beginning to accumulate which suggest it may be an important variable. In any event, more will have to be known about potentiation effects before they can be accommodated (or not) in other models.

Not only will recall tests affect subsequent performance on tested items, a test of one item will also affect performance on another item. The general effect is inhibitory, and it goes under the name output interference. In one study, Tulving and Arbuckle (1963) found that if one of the last few items in a list was tested early in output, then performance on that item showed a recency effect. If an early list item was tested at any output position, or if a late input item was deferred in its test position, then performance was at asymptote. Some results from their experiment with random input lists are shown in Fig. 5.6, and this figure illustrates the point. The other condition in their experiment made use of ordered input lists; they were essentially serial lists rather than paired associates and showed somewhat different results.

As Tulving and Arbuckle note, these effects can be attributed to output interference; any recent item can be driven down towards asymptote by testing some other item. Once at asymptote, however, items are no longer susceptible to additional input or output interference. Much the same results were reported by Murdock (1963c)

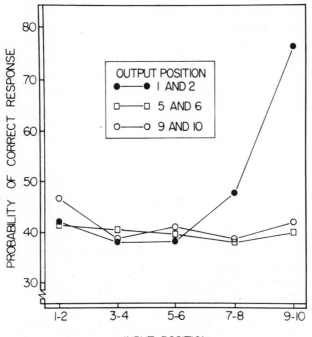

FIG. 5.6. Joint effects of input and output position in a list of ten paired associates. (Fig. 3 from Tulving & Arbuckle, 1963.)

who also systematically varied which input pairs were tested in which output positions. Items still in recent memory were affected by output interference but others were not. In a later study Tulving and Arbuckle (1966) suggest that output interference may actually be greater than input interference. The same conclusion was suggested by Baker and Organist (1964) for a continuous paired-associate task.

One of the popular metaphors in the current memory literature is short-term store. If the metaphor is apposite, then perhaps one should not only be able to enter information into the store but remove it as well. Consequently, testing items should effectively remove them from the store, thereby decreasing the load on memory. The above data show that the system certainly does not work that way, since in general testing one item decreases rather than increases the probability of remembering another. The one exception is very localized; testing the next-to-last item first helps performance on the last pair if the last pair is tested next (Murdock, 1963c). It might be suggested that studies of storage load and, in particular, storage-load reduction show essentially the same thing. However, in these studies it is perhaps more a question of reducing the number of items to be rehearsed so a limited-capacity mechanism has less to do.

Direct experimental manipulation of storage load has been attempted in the cuing-to-forget studies (e.g., Bjork, LaBerge, & LeGrande, 1968; Bjork, 1970b; Elmes, 1969a, 1969b). After a pair (or pairs) has been presented, the subject is given a cue informing him that he can forget the pair(s). It would be more accurate though more cumbersome to describe this cue as informing the subject that he need not remember the pair. He cannot forget the item in the sense of expunging it immediately from memory; it is probably more a matter of selectively rehearsing the noncued pairs and differentially grouping them to keep the cued and noncued pairs separate in memory (Bjork, 1972; Epstein, 1972; Epstein, Massaro, & Wilder, 1972). This topic will be considered further in Chapter 9.

ASSOCIATIVE SYMMETRY

In its strong form, the principle of associative symmetry as enunciated by Asch and Ebenholtz (1962) says that, "When an association is formed between two distinct terms, a and b, it is established simultaneously and with equal strength between b and a [p. 136]." In arguing for this principle, Asch and Ebenholtz were speaking against a long tradition which had held that backward associations were either epiphenomenonal or, at best, weak and of secondary importance. The traditional procedure for studying forward and backward associations had been to follow list learning of A–B pairs with recall tests in which B terms were presented and subjects instructed to respond with the appropriate A terms. The typical finding is that recall of A given B is less frequent than the recall of B given A (Ekstrand, 1966).

To explain this apparent asymmetry, Asch and Ebenholtz (and also Horowitz, Norman, & Day, 1966) suggested that differential accessibility was involved. As a consequence of many test trials the B members of the pair were more retrievable as responses than were the A members of the pair; consequently, it was this differential bias that produced superior performance in the forward direction, not associative factors *per se*. (In their article Asch and Ebenholtz use the term availability not accessibility, but in view of current usage the latter term is more descriptive of what they intended.) To document this point, Asch and Ebenholtz tried to have items equated for accessibility by preceding the paired-associate learning phase with free-recall learning of all the list items. Under these conditions which, they hoped, equated for accessibility, recall of A given B was as good as recall of B given A.

In general what Asch has suggested (Asch, 1962, 1968, 1969; Asch & Ebenholtz, 1962; Asch & Lindner, 1963) is (*a*) that associations are unitary; (*b*) they are all-or-none, rather than graded in strength; (*c*) that accessibility is graded rather than all-or-none; and (*d*) that recall depends upon recognition of the probe and availability of the response, as well as an intact association. Working in the Gestalt tradition, Asch has used different terms to express these ideas, but most of these views are accepted by those who find associationism or information processing more congenial. If the availability-accessibility distinction and the importance of stimulus recognition are acknowledged then the critical issue, as always, concerns the nature of the associative connection.

At this point associative symmetry is more a pretheoretical assumption than an experimental hypothesis to be proved or disproved. One may find it convenient to assume symmetry, and then asymmetrical results (which are not hard to produce) would be attributable to other factors (such as stimulus recognition or accessibility of the response). For instance, Waugh (1970a) found no reduction in latency on the test for backward associations after 15 trials in the forward direction that did decrease latency. She attributed this result to a performance factor and felt that it did not necessarily violate the principle of associative symmetry. Alternatively, one may assume that there are separate forward and backward associations which may be asymmetric.

Also, the whole question of strength *per se* is a theoretical issue as well. As stated in the previous chapter, I would argue that the most fruitful view is to assume (at least for single presentations) that associations are all-or-none, that they may fluctuate over time, and that there are separate forward and backward associations which may (though need not; see Wolford, 1971) have equal probabilities. Such a view seems best able to provide an accurate and economical description of data obtained under various recall and recognition procedures.

In several studies Murdock (1962b, 1965c, 1966b) found that after a single presentation of a list of six pairs, recall of A given B was as good as recall of B given A. Typical results are shown in Fig. 5.7 and, as can be seen, the forward and backward curves are essentially indistinguishable. Such results are obtained when the members of the paired associates are common words, selected and paired at random. Dichotic presentation ensures that the stimuli at least impinge on the organism simultaneously; this method of presentation does not change the finding. With simultaneous presentation, items may still be processed sequentially, and the order of processing may be inferred from the order of verbalization by the subject at the time of presentation. If one assesses directionality by order of verbalization there is still

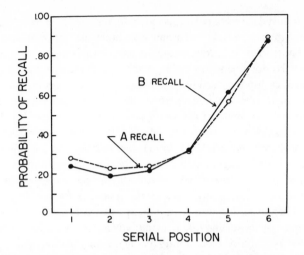

FIG. 5.7. Recall of B given A as the probe compared to the recall of A given B as the probe when the A–B pairs are constructed of common words selected at random. (Fig. 1 from Murdock, 1962b.)

symmetry in the recall performance. With random selection of items, prior language habits will make some pairs more meaningful in one direction than the other. Even when order of processing goes against the predominant order, backward recall (defined in this manner) was still as good as forward recall. Hence, in these cases recall was certainly symmetric, and it is hard to imagine that the underlying associations were not symmetric as well.

Recall asymmetry in short-term memory has been demonstrated for abstract-concrete and adjective-noun pairs (e.g., Kusyszyn & Paivio, 1966; Lockhart, 1969b). That is, recall will not be equally good in both directions if one member of the pair is an abstract noun and the other a concrete noun, or if one member of the pair is an adjective and the other a noun. For the latter, the noun is a more effective probe for the adjective than the adjective is for the noun. This effect occurs with appropriate pairs (e.g., SHORT–GRASS), anomalous pairs (e.g., ANGRY–GRASS), and both presentation orders (e.g., SHORT–GRASS and GRASS–SHORT), as well as when recall is forced so as to avoid one kind of criterion problem (Lockhart, 1969c). However, the adjective-noun effect disappears when the nouns are abstract, suggesting that both sets of effects can be subsumed under the principle that concrete probes are more effective retrieval cues for abstract targets than abstract probes are for concrete targets (Lockhart, 1969b). This conclusion has also been extended to adjective-noun triples (Lockhart & Martin, 1969).

Findings such as these need not disprove the principle of associative symmetry; even though it seems unlikely that a difference in accessibility of the items is involved, one could argue that the results do reflect stimulus recognition rather than associations *per se*. Thus, a concrete probe could be more effective in making contact with its memorial representation than an abstract probe, though the associations either way are equal. An alternative explanation would be to think that the forward and backward associations are characterized by different values of the transition parameters α and β, which values lead to the asymmetry in recall. These alternatives must remain speculative until some direct evidence can be obtained.

Horowitz and Prytulak (1969) have recently reported that, for asymmetric pairs, whichever member is the more effective retrieval cue will also be more likely to be recalled in a free-recall test of the pairs. Thus, for the pair HEAVY–CAKE the noun CAKE is the better retrieval cue, as well as the more likely term to be remembered if only one member of the pair is recalled. They explain this result in terms of redintegrative memory, suggesting that one can think of the pair as a unit. Then, whichever part of the pair is the more effective redintegrative cue is also the more salient. One need not use adjective-noun pairs to demonstrate unitization in paired associates. In an unpublished short-term memory study I probed for recall of a pair by its ordinal position. The lists were 2, 4, or 6 pairs long, the pairs were composed of common words, and the presentation rate was 2 sec/pair. The main results are shown in Table 5.1, which gives the frequency with which A and B terms separately were and were not recalled. Clearly A and B function as a unit; recall of B given A or recall of A given B is nearly .90 in both cases. And in this particular case symmetry certainly occurs.

In summary, whether the principle of associative symmetry is correct is a theoretical issue which is not going to be resolved by experiments. In a way, it is like the all-or-none issue where the data will not be decisive for any theory. What the experimental evidence does show, however, is that performance is about the same, sometimes exactly the same, whether A is the probe for B or B is the probe for A. These data clearly support the assumption of bidirectional associations made by interference theory and the cross-reference model.

MEDIATION AND IMAGERY

Recently there has been a considerable revival of interest in the question of mediation (e.g., Adams, 1967; Bower, 1970a, 1972c; Bugelski, 1970), stemming at least in part from the work of Paivio on imagery (e.g., Paivio, 1969, 1971). In paired associates a mediator converts a pair into a triplet which could perhaps be represented by A–M–B rather than simply A–B. An effective verbal mediator for the

TABLE 5.1

Recall Frequencies for the Components
of an A–B Pair Probed by Ordinal Position (Unpublished Data)

"A" member of pair	"B" member of pair	
	Recalled	Not recalled
Recalled	1817	243
Not recalled	261	1407

paired associate RING–LADDER might be RING–RUNG–LADDER. As has been noted, mediation was given formal theoretical status in the pure stimulus act of Hull (1930) and formed the basis for much work on transfer and mediated generalization in the 1950s. It is reappearing, though in a somewhat different guise, in current work on short-term memory.

An influential though unpublished paper was that of Wallace, Turner, and Perkins (1957) to which attention was drawn by Miller, Galanter, and Pribram (1960). Wallace et al. found that subjects could remember with at least 95% accuracy pairs of words presented only once for a single study trial. What made this result surprising was the fact that as many as 700 pairs were presented. Presentation was self-paced (subjects could have as much time to study each pair as they wished, up to 20 seconds), the pairs (at least those listed in the report) seemed to be composed of concrete nouns (e.g., FLOWERPOT–GRAND CANYON; DANNY KAYE–CATSUP; HAIRCUT–CLEAVER), and the subjects were instructed to form a mental image connecting each pair (e.g., Danny Kaye drenched in catsup). That subjects when probed could recall 496 pairs out of 500, or 664 pairs out of 700, is rather impressive evidence that memory for associations can be quite accurate.

A study by Glanzer (1962) explicitly introduced a possible mediator to make items triplets rather than pairs and found that triplets with mediating prepositions (tah of zum) and conjunctions (woj and kex) were better recalled than triplets with mediating nouns (yig food seb) and verbs (mef think jat). Montague, Adams, and Kiess (1966) studied natural-language mediators; they had subjects study paired associates comprised of CVCs and then asked them to write down the mediators if they had one. On a 24-hour retention test the subject tried to remember both the mediator and the B member of the pair, given A as the cue. Recall was over 70% if the subject recalled the right mediator, but no more than 6% if he gave a different mediator or had not formed one initially. Such results indicate the potency of mediators. In another study, Adams and Montague (1967) found less susceptibility to retroactive inhibition for mediated pairs than for pairs learned by rote. As suggested elsewhere (Adams, 1967, p. 93) mediated pairs may be immune to unlearning or, in terms of the Martin encoding-variability hypothesis, differentially encoded on second-list learning.

A similar absence of interference has been reported by Bugelski (Bugelski, 1968, 1970; Bugelski, Kidd, & Segman, 1968) when subjects learn six successive responses to the pegwords popularized by Miller, Galanter, and Pribram (one is a bun, two is a shoe, three is a tree, etc.). In effect, this experimental procedure can be represented as an A–B, A–C, A–D, . . . , A–G paradigm which, under normal conditions, would produce massive interference. However, if subjects are instructed to use imagery as they go through each list, then performance on final recall is quite high—over 60% for subjects in the imagery-instruction condition, but about 20% for the uninstructed subjects. Data from a similar study by Bower (1972c) is shown in Fig. 5.8. Each subject was given a single 5-second presentation of 20 concrete noun pairs, then tested. After five such cycles subjects were again tested, now on all 100 pairs. On both immediate and final test, subjects instructed to use imagery in associating the pairs far surpassed the control subjects not so instructed.

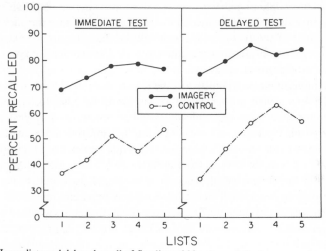

Fig. 5.8. Immediate and delayed recall of five lists of 20 pairs each for imagery and control subjects. (Fig. 3–1 from Bower, 1972c.)

In an analysis of this mnemonic device Bower (1970a) suggested that its important features seemed to be (a) that imaginal associations are formed between the known pegwords and the items to be remembered, and (b) these cues are used at the time of recall. Apparently the images need not be bizarre; he reports that subjects instructed to form familiar and sensible associative scenes remember as well as those instructed to concoct bizarre scenes. The cues must be used both at input and at output; that is, the pegwords must be used in forming the initial images and must be used at the time of recall. This principle seems generally characteristic of retrieval cues (Tulving & Osler, 1968). Bower suggests that there are dual memory systems, a verbal system and an imagery system. These systems may be richly interconnected, but imagery effects are not due solely to verbalization. One line of evidence is the work showing concrete word pairs to be more memorable than abstract word pairs. Another is the work of Brooks (1967, 1968) who has shown selective interference with visual and verbal material, depending upon the method of reporting.

One of the problems holding back work on imagery has been its dubious scientific respectability. In the era when Watsonian behaviorism was predominant in American psychology, it was clearly seen as a mentalistic concept which was beyond the pale. With more interest in internal processes the feeling has changed, and it no longer is in ill repute (e.g., Bower, 1970a; Bugelski, 1970; Hebb, 1968). However, it still would be nice if physiological indices could be obtained, as then one might have a powerful experimental handle on the problem. However, according to Bower (1972c) the prospects are not promising; he mentions discouraging results with eye movement recordings, pupillary dilation, and the electroencephalogram (EEG). In this connection, see also Paivio (1971, pp. 526–529).

A study by Tversky (1969) provides evidence for pictorial encoding. In her experiment there were names and cartoon-like faces, each varying along three binary dimensions. After learning the names for the faces, the subject had to respond "same" or "different" to two successive presentations where the modality (i.e., visual or verbal) of the second stimulus might be the same ($p = .8$) or might be different ($p = .2$) from the first stimulus. By varying the expectation of the modality of the to-be-presented (i.e., second) stimulus, it was hoped to manipulate the type of coding used by the subject, and the results suggested that, in fact, the subject used the appropriate coding (verbal or visual) as the basis for response. Thus, even though we cannot yet obtain physiological correlates of imagery, its existence can be inferred and its properties measured in a simple information-processing task.

Corroborative evidence with a different technique comes from a recent study by Wells (1973). Using the release-from-proactive-inhibition technique of Wickens (1970) to infer the dimension of encoding, she simply used words or pictures directly. The pictures were black and white line drawings, and the words were their names. There was approximately 70% release on the first shift, which is quite large. In a final free recall, subjects were about 95% accurate in denoting mode of initial presentation (given that they recalled the item), again suggesting different memorial representations for words and pictures.

Further analytic separation may be achieved in a paired-associate paradigm by comparing stimulus recall and recognition. Wicker (1970) found that pictures were better than words when used as stimulus terms for recall, but that recall conditional on recognition did not differ. That is, given that subjects recognized the stimulus term, recall accuracy was essentially equal for words and pictures. The implication is that the word-picture effect is in the encoding stage, not the associative stage. By contrast, Bower (1970c) compared interactive imagery (imagine the two members of the pair interacting) with noninteractive imagery. Interactive imagery produced higher recall, but there was no difference in stimulus recognition *per se*, suggesting that the interaction manipulation affected the association component rather than the encoding component.

One of the general points that emerges from this line of research is support for the concept of modality-specific memories. The necessity for memory modalities was clearly stated by Wallach and Averbach (1955), and in that paper a study by Kurtz and Hovland (1953) on the effect of verbalization on accuracy of recall and recognition was interpreted in a way that is very consistent with current thinking. Clearly we must have modality-specific memories in a very general sense, otherwise how would we remember words, sounds, and pictures? And we must have different systems for written and spoken language, otherwise we could not read or understand speech. Surely the existence of such systems can not be disputed; we simply need to understand more about their properties.

At this very general level, there is actually some evidence for localization of function in the nervous system. Separate auditory and visual experiential records are obtained in direct electrical stimulation of the exposed human cortex (e.g., Penfield & Perot, 1963), and the areas where stimulation gives rise to such reports are certainly not inconsistent with the possibility of separate stores (compare Figs. 9 and 10, pp. 669 and 671, in Penfield & Perot, 1963). More recently, evidence for hemispheric specialization has become available (Gazzaniga, 1972; Kimura, 1967; Milner, 1971; Sperry, 1968), with some evidence that the dominant (left) hemisphere processes speech, while the nondominant (right) hemisphere processes pictorial information. In fact, Crowder (1973) has even suggested that laterality effects may underlie short-term memory differences between vowels and stop consonants.

Regardless of what or where the physiological loci are, can we say anything else about differences in the underlying modality mechanisms? A common suggestion (e.g., Bower, 1972c; Murdock, 1969; Paivio & Csapo, 1969) is that the pictorial and verbal (or visual and auditory) systems are specialized for simultaneous (parallel) and successive (serial) processing, respectively. Speaking generally, vision is a spatially-distributed modality and audition a temporally-distributed modality, so the mode of processing in the nervous system may well—indeed, almost must—reflect this basic difference. One implication is that tasks that require retention of item and order information should be differentially affected by mode of presentation. This principle and some supporting data are detailed in Chapter 7 of Paivio (1971); see also Wells (1972).

One of the long-standing beliefs has been the importance of meaningfulness as a factor in paired-associate learning (e.g., Underwood & Schulz, 1960). Paivio (1969) has suggested that it may be more the concrete-abstract dimension than meaningfulness *per se*. He has done a number of experiments where he has pitted meaningfulness against concreteness and, apparently, the latter generally wins out. The comparison is made by taking comparable standard-score ranges from the normative data in Paivio, Yuille, and Madigan (1968). However, in isolating high- and low-imagery words there is always the danger of possible confoundings with other variables (Kintsch, 1972a).

Both the visual (imagery) and the verbal system can play a role in mediation. The former is primarily responsive to variation in concreteness, and the latter is primarily responsive to variation in meaningfulness. Extensive discussion of this and many other issues can be found in Paivio's recent book (1971). In this connection, one interesting point is mentioned by Haber (1969) who reports that children who can form eidetic images tend not to verbalize what they visualize because it interferes with the formation of a mental image.

While images can be vivid and realistic mental events, their role as a possible mode of representation of knowledge is quite another matter. They are probably derivative rather than fundamental, and we need to understand their basis. The fact that they are so readily available to introspection is no guarantee of their importance; in fact, it may suggest that we should be wary of them as an explanatory concept. For a critique of mental imagery and a discussion of several alternative modes of representation, see Pylyshyn (1973).

To conclude this section by returning to the topic of mediation, it seems abundantly clear that mediational aids in general, and verbal and imaginal mediators in particular, can result in dramatic improvements in memory for paired associates. However, work in this area is not an unmixed blessing. To be critical, in a way it may be a step backward rather than a step forward. The basic problem is to understand how people remember associations. To introduce mediators means we now have to explain how people remember mediators. Furthermore, we now have lost some degree of experimental control because these mediators are subject-generated rather than experimenter-controlled. To some extent, we are at the whim of the subject. And we are no longer studying memory and learning; we are studying transfer of training. After all, these mediators are part of the subject's language repertoire, and what we are really studying is how he uses his past knowledge in the experimental setting, rather than how he forms new memories under experimental observation.

Further, the low probability of success may not be generally recognized. Suppose mediation worked as follows: Associations from each member of an A–B pair are tested to see if there are any in common. (This is essentially the hook-up method of Underwood and Schulz, 1960.) Make the conservative estimate that the vocabulary size is 10,000 items and that, in a typical presentation period, 10 associations of each can be examined. Assume that each set of 10 is an independent random sample from the population; then it is not hard to show that the odds against finding a mediator (an association in common) are about 100 to 1. Clearly, success would be far too infrequent to countenance using a strategy of this sort. Mediational processes must have some inner direction; they are more complex than such a simple view would suggest.

There is yet another point. Certainly mediational devices are only a temporary expedient, an *aide memoire*, if you wish. With overlearning they drop out; we surely do not remember the names of people, the letters of the alphabet, the authors of novels, or the cities where our favorite athletic teams are located in that fashion. Even in experimental situations, I have had experienced subjects tell me that at first they try to use some sort (almost any sort) of association or mediating device; with practice, they say, they give it up because it is simpler to learn the pairs directly.

On the other hand, perhaps work on mediation will lead to new insights and understanding that we might not otherwise gain. Perhaps it will turn out to be valuable if only it serves to focus attention on a factor that we had been too prone to neglect. Or perhaps it is just a question of interest. If one takes as one's research problem the question of how associations are learned and forgotten then mediators are no panacea. (They may be more like Pandora's box.) Introducing mediation may have dramatic effects on one's data, but not on the depth of one's understanding. However, if researchers are interested in mediation *per se*, then certainly it is a bona fide problem, and one can only wish them well. But they should be advised that it is a problem with a long history, and judging by our progress to date, further advances will not come easily.

OPTIMIZATION

The last section in this chapter will deal with a rather different problem. It is the question of optimization. How can one structure the learning situation to maximize memory? In other words, what are the optimal conditions for learning to occur. This area of research is different from the usual theoretical investigations that go on in the laboratory in that the motivation behind the research is at least partly practical in nature. Clearly, from an educational point of view this question is important, so work on optimization is relevant to educational practices. However, it is also a test of our theoretical understanding. Clearly, any adequate theory of memory and learning should be able to specify what conditions should maximize memory.

Much of this work has been conducted by Atkinson and his colleagues at Stanford University. The general question they have investigated is as follows: In a paired-associates situation, given a fixed number of study trials how best can the pairs be presented. Clearly various options are available. The least imaginative would be to use a rectangular distribution; simply present each pair an equal number of times, as is the custom in verbal-learning experiments using an RTRT procedure. A second possibility would be self-selection; let the subjects decide themselves which pairs they would like to study, and when. Other presentation schedules depend upon the particular theoretical view under consideration.

One model is the linear model of Bush and Mosteller (1955), which says that the probability of an error on an item is reduced by some constant amount, after each presentation of that item. An interference-theory view would probably be similar. Thus, if the probability of an error on Trial 3 is .40 and the reduction had been 10%, then on Trial 4 the probability of an error is .36. When the error probability decreases to .10, the next presentation would reduce it to .09. It can be inferred from this example that the optimum strategy would be to present next that item that would show the biggest gain. That item would be the one with the largest error probability, which in turn would be the one least often presented. In sum, according to a linear model the standard RTRT presentation method should optimize performance, because one is always presenting items which should gain most.

A second model is the one-element model of Bower (1961, 1962). As described in the previous chapter, it says that items are either in the learned state or at a guessing level. One cannot observe directly when an item changes from the unlearned to the learned state, but the more correct recalls that occur after the last error on an item, the less likely that the item is still in the guessing state. Consequently, an optimum strategy here would be to keep track of each item, record the number of consecutive correct recalls, and present next that item for which this number is smallest. In the event that several items have the same low score (which will certainly happen), choose one at random.

A third model is the random-trial increments model of M. F. Norman (1964). It says that with probability c, a presentation reduces the error probability by a certain fraction, and with probability $1 - c$ there is no change in the error probability. Actually, both previous models are then special cases of this random-trial increments model; if $c = 1$ then you have the linear model, but if the error probability is reduced to zero, then one has the one-element model of Bower. However, we shall consider here the more general case where presentations decrease error probability on some proportion of the presentations.

The optimization schedule for the random-trial increments model is more complicated than the schedule for the other two models. It is necessary to have parameter values to characterize the learning ability of each subject and the difficulty of each of the pairs to be learned. At the beginning one has neither, but if one runs subjects in squads, then information will build up on item difficulty, and as a given subject is tested on more sessions, his learning rate will become known as well. This sort of an experiment is best run under computer control, which can do the bookkeeping required. That is, the computer stores and updates information on both item and subject parameters, and it selects the appropriate item to show the subject on each study trial according to these particular parameter values.

Experimental tests of these three models are reported in Atkinson and Paulson (1972), and the interested reader should look there for further references. In one test, subjects learned 300 Swahili vocabulary items in a mixed-list (within-subjects) design. Each day the subject studied 100 pairs, 50 according to an all-or-none (one-element) schedule and 50 according to the random-trial increments schedule. After 20 such training sessions there were two follow-up tests, one several days after the last session and the second approximately two weeks after the last session. The results seemed quite clear. On both the two-day and the two-week test, about 33% fewer all-or-none pairs were recalled than random-trial increments pairs.

These results suggest, then, that not only can optimization techniques be effective, but also that they can make a rather sizeable difference in learning time. As any language learner knows, learning a second language is a very time-consuming process, and reducing the time spent learning by a factor of one-third is really very impressive. Also, in several later studies Atkinson (1972a, 1972b) has reported that the random-trial increments schedule is more effective than either a uniform presentation schedule (which was worst) or a self-selection schedule in which subjects selected which pair they wanted to study next.

Although few psychologists have ventured into this area of optimization as yet, it will probably become more popular in the near future. For one thing, there is the obvious relevance of its application to education and educational practices. The techniques exist, and it is only necessary to make use of them. Also, it necessitates interactive presentation; what is shown to the subject next depends upon what the subject has done up to that point. There is a growing use of on-line small computers to conduct experiments in psychological laboratories, and the main rationale for computer-controlled experiments is to function interactively. Optimization then is a natural direction for computer-based research to take. Finally, as stressed by Atkinson, it provides a realistic and demanding test of our models and theories. If we really do claim to understand the formation, retention, and utilization of associations, then surely we should be able to make useful predictions in a naturalistic setting.

SUMMARY

We now know a fair amount about short-term memory for associations. These associations are formed immediately, almost automatically and effortlessly, after only a single presentation. These associations are also transitory, even if supported by imagery. Although most associations are quickly forgotten, some small number remain to support recall at surprisingly long intervals. Confidence judgments and latencies supplement the conventional accuracy measures, but their proper interpretation requires some theoretical assumptions. Repetition benefits retention, but the effect is somewhat dependent on lag. The Peterson Paradox characterizes this relationship, where later remembering is associated with earlier forgetting. Test trials potentiate performance, but output interference functions like input interference to depress performance. In the short-term case, forward and backward associations are equal, or nearly so, which supports the assumption of bidirectional associations. Optimal presentation schedules can facilitate paired-associate learning to an impressive extent.

Interference theory was not designed to interpret such short-term effects. Its basic principles may be applicable, but that is still an article of faith. The one-element model and multistate models are more applicable, but again many of them emphasize more long-term than short-term effects. A fluctuation or cross-reference model seems most suitable, at least for the data reported in this chapter. Whether associations really are all-or-none and fluctuate in the supposed fashion is still debatable, but at least one can interpret the data as if that was so.

Finally, the general implication of all these findings should be reiterated. The traditional view, from the Greeks through the associationists to the classical conditioners, seems to be wrong—or, if not wrong, misplaced in emphasis. It is not the case that associations are built up slowly and gradually with repetition. They are formed quickly and suddenly if not automatically, but are very rapidly forgotten. Long-term retention is then based on those short-term traces that have become resistent to forgetting. Repetition decreases the number of associations that are forgotten but not, perhaps, the rate of forgetting itself. It is in this way that long-term associations develop out of short-term memory.

6
THEORIES OF SERIAL ORDER

The third major topic to be discussed is serial order. The problem of serial order is basically the problem of how the brain encodes, stores, and retrieves strings of items presented in a temporally-ordered format. Or, more briefly, the concern is for one aspect of the problem of the temporal format of storage. How is temporal information represented in memory?

In this chapter we shall discuss five different theoretical approaches. They are retroactive- and proactive-inhibition models, models based on the concept of distinctiveness, the EPAM model, the filter theory of Broadbent, and models based on item and order information. The temporal format of storage is revealed by serial-order effects. So, we shall first try to clarify just what serial-order effects are and what needs to be explained. Also, we shall suggest a few terms which are useful in describing experimental procedures.

The basic paradigm consists of a single presentation and recall of a string of n items. Thus, I could read aloud the digits 634185 and ask you to repeat them to me. Two main characteristics of your performance are of interest here. The first is the memory-span function: how does the percentage of completely correct recalls decrease with list length? The second is the serial-position curve. If I score each digit as correct or incorrect, how does this score vary with the serial or ordinal position? That is, how often do you get the first, second, third, . . . , next-to-last, and last item correct. These are the two behavioral measures (or dependent variables) that we would like to be able to explain.

To illustrate, Fig. 6.1 shows memory-span functions for five different types of material. In each case, percent correct decreases from essentially 100% at the shortest list lengths to 0% at the longest list lengths. The exact values of the curves will vary with the method of scoring, which differs somewhat from experiment to

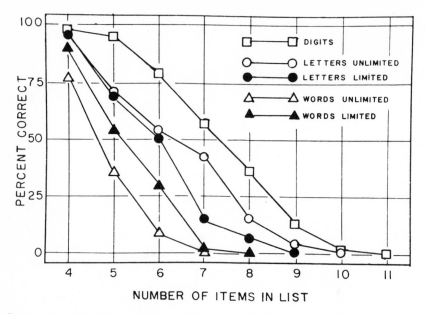

FIG. 6.1. Proportion of lists correctly recalled as a function of list length for different types of stimulus material. (Fig. 1 from Crannell & Parrish, 1957.)

experiment. However, the general relationships shown here are certainly typical. A numerical estimate of the memory span itself would be the length list that is correctly recalled 50% of the time. For these data, the span for digits would be about 7.3 items.

Serial-position curves are shown in Fig. 6.2. Here all subjects heard many 10-item lists, each a different random permutation of the ten decimal digits. Subjects were instructed to write down the digits in order from first to last, and each serial position was scored independently as correct or incorrect. Subjects were divided into quartiles in terms of overall performance. The primacy effect is quite extensive, there is no asymptote, and there is a brief but impressive recency effect. Recall of the last item was nearly always perfect. Note also that all four curves show a minimum at the same point (Serial Position 7). Generally, serial-position curves are asymmetric, with the minimum nearer the end than the beginning; this finding was an embarrassment to one of the early explanatory attempts (Hull, Hovland, Ross, Hall, Perkins, & Fitch, 1940). For other data see Conrad and Hull (1968), Crowder (1972), or Jahnke (1963).

There are three experimental or independent variables that are of major importance. The first is the value of n, that is, the number of items in the list. The second is the length of the retention interval, the amount of time that passes between the end of the list and the start of recall. The third is the number of prior lists, starting at zero for the first list of the experiment. A number of common experimental paradigms then fall out as special cases of this classification.

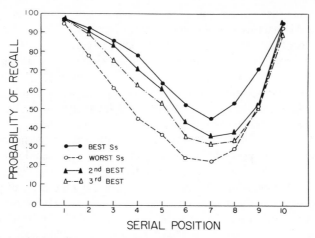

FIG. 6.2. Serial-position curves for serial recall of lists of ten digits, by subject quartiles. (Fig. 12 from Murdock, 1968c.)

Studies of memory span systematically vary n, use immediate retention tests (thus setting the length of the retention interval as defined above to zero), and employ many lists, so that steady-state conditions obtain for the number of prior lists. Studies employing the distractor technique of Peterson and Peterson (1959) use a constant value of n (typically three), systematically varying the length of the retention interval. They may or may not partial out the effect of number of prior lists. Studies of the build-up and release from proactive inhibition (Keppel & Underwood, 1962; Wickens, 1970) generally peg the values of the first two variables at some level and then systematically determine the effect of the third.

Instead of requiring recall of the entire list, one can ask for partial recall. There is the sequential probe technique popularized by Waugh and Norman (1965) where the probe is item i and the target is item $i + 1$. One can also use positional and reverse probes (e.g., Murdock, 1968c). In the former, the probe is i and the target is the item presented at position i; in the latter, the probe is the item presented at position i and the target is the value of i. Studies of the Hebb repetition effect (Hebb, 1961) are ostensibly memory-span studies but, every so often, the experimenter repeats an earlier list without informing the subject. Finally, studies of serial learning simply use an RTRT procedure to present the same n-item string repeatedly for immediate recall.

To comprehend what theories of serial order are trying to explain, it is useful to try to imagine this three-way classification (n, retention interval, and number of prior lists) with two somewhat different dependent variables. These two dependent variables are number correct per list and number correct per serial position. For the latter, one can use partial report (probe) or full report. Although it would be nice to have a theory to encompass the entire range, at this point we should be thankful if we could even understand in any depth any one of the special cases. In general most of the models to be discussed only attempt to cope with the special cases.

The preceding remarks are not meant to imply that this is all there is to serial-order effects. Many other independent variables could be (and have been) studied. However, I would suggest that they are of secondary importance; until we understand the primary variables, understanding of secondary variables will perforce be rather limited.

Since a variety of experimental procedures have been used, it is useful to provide labels for them here. I shall use the term "serial recall" to denote the case where the subject must reproduce the items in the order presented. The term "free recall" denotes the case where the subject need not reproduce the items in any particular sequence and is not responsible for showing the order of presentation in his report. Finally, the intermediate case will be called "constrained recall." Here the subject can write down the items in any order that he wishes, but the order of presentation must be represented in the final result. Thus, there might be 10 boxes for a 10-item list. The order in which the subject wrote down the numbers in the boxes is at his discretion but, whatever the order of report, the first box should contain the first item in the list, the second box the second item in the list, etc.

RETROACTIVE- AND PROACTIVE-INHIBITION MODELS

Models based on retroactive and proactive inhibition attempt to explain serial-order effects in terms of the joint effects of two independent variables. These variables are the number of prior items and the number of subsequent items. Any particular item in a list is preceded by some items and followed by others. The former produce proactive inhibition; the latter produce retroactive inhibition. To illustrate, Fig. 6.3 shows probability of recall as a function of the number of subsequent items, with the number of prior items as the parameter. With no prior items, forgetting is quite gradual; with four prior items, it is quite precipitous; and the other two cases fall in between. These data were obtained with a probe technique in a study in which the number of prior and subsequent items were orthogonal. Statistically speaking, both main effects and their interaction were highly significant. Thus, not only do number of prior and subsequent items affect recall, but also the effects of one depend upon the level of the other.

Foucault Model

The classical version of a retroactive-proactive inhibition model was presented by Foucault (1928). In an early study of serial-position effects, he presented lists of varying length for immediate recall. He took as his measure of retroactive inhibition the decline in recall of the first item in the list as list length increased. As one might expect, recall of the first item decreased, so retroactive inhibition increased as list length increased. His measure of proactive inhibition was the decline in the recall of the last item in the list as list length increased. Again as one might expect, recall of the last item decreased as proactive inhibition increased with list length.

In a list of length n, each item is preceded by anywhere from 0 to $n - 1$ items and followed by anywhere from $n - 1$ to 0 items. Thus, given known proactive-

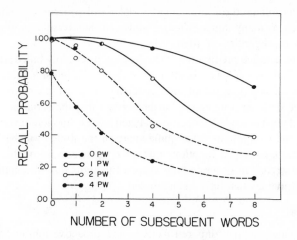

FIG. 6.3. Effect of number of subsequent words on probability of recall of a target item in a probe-recall experiment. The parameter is the number of prior words (PW). (Fig. 1 from Murdock, 1968c.)

and retroactive-inhibition functions for single items, it should be possible to predict recall level for any given item. Unfortunately, the predictions did not work out too well. Trying a simple additive model, Foucault suggested that perhaps the combined inhibition operating on any particular item was simply the sum of the proactive and retroactive components. The middle item, say, in a 7-item list is preceded by three items and followed by three other items. Since the first item in a 4-item list is forgotten 12% of the time and the last item is forgotten 9% of the time, then the predicted forgetting of the middle item of a 7-item list is 21%. Since the data showed it to be 81%, something seemed slightly amiss. Other predictions did not fare much better.

This theory, then, attempted to attribute interference effects to additive components based on temporal location. An alternative to this simple model that Foucault suggested was the possibility of an interaction. The further into the list a to-be-remembered item was, the more prior items there must have been, and perhaps there was a degraded registration. Then, the poorer the initial registration, the more serious effects of retroactive inhibition would be. Another possibility was that the initial and terminal items were unusually salient, by virtue of their first and last position. The implication then is that measures of retroactive and proactive inhibition based on their recall would be inappropriate when applied to other list items.

Even though the simple additive model could not make accurate predictions about specific serial positions, it was not too inaccurate when applied to the recall of the list as a whole. In another experiment with lists ranging from 5–13 items, the sum of the retroactive and proactive inhibition, as indexed by adding the number of forgotten first and last items from each list, produced a function for total inhibition (last column of Foucault's Table 7, p. 109). This function was not too discrepant from the overall percentages of forgotten items as a result of increasing list lengths summed over serial positions (last column, Foucault's Table 8, p. 110). It might be noted that Foucault used an augmented serial-recall procedure. Subjects were to recall, in order, as many items as they could, and then recall any other items they could remember, regardless of their order.

Although the detailed predictions of this approach certainly failed, this two-factor model of Foucault was at least a beginning. As he said (almost in these words) there is some value in applying established concepts of long-term memory to explain phenomena of short-term memory. Further, given that the serial-position curve is bow-shaped, it must be capable of being analyzed into two monotonic functions which combine to give a minimum value somewhere in the middle of the list. One can easily generate bow-shaped functions that have the necessary qualitative features. It is not quite so easy to generate bow-shaped functions that fit quantitatively over the range of variables that have been studied.

Melton Model

A related view emphasizing retroactive- and proactive-inhibition effects was suggested by Melton (1963). In a very influential review paper, he first identified a number of basic issues in the study of memory. They were the questions of autonomous decay of the memory trace over time, autonomous enhancement (fixation or consolidation) of the memory trace over time, the morphological characteristics of the memory trace (i.e., its form or structure), and the duplexity issue of storage (i.e., the question of one continuous system or two dichotomous systems, one for short-term memory and the other for long-term memory). Then, favoring a continuous view, he suggested several lines of evidence in support of this position. One was the continuity of repetition over the short- and long-term case; another was the continuity of interference effects over subspan and supraspan strings. It is here that the concept of intraunit interference becomes relevant.

Basically, Melton proposed that the same types of interference that occurred in long-term memory (i.e., proactive and retroactive inhibition) also occurred in short strings of items. That is, consider a string of n consonants or digits and focus on a single item. It has some number of prior items and some number of subsequent items. Together these provide the intraunit interference, and the greater the value of n, the greater the amount of intraunit interference. Unlike Foucault, Melton did not suggest a simple additive model. Instead, he relied for his argument on some recent short-term memory data.

These data were obtained from a study using the distractor technique of Peterson and Peterson (1959), and the number of items in the consonant string (i.e., the value of n) was systematically varied over a range of 1–5. The data from a replication and extension of this study are shown in the next chapter in Fig. 7.2, and in both cases (i.e., the original and the replication) the results were very clear. As the value of n varies, a family of curves fans out from a common origin, but the decay becomes more precipitous the larger the value of n. As Melton was careful to point out, the relevant parameter is the number of chunks in the string, not the number of letters *per se*. Thus, the string CATPIERED might well have $n = 3$ rather than $n = 9$, especially if spaces were used judiciously. In fact, Melton suggested that it might even be possible to use data from such studies to calibrate a chunk scale, as the term was intended by Miller (1956).

Intraunit interference, then, is an important concept even though a formal model of memory was not proposed by Melton. Interference effects result from prior and subsequent items; in some way they summate to increase with the length of the string, and there is a basic continuity in the source and the characteristics of the interference over short and long periods of time.

DISTINCTIVENESS

Another approach to serial-position effects is through the concept of distinctiveness. As mentioned above, perhaps the reason why the additive model of Foucault failed was that the quantitative estimates of retroactive and proactive inhibition were biased. If the end items were particularly salient or distinctive, then interference estimates based on their recall would not be accurate when applied to items in the middle of the list. There is evidence (e.g., Glanzer & Dolinsky, 1965) that the first and last items can be anchor points around which learning occurs, and there are various reasons why the end items could be the most distinctive.

A paper by Murdock (1960a) tried to make this concept more explicit. Basically, what I tried to do was to quantify the measure of distinctiveness and see how well it applied to data of various kinds. The initial point of departure was the serial-position effects one consistently finds in studies of absolute judgment (e.g., Garner, 1962). The absolute-judgment finding that has received most attention is the fact that the amount of information transmitted about unidimensional stimuli stays constant once the number of alternatives exceeds some rather small value. This finding has led to the important concept of channel capacity (Miller, 1956). However, it is also true that, in absolute-judgment studies, one finds serial-position effects much like those of Fig. 6.2, and perhaps this is not entirely coincidental.

As detailed by Murdock (1960a), a measure of distinctiveness called the D scale did in fact fairly accurately characterize serial-position effects in absolute judgment. Essentially all the D scale did was to transform scale value by a logarithmic transformation in accord with the Weber-Fechner Law and then express the distinctiveness of each item as a function of the sum of the differences in scale value between it and all other items in the list. Distinctiveness is the extent to which a given stimulus stands out relative to others in the ensemble, and the first and last stimulus in any ordered set would always be most distinctive according to the D scale. There is a clear affinity between the theoretical constructs underlying the D scale and the very extensive adaptation-level theory of Helson (1964).

The rationale for the application of the D scale to serial-position effects in verbal learning was based on the Hunter-McCreary Law. As reported by these investigators (McCreary & Hunter, 1953), serial-position curves for serial learning were invariant for massed and spaced practice at 2- and 4-second presentation rates, for nonsense syllables or familiar names, and for fast or slow learners, all provided that the serial-position curve was plotted in terms of proportion of total errors at each serial position. Since these variables are known to have large effects on learning, but since they apparently had no effect on serial-position curves, perhaps the serial-position curve is a consequence of some other factor. Distinctiveness seemed a reasonable possibility.

It was, then, a simple matter to apply the D scale to serial learning by assuming that the relevant dimension was temporal. That is, in absolute-judgment studies, stimuli vary on such dimensions as intensity, weight, size, and duration; in serial learning the stimuli are generally ordered on a temporal dimension only. Predicted serial-position curves were presented in the original article, and illustrative curves for the learning of 6-, 8-, and 10-item lists are shown in Fig. 6.4. It should be remembered that these are normalized curves; the area under each sums to unity.

As a basis for comparison, consider the curves shown in Fig. 6.5. These data are based on the serial learning of 8-, 13-, and 18-item lists and show mean number of errors at each serial position. As a first approximation, the theoretical curves of Fig. 6.4 seem reasonably similar to the empirical functions of Fig. 6.5, even though they are plotted in a different way. That is, both are bowed, both are asymmetric, both have more extensive primacy than recency, and in both cases the point of maximum difficulty shifts towards the right as list length increases. So, to the extent that the trends are the same, the D scale can be said to characterize the serial-position curve of rote learning.

However, quantitatively the D scale does not fare as well. A paper by Feigenbaum and Simon (1961) compared its predictions with those derived from the EPAM model, and found that the latter did somewhat better in accounting for some serial-learning data reported by Bugelski (1950). A more detailed description of EPAM will be presented in the next section; suffice it to say here that it assumes that subjects learn the list around end anchor points and then work in to the middle. For a list of eight syllables, the mean absolute error for the D-scale predictions was 1.8 per-

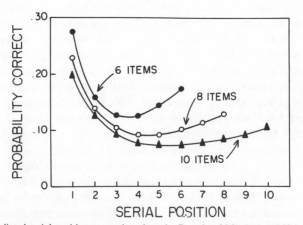

FIG. 6.4 Predicted serial-position curves based on the D scale of Murdock (1960a).

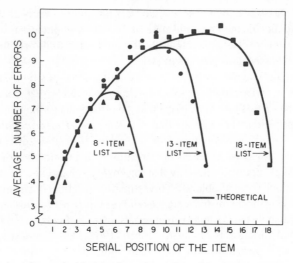

FIG. 6.5. Number of errors in 16 trials of practice on lists of familiar two-syllable adjectives. (Fig. 2 of Atkinson, 1957.)

centage points; for the EPAM model, it was only 0.8 percentage points. Clearly, in this one case the latter model was better.

Even though a distinctiveness model may not be quantitatively as good, it probably has greater generality than EPAM in that it can apply to judgmental tasks as well as memory tasks. Also, EPAM may be fine for list-learning situations, but it is not clear how it could handle similar serial-position curves based on single presentations. That is, if the bowing results from starting with end anchor points and slowly learning the items, one by one, from the outside into the middle, why do essentially similar bowed curves show up in memory span, where there is no opportunity for this gradual acquisition? Also, EPAM seems to make the serial-position curve a consequence of the learning process; if it is, why do the Hunter-McCreary variables that affect learning still leave the shape of the serial-position curve invariant? There is at least some evidence (Detterman & Ellis, 1971) that the D scale can characterize serial-position probe functions following single presentations.

Further evaluation of the D-scale model can be found in a recent paper by Bower (1971). On the critical side, he offers three points. The first point of criticism is several Gedanken experiments where nondiscriminable stimuli (e.g., 44.9, 45.0, and 45.1 db) are mixed with widely-separated stimuli (e.g. 5, 45, and 85 db). However, the model was never intended to apply to stimuli within a jnd. Bower's second point is that there is no way of incorporating in the predicted functions the effect of differences in the degree of learning. This point is certainly correct, and it was acknowledged in the original article. The third criticism is most serious—that the model is not a model at all; it simply provides a measure of distinctiveness without giving any insight into the mechanism. In one sense, this criticism is also correct. In another sense, however, the model is not quite so vacuous. If it turned out to be widely applicable then it would suggest, if only by implication, what the underlying processes or mechanisms might be. It would serve to direct attention to what should be represented in a process model.

Ebenholtz (1972) has recently suggested that the serial-position effect and serial learning may be independent processes. Though he feels that both are learning phenomena, the factors underlying one may be orthogonal to the factors underlying the other. In particular, he suggests that, "*. . .whenever discrimination occurs on the basis of dimensional location, the SPE* [serial-position effect] *will result* [p. 291]." Thus, in spirit he seems in sympathy with a distinctiveness-type notion, though he takes exception to the view that log energy values underlie the dimension. Ebenholtz has done considerable work investigating the effect of various dimensional manipulations, and the interested reader should see this paper for further details.

It is hard to dispute the contention that serial-position effects materialize whenever any dimensional variation is involved. Jensen (1962a) has demonstrated their existence with spatial variation, and they even show up in spelling errors (Jensen, 1962b). By now there are many paired-associate experiments with ordered stimulus terms that give the bow-shaped functions despite the usual randomized presentation order (see, for example, Bower, 1971; Murdock, 1960a; Siegel & Siegel, 1972). There is even a very similar function obtained in tachistoscopic recognition, and the correspondence between the two functions is very impressive (see Fig. 1, Harcum, 1967, p. 52). All things considered, it is difficult to avoid the conclusion that, in some sense, distinctiveness must be involved in these ubiquitous serial-position functions. But in what sense we certainly do not know, and much remains to be worked out.

EPAM

The acronym EPAM stands for Elementary Perceiver and Memorizer. In addition to various technical reports, the perceptual aspect of EPAM is described in Feigenbaum (1963), the mnemonic aspect of EPAM is described in Feigenbaum and Simon (1962, 1963), and an elaborated version is described most recently in Feigenbaum (1970).

The basic idea behind EPAM is that the brain is a serial processing system with a very limited capacity to form serial associations. Essentially, it does one thing at a time and takes a constant amount of time to do it. For serial learning, it starts at the end and works in. There is a small, immediate memory which holds an item or two, and initially these serve as anchor points around which to link adjacent items. It takes a constant amount of time to learn each new item, and by a random process the next item to be learned may be at the beginning or at the end. That is, either the beginning or the end will be selected at random, then the next item learned will be attached to that anchor point, and so on, one by one, until the list is learned. In this way a temporally-ordered structure will be formed.

A serial list need not have only two anchor points. One could have a two-part list as, for instance, in Wishner, Shipley, and Hurvich (1957) where half of the list was printed in black capital letters and the other half in red lower-case letters. On the assumption that subjects could either treat this as two sublists (consequently with three anchor points), or as one whole list (with the customary two anchor points), one could make predictions about the obtained serial-position curve by letting the proportion of subjects who used the first strategy be a free parameter. Perhaps one could also accommodate a von Restorff effect (improved performance on a single distinctive item embedded in the middle of a serial list), except that the only effect here seems to be an increased tendency for the salient item to be given as a response (Saltz, 1971, pp. 183-186). However, the results are somewhat different in a short-term probe situation (see Lively, 1972).

It might be mentioned that a very similar view of serial learning was quite independently suggested by Jensen (1962c). He proposed an empirical theory wherein subjects learn in sequential fashion around the end anchor-points. The degree of skewness in the curve would be a function of the subject's memory span (the larger the span, the more items learned in the first trial, so the fewer the items remaining to be acquired over trials; see Jensen & Roden, 1963). Also, group curves would be flatter than individual curves, since the averaging process would decrease the variability. One implication of this view is that items in the middle of the list could be re-ordered without cost before learning was complete (supporting evidence is given in Jensen, 1963).

EPAM is not limited to serial learning; it can also cope with the learning of a list of paired associates. An important concept here is the discrimination net, a way of sorting stimuli on the basis of their features so as to identify them. Suppose one had to learn the list XBN–1, RGP–2, XFM–3, and XQL–4. A possible sorting tree (Hintzman, 1968) is shown in Fig. 6.6. The first test when shown a probe is to determine whether there is an X in the first position. If not, respond 2; otherwise, see if there is an F in the second position. If so, respond 3; otherwise, see if there is a Q in the second position. If there is, respond 4; otherwise, respond 1. By this series of sequential tests one can sort a probe through this net until it reaches a terminal node which is a response. If new pairs were added to the list, additional test nodes (choice points) would have to be added to effect the necessary additional discriminations required.

The general view here is one of increased perceptual differentiation. One comes to notice distinctive features of the stimulus items in order to tell them apart. What features are represented in any particular discrimination net depends upon the stimulus ensemble. If all stimulus terms had the same initial first letter, clearly that would not be a very useful distinctive feature. Also, some features may be irrelevant. In the example of Fig. 6.6, the third letter is not even noticed. As is probably obvious, one attractive feature of such a view is that only binary tests are utilized, thus making this aspect of its realization in a computer program very simple and direct.

EPAM has been applied to experiments on paired associates which vary similarity, familiarization, and meaningfulness in an attempt to explain the effect of these manipulations (Simon & Feigenbaum, 1964). Also, it is claimed to be able to show that paired-associate learning will be all-or-none or incremental, depending upon the presentation rate and the strategy of the subjects (Gregg & Simon, 1967a).

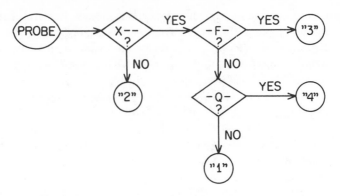

FIG. 6.6. A sorting tree to decide upon the correct response to the probe. The list of paired associates is given in the text. (After Hintzman, 1968.)

Hintzman (1968) has suggested an extension of EPAM he calls SAL (for Stimulus and Association Learner) which can be applied to such diverse phenomena as intralist stimulus-similarity effects, number of response alternatives, massed versus spaced item repetition, whole versus part learning, retroactive inhibition, and transfer paradigms. Actually, there are several versions of SAL; an enumeration of the particular assumptions and what they can account for is given at the conclusion of his article.

EPAM and SAL are particular instances of a general class of models commonly known as computer-simulation models. The model or theory is stated in the form of a computer program, which may be a list-processing language, FORTRAN, or any other computer language one wishes. To derive predictions one generally must run Monte Carlo simulations. That is, one designates the particular conditions to be studied and then runs the experiment with the computer rather than the college sophomore as the experimental subject. In effect, the computer functions in a triple capacity; it sets up the conditions of the experiment, it serves as subject, and then it again becomes an experimenter tabulating and analyzing the data. Many general accounts of computer-simulation techniques are available (e.g., F. F. Martin, 1968; Naylor, Balintfy, Burdick, & Chu, 1966).

Computer-simulation models are different from the more traditional quantitative models one associates with the scientific enterprise. For one thing, they are stated in programming language, not the language of mathematics. Further, one generally cannot draw specific deductions from a simulation model; instead, one must resort to a Monte Carlo procedure to discover what the model predicts. And on a more general level, scientific theories generally attempt to explain a variety a phenomena from a few basic principles or underlying assumptions, while in computer simulation the richness and complexity of the phenomenon under investigation is represented completely at the beginning.

There are several advantages to simulation models. For one thing, it is the easiest (and often the only) way one can represent the behavior of complex systems. One indication of this is the recent growth in the field of operations research, which uses simulation techniques on such complex systems as inventory control, transportation systems, marketing, etc. (e.g., Hillier & Lieberman, 1967). It may be suitable for another reason. Many of us are quite untrained in the standard mathematical techniques and skills often required for scientific theorizing, but we have learned to write computer programs with at least a modicum of skill. And it certainly is not difficult to develop a simulation model which very quickly becomes even more complex than we might wish.

On the other hand, there are two rather serious drawbacks to such models. One is practical: the cost involved. Each time one wants to make a new derivation from the theory one must do a Monte Carlo on the computer, and this can be expensive. Very expensive, at times, which itself may be a sufficient deterrent that can limit its usefulness. The other main problem is that one is often limited to qualitative, rather than quantitative, predictions. Since the predictions are really data, they have all the inherent variability of data, so one is restricted to probabilistic statements in the same way our data conclusions have confidence limits. With a mathematical model one can obtain parameter estimates and goodness-of-fit measures, and so make fairly unambiguous theoretical comparisons. It is far more difficult with simulation models.

The above comments by no means exhaust the topic; for further discussion the interested reader could start with Gregg and Simon (1967b) or Millward (1971). Whatever their advantages and disadvantages, computer-simulation models are scientific theories that in the last analysis must be evaluated as any other scientific theories. Do they help us to understand and predict the phenomena we are interested in?

As far as EPAM (and, for that matter, SAL) is concerned, my main criticism is the general point already expressed several times. Namely, they start with learning effects and try to explain them by certain (not unreasonable) assumptions. I would much rather start with short-term memory effects and derive such things as serial-position effects and other list-learning phenomena as a result of the specific way that memory builds up with repetition. If one assumes that the serial-position curve results from subjects learning a list slowly item by item, working from the end in, how does one explain that similar serial-position effects are manifest after a single presentation of a list? Or, still further, that serial-position effects show up almost everywhere that there is an ordered array, as noted in the previous section. One could claim that different processes are involved, and that may be. But at this point in the game it seems more promising to hope that the same fundamental process underlies them all, and that the slight differences that do occur from situation to situation represent local not global effects.

Also, it seems to me that EPAM in particular and computer-simulation models in general have had surprisingly little impact on the field as a whole. Very little research seems to have been done to test them other than by those directly involved in their construction. Also, one would be hard-pressed to name any new discoveries that have resulted from them. Even though there are several such models that really do have a fair degree of generality and cover an impressive range of phenomena, by and large one could almost say that they have been ignored by everyone else. As a specific instance, the EPAM model says that the human brain functions as a serial processing mechanism that does things one at a time, and in real time. This is exactly what the serial-scanning model of Sternberg says too (e.g., Sternberg, 1969a). But if one looks at the amount of research generated by the Sternberg model and the amount of research generated by EPAM there is no comparison.

One might wish to counter this example with the fact that serial-position curves have been around a long while, but linear reaction-time functions are relatively novel. But the fact remains that, to date, computer-simulation models have not been too productive. Whether this is a short-term or long-term effect remains to be seen.

FILTER THEORY

The next theoretical approach to be considered is the filter theory of Broadbent (1957b, 1958). This theory or model was intended originally to account for the split-span findings of Broadbent (1954, 1956, 1957a) and the immediate-memory work of Brown (1954, 1958), but it has turned out to have considerably more generality. It was the first of the information-processing models devoted explicitly to human memory, but its importance is more than just historical.

A split-span study is a memory-span study in which the list presentation is simultaneous over two different channels rather than successive over a single channel. Thus, if the list was 734215, in the split-span condition one channel might receive 734 at the same time that the other channel was receiving 215. In the first experiments the two channels were the two ears, so the subject would hear 734 in one ear at the same time as 215 was heard in the other ear. Originally this condition was referred to as binaural, but now the preferred term is dichotic (Broadbent, 1971, p. 135). Dichotic listening refers to the situation where separate messages are delivered to the two ears, while binaural indicates the absence of any channel separation. Mixed modes can also be used, so 734 could be presented visually while 215 would be presented auditorily; this presentation condition is generally called bisensory (Dornbush, 1968).

The main results are that performance is better when the two channels are reported successively, and there are more errors on the channel reported second. Even though a pair-by-pair order of report would be possible (e.g., 72, 31, 45) an ear-by-ear report is more accurate (e.g., 734, 215). There tend to be more errors on 215 than on 734. These findings do not depend upon whether presentation is dichotic or bisensory, but do depend upon rate of presentation. At a fast rate (a new digit arriving every one-half second on both channels) these effects are pronounced. They are attenuated, or disappear, at a slow rate (a new digit arriving every two seconds on both channels). Since at the slow rate the report was channel by channel, Broadbent originally felt that the difficulty was not in the fact that it is physically impossible to report two items simultaneously, but this issue has been reopened by Moray and Jordan (1966).

The memory effects reported by Brown (1958) were that immediate memory seemed particularly vulnerable to interference but was quite unaffected by similarity relations between the target information and the interpolated activity. When 1 to 4 items were presented and then a brief delay was introduced by an irrelevant activity, forgetting occurred though even a 4-item list is well within memory span. Forgetting increased as the number of to-be-remembered items increased from 1 to 4, but if they were consonant digrams it did not seem to matter whether the interpolated items (which had to be read aloud) were consonant digrams or digrams composed of digits. Such results were quite inconsistent with typical findings from the long-term memory literature.

The general idea behind the filter theory was that there are two separate systems or mechanisms, an S system and a P system, which have different characteristics. The S system (where S represents storage) holds information that arrives simultaneously, hence it works in parallel; the P system (where P represents perceptual) processes information sequentially, so it is essentially a parallel-to-serial converter. The filter mechanism (a switch, if you will) controls the parallel to serial conversion (or the processing of information), and it is not unlike the well-known concept of attention.

To illustrate these concepts, Broadbent first suggested a mechanical model, and then a more flexible flow-chart. The mechanical model is illustrated in Fig. 6.7, and it is essentially a Y-shaped tube with return loops and a valve or filter to control the flow. Let us represent items of information in a memory-span task as little metal balls dropped into one or both stems of the Y. If they are dropped, one by one, into a single stem, and if the filter (shown pivoted at the junction) is appropriately set, then the balls will pass straight through. This is the conventional memory-span situation. In the split-span case, simultaneous entries are made into each channel, and what happens next depends on the filter. It can be set to let all balls from one branch through, then switch to the other branch; this seems to happen at fast presentation rates. It can alternate, in a left-right-left-right-left-right order, which can happen at slow rates even though it still may not be the preferred method. Such an interpretation can obviously be related both to attention and to the characteristics of the switching mechanism. The temporal format of storage is represented by the position of the metal balls in the system.

To account for the fact that the channel reported second is less accurate, assume that the branches contain a destructive acid. Then the delay necessitated by the time taken to process the first channel will result in deterioration of the memory traces of the items held in the second channel; there is decay because the acid eats away the metal balls, and the longer the delay the more the decay. The return loop is designed to counteract the decay effect, so with recirculation an enforced delay may not have a deleterious effect on the trace. Subjectively, recirculation is akin to rehearsal, and a neural analog often suggested to account for short-term memory effects is reverberatory circuits (e.g., Hebb, 1949).

In order to account for the immediate-memory effects of Brown, and the Y-shaped tube being a single-channel mechanism, it is impossible to have simultaneous recirculation of the target items and shadowing of the interpolated items. Consequently, the target items must be delayed, with the resulting decay producing the poorer performance. Since the items can be portrayed as discrete metal balls, the nature of the

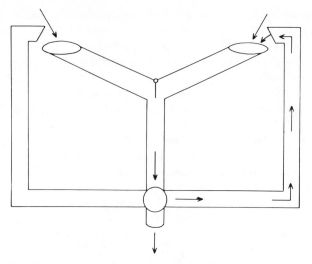

Fig. 6.7. Mechanical model to illustrate the main concepts of filter theory. (Fig. 2 from Broadbent, 1957b.)

items being processed during the retention interval should not be expected to affect the other items held temporarily in store; thus, similarity effects would not be expected.

In this model the branches of the tube correspond to the S system, where information may be stored in parallel. There is no necessity to restrict the number of incoming branches to two; clearly, we have many sensory modalities. The stem of the tube is the single-channel P system, where items are processed or pass through one at a time. The valve controlling entry is the filter. Broadbent believed in the possibility of decay from short-term memory, so the hypothetical acid reflects this time-dependent process. As noted, recirculation represents rehearsal, and information is represented by the metal balls. In Fig. 6.7 the arrow pointing directly down from the bottom of the stem goes to output (the response given by the subject).

This model is a model in the real sense; an analog (physical, as it happens) that portrays in vivid fashion hypothetical processes going on in the nervous system. It is quite easy to make deductions from the model; for instance, how this system could output the balls in the opposite order from their entry (which is backward memory span, i.e., given 734215, report 512437), and how the accuracy of backward recall should compare with the accuracy of forward recall. Not only is it a concrete and descriptive model, but also it is in good correspondence with a number of experimental findings. Of course it is hypothetical and a bit on the fanciful side, but it does have an heuristic value. Actually, if one lets one's imagination roam still further one can envision the arrow pointing downward feeding an endless conveyor belt onto which the metal balls fall. As they recede continually into the past, some of them drop off. So some tiny fraction of what continually is present in consciousness achieves stability of representation in long-term memory.

A more elaborate representation of filter theory is the flow chart shown in Fig. 6.8. Here the S system is represented by a box labelled short-term store, and the P system by a second rectangle following the (selective) filter. The S system follows the senses because Broadbent felt that it was more than simply after-discharge of the end organs. The recirculation feature is represented by the upper return arrow from the P system to the short-term store, and one branch from the P system goes eventually to the effectors and some observable response. Broadbent interprets the formation of associative relationships as changes in conditional probabilities, so this box in the lower right-hand corner is a somewhat oversimplified representation of long-term memory. Since the setting of the filter is modifiable by instructions (and in many other ways too), there is another return arrow to denote this control feature.

One of the very general implications of this filter theory of Broadbent is that there is no sharp dividing line between perception and memory; or, that the same mechanisms may be involved in both. With the further concept of a limited-capacity channel, demands of one cannot be satisfied without cost to the other. This general point was nicely illustrated in a subsequent study by Broadbent and Gregory (1963). At the same time that a list of six digits was presented to one ear a burst of white noise was presented to the other ear, and this noise might or might not be accompanied by a brief tone. In effect, this task is a mixture of signal detection and memory span. Sometimes subjects disregarded the digits and reported only the presence or absence of the tone. Other times they reported both the digits and the tone. The detection performance (d') was affected by the requirement to report the digits; therefore perception is affected by demands on the memory system.

Another general implication of this model of Broadbent is that if the P system is kept very busy processing one channel of information, any stimuli momentarily presented through another channel could not later be recalled. At first this seemed to be correct. Using the shadowing technique of Cherry (1953), where one has to report (shadow) the message presented on one channel and then subsequently recall any

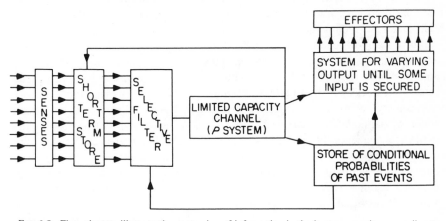

FIG. 6.8. Flow chart to illustrate the processing of information in the human organism according to filter theory. (Fig. 7 from Broadbent, 1958.)

message concurrently presented on the second channel, Moray (1959) found that subjects could not even recognize a short list of words presented many times over while shadowing a prose passage. However, Mowbray (1964) found that visually-presented words were somewhat better recalled than auditorily-presented words (with auditory shadowing), and recently considerable evidence has accumulated to indicate that visually-presented information can in fact be remembered very well (e.g., Kroll, Parks, Parkinson, Bieber, & Johnson, 1970; Parkinson, Parks, & Kroll, 1971; Parkinson, 1972).

Yet another aspect of the filter theory in general and the limited-capacity hypothesis in particular is the work on the psychological refractory period. As reviewed, for instance, by Welford (1960), Bertelson (1966), Smith (1967), or Broadbent (1971), there is much evidence to indicate that reaction time to a second signal coming shortly after a first is delayed, and the amount of delay is (within limits) a decreasing linear function of the interstimulus interval. That is, if the subject has to make a choice response to the first signal and then a choice response to the second signal, it is as though the P system is exclusively preoccupied with the first and must wait for completion before processing the second.

Clearly the filter theory seems capable of explaining the main features of split-span and immediate-memory effects. It can probably also explain why the serial-position curve is bow shaped. When a list of items is presented to the subject there is not only the presentation rate to be considered, but also the rehearsal rate and the re-call rate as well. The rehearsal rate will be faster than the recall rate. Since rehearsal is faster than recall, early items will tend to spend less time in the S system than later items. On the other hand, if the presentation rate is slower than rehearsal then, because the first items are delayed in the P system, there will be a recency effect. The combination of these two factors should then produce a U-shaped function (Broadbent, 1958, p. 235).

Although filter theory has considerable explanatory value, it has turned out to be wrong on many specific points. With the advantage of hindsight, we can now point out some of its inaccuracies. Aside from its incompleteness (which will be a criticism of any model of memory until we understand the workings of the human mind), there are three main difficulties. First, additional work on attention has suggested some different views on the detailed operation of the filter and what a "channel" is. These ramifications are outside the scope of this book; those interested in the matter are referred to works by Moray (1969), Norman (1968), or Treisman (1969).

Second, it seems that Broadbent was wrong on the similarity point. He felt that similarity did not affect short-term memory, and in a later paper (Broadbent, 1963) used this as evidence for separate short- and long-term stores. However, it turned out that people were looking for the wrong kinds of similarity. Conrad (1964) showed that acoustic similarity did indeed have a very considerable effect in short-term memory, and now there is ample evidence to document this contention. This work will be discussed at greater length in the next chapter.

Third, the evidence for decay has been weak at best, and one could even make the flat statement that forgetting through the passage of time *per se* just does not occur in short-term memory. Much work has shown that interference accounts for the majority of the forgetting in short-term memory (e.g., Murdock, 1961a; Waugh & Norman, 1965), and there is recent evidence of a more direct sort that argues against a decay process. Reitman (1971) introduced a signal-detection task during the retention interval to allow time to pass with a minimum of interference and found no evidence of forgetting. This result was also corroborated by Atkinson and Shiffrin (1971). This procedure seems the closest approximation yet to filling the retention interval with empty time, and on the basis of current evidence the verdict on decay effects seems negative.

Despite these particular difficulties with filter theory, its general advantages should not be overlooked. As has been noted, it was the first real information-processing model for memory, and this approach has become steadily more popular as a way of looking at short-term memory phenomena. It suggests a useful research strategy as well. Although we cannot open up the head and look inside, with appropriate experimental manipulations we can at least attempt to trace the flow of information in the organism (Broadbent, 1963) and draw inferences about stages of processing. And, of course, it can explain at a qualitative level a number of experimental findings. It is not a quantitative model, but Broadbent has argued that the time for quantitative theorizing has not yet come. Finally, in this model temporal order is clearly represented in memory, and serial-order effects in the data are seen to be the result of a temporal-to-spatial transformation applied to the memory trace.

ITEM- AND ORDER-INFORMATION MODELS

The final type of model to be considered in this chapter are the models based on a separation of item and order information. Item information means what the *item* is; order information means the ordinal location or serial position of an item. If I present the string 6BQ327 and you recall 6DQ237, then one error of each type is suggested. The fact that you have substituted D for B in the second position would be an item error (or a loss of item information), while the fact that you have transposed the digits 3 and 2 would be an order error (or a loss of order information). Models of serial-order effects based on item and order information essentially suggest that separate retention mechanisms are necessary to account for the preservation of these two different types of information. With varying degrees of specificity such models have been suggested by Brown (1958, 1959), Conrad (1959, 1965), Crossman (1961), Estes (1972), and Wickelgren (1965b, 1966a, 1969a). Experimental methods of separating item and order information have been suggested by Murdock and vom Saal (1967) and Donaldson and Glathe (1969).

These models are the most explicit of all in treating the temporal format of storage. They were developed originally in an attempt to solve a problem for information-processing views of human short-term memory. As exemplified, for instance, by the filter theory of Broadbent, such models suggest that the basic unit of analysis in memory should be some informational quantity, perhaps a "bit" of information (where bit is a contraction of binary digit). If this is the case, why then is memory span relatively insensitive to variations in information load? This fact was pointed out by Miller (1956), whose suggestion was to substitute chunks for bits. This line of development has been followed by those interested in organization theory. The other line of development has been to preserve the informational assumption but distinguish between two types of information, item information and order information.

Brown Model

Brown (1958) suggested that the limitation reflected in memory span was one of order information rather than one of item information. That is, assume that remembering what items are presented is separate from remembering what the order of these items is. Then, if the memory load represented by order is much greater than the memory load represented by the items, it is the former that will determine span in the conventional procedure. What items are presented, binary digits or common words, will be relatively unimportant, since in all cases the difficult thing to remember is their presentation order. Consequently, the results reported by Miller (that memory span is relatively independent of the nature of the items used) are not contradictory to this information-processing view.

This view was elaborated somewhat in a subsequent paper (Brown, 1959). It was suggested that traces were stored with some redundancy; consequently, decay of the underlying trace (a decrease in the signal-to-noise ratio) need not bear a one-to-one relation with observed performance. Within a limited-capacity system, storage capabilities were flexible and would be allocated as the encoding process demanded. For memory span, order information was assumed to be stored with little redundancy, and consequently it was quite vulnerable to any forgetting. As a result, transpositions (loss of order information) might be observed, since this loss could precede loss of item information. Though of less relevance here, Brown attempted to show how a decay theory of memory, then (and now) unpopular, could account for some of the general findings typically cited in support of interference interpretations of forgetting. As has been mentioned, these concepts are not unlike those of later applications of signal-detection theory to short-term memory.

Crossman Model

In an elaboration of this viewpoint, Crossman (1961) suggested a random-address model for immediate memory. Suppose the brain has a limited number of storage registers or addresses which can store the typical material presented in a memory-span task. Further, assume that they are essentially unordered, but that some means of representing order can be encoded in them. Then, at the time a memory-span list is presented, the subject will store in each register both what the item is and some identifying code to designate the serial position of this item in the list. For the latter, the obvious way would be just to use single digits to code positions. Then, at the time of recall, the subject would search these addresses randomly, recover both item and order information, arrange the items on the basis of their serial position, and then give his overt response.

With this type of model, then, separate information is stored to represent item and order information. To understand how a transposition could occur, remember that loss of the serial designation would not require loss of item information, since these two features are separately represented. The amount of item information would be proportional to the size of the source vocabulary, while the amount of order information would be proportional to $n!$ where $n!$ represents the number of possible permutations of a string n items long. (The proportionality would be logarithmic from a strict information-theory view.) One implication of this view is that efficiency is greatest with shortest lists. Thus, if recoding were possible to shorten the number of items, even at the expense of increasing the entropy of the ensemble, there would be a net gain in terms of reduced total information load. This view, then, is compatible with the recoding efficiency reported in the original Miller (1956) paper.

Although little more has been done with this random-access model, it at least provides a link to the role of errors in short-term memory. In an early paper on this topic Conrad (1959) pointed out their significance. Speaking generally, one of the best ways of studying the human memory system is to overload it to the point where breakdowns occur, then discover where and how it does break down. At the risk of slight overstatement, errors are to the study of human memory what Freud claimed dreams were to the study of the unconscious. (This assertion will not be found in the Conrad paper.) Conrad did however classify errors by types, enumerating transpositions, omissions, substitutions, and serial-order intrusions. Transpositions are rearrangements of order as in the example given at the beginning of this section. Omissions are failures to respond. Serial-order intrusions are quite special; they are responses from the previous list and the same serial position. Thus, if one string was 614 and the next was 792, and if the subject recalled the latter as 794, then the importation of the digit 4 would be a serial-order intrusion. Substitutions are essentially a wastebasket category—errors that can not be classified either as transpositions or serial-order intrusions. In the above example, the digit 3 would be a substitution error if the recall had been 793.

In scoring data from memory-span studies, such a classification is useful but not completely satisfactory. There will always be some cases that are difficult or even impossible to classify. A simple transposition or a single serial-order intrusion is straightforward and easy to spot, as are single substitution errors. Beyond that, complications begin to develop, and it does not take much imagination to conjure up cases which are quite indeterminate. In effect, one is trying to infer base structure from suface structure, and that is always difficult. It is far more satisfactory to hypothesize some base structure (underlying process) and deduce what the empirical results (surface structure) should be. This procedure requires a model but permits evaluation in terms of agreement between expected and obtained results.

Conrad Model

In a later paper Conrad (1965) proposed a bin model to explain serial-order effects. Imagine that there are a set of ordered bins, or storage registers, each of which holds a single item. The first item goes in the first bin, the second item in the second bin, the third item in the third bin, and so on until one runs out of space. To recall, the subject simply reports the contents of the bins in the requisite (forward) order. Conrad further assumed that items in each bin could decay, but there is no way in which the contents of the bins could interchange.

To Conrad, decay meant a fall in the signal-to-noise ratio, as in the Brown model described above. Decay was gradual, so partial forgetting might result in an error somehow similar to the correct item. Substitution errors might be spotted in this way. Further decay would result in memorial illegibility and perhaps the consequent omission. The subject might simply say, "I can't remember the next digit." Serial-order intrusions could result if decay of a particular item from one list was more extreme than decay of the comparable item in the immediately preceding list. What remains in the error category is transpositions, and these are a bit less obvious.

In effect, Conrad suggested that transpositions were more apparent than real. Take the model literally, and assume that the subject is simply reading out the contents of the bins one at a time. He comes to a point where decay has occurred, and as it happens makes a substitution error. Then, assume that later in the list this substitution happens to be an actual list member. The subject knows that no items are repeated, so he cannot say the same item twice. Nor can he go back and change his previous response. The only option open to him is now to disbelieve his memory and report the next best thing, which is probably the correct item at the point of the substitution error. As a consequence, a transposition has occurred. The experimenter thinks that there has been loss of order information, but in fact there has not. In the base structure there are two substitution errors, and it is in this sense that the transposition is more apparent than real. An illustrative example of the assumed processes is shown in Fig. 6.9.

The important point to remember, then, is that in the Conrad model transpositions are a phenomenon of surface structure, not base structure. In the underlying memory trace there is no rearrangement of order. Instead, there is simply decay, and a combination of the structure of the list and the strategy of the subject gives rise to a recall protocol in which the items are rearranged relative to the order of presentation.

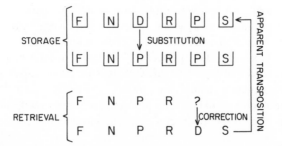

FIG. 6.9. Illustration of a "transposition" in terms of the model of Conrad (1965). The first row shows the initial stored representation of the list. The second row shows a single substitution error. The third row shows the subject's recall up to the point where he detects a repetition. The fourth row shows his correction, resulting in an apparent transposition.

One prediction that would seem to follow is that pairs of confusable items should show more transpositions than pairs of nonconfusable items. Conrad (1965) showed this prediction to be true; there were more than five times as many transpositions of confusable pairs as nonconfusable pairs. Also, when a transposition did occur, there was a very sharp gradient effect. If the transposition occurs between items i and j, the proportion decreased both sharply and monotonically as the number of items intervening between i and j increased from zero to four. (All lists were six-items long, so four is the maximum.) Conrad considered that this finding was also consistent with the model; for reasons given in the original paper he felt that, when decay occurred, substitution errors were most likely to be the immediately following item.

As Conrad (1965) concluded, "What would be crucial is a variable that, in the defined case, could be shown to affect order of items differentially from the items themselves [p. 169]." Murdock and vom Saal (1967) found such a variable, category membership. Words from the same category (e.g., GRAY BROWN RED) were more accurately recalled than words from three different categories (e.g., EEL SCREW LOUNGE), but they were more liable to be transposed. Thus there was better retention of item information for words of the same category, but better retention of order information for words of different categories. These results were interpreted as inconsistent with the Conrad model, which would seem to predict that loss of item and order information should be positively correlated. As an alternative, it was suggested that not only could transpositions occur in storage, but also they might be more basic than loss of item information. As argued in the original paper, it could be that transpositions are disruptive; the probability of loss of item information is greater when a rearrangement in the memory trace occurs than when it does not.

Wickelgren Model

Wickelgren (1965b, 1966a) has reported several tests of what he refers to as an associative and a nonassociative model of short-term memory. The nonassociative model is essentially the bin model of Conrad. Items are stored in ordered locations, and there are no direct associations between items *per se*. An associative model is essentially a chaining model, where item representations in memory are used and the record of serial order is given by direct item-to-item associations. A discriminating test would be to repeat an item in the list. According to a nonassociative model, the contents of the bins or registers is quite immaterial, so there should be no difference between lists with and without repeated elements. According to an associative model, since item-to-item associations provide the underlying base structure, repeating an item should make the item immediately following the repeated item more vulnerable to error, since one would have two possible pathways leading from the single memorial representation of the repeated item.

The Ranschburg effect (Crowder & Melton, 1965; Jahnke, 1969, 1970, 1972) provides some relevant data. This effect refers to the inferior serial recall of lists with repeated elements compared to a control condition with unique items. The poorer performance may be on the repeated item itself or on its neighbors, and it seems to depend somewhat on the particular serial positions i and j which the repeated item occupies. Wickelgren has pointed out in particular that there are cases where the items in position $i + 1$ and $j + 1$ are at a disadvantage in recall in the experimental condition, and he interprets the data as generally supportive of an associative model. However, the effects tend to be small in magnitude, rather inconsistent across serial positions, and even Wickelgren points out (Wickelgren, 1966a) that a nonassociative model could be elaborated to account for such effects. Recently Wickelgren (1969a) has extended this associative model to phonemic production in speech; for a criticism of this view see Halwes and Jenkins (1971).

Estes Model

The most detailed model of this genre is a structural model recently proposed by Estes (1972). It is designed to account for immediate memory, grouping, and learning effects with serial lists. Associations are formed between control elements and items, not between items. Suppose I have to remember (or learn) the telephone number SP60516. A theoretical representation is given in Fig. 6.10. Assume I make two groups, the prefix SP and the five digits 60516. Control element $C_{2,1}$ codes the former; control element $C_{2,2}$ codes the latter. The first subscript denotes the level of the control element. They are assumed to be hierarchical, and in this case they are second-level elements as C_1 codes the full string. They are ordered as denoted by the second subscript, so the fact that SP is coded as $C_{2,1}$ means it is the first second-level control element. Without grouping, this string would be represented simply by C_1 with seven arrows radiating out to the seven elements. If the grouping were 4-3 (i.e., SP6-0516) then $C_{2,1}$ would have the three terminal nodes S, P, and 6, while $C_{2,2}$ would have the four terminal nodes 0, 5, 1, and 6.

In an immediate memory test, assume I am presented the string and encode it as shown in Fig. 6.10. To recall, I start with C_1, read down to $C_{2,1}$, follow the two arrows to the letters S and P which I report, then go to $C_{2,2}$, follow its branches, and report in order 60516. Thus, reporting simply involves decoding the tree, and one might expect a brief pause between the two groups. If delayed recall is required, as would be the case if some interpolated activity intervened between presentation and recall, then some rehearsal would be necessary to prevent decay. Estes suggests that this rehearsal may be viewed as some sort of reverberatory process, cycling through as often as necessary to tide the trace over the period of interpolation.

However, errors in timing can occur. Assume some variability in timing is characteristic of each item. Then, purely on the basis of random variation, eventually some item will fall ahead of or behind one or more of its neighbors, so there will be a transposition between list items. The immediate prediction is that transpositions would increase with the duration of the interpolated activity. In addition to evidence reported by Estes, studies by Henley, Noyes, and Deese (1968) and by Murdock and vom Saal (1967) show that transpositions do indeed increase as recall is delayed.

Not only are the groups coded by control elements, but the individual items themselves might be as well. Thus, a letter or a digit can be broken down into features (e.g., phonemes in a spoken utterance), and each feature may require a control element. With perturbation in timing, rearrangement of features may occur, which

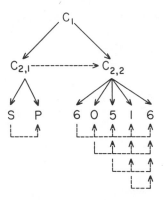

FIG. 6.10. Illustration of the coding of the string SP60516 according to the structural model of Estes (1972). Each subscripted letter C represents a control element, and the dashed arrows represent the inhibitory associations which are presumed to develop with learning.

in turn may lead to item errors. What particular error occurs depends upon the particular feature-system envisioned and the particular timing error made, but if an illegal feature combination occurs then omissions are presumed to result. Perhaps the important point to note here is that, as Estes emphasizes, order errors are primary and item errors are derivative. That is, the basic forgetting mechanism is seen as perturbation in timing during the recycling process, and what item errors do occur are viewed as a consequence of this process.

Since the reverberatory process is seen as a recycling through the string from beginning to end, and since misalignment in either direction is equally possible, the resulting serial-position curve for loss of order information is bowed and symmetrical. Items in the middle are most vulnerable because they have the furthest distance to move, while end items can only migrate into the middle. The loss of features is seen as monotonic, increasing from beginning to end. Estes presents some curves that show good agreement between predicted and obtained errors at different retention intervals.

So far all we have considered is immediate recall and rehearsal over the short term. Estes suggests another mechanism to accommodate learning effects, namely, inhibitory connections from each item to all following it in that chunk. These inhibitory connections are illustrated by the broken arrows of Fig. 6.9. Evocation of $C_{2,1}$ simultaneously inhibits $C_{2,2}$. Within the chunks, S inhibits P, and each digit inhibits all that follow. This inhibition is momentary; once the response is evoked, the inhibition is released and the process moves smoothly to the next item or chunk in the string. These inhibitory connections are seen as developing out of the rehearsal process, so learning develops out of short-term memory. If there has been partial loss of information, the rehearsal process can still pick up on what is left and consolidate that to prevent further decay.

One implication of this view is that chunking can be seen as a useful way of minimizing the total number of associations required to remember a string. Suppose

12 items are presented, and one simply totals the combined number of excitatory and inhibitory connections required as a function of how the grouping is done. As Estes shows, one chunk of 12 is the least economical, 6-6 is appreciably better, and 2-2-2-2-2-2, 4-4-4, and 3-3-3-3 are better yet (in that order). Also, it seems reasonable that the transitional error-probability data reported by Johnson (1970) would be consistent with this view. However, Estes does not go much beyond the simple suggestion of inhibitory processes, so it is not clear yet what the model can and cannot do in the area of long-term memory and learning.

This structural model is interesting for two historical reasons, one discussed by Estes and one not. The first is in reference to the serial-order problem as stated so effectively by Lashley (1951). Lashley criticized the then-popular view of serial ordering as simple chaining, wherein the first response to an item in a string became the stimulus for the second item, it in turn became the stimulus for the third item, etc. Two of the criticisms advanced by Lashley were that it could not begin to cope with the complexities of such rule-governed behavior as language, and that even relatively simple serial chains in skilled acts could run off at speeds impossible for a mechanism such as simple chaining. Today no one would seriously try to portray language in any simple chaining fashion, but there is still the interresponse-time problem for skilled acts.

The structural model of Estes would not be embarrassed if (or when) the interresponse times were found to be less than some minimum possible by a proprioceptive chaining mechanism. No item-to-item associations are postulated; responses are under control elements. Estes points out that there is no particular reason why some limiting delay would be necessary, so he is saying that skilled acts can be under central control just as Lashley assumed. Actually, there is still much more speculation than data on this point. I once measured interresponse times of subjects practicing a simple chain of eight motor responses and found that the learning curve seemed to be approaching quite nicely the (separately measured) proprioceptive reaction time as the asymptote. With high degrees of overlearning, skilled acts can surely run off more rapidly, but then we still don't know what the appropriate units of measurement might be.

The other point is that this model of Estes seems to be a more formal and rigorous elaboration of a view that was earlier suggested by Hebb (1949). That is, Hebb suggested that short-term memory was mediated by an activity trace, reverberatory loops were mentioned as a possibility, and with repetition the trace could consolidate into a long-term structural trace. In many ways this is exactly what Estes is saying. What is interesting is that Hebb subsequently rejected this view on the basis of evidence to be considered in the next chapter, and one would like to know how the model of Estes could cope with the so-called Hebb repetition effect (Hebb, 1961; Melton, 1963). Actually, there are many aspects of serial-order effects to which the Estes model could apply, but whether it can be applied successfully remains to be seen. The model is still in a provisional stage, and much work remains before we can realistically assess its adequacy.

SUMMARY

The basic serial-order problem is the representation and utilization of the temporal order of events. The main independent variables in serial-order studies are the number of items in the string, the length of the retention interval, and the number of prior lists. The main dependent variables are the percentage of completely correct recalls and serial-position effects. Theories of serial order attempt to explain the inter-relationships.

The two main retroactive- and proactive-inhibition models are those of Foucault and Melton. The Foucault model tried to explain serial-position effects in terms of a simple additive model, where the interference acting upon a particular item was the sum of two components (the proactive inhibition from prior items and the retroactive inhibition from subsequent items). In general, the model underestimated the amount of interference. Melton emphasized the importance of intraunit interference. As in long-term memory, similar processes could be demonstrated to be operating on a more molecular level within a single n-gram, and the total amount of interference increased with n.

Another approach is to assume that serial-position effects are manifestations of variations in distinctiveness. The first and last items in a list are most distinctive, and the distinctiveness of any particular item is related to its distance from other items in a string. Qualitatively, such a view can generate reasonable serial-position effects, but quantitatively the EPAM model may fit better.

The EPAM model suggests a serial processing view where discrete associations are built up one at a time, starting from the end and working inward. It takes a certain amount of time to form these associations, so there is a slow development over trials. A similar model, SAL, has been developed for paired-associate learning. EPAM and SAL are examples of computer-simulation models; some of the advantages and disadvantages of this type of model have been discussed.

The filter theory of Broadbent was the first extensive application of an information-processing approach to human short-term memory. Many parallel inputs converge upon a limited-capacity single channel (P system), and a filter mechanism controls the parallel-to-serial conversion. With simultaneous (multichannel) presentation, some information may be held briefly in a short-term store where it is vulnerable to decay. Recirculation is possible in the form of rehearsal but, given the capacity limitations, preoccupation with past events may interfere with the perceptual processing of incoming information.

The item- and order-information models are the most explicit in treating the temporal format of storage. An early model by Brown made the distinction between remembering what the item was (item information) and remembering its location in a string (order information). Crossman proposed a random-address model, and it is one way of solving the difficulties for an information-processing view previously noted by Miller. Conrad proposed a bin model wherein no loss of order information occurred; transpositions were interpreted as stemming from loss of item information.

Wickelgren has reported some tests of an associative versus a nonassociative model, with results supporting the former. Finally, Estes has suggested a structural model with control elements to provide a hierarchical arrangement. Grouping effects are represented, and errors of timing in a recirculation loop are suggested as the mechanism for loss of order information. Loss of order information brings about loss of item information, and long-term stability results from the development of suggested inhibitory connections.

7
DATA ON SERIAL ORDER

In this chapter we shall discuss some of the main empirical findings from studies of serial-order effects in human memory. The topics to be covered are forgetting functions, repetition effects, limitations in capacity, chunking, similarity effects, proactive inhibition, and multichannel effects.

FORGETTING FUNCTIONS

Basically there are three different forgetting functions that we need to consider. The first is the forgetting function of memory span, which is simply the serial-positive curve. It is a forgetting function in the sense of Foucault (1928); each item is preceded and followed by some varying number of other items in input and output. The second is the forgetting function obtained with the distractor technique introduced by Peterson and Peterson (1959). The third is the forgetting function obtained with a probe technique, in particular the sequential probe popularized by Waugh and Norman (1965). All three are simply special cases of the general formulation suggested at the beginning of the previous chapter.

Memory-span serial-position curves were presented and discussed in the previous chapter. The point that remains in need of further discussion is the effect of presentation rate on these functions. Early studies by Conrad and Hille (1958) and Fraser (1958) gave some support to a decay theory of memory by their finding that fast presentation coupled with fast recall led to better performance than slow presentation coupled with slow recall. In the Fraser study only these two conditions were used, but the difference was quite considerable (.58 versus .37) for older subjects (30–55 age range). In the Conrad and Hille study, presentation and recall rates were varied orthogonally, and the proportion of lists correctly recalled decreased monotonically as mean delay between presentation and recall of individual digits increased (see their Table 1, p. 3). However, other experiments have given opposite results, and Posner (1964a) showed that the decay effect washed out with constrained recall. A review of these early studies will be found in Posner (1963).

By and large, the many studies that have been done are so equivocal that it seems unlikely that any major effect is involved. My own feeling is that presentation rate has no effect on memory span, at least for auditory presentation and ordered recall. I once did some experiments varying presentation rate from 6 digits/sec to one digit every 1.5 seconds, and found no differences at all. (With visual presentation, however, the span may increase with slower presentation rates; see Mackworth, 1962a, 1962b, 1962c). The other point is that investigators have generally given up on the idea of testing decay theory by the simple expedient of varying presentation rate. Although different presentation rates do allow differential time for decay, they also allow differential time for rehearsal, for encoding, and probably for other processes too. All in all, it is not a very analytic technique.

By contrast, the distractor technique introduced by Peterson and Peterson (1959) was a major breakthrough. This technique made it possible to study forgetting in short-term memory over brief periods of time. In retrospect it is simplicity itself, and one wonders why it took so long to be discovered. However, knowledge is often advanced in this way, and problems that appear insolvable at one point in time suddenly appear trivial once the key insight has occurred. Though the distractor method has problems, it continues to be widely used and is still one of the better methods for obtaining forgetting functions in short-term memory.

In the distractor technique, a string of n items is presented to the subject and followed by some interpolated activity designed to prevent the subject from rehearsing the string of items. If you wish, the interpolated activity is designed to distract the subject's attention from the to-be-remembered material. After a designated retention interval, the subject's memory for the string is tested, generally by recall. This presentation-test sequence defines one trial, and usually each subject is given many trials. By varying the length of the retention interval over trials, one is able to trace out a retention curve for each subject, though generally the results are pooled over subjects.

Forgetting functions from an early study are shown in Fig. 7.1. It is clear that the curves are much the same for words and letters, but the value of n (here 1 or 3) makes a large difference. The retention curves shown here for trigrams are quite typical; they fall off rapidly over the first 5–10 seconds, then seem to level off. These (pooled) data are based on practiced subjects; when we come to the section on proactive inhibition the picture will change somewhat. In the particular experiments shown in Fig. 7.1, the interpolated activity happened to be counting backwards from a three-digit number by threes or fours. Many different interpolated activities have been used and, provided similarity relations are controlled, it seems to be relatively unimportant what rehearsal-prevention technique is employed. However, different information-processing demands do affect the retention curve (e.g., Dillon & Reid, 1969; Neimark, Greenhouse, Law, & Weinheimer, 1965).

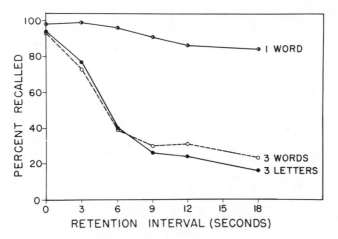

FIG. 7.1. Forgetting functions obtained with the distractor technique. (Based on data from Murdock, 1961a.)

As mentioned previously, a critical parameter of the forgetting function with a distractor technique is the value of n, the number of items in the string. This parameter seems to characterize the number of chunks of information presented, not the number of bits of information presented (Murdock, 1961a). The larger the value of n, the greater the amount of intraunit interference (Melton, 1963). Although Melton presented a family of curves to show how retention varied with n, several additional experimental precautions seem necessary to avoid any possible confounding. Exposure duration should be proportional to the length of the string, so that the subject will not have extra time to rehearse brief lists. The test should be on individual elements of the string rather than on all n elements, since as the value of n varies, not only is there more to remember, but there is also more to recall.

Such a study has recently been conducted at Toronto by Steven T. Carey and Ronald Okada. Each subject was pretested to determine an appropriate reading time for him for each value of n, and this presentation time was then used throughout the experiment. Elements in the string were probed; if $n = 4$, a test might be *?** indicating that the second item was requested. The stimuli were 1–5 consonants selected randomly from a pool of 10 consonants chosen to be low in acoustic similarity. Six different retention intervals were used, and since the experiment was run on a laboratory computer (see Murdock, Dufty, & Okada, 1972, for further details) the stimuli and the order of conditions were randomized. The main results (pooled over the eight subjects) are shown in Fig. 7.2. One does indeed find a family of retention curves fanning out from (approximately) a common origin. As Melton suggested, intraunit interference seems to be a potent factor in short-term memory.

The third retention function is that obtained with a probe technique. Unlike the distractor technique where one usually presents a subspan string for delayed recall, here one generally presents a supraspan string or list for immediate recall. An early study by Anderson (1960) tested for part of the list. In later probe studies only one of

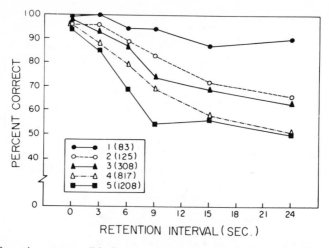

FIG. 7.2. Proportion correct recall for 8 subjects shown 1–5 consonants in a distractor task and tested on only a single consonant. Mean presentation duration is shown in parentheses in the figure legend key. (Unpublished data of S. T. Carey and R. Okada.)

the list items was tested, and the general presumption is that the other list items are in effect the distractors. That is, the subject is encouraged to pay equal attention to each item in the list as it is presented, and the duration of the retention interval is determined by the selection of the target item. With a sequential probe, the probe is item i and the target is item $i + 1$.

One set of results (Waugh & Norman, 1965) with a sequential probe is shown in Fig. 7.3. On each trial, a list of 15 digits was presented and followed by a probe,

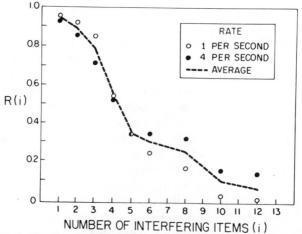

FIG. 7.3. Forgetting function obtained with a sequential probe technique. The ordinate $R(i)$ is proportion of items recalled as a function of number of interfering items i. (Fig. 1 from Waugh & Norman, 1965.)

i.e., one of the (once-presented) items from the list. The subject was to recall the item that had followed the probe. Two different presentation rates were used, but since the differences were not large, one function is shown to characterize the probe-digit forgetting function. Here it is seen to be S-shaped, extending over about the last 8–10 items.

In this article Waugh and Norman show that the function depicted in Fig. 7.3 is characteristic of a number of different experimental paradigms. The fact that it does not vary (very much) with presentation rate is commonly taken as evidence that forgetting in immediate memory is more a function of interference than decay. Other types of probe tests are possible; as has been mentioned, one can use sequential probes, positional probes, even reverse probes. With serial lists the curves are by and large pretty much the same. However, what is very clear is the considerable difference between these functions, singly or collectively, and the probe function for paired associates. The latter spans only the last 2–3 pairs in the list and has a stable asymptote well above zero. Also, serial probe curves generally show a primacy effect when the first position is tested (which it was not here). These differences in the retention functions for serial probes and paired-associate probes are one of the reasons for the view that different theoretical processes are involved in the two cases.

Although considerable theoretical significance has been attached to the probe-digit function shown in Fig. 7.3, a word of caution is in order. Since this experiment used a fixed list length, the number of prior and the number of subsequent items co-varied. As shown in Fig. 6.3 and discussed in the last chapter, different retention curves would be expected to result, depending upon the number of prior items. Thus, there is not a unitary probe-digit forgetting function, and a simple displacement concept would not seem to explain the data even for this one type of forgetting function (Murdock, 1968c).

REPETITION EFFECTS

Since we have three different types of experimental paradigms with which to study serial-order effects, we must consider repetition effects in each. The serial-position curves of memory span map onto the serial-position curves of rote serial learning, and repetition can easily be manipulated with either a distractor technique or a sequential probe technique, or both together. Also, the Hebb repetition effect is a special topic to be considered because of its considerable theoretical interest (Hebb, 1961).

Since it provides a convenient transition, let us start with the Hebb repetition effect. In a typical memory-span experiment, single lists are presented and tested, but each list is a different configuration of items. No lists are repeated. The rationale, of course, is that many replications are necessary to obtain stable data. Suppose, however, that every now and then one particular list is repeated without telling the subject. To be more precise, suppose there is one critical list, and every third trial that is the one shown to the subject. With the presumption that short-term memory is purely a transitory phenomenon consisting only of some ephemeral excitatory activity in the brain, no effects from this manipulation would be expected. That is, performance on this critical list should in no way differ from performance on control (nonrepeated) lists, assuming that the necessary experimental precautions were observed.

Consequently, when this experiment was first performed by Hebb (1961), it came as a surprise to find that, in fact, memory for the repeated list did improve gradually the more it was repeated. These results are shown in Fig. 7.4 and, as can be seen, performance on the repeated series improved consistently. The necessary implication, then, is that something more than very transitory excitatory activity is involved in memory-span tasks.

This effect was replicated and extended by Melton (1963), who showed that the benefits of repetition decreased as the number of lists intervening between successive repetitions increased. More recently, Bower and Winzenz (1969) reported a series of studies in which different group structures were studied. When the grouping is changed (e.g., from 12,345,6789 to 123,4567,89) the repetition effect disappears. Also, when a constant group structure is preserved but only some of the chunks are repeated, it seems necessary to repeat the initial chunk if improved memory is to be obtained. These results were taken as evidence against a nonassociative or bin model. As an alternative, the authors suggested a reallocation hypothesis, wherein grouping determined the storage location in memory and the benefits of repetition were con-

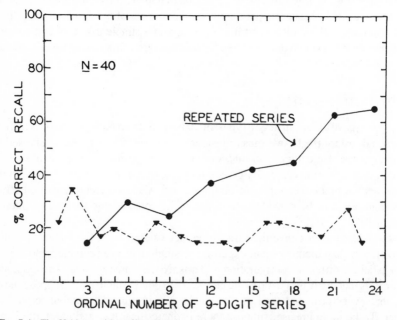

FIG. 7.4. The Hebb repetition effect. One list in a memory-span experiment was repeated every third trial, and this graph shows how its performance improved relative to control (nonrepeated) lists. (Fig. 1 from Hebb, 1961.)

tingent on the correspondence between current presentation and previous memorial representation.

One use of the Hebb repetition technique is as a method of distinguishing between short-term and long-term memory (by those who believe in such a distinction). In one such study, Baddeley and Warrington (1970) compared the performance of amnesic patients and normals when every other list was repeated. Somewhat to their surprise, both groups showed about equal improvement. Two possible explanations they suggest are that amnesic patients are in fact not deficient on one type of long-term memory, or that long-term memory may not underlie the Hebb repetition effect. A further discussion of these and related issues may be found in Warrington (1971). Bartz (1969) found that repetition facilitated both immediate and delayed recall, though the latter benefited more than the former. In a somewhat different vein, Bartz (1972) found that repetition in a dichotic situation benefited only the channel reported second, a finding he interpreted as contrary to a filter-theory interpretation.

Under more conventional procedures where the same list is immediately repeated trial after trial, the serial-position curve gradually flattens out. A reasonable analogy (for the graphs, not the process) might be a weighted sling suspended from two trees, where the length of the sling is gradually shortened by pulling simultaneously at the two points of attachment. Some data from Ward (1937) are shown in Fig. 7.5. A list of 12 nonsense syllables was learned by the serial-anticipation method, and the five curves shown in Fig. 7.5 are the serial-position functions when 3, 5, 7, 9, or 11 of the 12 items were correctly anticipated. There is much similar data of this kind in the early literature, reviewed for instance by Hovland (1951) or McGeoch and Irion (1952). Separation of item and order information has been attempted by Voss (1969).

Explaining serial-position effects and how they change with practice is a very important problem, but analytically this method is probably not as good in studying

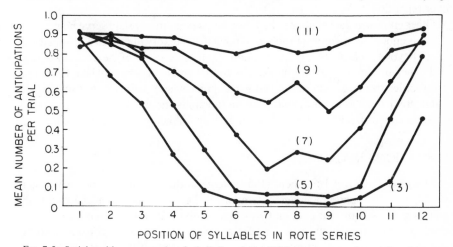

FIG. 7.5. Serial-position curves when 3, 5, 7, 9, and 11 of 12 items are correctly anticipated in rote serial learning. (Fig. 8 from Ward, 1937.)

repetition effects as either the distractor technique or the probe technique. One opinion sometimes expressed is that repetition slows down the rate of forgetting in short-term memory. In fact there is data from the original Peterson and Peterson (1959) study showing that such may not be the case. In Experiment II they varied the duration of the original exposure, so subjects had time for 1, 2, or 4 rehearsals of the trigram before interpolation began. If the data for the vocal group shown in their Table 1 (p. 197) are plotted on semi-log graph paper, it will be seen that all three groups showed essentially the same rate of forgetting; what did change was the asymptote. The implication is that repetition affects the level of forgetting, not its rate.

More extensive data were reported by Hellyer (1962). He had subjects repeat each trigram one, two, four, or eight times before interpolation, and the interpolated activity persisted for 3, 9, 18, or 27 seconds. If one plots these data on semi-log paper it will be found that the asymptote increases appreciably with repetition; by a very approximate technique, I found values of .10, .18, .36, and .55, respectively. However, the rate constant seemed to vary with repetition as well. Actually, there appeared to be one decay rate for one or two presentations but a more gradual decay rate for four or eight presentations.

Repetition effects with a sequential probe technique can be determined by varying the number of presentations of the list which precede the presentation of the probe. It is an RRT paradigm. One set of data from a study by Woodward (1970) is shown in Fig. 7.6. In this experiment one, two, or four presentations of a serial list of ten common English words preceded the presentation of the (sequential or positional) probe. Qualitatively, these results seem a bit different from those results shown in Fig. 7.5. To continue the analogy, here it is as if the front point of the sling's attachment moves up, but the rear point of attachment stays fixed. These functions do seem characterized by an asymptote, and the recency span appears reasonably invariant over repetition.

Other empirical data could be cited, but at this point they would serve no purpose. There is enough to document the obvious point that memory improves with repetition. To go beyond such an obvious observation requires some sort of theoretical position, and it then becomes a meaningful exercise to try to relate theory and data. Few of the serial-order theories seem developed to the point where they can start making detailed predictions as to how serial-position functions should change with repetition, so further understanding of these effects must wait for theoretical developments.

LIMITATIONS IN CAPACITY

The filter theory of Broadbent (1958) suggests that the human memory system should be seen as part of a larger system, one designed to process information in the continual interaction that goes on between an individual and his environment. As a consequence, information-processing demands should have an effect on the encoding, storage, and retrieval of information that occurs in many of the short-term memory tasks that we use. In fact, there is a fair amount of evidence that serial reproduction

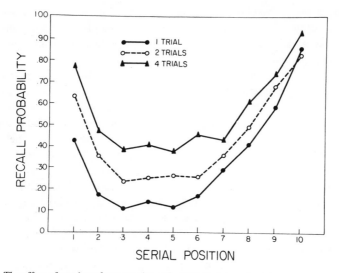

FIG. 7.6. The effect of number of presentations of a 10-item list on short-term memory as tested by a sequential or positional probe. (Fig. 1 from Woodward, 1970.)

is affected by the information-processing load. Before considering such limitations in capacity, let us consider again what is meant by information processing.

Suppose an individual is shown a multi-attribute stimulus such as a large red triangle inverted in the lower right-hand corner of a large card with the figure cross-hatched but the background plain. He is then shown different figures and told to report as quickly as possible whether they differ on an odd or even number of dimensions. For instance, a green upright triangle would differ on two dimensions, but an inverted red triangle without cross-hatching would differ on only one. Hence the responses should be even and odd, respectively. Since regardless of the test stimulus only one of two responses is required, one might claim that the subject was transmitting just one bit of information. Even as the number of relevant dimensions varied over some wide range, still only one bit of information would be transmitted. However, what would seem to be important is the number of relevant dimensions, and that would presumably determine the latency of the binary response. In other words, in order to assess information-processing demands realistically we must determine what internal processing is required, not simply the overt response *per se*.

A simple example of this point comes from Broadbent and Gregory (1965), who found that the compatibility of a simple motor response affected memory for repetition of digits that were concurrently presented. A study by Broadbent and Heron (1962) illustrates the importance of information-processing demands. They gave subjects a digit-cancellation task concurrently with a modified memory-span task. In effect, the subjects had to listen to spoken letters of the alphabet and report the one letter in ten that was repeated, while at the same time crossing out digits with the target digit varying haphazardly. The former was considered to be the subsidiary task, and performance on the primary task (digit cancellation) varied both with the memory load and the age of the subjects. (Aging and memory is a topic on which a fair amount of research has been done, but it will not be considered here. The interested reader might consult Broadbent, 1971, or Drachman & Leavitt, 1972.)

Probably the most extensive work in this area is that of Posner. In an early paper (Posner, 1964b) he proposed a three-fold classification of information-processing tasks in terms of information-conserving, information-reducing, and information-creating operations. In a conservation task all the information in the input would be represented in the output. In a reducing task there would be less in the output than in the input (i.e., a many-to-one mapping), while in a creation situation it would be the other way around. There are applications, particularly in the reaction-time area, but also in the area of coding. As illustrated in Murdock (1968d) this classification is similar to the redundancy-reducing, redundancy-preserving, and redundancy-increasing codes of information theory (e.g., Abramson, 1963).

Posner and Rossman (1965) required subjects to perform information transforms of varying degrees of complexity and assessed their effect on memory. On each trial a list of eight digits was spoken to subjects at a rate of 30 digits per minute. Subjects were to transform either the last zero, one, two, or three pairs in one of four ways: reverse them, add them, report high or low and odd or even, or give a binary response according to the interaction. (The number of transforms and their complexity were orthogonal.) Memory for the first pair of digits was tested, and it decreased appreciably as a function of both number and complexity of the transforms. Thus, the more information processing performed and the greater the information reduction achieved, the less accurate memory was.

The importance of similarity effects in long-term memory has long been known, and now there is considerable evidence for similarity effects in short-term memory. They will be discussed in a later section of this chapter, but here it should be noted that this work on informational transforms and their difficulty can provide a dimension independent from that of similarity. This point was made again by Posner and Konick (1966), who were able to show that forgetting can proceed quite independently of the similarity of the interpolated task. Also, they attempted to determine whether forgetting was more a function of differential forgetting during the retention interval or competition among traces at the time of recall. They referred to these two views as an acid-bath versus a trace-comparison process. Since the level of performance seemed to vary more with the length of time an item was in store, and also seemed to be independent of the strength of the item, the authors preferred the acid-bath to the trace-comparison interpretation. These and related matters were later discussed in a review article by Posner (1967).

An even simpler demonstration of capacity limitations is the prefix effect first reported by Conrad (1958, 1960a). In a standard memory-span task, the subject is instructed simply to prefix his recall with the redundant digit zero. That is, if the string is 7660516 then the subject is to report 07660516. The digit zero is redundant since it is known to the subject in advance and given in the instructions, not in the list. When the presented list is eight digits long, Conrad found that adding the redundant digit zero appreciably reduced the frequency with which the string could be accurately reproduced. Thus, even such a simple requirement as adding a prefix can, under the right conditions, have a considerable effect on performance.

This work has been considerably extended in the collaborative research of Crowder and Morton (e.g., Crowder, 1971; Crowder & Morton, 1969; Morton & Holloway, 1970). They have found both prefix and suffix effects, where a suffix is simply an extra item presented by the experimenter which need not be recalled by the subject. Both a prefix and a suffix depress the serial-position curve, though for different reasons (Morton, 1970). Whether or not an effect (i.e., impaired recall) is obtained depends upon the particular conditions. These authors have also suggested a model to accommodate some of the effects of short-term memory (Crowder & Morton, 1969). They suggest precategorical storage of both acoustic and visual information, though with rather different time constants. This model is closely related to that of Sperling (Sperling, 1963, 1967; Sperling & Speelman, 1970) in that both emphasize the importance of brief sensory memory and the transfer of information from a precategorical to a postcategorical form.

Although the experimental data seem clear enough, there are several interpretive problems with prefix and suffix effects. One is simply the comparison problem. To say that the magnitude of, say, the prefix effect is large means that recall of eight digits alone will be much better than the recall of eight digits prefixed with a redundant ninth digit. But presumably recall of eight digits prefixed with a redundant ninth digit is better than the recall of nine (nonredundant) digits. Around the memory span, differences in list length have a large effect, so that adding a single item can drop the curve perhaps 25 percentage points. But the redundant prefix (or suffix) falls in between, so from this point of view the effect does not seem quite so large. Prefix and suffix effects must be intermediate between list-length effects, and list-length effects are the proper basis of comparison.

Further, their proper interpretation is probably secondary to serial-position effects. That is, variations in the serial-position curve as a function of such independent variables as have been studied in this connection will be difficult to interpret properly until we have a firmer grasp on the basic serial-order effects themselves. Thus, it seems to me, one should concentrate on trying to understand why serial-position functions are as they are, before we try to explain why variations in redundant elements have the effects that they do. However, these points aside, it is still true that the well-documented prefix and suffix effects are yet another illustration of the capacity limitations in short-term memory. Also, they seem to be useful tools to study modality effects and processes related to speech perception (e.g., Crowder, 1973).

Finally, an interesting linear relationship between memory span and scanning rate has been reported by Cavanagh (1972). It seems that the greater the memory span as measured by conventional means, the faster the scanning rate as measured in the paradigm of Sternberg (1966). The slope of the function is very close to 250 msec. One way such a result could occur would be if there was a fixed limitation or capacity to short-term memory, and one interrogation of the system required 250 msec. As one varied the type of material from digits to nonsense syllables, the span would decrease and the scanning time per item would increase, but the product of these two would stay constant. Unfortunately, as Cavanagh notes, there are several alternative explanations. Also, interpretive problems with the scanning paradigm may make this invariance hard to explain.

CHUNKING

Given the severe capacity limitations of short-term memory, one method of reducing these limitations and so expanding our capacities is by chunking. As commonly used, this term refers either to regrouping or recoding the stimulus information presented. Thus, if the unbroken seven-item string 7321408 was translated into 732, pause, 1408 one would have one type of chunking (regrouping); or if 110100000011 (binary) was translated into 6403 (octal), one would have the other type of chunking (recoding). The importance and usefulness of chunking was first suggested by Miller (1956), and as experimental evidence he actually used a demonstration similar to the binary-to-octal translation example given above.

This influential paper by Miller demonstrated two main points about chunking in short-term memory. First, that memory as measured by memory span was more a function of the number of chunks of information than the number of bits of information. Second, that memory span, at least for binary digits, could be dramatically increased by a recoding technique. This latter point has recently been documented by Slak (1970), who used a phonemic recoding for decimal digits. For some experiments, two dedicated subjects learned the code (how to translate digit triples into phoneme syllables), and their memory span increased from 9.3 to 13.6 digits. In another experiment, a group of 20 subjects learned the code for a reduced ensemble, and their serial-learning performance was considerably better than a control group. These experiments by Slak clearly support the utility of recoding, but the results were not in perfect agreement with a constant-chunk hypothesis. If three decimal digits are considered to be three chunks, but one recoded phonemic syllable is considered to be a single chunk, then the memory span should have increased by a factor of three. It clearly did not. Perhaps one interpretive difficulty here is the *a priori* definition of the unit of measurement (i.e., chunk).

An early study by Murdock (1961a) showed that chunks were a viable concept in a Peterson and Peterson distractor task. As shown in Fig. 7.1, three words were forgotten much as three letters (CCC trigrams), but three letters (these CCC trigrams) which did not make a word were much different from other constellations of letters which did in fact make a word (top curve in Fig. 7.1). These findings were extended by Melton (1963), who presented a family of curves much like those shown in Fig. 7.2, and this regularity was one line of evidence he cited in arguing for the continuity of short-term and long-term memory.

Evidence of a different sort comes from a study by McLean and Gregg (1967). Their subjects learned a 24-letter serial list by a study-test method in which different groupings were used. The subjects examined index cards one at a time at their own rate, and on each card there was a group of 1,3,4,6, or 8 letters. Interresponse times were obtained both for the final study trial and for an (unexpected) backward recall test; when they finished learning, the subjects had to recite the list in reverse order. The authors used a derived measure and showed that in fact interresponse times within and between what the experiments had defined as chunks for that subject were clearly reflected in the latency of recall. Even in the one-letter condition, grouping effects existed, but they were of course more idiosyncratic than the other conditions.

Severin and Rigby (1963) found that, for telephone numbers, a 3-4 grouping gave better results than groupings of 1-3-3, 2-2-3, or 1-2-2-2. In several studies Wickelgren (1964, 1967) varied the size of the rehearsal grouping. Digits were presented at a one-second rate and subjects were instructed to rehearse in nonoverlapping sets of two, three, four, or five. In the various experiments, list length ranged from 6–10. In general, a rehearsal group or chunk of size three was optimal, both for ordered and free recall. For rehearsal, a chunk size of four was only marginally inferior, so these data suggest that a chunk size of 3–4 digits is best for short serial lists.

In a different vein, a series of studies by Lindley (Lindley, 1963, 1965; Lindley & Nedler, 1965; Schaub & Lindley, 1964) demonstrated the efficacy of recoding cues in remembering trigrams. In a Peterson and Peterson task, the subject might be presented eXPOse, or SOUth, or BUTter. He was to verbalize and remember only the three letters appearing in capitals, but in all cases the letters were part of an English word. Under these conditions the recoding cues (the English words themselves) facilitated retention of low meaningful trigrams, as did decoding cues as well (i.e., presenting dou---ess at the time of recall, given the initial presentation of douBTLess). One need not embed the trigram in words but can instead obtain similar results by using associations (e.g., zodiac is a common associate to ZOJ, but zig is uncommon). An additional finding of these studies is that the ease of decoding (i.e., the ease of extracting ZOJ given that one remembers zodiac or zig) is another important variable, an effect also reported by Underwood and Erlebacher (1965) for multitrial free recall and for paired-associate learning.

Several studies have tried to compare the relative effectiveness of meaningfulness and pronounceability as mnemonic aids. One can do this by varying independently these two factors, and the critical comparison is between low-meaningful units that are easy to pronounce versus high-meaningful units that are difficult to pronounce. Unfortunately, conflicting results have been reported. Gibson, Bishop, Schiff, and Smith (1964) used trigrams such as OKR and IFB and made them either pronounceable (KOR and BIF) or meaningful (RKO and FBI). Both on item recognition and on free recall, the meaningful arrangement led to better performance than the pronounceable relationship, in this study.

Contrary results have been reported by Laughery and Pinkus (1968). They used 12-letter strings, and an example of the 2 × 2 conditions is UOBJCBAIRGFT, GOCDERTEGDOS, CIABTUCIODDS, and BINREDGETSOD. They presented the letters sequentially on an in-line display, and they used five different presentation rates. Their main results are shown here in Fig. 7.7 and, as can be seen, pronounceability conferred a greater advantage than meaningfulness at all presentation rates. The fact that the four curves are more or less parallel (even though the interaction was statistically significant) seems to rule out several possible explanations in terms of differential encoding times for the two types. The reason for the Gibson *et al.* results conflicting with those of Laughery and Pinkus is not at all clear. It could be a reflection of the fact that serial ordering was required in the latter study but not the former, or it could be the difference between simultaneous versus successive presentation of the stimulus material.

Actually, there is little point in trying to determine if one study is correct and the other incorrect. After all, pronounceability and meaningfulness are quite different dimensions, and (at least at present) there is no way one can compare variations in one with variations in another. They are incommensurable, so while one can make sensible comparisons within either dimension singly, crossdimensional comparisons are of necessity less fruitful. The important point is that, taken together, these studies demonstrate that both meaningfulness and pronounceability can affect chunking in short-term memory. (The Gibson study actually compared the effect of these manipulations on perceptual thresholds, as well as on memory, and found the opposite direction in the difference there. The commensurability point obviously does not apply to this comparison.)

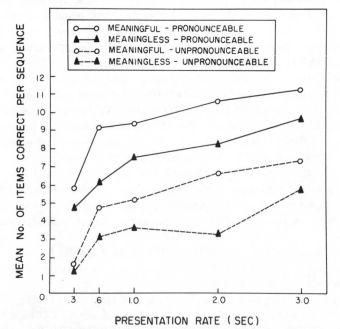

FIG. 7.7. Recall of 12-letter strings presented at different rates and varying both in pronounceability and meaningfulness. (Fig. 1 from Laughery & Pinkus, 1968.)

The importance of grouping as a basis for organization has recently been reviewed by Bower (1972a). In addition to the work reported in the Bower and Winzenz monograph, there are indications that one can obtain facilitation in a variety of ways. Not only is there temporal grouping, but there could be proximity in time or space, category membership, or even syntactic constructions. It is interesting to note the re-emergence of the old Gestalt principles of figure-ground relationships as a possible basis for memory organization. If these principles turn out to be useful in understanding chunking, then it would be yet another illustration of Broadbent's point that perception and memory have many aspects in common.

A theoretical framework for conceptualizing chunking and coding in serial lists has been proposed by Johnson (1970). He suggests that (*a*) a code is the memorial representation of information, (*b*) a chunk is a sequence represented in memory by a single code, (*c*) the code includes not only the item, but also the order information, and (*d*) one must first recover the code before it is possible to recall overtly any of the information represented in a chunk. The basic dependent variable is a conditional probability. Specifically, this variable is the probability of an error in the recall of item $i + 1$, given correct recall of item i. The transition-error probability, or TEP, can go across a chunk boundary. If the grouping were 769, pause, 0516, then the TEP would be the probability of incorrectly recalling 0, given the correct recall of 9.

This work began by investigating TEPs of sentences from the point of view of a phrase-structure grammar. Discussion of this work can be found in Johnson (1968) or Kintsch (1970b). For unrelated items, the grouping is provided by the experimenter in terms of the format of presentation, so one could simply show the subject a list of items with spaces to correspond to whatever groupings one wishes. The general finding is that TEPs at chunk boundaries are higher than they are within chunks, which suggests that the difficulty is in gaining access to a chunk.

Johnson's data consistently show that the TEP across chunk boundaries is greater than TEPs within chunk boundaries. Within the first chunk, TEPs reflect the amount of information yet to decode, whether measured by the number or by the size of the remaining chunks. Also, when lists are constructed of strings and a given sequence is practiced for a number of trials, changing the order of items within chunks had an adverse effect on performance, though not as much as replacing items within a chunk.

To conclude this section on chunking, it should be noted that these effects are not restricted to serial-memory tasks. They seem to show up more generally in such sequential tasks as motor skills. Here the concepts of information theory are probably more strictly applicable, and by now there is a fair amount of evidence attesting to their utility. For an experimental example see Murdock (1968d); for further discussion see Broadbent (1971) or Fitts and Posner (1967).

SIMILARITY EFFECTS

In this section we shall consider some of the more important studies of the effect of similarity on memory for serial order. To be consistent, we should first have a clear theory of loss of item and order information. Then, it might be the case that similarity affected memory for item information or memory for order information, or that one type of similarity affected one, and another type of similarity the other. However, we do not yet have an established model accommodating item and order effects, so we must blur the distinction. This is a pity, because it might be more profitable to study similarity effects in a theoretical framework than to ask whether short- and long-term memory can be isolated by appropriate similarity manipulations.

The classic study in this area is by Conrad (1964), who showed that acoustic similarity had a deleterious effect in a memory-span task. On each trial, a list of six consonants was shown to subjects who had to recall them in order. The vocabulary or ensemble was the 10 letters B,C,P,T,V,F,M,N,S, and X, of which six were selected at random for presentation on each trial. Because of the ambiguities that would otherwise arise, Conrad here limited his analysis to single substitution errors, those cases where there was exactly one erroneous consonant reported. Since the ensemble was restricted to 10 letters, a 10 × 10 confusion matrix was constructed, where the columns represented the letter presented and the rows the letter recalled. The off-diagonal entries in this matrix were clearly unequally distributed, showing systematic patterns of some sort in the error data. To determine of what sort, Conrad compared this confusion matrix with the comparable one obtained from a listening test. These consonants were spoken against a background of white noise, and the errors were perceptual in nature. The similarity between these two error matrices was striking, and Conrad (1964) suggested that ". . . the memory trace, in this kind of situation, has an acoustic or verbal basis . . . [p. 82]."

Confirmation was not long in coming. Wickelgren (1965a) used the full alphanumeric vocabulary (letters and digits) with slightly longer lists and found that, for consonants, acoustic errors predominated. There were no systematic confusions involving digits, which are acoustically more distinctive than letters. Wickelgren also pointed out that the source of confusions could either be acoustic (stimulus determined) or articulatory (speech-motor), since these dimensions were perfectly correlated in the stimulus material.

In a subsequent paper Wickelgren (1965c) tested a distinctive-features model for short-term forgetting. Neither vowels nor consonants are unitary, but both can be analyzed into constituent features, such as place of articulation, openness of the vocal tract, etc. Using random permutations of words which differed only in the vowel sound (e.g., LICK, LECK, LACK, LOOK, LUCK, and LOCK), Wickelgren examined recall errors in terms of different distinctive-feature systems of phonetics. He suggested that a two-dimensional phonetic classification was appropriate (the two mentioned above) and that a vowel may be coded as a set of two distinctive features which may be forgotten independently. A similar analysis (Wickelgren, 1966b) was also suggested for English consonants, but with a four-dimensional feature classification (voicing, nasality, openness, and place of articulation).

Several studies also raised the question of the theoretical status of similarity effects. Wickelgren (1965d) showed that, in a retroactive-inhibition short-term paradigm, acoustic similarity played much the same role as the more traditional similarity manipulations in long-term memory. Wickelgren notes that, for serial learning, the transfer and retroaction surface of Osgood (1953, p. 532) suggests negative transfer and retroaction as similarity increases, which is what he found. Then, a separate manipulation of proactive and retroactive effects showed comparable results for the retention of single letters (Wickelgren, 1966c). Finally, differential results for item and for order information were reported (Wickelgren, 1965e). When phonemically similar or phonemically different lists were to be recalled, order recall was worse for the former but item recall was either no different or better. These results, along with other findings reported earlier, were considered to be more consistent with an associative rather than a nonassociative model of short-term memory.

Separation of acoustic and articulatory factors has been attempted by Hintzman (1965, 1967). In the first study it was pointed out that the letter P, on an articulatory basis, is more similar to B; but on an acoustic basis, it is more similar to T as both P and T begin with an unvoiced stop. The Conrad listening data showed that the P-T confusion was more frequent than that between P and B, but the recall confusion went the other way. In the second study, Hintzman used the data reported by Miller and Nicely (1955) to suggest that the place of articulation (front, middle, back) was not a particularly salient dimension for perceptual (acoustic) confusions. Consequently, if that was represented in the memory data, it would suggest an articulatory basis for encoding. With the unvoiced consonant sounds pa, ta, ka, and the voiced consonant sounds ba, da, ga (in each case place of articulation being front, middle, and back, respectively), he found both dimensions represented in the memory errors. The general import of these two studies then is that the underlying mechanism is more likely to be articulatory than acoustic.

If the internal representation (and consequently the confusion data) were acoustic, it might mean some auditory image was evoked by the visual presentation of a verbal item. If on the other hand it were articulatory, then it might mean there was some vocal, or subvocal, pronunciation or rehearsal of the item, and this kinesthetic or proprioceptive feedback would underlie the memory trace. While Hintzman favors the latter, he points out that the articulatory hypothesis could also assign it a more central locus. To test the central versus peripheral issue, one could monitor the subvocal activity of a subject and determine its role in the memory confusions. In one such study Glassman (1972) did exactly this; subjects either inhibited their subvocal activity or did not, which was assessed by electromyographic records. It turned out that the proportion of errors that were phonemic decreased appreciably under the inhibition condition, thus implicating the peripheral speech-motor activity as a significant factor in the so-called acoustic confusion effect.

Conrad (1967) has used acoustic confusions as a means of trying to compare an interference-theory prediction with a decay-theory prediction of forgetting. He suggested that differential similarity patterns would be predicted over a retention interval in a Peterson distractor task, and the results were interpreted as a loss in discriminative (i.e., acoustic) characteristics in accord with the decay prediction. In another line of research he has studied short-term memory processes in the deaf (Conrad, 1970, 1971; Conrad & Rush, 1965), and his general findings seem to suggest two kinds of deaf children. One type seems to rely on articulatory coding, while the other type depends upon a different coding which may be based on shape. Reading consonant sequences aloud or silently made no difference for the first group, but the second group performed worse under the vocalization condition. This result is to be contrasted with normal subjects, where vocalization facilitates recall (Conrad & Hull, 1968; Murray, 1965, 1966, 1967, 1968). In a recent developmental study Conrad (1972a) found that vocalization instructions affected the naming behavior of children but that, with vocalization constant, the naming facilitated recall.

Given the importance of acoustic encoding in short-term memory, the nature of the memory deficit (if any) in the deaf becomes particularly interesting. One suggestion made by Hermelin and O'Connor (1973) is that deaf children suffer an impairment in the retention of order information. In one study they presented the three letters of a trigram so that the temporal (first to last) order was uncoupled from the spatial (left to right) order. On a recognition test the three letters were presented sequentially, either in the same temporal or the same spatial order. A "yes" response was appropriate only when the temporal order of the probe matched the temporal order of the trigram, and control children seldom erred. In contrast, the deaf children showed a high false-alarm rate, thus suggesting that perhaps an initial spatial encoding was overriding whatever temporal encoding might have occurred. Other interpretations are possible, of course, but the general point is that deaf children seem to differ from normal children in the encoding or retention of order information.

Of course, the picture is not anywhere near as clear as has been suggested so far. Wickelgren (1969b) has pointed out some of the problems involved in trying to infer, from data from confusion matrices, the coding dimensions actually used. Shulman (1970, 1972) and Raser (1972b) have presented evidence implicating semantic coding in short-term memory, and Bregman (1968) has found forgetting curves for semantic, phonetic, graphic, and contiguity cues spanning an extensive range, and they do not look all that different. Also, if in fact subvocal articulatory factors were crucial, then one would expect a manipulation such as delayed auditory feedback to have an adverse effect on recall. In fact it does not, at least not with a sequential probe technique (Murdock, 1967d). Even when intralist similarity was increased on an associative, acoustic, or visual similarity dimension (in the hopes of thereby making the articulatory dimension more important), delayed auditory feedback still had no deleterious effect on recall (Levy & Murdock, 1968). A possible rapprochement suggested by various authors (e.g., Glassman, 1972; Levy, 1971; Peterson & Johnson, 1971; Shulman, 1971; Tell, 1972) is that short-term memory is a flexible system which can encode on a multiplicity of dimensions. No one dimension is crucial, but when the experimental conditions are such as to make one dimension relatively useless, another dimension or dimensions will be used instead. Clearly one can process or encode stimulus information along a variety of dimensions (Craik & Lockhart, 1972); whether the errors we obtain in our confusion matrices reflect this chameleon-like process is not yet a settled matter.

At a more general level, one of the conclusions frequently encountered in the current literature (e.g., Adams, 1967; Baddeley & Patterson, 1971; Kintsch & Buschke, 1969) is the assertion that short-term memory is an acoustic system or uses acoustic coding, while long-term memory is a semantic system or uses semantic coding. Baddeley (1966a) compared immediate serial recall from an acoustically similar ensemble (MAD, MAN, MAT, MAP, CAD, CAN, CAT, CAP) with serial recall from a semantically similar ensemble (BIG, LONG, BROAD, GREAT, HIGH, TALL, LARGE, WIDE) and, compared to a control group, the former was recalled much worse. To separate acoustic and formal similarity he compared sets like BOUGHT, SORT, TAUT, CAUGHT, WART with sets like ROUGH, COUGH, THROUGH, DOUGH, BOUGH and found the former were more poorly recalled. Then, in a comparable experiment on long-term memory (20-minute retention interval), Baddeley (1966b) found that, after four original learning trials, performance on the retest was worse for the semantically similar lists. The implication he drew from these results was that short-term memory used an acoustic coding system while long-term memory used a semantic coding system.

To isolate encoding, storage, and retrieval, Baddeley (1968) made the acoustic-semantic similarity comparison under a variety of experimental conditions. In a distractor task the slopes of the two functions (i.e., the forgetting curve for semantically-similar and acoustically-similar strings) were parallel, thus ruling out different decay rates. If encoding was on an acoustic basis then white noise during the retention interval should lower performance, but it did not. Finally, for retrieval effects the Wickelgren phonemic-associative hypothesis might predict difference in the items following similar items (i.e., Ranschburg-like effects with similar rather than repeated items). This effect was not found; instead, the difficulties occurred on the acoustically-similar items themselves. Thus, the effects of acoustic similarity were seen as occurring in retrieval, and possibly they were due to the overloading of retrieval cues.

However, it is a long inferential step from finding the presence or absence of a particular similarity manipulation to drawing conclusions about the nature of the encoding dimension in human memory. The main problem is to isolate encoding, storage, and retrieval; that is, to insure that the similarity manipulation affects only one of them. The experiment by Baddeley (1968) is at least a first step in this direction. However, by now there seems to be such a variety of positive results that have been obtained that one is tempted to assert that almost any type of similarity manipulation could in principle be effective, if only one were ingenious enough to find the appropriate conditions of testing. And there is certainly evidence for acoustic effects in long-term memory (e.g., Brown & McNeill, 1966; Bruce & Crowley, 1970; Dale & McGlaughlin, 1971; McGlaughlin & Dale, 1971; Nelson & Rothbart, 1972).

It seems that the question of whether or not semantic similarity affects short-term (or, more accurately, primary) memory is still with us. On the one hand, Shulman (1971) argues that it can, though whether it does will depend upon the task demands. On the other hand, Baddeley (1972b) argues that there is no evidence that it can, and those cases where it does can be attributable to retrieval rules. The evidence I find reasonably compelling is a finding from Murdock and vom Saal (1967) that the proportion of correct recalls at a 3-second retention interval in a distractor task was .43 for different-category trigrams (e.g., EEL SCREW LOUNGE) but .67 for same-category trigrams (e.g., GRAY BROWN RED). *Post hoc* one could claim that retrieval from a single category was somehow easier than from three different categories. Equally plausibly, on a *post hoc* basis, one could argue that there is more intraunit interference to lead to more forgetting in the one-category than the three-category case. Whichever *hoc* one postulates, the fact remains that after a very short retention interval there are large differences in recall as a function of semantic (category) similarity. It might be suggested that the two curves asymptote at different levels, so a correction for secondary-memory effects would eliminate these so-called primary-memory differences. In reply, it has been noted that secondary-memory effects are not all that permanent, so corrected against a long-term asymptote of zero these effects are genuinely short-term.

However, it is still the case that the original Conrad findings demonstrating the importance of phonemic factors in short-term memory have stood up very well. They have been extensively replicated, and there really can be no doubt about them. The empirical results are quite clear; what is less so is the proper theoretical interpretation. It now seems very unlikely that we shall be able to infer the basis of memory coding from examination of errors under experimentally controlled conditions. Instead, we shall have to start with theories or models and see if the experimental consequences agree with the extant data. About the only extensive work of this kind has been the phonemic model of Sperling and Speelman (1970). Whatever the deficiencies of this model, it is at least a serious attempt to cope with some of the acoustic effects of short-term memory. The interested reader is encouraged to use this paper as a point of departure and see if he can increase our theoretical understanding of similarity and confusion effects in human memory.

Finally, let me close this section on similarity effects with an editorial comment. It is quite popular these days to try to infer the nature of the encoding dimension(s) from manipulations of similarity in the stimulus material. Thus, papers include phrases such as semantic encoding or phonemic encoding. In addition to the comments made above, it should be remembered that (*a*) we have no adequate measures of similarity as a dimension, and (*b*) we have no adequate methods for isolating memory effects in the encoding process. In terms of the first point, we are still measuring similarity in the same way researchers in the verbal learning area did fifty years ago. The doctrine of identical elements is with us again; just as the nonsense syllables TGR, GLT, LRG, and RLT were considered similar because they contained repeated letters, so today the words ROUGH, TOUGH, GUFF, and LUFF would be considered similar because of common phonemes. More powerful methods of scaling exist.

As for the second point, while perhaps we can separate storage processes from retrieval processes, there is no model-free way to isolate encoding processes from either. It is sometimes claimed that any dimension that demonstrates release from proactive inhibition must be an encoding dimension, but how does one separate retrieval and encoding? In the last analysis, they cannot be independent. Everything that is stored must have been encoded, and everything that is retrieved must have been both encoded and stored. At least until we are wiser than we are now, we had best remember that encoding, storage, and retrieval are sequential and inter-dependent processes, and one localizes the effect of a particular experimental ma-nipulation only at the cost of an extensive set of theoretical assumptions.

PROACTIVE INHIBITION

The importance of proactive inhibition as a factor in forgetting from long-term memory has been recognized since the influential paper of Underwood (1957). At first, proactive inhibition seemed to play no role in forgetting from short-term mem-ory, and this result was one of the reasons that people once thought that short-term and long-term memory were fundamentally different. The proactive-inhibition evidence came from studies of the distractor technique which, typically, tested sub-jects for many (e.g., 48) trials. If this inhibition did operate, then (it was thought) performance should gradually deteriorate over the course of the testing session. But, when one looks at performance in successive blocks (say quarters; Trials 1–12, 13–24, 25–36, and 37–48) it does not. Ergo, there is no proactive inhibition in short-term memory.

The problem was that we took too large a block. If instead of looking at perfor-mance in the first, second, third, and fourth block one looks at performance on the first, second, third, and fourth trial, quite a different picture emerges. As first report-ed by Keppel and Underwood (1962) and soon replicated by Loess (1964), there is little or no forgetting over the retention interval of the very first item presented. How-ever, the second item shows some forgetting, the third still more, and perhaps the fourth as well, though a steady state is soon approached. Illustrative data is shown in Fig. 7.8, where proportion of correct responses as a function of retention interval is

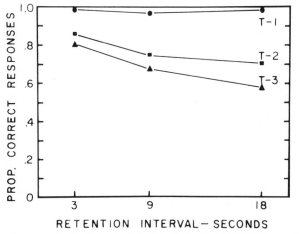

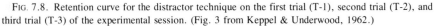

FIG. 7.8. Retention curve for the distractor technique on the first trial (T-1), second trial (T-2), and third trial (T-3) of the experimental session. (Fig. 3 from Keppel & Underwood, 1962.)

shown for the first trial (T-1), the second trial (T-2), and the third trial (T-3). The progressive decrease in these curves illustrates proactive inhibition.

Not only is there proactive inhibition in short-term memory, but there is also release from proactive inhibition. As first demonstrated by Wickens, Born, and Allen (1963), if one changes the nature of the to-be-remembered item say on Trial 4 then, compared to an unchanged control group, recall of the post-shift material improves dramatically. In some cases recall is restored to its original (Trial 1) level, so the release may be complete. In the original study the material was either letters or digits. The two experimental groups started either with letter- or with digit-trigrams and then shifted on Trial 4 to the other class of material. The two control groups continued on with whichever class they had started with. Comparable effects seem to occur with recognition (Carey, 1973; Fozard, 1969; Gorfein & Jacobson, 1972; Petrusic & Dillon, 1972).

Since this original paper, Wickens has investigated release from proactive inhibition along many different conceptual dimensions. A summary of some of these findings is given in a theoretical paper (Wickens, 1970) in which he reports that release will occur if the change is in orthography, taxonomic class, semantic differential, sense impression, word frequency, acoustic-articulatory dimensions, imagery, or mode of presentation. More recently he has suggested that these dimensions may be grouped into three main categories, with semantic categories showing the greatest changes, physical categories the next, and marking-syntactic categories having little or no effect (Wickens, 1972). The theoretical interpretation he suggests is in terms of encoding processes, where the characteristics of the stimulus material determine how the subject will encode the material at the time of presentation. The magnitude of the release effect tells us how salient or important this encoding dimension is in memory.

One of the variables that turns out to be important in determining proactive effects in short-term memory is the time between items, or intertrial interval. As demonstrated by Peterson and Gentile (1965) and by Loess and Waugh (1967), interference effects seem to dissipate as the intertrial interval increases. The latter study showed that the effects essentially disappear at about two minutes. Another manifestation of this effect is in the intertrial dependencies in a distractor technique. Successive trials are not independent. In some unpublished data analyses, I have found that the probability of correct recall on Trial $n + 1$ was about .6 given incorrect recall on Trial n, but only about .4 given correct recall on Trial n. The obvious interpretation is that when an item is correctly recalled it will function as a source of interference for the next trial, with a very short intertrial interval. When it is not recalled, whatever intertrial interval there is derives from the item presented, and the intertrial interval measured this way is much longer. Of course, this temporal comparison is confounded with differential interference effects from remembered and forgotten items, and careful experimental control would be necessary to sort them out.

One possible interpretation of proactive-inhibition effects is in terms of a limited-capacity notion. The so-called proactive-inhibition effect could be simply a manifestation of the more general reduced-primacy effects one usually sees with subjects who have had practice on short-term memory tasks. If so, then in terms of a limited-capacity hypothesis there might well be an increased recency effect. This would show up in improved retention of the interpolated task over trials. Retention of the interpolated task is seldom measured but, when it was, Murdock (1966c) found the expected results. However, others (e.g., Crowder, 1968; Frost & Jahnke, 1968) have criticized this view, and by now there is enough published and unpublished data to make me less confident that my original suggestion is the correct interpretation of proactive-inhibition effects in a distractor task.

Another suggestion, which is perhaps less contentious, is the distinction between inter- and intratrial inhibition. As in studies, for instance, by Murdock (1961a) and Wickelgren (1966c), one can vary systematically the number of (irrelevant) items preceding the to-be-remembered item (see Fig. 6.3). Then, when one is looking at intertrial proaction effects, one varies the number of preceding trials; but when one is looking at intratrial proaction effects, one varies the number of preceding items. Actually, both inter- and intratrial effects qualitatively seem to be much the same. Both seem to increase over the range 0–4 and thereafter either stay constant or decrease. As the number of prior trials or the number of prior items increases over this range, proactive inhibition increases, but further increases in either the number of prior items or prior trials seem to have no further adverse effect on memory.

Despite the admitted importance of proactive inhibition in human memory, statements to the effect that it is the "cause" of forgetting are perhaps an exaggeration. Imagine a family of retention curves fanning out from a common origin, as shown for instance in Figs. 7.8 or 6.3. What such data mean is that there are two "causes" of forgetting: inhibition and time. If you conditionalize on the time dimension, then indeed number of prior items has a clear effect. But if you conditionalize on inhibition, then number of subsequent items (or time) has a clear effect. Thus, it is (at least) a bivariate situation with number of prior and number of subsequent items affecting memory. It is an oversimplification to focus only on one of them and elevate it to causal status.

Another interpretive point is that proactive inhibition is basically an empirical effect not an explanation. That is, retention does deteriorate as the number of prior items increases; why? An interference-theory explanation might be that presentation of an item changes the associative hierarchy but that these changes spontaneously recover over time. If these changes were restricted to recent items, then such a mechanism might constitute an explanation. Another possibility might be that the more items presented, the more items the subject remembers, but the more difficult recall would be because of the selection problem. If a three-word triplet were presented with 0, 1, 2, or 3 prior triplets (either inter- or intralist), surely the subject's recognition ability would be quite good, so from that point of view he could be said to remember them. Perhaps the poor performance on the recall task reflects the increasing difficulty of retrieving a specified subset from a growing ensemble under conditions of poor discriminability.

From this point of view it is not surprising that there is no effect of intertrial interval in memory span (Conrad, 1960b). Past three or four items there is no further effect, and since memory-span lists tend to be six or more, the availability of prior lists would not have any effect on memory for the current list. Or, more accurately, since the difference between two and four prior items or trials is very slight in a distractor task, so the spacing of prior lists in a memory-span task should be quite inconsequential.

A further implication of this view is that proactive inhibition with cued recall should be quite different from proactive inhibition with serial lists, and so it is. At least with paired associates, primacy decreases and recency increases, but there is no overall impairment with practice (Murdock, 1964). This point is discussed by Broadbent (1971), and I would agree completely with his statement that, "The antithesis . . . is sufficiently clear to make one confident that it is the difference between the two techniques for assessing memory which is responsible [p. 342]." We must be very careful, then, when we talk about forgetting from short-term memory. It is very task-dependent and, for that matter, very measure-dependent. We should be wary of overgeneralizing our results.

Very generally, then, what I am trying to suggest is that proactive-inhibition effects in short-term memory may be less a forgetting phenomenon than a discriminability phenomenon. Said slightly differently, we may have considerably overestimated the amount of forgetting that occurs in a distractor task. If the subject completely forgets all previously presented items (or waits two minutes or has not experienced any previous trials), then the data clearly show that he does not forget while counting backward. If he remembers the previous trials or items, then he is quite likely to err in his attempted recall. But failing to recall is not necessarily equivalent to forgetting. Data and interpretation not inconsistent with this viewpoint may be found in Gardiner, Craik, and Birtwistle (1972).

MULTICHANNEL EFFECTS

All of the topics considered so far have used single-channel presentation. That is, items are presented visually or auditorily, but there is only a single stream of information to which the subject must attend. In the multichannel case two or more streams of information are used, and the subject must process these several streams as best he can. Much of the early experimental work on which Broadbent's filter theory was based used multichannel presentation.

One of the first questions which comes up in such work is the definition of a channel. As it happens, information theorists have a very simple and satisfactory definition of a channel, and this definition is abstract enough to be widely applicable. A channel is simply a matrix of transition probabilities which map input into output (Abramson, 1963, p. 94). Thus, one has a source ensemble, a message ensemble, and a set of transition probabilities which specify the probability of each message (output), given each source (input). The physical embodiment of a channel (be it telephone, telegraph, computer, or the human auditory or visual system) is quite immaterial. In all cases we can determine the characteristics of the channel once we know the characteristics of the source and the message.

This definition has not been much used by psychologists studying memory and attention, at least partly perhaps because the input and output ensembles could not be so circumscribed. If, for instance, one is interested in errors, then one generally includes extralist intrusions, which by definition are outside the ensemble. In early work there was a tendency to associate channel with mode of presentation, so in dichotic presentation the channels were the two ears (and, of course, auditory pathways as far into the nervous system as one cared to speculate). In the bisensory case the two channels were eye (plus visual system) and ear. However, work on attention (e.g., Broadbent, 1971; Treisman, 1969) showed that factors of meaning would also intrude, so consideration only of sensory systems was insufficient to account for the obtained effects.

Here we shall be concerned only with memory, though at the risk of violating the very precept stated earlier. That is, just as memory involves encoding, storage, and retrieval, which are almost surely interdependent processes, so memory in turn depends upon attention. What we remember depends upon what we attended to, so how can one understand memory without first understanding attention? There is an infinite regress here. Since attention is selective perception, we must first understand perception. But perception depends upon sensation, which in turn depends on photochemistry and neurophysiology; these in turn involve more molecular processes yet. Perhaps for ultimate understanding all these must be known, but surely we can make some progress by focusing our efforts on a restricted domain of inquiry. Where one draws the line is probably a matter of personal preference, but that some line needs to be drawn seems clear.

One of the methods used in multichannel tasks is the shadowing technique (Cherry, 1953; Mowbray, 1964), where a steady stream of information is presented on one channel (i.e., auditory or visual) with an occasional to-be-remembered item or items on the other channel. The hope here is that one can study the persistence of unattended information. Since the steady stream must be echoed (repeated back or shadowed), if this shadowing task is sufficiently demanding it will completely absorb the limited channel capacity and so make it possible to track the fate of unattended information over time.

That the two channels are not independent is clear from a study of Mowbray (1964). He found that performance on the shadowing task falls to under 20% at the point of insertion of the target word. On the one hand, this effect would seem to cast doubt on the assumption that one really is studying the persistence of unattended information. On the other hand, his data showed no differences in shadowing for recalled and nonrecalled items, which seems a bit surprising. In any case, it behooves investigators using this technique to make careful measurement of performance on the shadowing task to see if observable performance decrements do occur. In the absence of such measurements, any theoretical conclusions would seem a bit suspect.

In a carefully performed experiment, Norman (1969b) presented a list of four two-digit numbers in one ear while material to be shadowed (rapidly-presented monosyllabic words) was presented in the other ear. The subjects were given extensive training on shadowing, and performance was monitored throughout. Memory was tested by a recognition procedure, and the important result is that a fairly typical serial-position curve was found under shadowing conditions for an immediate-memory test. Under delayed tests, the typical finding of chance performance was obtained, so the implication drawn was that verbal material presented on the un-attended channel in fact enters into short-term memory but is not permanent. Similar results have also been reported by Peterson and Kroener (1964) and Glucksberg and Cowan (1970). Lewis (1970, 1972) has even shown that reaction time to signals on the attended channel vary with the semantic similarity of items on the unattended channel, suggesting a deeper level of processing for the unattended items than is generally assumed.

However, this conclusion is not unanimously accepted. Davis and Smith (1972) suggest that repeated testing of the unattended ear makes it functionally relevant, so it may in fact not be completely unattended regardless of the difficulty of the shad-owing. They tested recall of the attended channel as a function of information pre-sented on the unattended channel, reasoning that if the latter was processed there should be, from all we know about probed recall, some interference effects. There were not, so they argued for early selection.

We now seem to have come full circle. The early results showed no memory for the unattended channel. Then we found that one's name breaks through; then crossover effects were found as a function of sequential redundancies. Then immediate tests of the unattended channel showed above-chance performance, suggesting that the material does get in somehow. But finally, if the unattended channel is never tested then it might as well not be there. Theories of selective attention will have to be developed a bit further to account for all this. However, it is still the case that shad-owing can be a useful technique for studying memory, as the next set of studies will demonstrate.

Some recent studies show that memory need not be so transitory if the bisensory condition is employed. Kroll, Parks, Parkinson, Bieber, and Johnson (1970) reported 75% recall 25 seconds after visual presentation with auditory shadowing. Parkinson, Parks, and Kroll (1971) used a similarity manipulation and concluded that, under comparable conditions, persistence was essentially in terms of the visual properties, not the name of the letters. Parkinson (1972) even found a typical serial-position curve for eight letters after 20 seconds of shadowing, and it was not far down from the comparable curve obtained at a 1-second interval. These results are shown in Fig. 7.9. In general, these results would seem to provide impressive testimony for reten-tion of visually-presented information, even though the limited-capacity system was at least reasonably preoccupied with shadowing. (It might be mentioned that the shadowed message went off momentarily when the target was presented, so strictly speaking the presentation was not bisensory).

The other broad class of multichannel research relevant to serial ordering is that work wherein two or more streams of information are simultaneously presented and the subject is to attend to all of them. In studies that use a shadowing technique, there is only one stream of information to which the subject needs to attend. In what may be

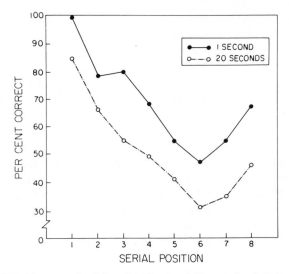

FIG. 7.9. Serial-position curve for 8-item list after 1 and 20 seconds of shadowing the attended channel. (Fig. 4 from Parkinson, 1972.)

called a "fireworks" technique, the subject is presented with a burst of information, either auditory or visual, sudden in onset but brief in duration. This burst momentarily overloads the subject's sensory capacities, but soon it is gone for good. Then the subject reports what he has seen or heard and, from his report, we draw inferences about the persistence of rather short-term memory.

Early work in this area was that of Broadbent, who used dichotic presentation. Here the two channels were the two ears, and this technique has already been described. As noted, the main results were (a) channel alternation in the order of report was difficult at rapid rates of presentation, and (b) the channel that was reported second was more prone to error. Subsequently, an analysis of order of report was given by Bryden (1962), who suggested that the channel-by-channel order may well be the more natural one for dichotic listening. More recently he has suggested a model for sequential organization (Bryden, 1967) that emphasizes the similarities between tachistoscopic recognition and dichotic listening. The two have much in common from the point of view of the spatio-temporal distribution of information.

The ear-by-ear order of report found by Broadbent and many others may be more a characteristic of the auditory system than of dichotic presentation *per se*. A study by Savin (1967) showed that sequential report occurred even though there was no channel separation at all. Presentation was binaural, not dichotic, yet still the two streams tended to be reported sequentially rather than simultaneously. Bryden (1971) separated experimentally the attended channel and the channel reported first. Some subjects had to report first the attended channel, others had to report first the unattended channel. The results suggested that output interference might play a larger role in dichotic performance than attentional factors *per se*.

Whether one finds a channel-by-channel order of report at fast presentation rates also depends somewhat on what the channels are. Sampson and Spong (1961a, 1961b) found a temporal order of report with dichoptic presentation. Dichoptic presentation is the visual analog of dichotic presentation; one message goes to the left eye and the other message to the right eye. In a temporal order of report the items are recalled pair by pair. In the bisensory case one channel is the ear and the other is the eye. In a series of bisensory studies, Madsen, Rollins, and Senf (1970) found a channel-by-channel order of report at the fast rates but a temporal order of report at the slow rates. They found little evidence for the cross-channel switching reported by Yntema and Trask (1963), so the latter results may tell us more about auditory segregation than about channel separation. Finally, Corballis and Luthe (1971) extended an earlier study by Sampson (1964) and treated two properties of visual stimuli as the two channels. Words were printed in color as in the Stroop technique (Stroop, 1935), and the two channels were the names of the words and their color. At least under some conditions there was the Broadbent effect, namely, channel-by-channel report at the fast presentation rate (see also Corballis & Philipp, 1966). So, taken together, these studies would seem to suggest that the one reasonably clear exception is the dichoptic condition.

Actually, a stronger caveat should be mentioned here. One should be very careful about drawing conclusions, in terms of channels, from studies that use dichotic presentation. Results from such studies tell you something about dichotic listening, but there is a very poor channel separation with the two ears. If the two "channels" are the eye and the ear (or, for that matter, the two eyes) the results can be very different. Examples would be the difference between temporal and channel order of report with dichotic and dichoptic presentation, or the failure to find the crossover effect of Yntema and Trask (1963) in the bisensory case (Madsen et al., 1970). In a word, if one wants to study multichannel effects, one should make sure that a reasonable sample of the many possible channels is studied.

A methodological precaution might also be mentioned here. In varying presentation rate to determine its effects on memory, one should make sure that the stimuli as stimuli are constant and only the silent period varies. This precaution is not merely academic. Both in vision (Purcell, Stewart, & Dember, 1969) and in audition (Aaronson, Markowitz, & Shapiro, 1971) it has been found that the duration of the quiet period between stimuli has a considerable effect on the observed performance, at least in the 0–250 millisecond range.

Although spatio-temporal effects are not generally considered under the rubric of multichannel effects, perhaps they should be. The general point is that space and time are two separable dimensions of stimulus presentation. Also, they have a natural correspondence with visual and auditory presentation. That is, in a very general sense audition is a temporally-distributed modality and vision is a spatially distributed modality, and these dimensions are surely represented in memorial processing (e.g., Mayzner, Tresselt, & Helfer, 1967). There has been a limited amount of experimental work in long-term memory (Ebenholtz, 1963; Heslip, 1969; Slamecka, 1967b) and in short-term memory (Mandler & Anderson, 1971; Murdock, 1969) that has explicitly tried to separate the temporal and spatial arrangements of the display. Of the two, the temporal dimension is probably more critical, but the interaction is appreciable. That is, when the spatial and the temporal dimensions are both in the natural order (for us, left-to-right associated with first-to-last), then serial memory is far better than when either is not. However, so far we have not progressed much beyond this point. I am convinced that it is very important to understand this problem, but so far our theoretical conceptualizations have not been very profound. One of the more provocative papers on this subject is one by Milner (1961), but unfortunately neither he nor anyone else seems to have done much to follow it up.

An extension of the dichotic condition was reported by Corballis (1967a) who investigated the presentation-rate effect with three-channel presentation. In this case, one set of items was presented to the left ear, another set of items to the right ear, and yet a third set of items to both. At the slow rate a temporal order of report predominated. However, as presentation rate increased, the channel-by-channel order of report did not seem to be very effective here. As Corballis notes, it is hard to say whether there is something fundamentally different between two and three channels, or whether discriminability effects militate against the Broadbent effect. Further three-channel effects are reported in Darwin, Turvey, and Crowder (1972). In an earlier study Moray, Bates, and Barnett (1965) had gone up to four channels to determine whether the memory span of eight was constant regardless of whether the distribution was eight items successively on a single channel, four items concurrently on two channels, or two items on each of four channels. In fact it was not; the four-eared man did not hear (or remember) very well.

In the visual domain, Harris and Haber (1963) and Haber (1964) used cards from the Wisconsin card-sorting test which varied in color (red, blue, green, yellow), form (star, circle, cross, triangle), and number (one, two, three, four). A pair of these cards was presented tachistoscopically, and subjects were asked to recall either by objects (e.g., two red circles; four blue stars) or by dimensions (e.g., two, four; red, blue; circles, stars). In a sense, the former corresponds to channel-by-channel report whereas the latter corresponds to temporal order of report, if it is remembered that the attributes in vision correspond to sequence in audition. Object encoding seemed somewhat faster and more accurate than dimension encoding, but it could be modified by pre-training.

A final example of a fireworks technique is a four-channel display studied by Murdock (1971a). At the same time that two words were presented dichotically, two additional words were presented visually, both for the same duration. This duration was approximately 500 msec, so it was a brief burst of information. The subject was to report what the words were (free recall), then he was probed on one of their attributes. Of the two auditory words, one had been spoken in a male voice and the other in a female voice; of the two visual words, one had been typed in upper case and the other in lower case. It was this representational aspect that was probed. Not only could the subjects free recall the four words with a reasonable degree of accuracy (in some cases, without error), but generally they could correctly identify the probed attribute as well. There was also clear-cut evidence for channel-by-channel report. These results were interpreted as suggesting that representational information can persist in essentially unrehearsed form, at least up to 4–5 seconds.

What has been learned from these various multichannel studies? There are several clear-cut and quite reproducible experimental findings. Order of report is one, and effects of presentation rate another. Pre-cuing seems to affect the results, and attentional strategies should be controlled unless they are the object of investigation. Theoretically, however, the picture is less clear. The concept of the channel seems useful, probably necessary. Good channel separation can be obtained with experimental care. However, the interpretive picture is quite jumbled and confused. When selection takes place, where (and if) parallel-to-serial conversion occurs is certainly not agreed upon, and clear-cut separation of encoding and read-out has not been obtained. We are capable of studying memory over very brief periods of time (the "short" in short-term memory gets shorter every year), but we still do not have acceptable analytic techniques for separating the underlying processes. The flow of information may be as described in the flow-charts of Broadbent, but we do not yet have the techniques for isolating and identifying the separate stages of processing.

SUMMARY

There are three different forgetting functions for serial order. They are the serial-position curve of memory span, the distractor technique of Peterson and Peterson, and the probe technique for serial lists. The latter two are quite similar and have been useful in investigating a variety of empirical effects. Among the more important are the number of items to be remembered, repetition, similarity, interpolated information-processing, and proactive inhibition.

The Hebb repetition effect refers to the fact that a repeated list will be more accurately remembered in a memory-span paradigm. With a probe technique, repetition serves to elevate the asymptote without affecting the recency span. In the Peterson paradigm, repetition also raises the asymptote; whether it also affects the rate of forgetting is less clear.

Capacity limitations are clearly evident in many serial-order tasks. The greater the information-processing demands during an interpolated interval, the less the subject will remember at the end. Even in memory-span tasks, adding a redundant prefix or suffix will reduce the amount recalled. One way to overcome these limitations in capacity is by chunking, or transforming the material to a more memorable form. Grouping is one method, and recoding cues is another; meaningfulness and pronounceability also play a role. The work of Johnson on transitional-error probabilities is a way of revealing some of the microstructure of these effects.

The deleterious effect of phonemic (acoustic or articulatory) similarity on short-term memory is clearly established. In memory span, for instance, consonant strings with common phonemes will be harder to remember than ones with distinctive phonemes. Whether short-term memory is an auditory system is less clear. It seems quite clear that both phonemic and semantic similarity can affect long-term memory; whether semantic similarity can also affect short-term memory is more debatable.

Proactive inhibition operates in short-term memory as well as in long-term memory. Not only is there the build-up of proactive inhibition, but there is also release as well. Changing the characteristics of the material will re-set the subject to his original high level of performance; so too will an interpolated quiet period. Poor performance in a Peterson paradigm may occur because the subject remembers too much; the ostensible forgetting may at least partly reflect a problem of discriminability.

Multichannel techniques have been devised to test aspects of Broadbent's filter theory, including his concept of attention. The shadowing studies now seem to suggest that interference effects (between remembered and shadowed material) are critical; when the interference is reduced, so is the forgetting. There is current disagreement as to whether a shadowing task is a good method of studying retention of material on an unattended channel. An alternative is a fireworks technique, where the subject is suddenly given a brief information overload. Characteristics of performance seem to depend upon the sensory modalities selected as channels. There is some evidence to suggest that persistence of representational information exceeds the range normally associated with echoic and iconic memory.

8
THEORIES OF FREE RECALL

The fourth and final topic to be discussed is free recall. In this chapter we shall discuss seven different theoretical approaches. They are temporally-structured models of memory; the buffer model of Atkinson and Shiffrin (1971); organization theory as developed by Mandler (1967) and by Tulving (1968); the address-register model of Broadbent (1971); sampling models as suggested by Shiffrin (1970a) and others; the levels-of-analysis model of Craik and Lockhart (1972); and the FRAN model of Anderson (1972), Anderson and Bower (1972a), and Bower (1972a). As before, we shall first describe some of the important experimental results which call for explanation.

In single-trial free recall a list of items is presented to the subject who is then asked to recall as many of these items as he can in any order. He is given credit for every item recalled regardless of order. What is free about free recall is the order of recall; it need not bear any prescribed relationship to the order of presentation. In multitrial free recall the list is repeatedly presented, generally in study-test or RTRT form, still with unspecified output order. Generally the presentation order is randomly determined on each study trial. Practice may be continued for a fixed number of trials or until some performance criterion has been reached.

There are four basic empirical findings which any theory of free recall must consider. From molar to molecular, they are as follows. First, in multitrial free recall the acquisition curve is negatively accelerated or exponential. This would occur if there was a constant probability of recalling any item not recalled on the previous trial. If the probability of recalling an item that had been recalled on the previous trial was also unity, then the result would be a negatively-accelerated or exponential acquisition curve. An example is depicted in Fig. 8.1, which shows three different learning functions. Two are for 40-item lists, and the third is for a 20-item list. Con-

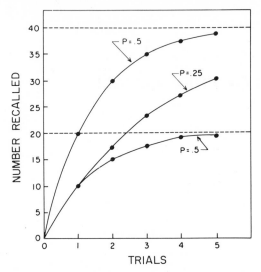

FIG. 8.1. Typical learning curves for multitrial free recall. Three curves are presented, two for 40-item lists and one for a 20-item list. The probability value is the probability of recalling on Trial $n + 1$ an item not recalled on Trial n.

stant probability values (P) are assumed, and they are indicated in the graph. In all cases, list length is taken as asymptote, and these idealized curves are reasonably representative of the results one obtains from individual subjects in multitrial free-recall procedures (Murdock, 1960b).

The second empirical finding is the total-time effect. If a list is presented for a fixed amount of study time, how that study time is divided up into number of items and presentation time per item does not affect the number of items recalled (Murdock, 1960b; Postman & Warren, 1972). Thus, a 20-3, a 30-2, and a 60-1 list all require 60 seconds to present, but the same number of words will be recalled from each. (In a 20-3 list, 20 words are presented each for 3 seconds.) A further aspect of the total-time effect is how recall varies when the total presentation time is varied. In an early study Murdock (1960b) found that the number of items recalled after a single presentation was a linear function of total presentation time. This relationship can be expressed as

$$R_1 = kt + m \qquad (8.1)$$

where R_1 is first-trial recall, t is total presentation time (the product of list length and presentation time per item), and k is the rate constant. This function adequately describes the data when the total presentation time does not exceed a minute or two; over a more extended range, the function may drop off and become logarithmic or exponential (Roberts, 1972).

The third finding is the serial-position effect. This effect is illustrated in Fig. 8.2, which shows data from Murdock (1962a) for 10-2, 15-2, 20-2, 20-1, 30-1, and

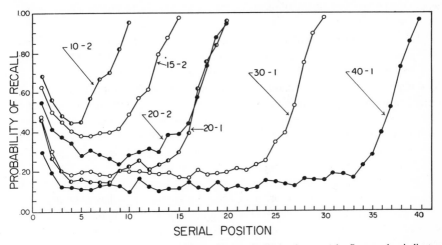

FIG. 8.2. Serial-position curves for single-trial free recall. For each curve, the first number indicates list length and the second number indicates presentation time per item. (Fig. 1 from Murdock, 1962a.)

40-1 lists. There is a recency effect which spans the last 7 or 8 serial positions, a primacy effect which spans the first 2 or 3 positions, and a flat middle section or asymptote. The terms primacy and recency effect simply refer to the superior performance on the first and last items in the list. As noted elsewhere (Murdock, 1972), a reasonable description of the recency effect is given by the Gompertz double-exponential function

$$P(i) = 1 - (1/L)^{.5^i} \qquad (8.2)$$

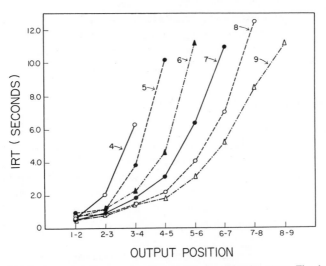

FIG. 8.3. Mean interresponse time as a function of ordinal position in output. The data have been partitioned in terms of total number of words recalled (4–9). (Fig. 1 from Murdock & Okada, 1970.)

where $P(i)$ is the probability of recalling the ith item from the end of a list ($i = 0,1$, $2, \ldots$) of length L.

The fourth and final result to be noted here is the interresponse times. Data shown in Fig. 8.3 are from a recent study by Murdock and Okada (1970). The data were partitioned on the basis of the number of words recalled (4–9), and the curves show how interresponse times increased with ordinal position in output. In all cases, interresponse times increased from less than 1 second between the first two words recalled to approximately 10 seconds between the last two words recalled. Not only is each function monotonic, but also one has a family of curves fanning out from a common origin with no crossovers. At any given output position, interresponse time is a good predictor of the number of words yet to recall.

There is another set of findings that I would very much like to add to the above list, but cannot. These are output-order effects. As anyone who has ever done free-recall experiments knows, free recall is free in name only. The order in which the words are recalled is quite stereotyped. Generally subjects start with the last few items then, after running them off in serial order, jump back into the middle (or beginning) of the list, though still with a forward bias. While these trends seem clear on inspection, we have no satisfactory way to characterize them. Although it is a pity, the list must stop at four rather than at five because, at least so far, no one has been able to provide a simple and succinct description of this aspect of single-trial free-recall data. Experimental data, however, may be found in Deese and Kaufman (1957).

To summarize, in multitrial free recall the acquisition curve is negatively accelerated or exponential. On the first trial, if total presentation time is constant, then concurrent variation in list length and presentation rate will not change the number of items recalled. The serial-position curve of free recall has three components: a brief primacy effect, a more extensive recency effect, and an asymptote between the primacy and the recency effect. Finally, in the act of recalling, each additional retrieval comes only at the cost of additional time spent trying to recall. Interpretation of these findings is model-dependent, so we shall turn to the models forthwith.

TEMPORALLY-STRUCTURED MODELS

Temporally-structured models of memory are those that partition the contents of memory on a temporal basis. They may dichotomize memory into a short-term and a long-term store, or they may trichotomize memory into sensory, short-term, and long-term stores. The distinguishing features of these models are the temporal compartments or stores and the transfer of information from one store to another. A necessary, though often unstated, consequence of such models is that a mechanism must be provided for the encoding, storage, and retrieval of information from each of the postulated memory stores.

Let us start with an overview, a synthesis of various approaches, or the modal model I described (but did not particularly favor) in a paper published several years ago (Murdock, 1967a). A very simple block diagram is shown in Fig. 8.4, where

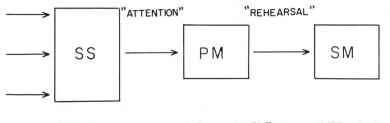

FIG. 8.4. A simple flow chart to illustrate the main features of temporally-structured models of memory. The major divisions are sensory stores (SS), primary memory (PM), and secondary memory (SM). (Fig. 8 from Murdock, 1967b.)

the three rectangles represent sensory stores (SS), primary memory (PM), and the secondary memory (SM). It is generally assumed that the sensory stores contain representational information from the world around us: the end-organ stimulation from the various receptors throughout the body activated by physical energies in our environment. That which is attended to is transferred to or enters primary memory, a short-term store of limited capacity variously implicated in memory span, the span of apprehension, recency effects, and perhaps even consciousness. Transfer of information from primary to secondary memory occurs on the basis of rehearsal. Not all of the information in sensory stores reaches primary memory, and not everything in primary memory reaches secondary memory, but while there is this progressive reduction, that which does finally enter secondary memory is presumed to be relatively permanent.

Each store then has different capacities and, as a corollary, different time constants are associated with the forgetting process. Loss from sensory stores is generally thought to be of the order of 250 msec (Averbach & Coriell, 1961; Massaro, 1970; Sperling, 1960). Loss from primary memory is perhaps of the order of 5 seconds, though this value is more task-dependent and less time-dependent than the estimate for sensory decay. Time constants associated with secondary memory are far greater yet; estimates range from minutes to years. Actually, the exact values are not particularly important. What does matter is the relative order of magnitude.

As Fig. 8.4 shows, the presumed forgetting mechanism also differs for each store. Loss from sensory stores is by decay, or merely the passage of time *per se*. Loss from primary memory is a more active process, where current occupants are displaced by items coming after them. As in the Conrad model described earlier, if within primary memory itself there are only a limited number of storage registers or bins, then when they are full a new item can only gain admission by displacing one of the items already entered. Displacement then is the replacement of an old item by a new item. Loss from secondary memory is less precisely defined or understood. It is characterized here as due to interference, with no commitments intended as to the relative contributions of such potential factors as retroactive interference, proactive interference, unlearning, or response competition.

Perhaps the major application of this model to experimental data has been in terms of the serial-position curve of single-trial free recall. This application is illustrated in Fig. 8.5, which shows a smoothed serial-position curve much like those depicted in Fig. 8.2, along with the theoretical constructs of primary and secondary memory. The general idea is as follows. During list presentation all items are attended to and so enter primary memory. For items in the middle of the list there is some low but constant probability of transfer to secondary memory, and this probability is represented by the asymptote of the serial-position curve. Early items receive more rehearsals, and late items receive fewer rehearsals (Rundus, 1971), so the early part of the secondary-memory curve points up, and the latter part drops down. This area is shown in the figure as cross-hatched down to the left.

In recall, the subject is assumed to dump primary memory first; that is, the subject outputs those items still in the limited-capacity primary-memory store. Since the probability of an item being in this store drops off the further back into the list one goes, the recency effect is seen as monotonically decreasing as one goes back into the list. The recency effect spans approximately the last eight items, so the probability of an earlier item still being in primary memory is essentially zero. The vertical line at Serial Position L−7 is intended to represent this span. The area under the primary memory component is cross-hatched down to the right, and there is an area of overlap. This overlap will be discussed shortly.

Temporally-structured models such as this have been suggested or accepted by a number of investigators. These include Bower (1967a, 1967b), Glanzer (1972), Kintsch (1970b), Laughery (1969), Norman (1969a), Norman and Rumelhart (1970), Waugh and Norman (1965), and Wickelgren (1970a). The details and the emphasis vary somewhat from model to model. Rather than describe all of these models separately, let me simply consider some of them and indicate their distinctive features.

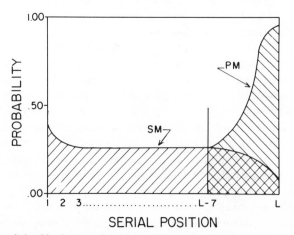

FIG. 8.5. The relationships between the serial-position curve of single-trial free recall and the theoretical constructs of a temporally-structured memory model.

The short- and long-term components of Fig. 8.4 were dubbed primary and secondary memory by Waugh and Norman (1965). Further, they called attention to the fact that these two stores were independent. That is, an item could be stored in primary memory, in secondary memory, or in both. As a consequence, by simple probability theory it follows that

$$R(i) = P(i) + S(i) - P(i)S(i) \qquad (8.3)$$

where $P(i)$ is the probability that an item in Serial Position i is in primary memory, $S(i)$ is the probability that an item in Serial Position i is in secondary memory, and $R(i)$ is the probability than an item in Serial Position i is recalled. Then by simple rearrangement of terms it follows that

$$P(i) = \frac{R(i) - S(i)}{1 - S(i)}. \qquad (8.4)$$

This equation provides a model-dependent way of obtaining a primary-memory curve from the data. It is to be contrasted with Eq. (8.2), which is a description of the curves that are obtained. These empirical curves are sometimes referred to as normalized curves, since they are corrected for asymptote. That is, the scale goes from 1.0 to whatever value $S(i)$ assumes, and what Eq. (8.4) does is to make a rubberband transformation; namely, it converts this range to a 1.00 to 0.00 scale. An exam-

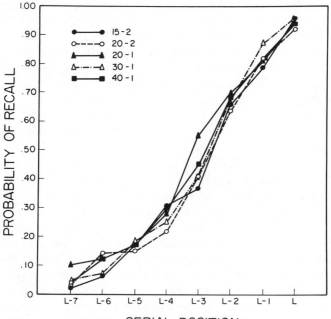

FIG. 8.6. Normalized recency curves for single-trial free recall. The last eight points of each curve in Fig. 8.3 have been corrected or normalized by Eq. (8.4). (Fig. 4 from Murdock, 1971c.)

ple is illustrated in Fig. 8.6, which shows the recency curves of Fig. 8.2 redrawn in this manner.

These normalized recency curves are model dependent because the transformation is based upon a theoretical assumption. The assumption is that primary memory and secondary memory are independent in a probabilistic sense. An analogy would be drawing one card at random from a deck of playing cards; the probability that it is a face card and the probability that it is a spade are independent. Obviously, the drawn card can be both a face card and a spade. In the Waugh and Norman model, primary and secondary memory are of course assumed to be independent, and this assumption has certain empirical consequences, as we shall see.

However, it might be well to point out that different methods of measuring primary memory involve different assumptions and are not necessarily equivalent. Another measure used by some investigators (e.g., Tulving & Colotla, 1970) is to use lag, the number of items (presented or recalled) intervening between presentation and recall of each item. A cutoff point (e.g., 7) is selected; all items with a greater lag are assumed to be secondary-memory items, while all items with a shorter lag are assumed to be primary-memory items. In this way one can assess the effect of various experimental manipulations separately on the primary- and secondary-memory components. This method assumes that primary- and secondary-memory items are mutually exclusive. Although a lag measure such as this is quite convenient (especially with computer analysis of data), it should be noted that it is not consistent with the underlying framework of the Waugh and Norman model. Of course, one may indeed have a model where primary and secondary memory are disjoint, but then that is no longer the model proposed by Waugh and Norman.

One of the implications of temporally-structured models in general, and the independence assumption in particular, is that it should be possible to eliminate the recency component of the curve without affecting the asymptote. This effect was in fact demonstrated by Postman and Phillips (1965), who interpolated 0, 15, or 30 seconds of counting before recall of 10-, 20-, or 30-item lists. Their data are shown here in Fig. 8.7, and it is quite clear that the interpolated distraction eliminates the recency effect without changing the asymptote.

In a way this was a serendipitous finding, since the study was motivated by theoretical considerations of a rather different sort. However, a direct attack on this issue was reported by Glanzer and Cunitz (1966), who tried to find experimental variables which would actually have separable effects on the recency and asymptotic components of the serial-position curve. They clearly succeeded, and for recency their experimental manipulation was essentially that of Postman and Phillips. Thus, it seems quite clear that in fact the recency component of the serial-position curve of single-trial free recall can be flattened right out. One interpretation is that primary memory has been emptied but secondary memory left undisturbed. Other variables that seem to affect only recency are mode of presentation (Craik, 1969; Murdock & Walker, 1969; Watkins, 1972) and temporal grouping (Gianutsos, 1972). By contrast, variables that affect the asymptote (but not recency) are presentation rate and list length (Glanzer & Cunitz, 1966; Murdock, 1962a), word frequency (Raymond,

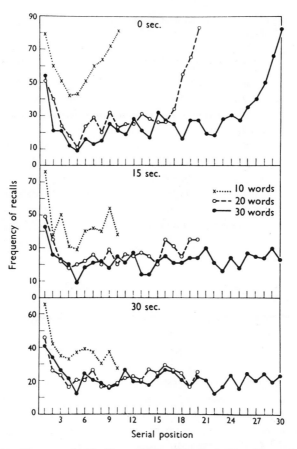

FIG. 8.7. Serial-position curves for 10-, 20-, and 30-item lists after 0, 15, or 30 seconds of interpolated distraction. (Fig. 1 from Postman & Phillips, 1965.)

1969), addition of a subsidiary task during list presentation (Baddeley, Scott, Drynan, & Smith, 1969; Murdock, 1965d), semantic-associative attributes (Craik & Levy, 1970; Tulving & Patterson, 1968), and multilingual lists (Tulving & Colotla, 1970).

A thorough and comprehensive account of this work can be found in Glanzer (1972). Much of it is fairly straightforward theoretically and needs no further comment here. Other theorists have diverged somewhat from or elaborated upon the very simple model shown in Fig. 8.4. Bower (1967a, 1967b) emphasized that the input to the primary-memory component was the output from a pattern-recognition memory, and (particularly in the latter paper) his concern was to develop a reasonable model for the format of storage. Some of these views were considered earlier in Chapter 2.

Norman and Rumelhart (1970) present a very comprehensive model, but they too concentrate on the initial representation (and some of its consequences) as a vector of attributes. This perceptual vector is translated into a memory representation by a naming process, which in turn has short- and long-term representation. Of all those mentioned earlier, perhaps the most distinctive model is that of Wickelgren (1970a). He favors a strength representation in memory with differential decay rates for sensory, short-term, intermediate-term, and long-term memory. The measure here, of course, is the d' measure discussed previously, and Wickelgren has reported much data to support his contention that there are in fact at least four different decay parameters to characterize these different memory stores.

To conclude this section, temporally-structured models have been quite popular and useful. They help in remembering and organizing a number of experimental findings. The model we shall consider next is the buffer model of Atkinson and Shiffrin. It too is a model of this type, but it is so extensively used and cited that it deserves special treatment. Consequently, it has not even been mentioned in this section, but will be considered on its own in the next section.

THE BUFFER MODEL

The buffer model of Atkinson and Shiffrin (1965, 1968, 1971) is really the model on which the modal model is modelled. It has the three compartments of sensory, short-term, and long-term stores, the transfer processes, and decay and displacement. However, it has much more, and some of its ramifications become quite complex. An important feature emphasized in the latter two papers cited above is the matter of control processes. The so-called structural and control processes correspond to the distinction between fixed properties of the system and those features elected by the user. Thus, there might be a capacity to store a certain amount of information, which would be a structural feature, but how this capacity was allotted to conflicting demands might be a function of the strategy used by the subject, and thus a control process. The user is the individual himself or, if you wish, the central processing mechanism, a currently fashionable phrase for an homunculus whose computer origin obviates some of the opprobrium generally reserved for such mentalistic operators.

A slightly more detailed flow chart for the buffer model is shown in Fig. 8.8. The rehearsal buffer is seen as part of the short-term store. The buffer is composed of a certain number of storage locations (slots or bins, as in the Conrad model); the number of such slots is designated by r. These slots are temporally ordered as in a push-down stack, with the ordering indicated by the notation $r, r - 1, r - 2, \ldots,$ 1. Each incoming item may or may not be entered into this buffer. If not, it can be recalled from the sensory register with probability 1.0 if it is tested immediately. Consequently, immediate recall need not necessarily be very informative about the contents of the buffer. The probability that an item is entered into the buffer is denoted by α.

Since there are only a fixed number of slots in the buffer, if all are filled then entry of a new item can only be achieved by displacing an old item. The new item always goes on top (i.e., in Slot r), but which item is displaced is probabilistic.

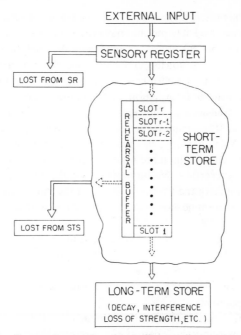

FIG. 8.8. Flow chart to illustrate the operation of the buffer according to Atkinson and Shiffrin. (Fig. 2 from Atkinson & Shiffrin, 1968.)

As detailed, for instance, in Phillips, Shiffrin, and Atkinson (1967) the oldest item (Slot 1) is displaced with probability δ, the next oldest item (Slot 2) is displaced with probability $\delta (1 - \delta)$, the next is displaced with probability $\delta(1 - \delta)^2$, etc. In other words, displacement from the buffer is characterized by a geometric distribution. More specifically, $d(i)$, the probability that the ith item in the buffer is displaced, is given by

$$d(i) = \frac{\delta(1 - \delta)^{i - 1}}{1 - (1 - \delta)^r} . \tag{8.5}$$

Slot 1 represents the oldest item and Slot r represents the newest item. It may be appreciated that this equation permits different results depending on the numerical value of the parameter. As δ approaches 1, the more likely it is that the oldest item is lost first; as δ approaches $1/r$ all items are lost with equal probability. Furthermore, this variation will also determine whether the recency effect is S-shaped or a simple exponential decay (e.g., Kintsch, 1970b, p. 213).

Since the newest item goes on top, and one of the items near the bottom may be displaced, rearrangement is necessary to accommodate all the buffer items. According to the theory what happens is that, relative to the displaced item, all newer items move down one slot while all older items keep their place. Thus, to summarize, when an item does enter the buffer, it enters on top, some one other item is displaced, older items than the one displaced stay put, but newer items move down one slot. As may be apparent, this hypothetical process complicates the analytic expressions somewhat, since separate consideration has to be paid to the older and newer items.

While an item resides in the buffer, transfer to the long-term store occurs. This process is seen as transfer of information, and the longer items stay in the buffer the more information is transferred. The transfer rate is specified by the parameter θ. So, for a given period of occupancy, the greater the value of θ, the more information that is transferred. As an analogy, imagine an object with variable buoyancy suddenly released under water. The more time that passes after the release, the closer the object will be to the surface, but this depends on the buoyancy as well. Thus, in the buffer model, it is both the length of time that the item is in the buffer and the transfer rate θ that determine how much information is transferred to long-term memory.

Once an item is displaced from the buffer the transfer necessarily ceases. At that point decay from the long-term store begins. Here too there is a parameter to characterize the decay rate, and it is τ. The greater the value of τ, the faster the decay from the long-term store. As in the last example, decay here also involves both length of time and a rate parameter.

We have, then, five parameters in all to characterize the operation of the buffer model of Atkinson and Shiffrin. There is r, the number of slots in the buffer; there is α, the probability an item enters the buffer; there is δ, the parameter governing displacement from the buffer; there is θ, the transfer rate from the buffer to the long-term store; and there is τ, the decay parameter to characterize loss of information from the long-term store. The basic equations for the model are as follows:

$$\beta_j = \begin{cases} 1 - \alpha, & j = 0 \\ (1 - \beta_0)(1 - \alpha/r)^{j-1}\alpha/r, & j > 0 \end{cases} \tag{8.6}$$

$$Pr(C_i) = \left[1 - \sum_{k=0}^{i} \beta_k \right] + \left[\sum_{k=0}^{i} \beta_k \rho_{ik} \right] \tag{8.7}$$

$$\rho_{ij} = 1 - (1 - g) \exp\left[-j\theta(\tau^{i-j}) \right]. \tag{8.8}$$

These equations were actually developed for the paired-associate situation, but let me interpret them as if they applied to a free-recall situation. When the retrieval of an item is attempted there is some probability that it will succeed, and this probability is given by Eq. (8.7). The first term in this equation is the probability that the item is in the buffer at the time of attempted retrieval (and if it is, the retrieval attempt will succeed). The second term is the probability it is not in the buffer; then successful retrieval will depend upon its being in long-term memory, as given by Eq. (8.8). Here g is the guessing probability, i is the lag (number of items intervening between presentation and attempted retrieval), and j represents length of stay in the buffer. Equation (8.6) gives the probability that an item stays in the buffer for exactly j trials, given that retrieval is attempted at some lag greater than j. The parameters r, α, θ, and τ are as explained above.

This description provides only the flavor of the model, and the interested reader is referred to original sources (a good exposition is given in Atkinson, Brelsford, & Shiffrin, 1967). The critical reader may wonder about the extension from paired associates to free recall. This extension is quite straightforward in the case of cued recall; in the case of noncued recall, one need only make some assumption about the interference effects of each attempted recall. However, such an assumption is in principle no different from the assumption one must make about output interference with paired associates, so the only problem is to decide how much to weight each test trial or attempted retrieval. The numerical value of the weighting given may be debatable, but the need for some weighting probably is not (e.g., A.D. Smith, 1971).

Perhaps it is worth pointing out that deductions from the model and inferences from the data do not necessarily converge. That is, the model says that an item in the buffer at the time of attempted retrieval will be recalled with probability 1.0, and it also says that the shorter the lag, the higher the probability that an item will in fact be in the buffer. However, given that an item is recalled at a short lag, there is no guarantee that in fact it came from the buffer. It may have come from the long-term store. Thus, one can make clear predictions from the model, but inferences from the data about the underlying states cannot be made with certainty. This point is of course generally true about theory and data, but perhaps is not as clearly appreciated as it might be.

In order to make specific predictions from the model it is necessary to know what numerical values to assign to the various parameters. What values should they have? Here one encounters the estimation problem; it is necessary to estimate the values of these parameters from data. The estimation problem has been mentioned before, and useful references are Atkinson, Bower, and Crothers (1965), Bush (1963), and Restle and Greeno (1970). A simplex method of function minimization has been described by Nelder and Mead (1965), and it provides a quick and efficient means of solution.

The buffer model has been fairly extensively tested on data obtained in a continuous paired-associates paradigm, and it seems to fit quite well (Atkinson & Shiffrin, 1968; Loftus, 1971). In one attempt to apply it to a discrete-trials paradigm it did not come off quite as well, and a fluctuation model seemed at least as good (Murdock, 1972). Also, there are various experimental findings in the literature which would seem embarrassing, if not directly contradictory, to the model. For instance, it is not clear how auditory and visual presentation can result in differences in the recency part of the serial-position curve and not be reflected in the asymptote (Murdock & Walker, 1969). It is not clear how Kenneth, a neurological patient with a memory span of 1.5 items, can show a learning curve for multitrial free recall which has a slope indistinguishable from normal subjects (Warrington & Shallice, 1969). In a Peterson and Peterson distractor task, an interpolated period of nonverbal signal detection allows longer residency in the buffer, yet the data show no improvement in the long-term component of memory (Atkinson & Shiffrin, 1971). For that matter, there is no assurance that the buffer model can even fit the serial-position curve of single-trial free recall. To my knowledge there have been no published reports that give parameter estimates or some quantitative estimate of goodness of fit.

By way of summary, my own feeling is that the buffer model has been useful in bringing some semblance of order into a burgeoning field and providing a theoretical framework to integrate old findings and assimilate new findings. But signs of defection are beginning to appear, and the initial excitement seems to have abated somewhat. As I have stated before, I am not enthusiastic about partitioning of memory into discrete temporal stores, and some of the other possible models are beginning to provide viable alternatives to the buffer model of Atkinson and Shiffrin.

ORGANIZATION THEORY

We turn now to quite a different line of approach, a viewpoint which goes under the name of organization theory. As pointed out by Bower (1970b), it is more a slogan or a banner than a formal or precise model or theory. In one sense, its origins can be traced back to the Gestalt school of psychology, and the principles of perceptual organization (e.g., figure-ground relations, similarity, proximity) are re-emerging in mnemonic contexts. In another sense, current organization theory represents an attempt to extend and document the principle of chunking suggested by Miller (1956).

The importance of organization was manifest in the work of Bousfield in the 1950s. Thus, Bousfield (1953) and Bousfield and Cohen (1953, 1955, 1956) studied free recall with categorized word lists composed, say, of 15 items in each of four different taxonomic categories (e.g., animals, names, professions, and vegetables). Even though the items (category members) were randomly dispersed throughout the list, they tended to cluster by category in recall, even though there was nothing in the task demands to require it. While the existence of clustering seems indisputable, its measurement is still something of a problem (e.g., Bousfield & Bousfield, 1966; Dalrymple-Alford, 1970; Frankel & Cole, 1971; Roenker, Thompson, & Brown, 1971; Shuell, 1969). However, measurement considerations cannot be divorced from theoretical considerations; the former depends on the latter (Colle, 1972).

The role of interitem associations in clustering was shown by Deese (1959a). From normative data he found it was even possible to predict, with fair accuracy, the occurrence of a particular intrusion into a free-recall list, even though the word was not actually presented in the list (Deese, 1959b). A discussion of some of the early views on this subject may be found in Deese (1961). Cofer (1965, 1967) and Cofer, Bruce, and Reicher (1966) have reported a number of experiments on clustering and free recall, and among other things they have tried to compare associative clustering and categorical clustering. Initially the attempt was made to contrast them, but the favored interpretation seems to be that both are necessary. Interlingual clustering, with and without category clustering, has also been investigated in multi-lingual subjects; see, e.g., Dalrymple-Alford and Aamiry (1969) and Lambert, Ignatow, and Krauthamer (1968).

The measurement of clustering was extended to noncategorized word lists by Tulving (1962) with his measure of subjective organization. He showed that one could use a measure based on the stereotypy of order of responses over successive pairs of trials and that this measure increased with repetition (practice) much as did the standard measure of number of items recalled. As Tulving noted, his measure of clustering was a coarse measure in that it required rigid sequences of responses to be repeated over successive trials. Undoubtedly the organization processes are much more complex and elaborate than such a measure would indicate. Unfortunately, a measure (or a theory) adequate to cope with this diversity is as elusive today as it was a decade ago.

A subsequent analysis of multitrial free recall attempted to account for learning data by partitioning items into four categories: CC, NC, CN, and NN (Tulving, 1964). These letters designate recalled (C) and nonrecalled (N) items on Trials n and $n + 1$, respectively. Tulving suggested that the CC component increased logarithmically over trials, while the NC component remained essentially constant with practice. This attempt to synthesize the learning curve for multitrial free recall results in a different quantitative function than the exponential function described above, but this attempt of Tulving's was based on data averaged over subjects of varying ability. In data I have collected the exponential function seems quite adequate for individual subjects.

Another issue which developed from this paper was the role of repetition and chunk size. Tulving (1964) and Tulving and Patkau (1962) suggested that what happened with repetition in free recall depended upon the unit of measurement. While the number of words recalled increased, the number of chunks increased much less, if at all. Perhaps what was happening was that the number of chunks was invariant, and repetition simply increased the chunk size. Much the same argument can be advanced in connection with number of items and number of items per category (Tulving & Pearlstone, 1966). In a list of categorized items, cued recall (presenting the category names to the subjects) increases the number of words recalled but not the number of items per category recalled. Thus, the category instances may be considered chunks. Compared with noncued recall (no category names provided), cued recall provides access to these chunks but does not affect performance on the chunk *per se*.

Terms such as availability, accessibility, and retrieval cues are common parlance among organization theorists. The availability of mnemonic information refers to its existence, while the accessibility refers to its utilization. Information which is available but inaccessible is like a misshelved book in a library; it's there, but hard to find. A question (or probe, or pointer) denotes target information, the answer to the question. A retrieval cue is a memory aid, additional information over and above the probe, which increases the probability of recall. For instance, Tulving and Osler (1968) found that weakly [sic] related associates such as FAT or LEG to MUT-

TON, VILLAGE or DIRTY to CITY, EMBLEM or SOAR to EAGLE were retrieval cues (i.e., facilitated recall) if and only if they were present both at input and at output. Thus, if FAT was presented with MUTTON at presentation but LEG was presented at recall, performance was little different from control conditions. However, if either FAT or LEG was used both at presentation and at recall, performance was almost twice that of the control conditions.

Another distinction which may become popular is the one between episodic memory and semantic memory. As suggested by Tulving (1972), the former refers to temporally dated episodes or events, while the latter refers to the knowledge accumulated by an individual over his lifetime. Thus, your knowledge that the battle of Hastings was in 1066 would be information stored in semantic memory, while your knowledge that the retrieval cue example in the previous paragraph was LEG or FAT would be information stored in episodic memory. Some subset of episodic memory persists and becomes part of semantic memory. Generally, experiments on human memory concern themselves only with the former, but there is a growing tendency to spread out and include the latter. Thus, experiments on retrieval of information from memory may make use of information pre-existing in the long-term store. Landauer and Freedman (1968) investigated the question of whether the time to make decisions about category instances varied with the category size (it did, to some extent); in a similar vein, Collins and Quillian (1969, 1970) studied the time to answer questions (make decisions) about information that might be hierarchically structured in semantic memory. Some interpretive difficulties have been pointed out by Conrad (1972) and by Rips, Shoben, and Smith (1973).

Work on semantic memory *per se* is also in full swing. One line of development is computer simulation models such as have been proposed by Collins and Quillian (1972) and Rumelhart, Lindsay, and Norman (1972). Methods of measuring semantic memory have been discussed by Meyer (1970). A review of this area may be found in Frijda (1972). In a somewhat different vein, Kintsch (1972b) has also been working on semantic memory. His approach is to develop a formal theory of semantic memory and then test some of its empirical implications. The problems involved in construction of a computer simulation model are quite different. The simulation models are essentially in the artificial intelligence tradition, while the work of Kintsch is what psychologists have been doing all along, namely, constructing and testing theories of human behavior. Although dissenting opinions abound, it seems to me that in the long run work in the latter tradition is more likely to advance our understanding of what we as psychologists should deal with, that is, the mechanisms and processes by which human beings encode, store, and retrieve information.

To return to the main experimental work, another major contribution has been the work of Mandler (1967, 1968, 1970, 1972). One of the clustering effects he has investigated extensively is the relationship between number of categories and recall. In a sorting task, subjects are given a pack of cards, each with a single word. They are to sort them into separate categories, as many as they wish up to seven. Then, they are subsequently asked to recall as many items as they can. The general finding seems to be that total recall is a linear function of the number of categories used in sorting. If you wish, they are retrieval cues; if there was some fixed limit to the number of items per category that could be recalled, then clearly the linear function relating word recall to number of categories would be found. More recently (Mandler, 1972; Mandler, Pearlstone, & Koopmans, 1969) he has been studying the effects of organization on recognition memory.

Another main contribution has been the recent experimental and theoretical work of Bower (1970b, 1972a). These two papers provide the best survey and introduction to the field that I know of, and the interested reader would be well advised to put them at the top of his reading list. Bower has reported a number of clever and ingenious experiments which demonstrate in very striking fashion the benefits of organization processes on memory. These are not restricted to free recall; they include paired associates and serial ordering as well. As his work has shown, the empirical effects can be very large indeed. No longer do we need to rely on our intuition; there are by now many different experimental paradigms which seem to work quite well.

By this point, the reader will perhaps have come to appreciate the sentiment expressed in the opening paragraph of this section. Organization theory is not so much a theory as a point of view. It is a belief, if you will, that there is more to human memory and learning than the simple associations studied under the aegis of behaviorism and interference theory. As one might expect, a certain polarity seems to have developed; on the one hand, there are those with an organization orientation who deprecate the more traditional work as unimaginative, pedestrian, perhaps even benighted. On the other hand, there are those who feel that associationistic concepts can accommodate most, if not all, of the organizational findings to date, and they raise their eyebrows politely at what they feel to be the overstated claims and exaggerations of their opponents. I certainly have no wish to enter into this argument; theoretical preconceptions are one's own prerogative, and it is seldom fruitful to challenge them on such grounds. For a more scholarly discussion of these and related topics, the interested reader should see Postman (1971, 1972) or Voss (1972).

More particularly, Postman (1971) discusses the question of whether there are fundamental differences between organization theory and interference theory. While they use different concepts and prefer different paradigms (free recall and paired associates, respectively), the subjective organization in free recall may be based upon or involve the pairwise linkages or associations so fundamental to interference theory. Postman seeks a rapprochement, and in addition to theoretical analyses he introduces some important experimental evidence. This evidence involves transfer studies, from free recall to paired associates and vice versa. In the former, negative transfer should (and does) result. The (random) pairwise associations should overall be incompatible with the subjective groupings from free recall and so make second-task learning (paired associates) more difficult for the experimental group than for a control group which has free recall and paired-associate lists with no items in common. This negative transfer holds for recall and recognition measures, and also for categorized and noncategorized lists. For transfer in the other direction (paired associates to free recall), the transfer should be positive, since whatever pairings are remembered from the first task should facilitate organization, hence learning, on the second task. Both for recall and recognition these results were obtained, at least over the early trials. (The imposed first-task groupings may not have been optimal for free-recall learning, and a crossover effect was obtained in the recognition condition; see Postman, 1971, Fig. 2, p. 295. A similar point will come up in consideration of part-to-whole transfer in the next chapter.) The general conclusion reached by Postman was that the subjective groupings in free recall may display the traditional associative properties assumed by interference theory.

Finally, let me conclude this section with a few general criticisms of organization theory. First, it is not a theory but a point of view. Perhaps its proponents would claim no more. Second, no very profound concept of organization has emerged. In fact, the way it is generally measured (the intertrial repetition measure) is in terms of the occurrence on two successive trials of particular two-item chains. Such a view of organization is not at all what the Gestaltists had in mind. Third, the measures themselves are not based on a theoretical model of the processes involved in organization, and often they are not even able to measure on an ordinal or ratio scale the amount of organization occurring under different experimental conditions. Finally, some of the empirical effects claimed by organization theorists may be interpreted in rather different terms (e.g., Carey & Okada, 1973; Slamecka, Moore, & Carey, 1972). It is certainly true that the organization theorists have uncovered some large, reliable, and impressive empirical effects. Perhaps it is time for those interested in these effects to work toward a more adequate theoretical explanation of the data.

THE ADDRESS-REGISTER MODEL

We have already discussed the filter theory of Broadbent, which was presented in 1958 in his book *Perception and Communication*. A revised version of this model was presented in 1971 in *Decision and Stress*. While in no sense a new model, it is sufficiently different to warrant a different name. Since its novel feature is an address register, that seems like an appropriate characterization. Further, it is discussed here rather than in connection with serial-order effects because, unlike its predecessor, it seems primarily oriented towards explaining results from studies of free recall.

For the uninitiated, Broadbent is not the easiest writer to read, and *Decision and Stress* is a rather long book. For one interested in primary sources, the following is suggested. Broadbent (1966b) provides a general preview of things to come. Broadbent (1969), Broadbent (1970), and then Broadbent (1971) provide progressively more detailed elaborations of the model and could well be read in that order. And in the 1971 book, Primary Memory (Chapter VIII) is the critical chapter, with judicious cross-referencing to other sections as necessary. Here we shall try to provide an overview, but the interested reader certainly should consult the primary sources, if only to make sure that he has not been misinformed here.

The address-register model of Broadbent is a temporally-partitioned model with four components, three of which are already familiar. They are the sensory stores, primary memory, and the long-term store. To these Broadbent adds an address register, after primary memory but before the long-term store. The address register holds information about the items, not the items *per se*. In categorized word lists, it might hold the category names. It could also hold representational or similarity information. Whatever the contents, they are seen primarily as retrieval cues. They contain information, in free recall, about the items presented, which will be useful in the retrieval required at the end of list presentation.

Perhaps the clearest explanation is in terms of the analogy suggested by Broadbent (1971, p. 376). Imagine the desk of a college professor with a few letters that came in today which require answering, a few notes scattered about the desk-top to remind him of urgent items, and a near-by file cabinet containing more long-range information. The letters correspond to the type of information stored in primary memory, the contents of the file cabinet to the organized and classified (?) information in long-term memory, while the notes pointing to high-priority events correspond to the information stored in the address register(s). This analogy has sufficient verisimilitude so that it may be pursued a bit further.

The information in primary memory is partly representational so, for instance, information about orthographic or phonemic attributes might be available. So too with the letters on the desk. The address register points to actions to be taken, not the information *per se*. Thus the scattered notes on the desktop are only reminders. The pointers may refer to primary memory or to long-term memory, just as the notes may refer to today's letters or filed information. Information in long-term memory is filed or classified in various ways, not necessarily in neat and tidy fashion. So too with the contents of many file drawers.

The general mode of processing information is still in terms of selection or categorizing. However, in this new model of Broadbent there are two types of categorizing. One is filtering; the other, pigeon-holing. Filtering is essentially stimulus selection; pigeon-holing, essentially response selection. Filtering is early in the information-flow process; pigeon-holing comes later. Operationally, they could be distinguished by the two measures of signal-detection theory. Filtering would be manifest in the sensitivity parameter d', while pigeon-holing would be manifest in the criterion parameter β. As an experimental example, in a tachistoscopic display one could show red and black letters, or letters and digits. Precuing could help in selective recall by color and this would be filtering, but precuing might not help in the selection, say, of letters since pigeon-holing comes later in the system. The term pigeon-holing is intended to denote ready-made categories into which items are fitted. There is also some probable loss of information. Thus, all mail with Zip Code 43210 goes in the same slot for Columbus, Ohio regardless of the handwriting on the envelope.

One line of research that seems to have played an important role in this theorizing of Broadbent's is the experimental separation of recency effects and asymptote as reported, for instance, by Glanzer and Cunitz (1966). In his analyses Broadbent seems to use interchangeably two empirical effects noted at the beginning of this chapter. One is the linear relationship between R_1 and t given in Eq. (8.1), and the other is the serial-position effect of single-trial free recall shown in Fig. 8.3. If I understand him correctly, he seems to be saying that the intercept m in the equation is to be identified with the recency effect of the serial-position curve and the slope k with the area under the asymptote. Thus, when interpolated counting eliminates the recency effect this is equivalent to setting m to zero, while variations in the asymptote with, e.g., presentation rate are affecting the slope constant k. Although this possibility is attractive, the numbers simply do not work out right. The area under the normalized recency curve is 3.0 ($\pm$ 10%) items (Murdock, 1972), while the intercept of this linear function is about 6.0 items (Murdock, 1960b). Further discussion of this point may be found in Craik (1971).

In this same connection, Broadbent (1969) suggests that the two constants of this linear function may enable an experimental separation of the address register and the long-term store. The intercept m would be a measure of the size of the address register, while the slope k would represent the transfer of information to the long-term store. To interpret this possibility literally would suggest that there were three possible address registers, and one would want to use them efficiently. However, to my knowledge this possible identification is not suggested (this specifically, at least) in the latter two presentations of the model, so perhaps this possibility has been consigned to the wastebasket.

Although a few pages such as this cannot hope to do justice to the richness and diversity of topics covered in *Decision and Stress,* at least it should indicate the outlines of this address-register model. What experimental findings does Broadbent adduce in its support? In addition to the experimental separation of recency effects and asymptote noted above, there seem to be three main points. One is the fact that decay effects are manifest in primary memory. This is the interpretation presumably excluded by Waugh and Norman (1965), but it is claimed careful examination of the data suggests otherwise (and see also Baddeley, 1972a). A second point is that modality of presentation affects the recency part of the serial-position curve but not the asymptote (Craik, 1969; Murdock & Walker, 1969). As has been noted, such an effect is at least embarrassing to simple primary-secondary memory models. The third point is that the effects of acoustic similarity seem to span the full range from the most recent items to items in long-term memory (Bruce & Crowley, 1970; Craik & Levy, 1970; Glanzer, Koppenaal, & Nelson, 1972).

These three findings are not so much specific deductions from the address-register model as they are embarrassments to other models which are otherwise consistent with the general Broadbent view. Thus, Broadbent has always been partial to a decay theory of memory, and evidence that decay may occur in primary memory runs counter to any primary-memory model that works only on a displacement or interference basis. The modality point should be clear; in a strict transfer model, such as the buffer model of Atkinson and Shiffrin, it is by no means evident how some independent variable (such as mode of presentation) can affect recency but not the asymptote. In the Broadbent model representational information is not precluded from primary memory, and the address registers could also store information about this feature. Consequently, there would seem to be two ways that the Broadbent model could talk about modality effects. The point about similarity is that a neat and tidy distinction between only two stores, one responsive to phonemic similarity and the other to semantic similarity, is too pat. Thus, some of the same features may be represented in all parts of the system.

By and large, this address-register model of Broadbent does not seem all that different from other temporally-structured models of memory. Basically it preserves the distinction between short- and long-term stores but uses an address register to mediate access to either and allows similarity of representation in these different systems. Obviously it is more concerned with retrieval considerations than some other similar models, and what Atkinson and Shiffrin discuss in terms of control processes might be embodied in this address register, since clearly its contents are optional and at the discretion of the subject. While its chief distinctive feature is the address register, such a concept is not novel. Buschke (1966) distinguished event stores, marker stores, and address stores and tried to test them by comparing temporally-ordered and numerically-ordered recall of short lists of digits. The concept of address register also has a certain affinity with the Tulving concept of retrieval cues.

It seems to me that the contribution of the Broadbent model is that it is essentially a useful way of talking about certain aspects of the data on free recall. Empirical findings can be interpreted in its terms, but the model is more inferential than deductive. That is, it does not seem to lend itself to very many *a priori* deductions; it is not a model easily capable of disproof. If you wish, it is a point of view rather than a rigorous theory. However, this feature is not unique to the address-register model. Theories and models of free recall are probably the most elusive and slippery of all those considered in this book. Even the buffer model, which started out in quite rigorous and precise terms, has become watered down to the point where it becomes capable of explaining (i.e., talking about) almost any effect. What seems to be happening is that current models are viewed as expository devices, and one does experiments to find out which of several alternative characterizations is most nearly correct. At this stage in our knowledge such a view is certainly not unreasonable. But one should perhaps put the term model in quotation marks.   .

SAMPLING MODELS

In this section we shall consider models of free recall that emphasize a sampling process. There is a natural affinity between the classic urn models of probability theory and retrieving items from memory. In the former, one is drawing marbles from an urn and sampling with or without replacement. Various statistics of the process can be calculated by standard methods. In the latter, the subject has a comparable task—to enumerate all members of a set (draw marbles from an urn) by retrieving or sampling them one at a time. One such model which relates interresponse times to trials for categorized and noncategorized lists has been suggested by Albert (1968).

Perhaps the best-known model of this type is that of Shiffrin (1970a). Think of information stored in long-term memory as comparable to marbles in an urn. Then to retrieve a specific item of information from this store, a random sample is drawn which may or may not contain the target item. This information is placed in short-term memory, now functioning like work-space, and the contents examined one by one, perhaps in serial fashion. If the search is successful, the process concludes with a response. Otherwise, re-sampling occurs. The process continues until either a successful conclusion occurs or further tries appear unfruitful.

Obviously, the process cannot be quite this simple or quite this random. The long-term store is organized, probably along various dimensions, and the sample is certainly not completely random. One possible dimension is temporal, and then the sampling would be confined to information which has been entered at approximately the correct point in time. An ingenious experimental test was reported in Shiffrin (1970b). In a single-trial free-recall paradigm the subject had to recall not the list presented, but rather the one presented just prior to it. The fact that the subjects could do this with a reasonably low intrusion rate suggests that sampling can in fact be organized along a temporal dimension. Further, since a double-alternation (AABBAABBA . . .) pattern of list-length was followed (lists were either 5 or 20 items long), it was possible to separate out target-list length and amount of interference. It turned out that the former was the critical variable; amount recalled depended upon length of the target list, not length of the intervening list.

Probability of retrieval of an item is assumed to be proportional to its strength in memory. An example given by Shiffrin (1970a, pp. 389–390) can illustrate this point. Suppose the stored information consisted of two cities in New Jersey with strengths 1 and 2 and two cities in New York with strengths 1 and 2. Then the probability of retrieving a particular city is either 1/6 or 2/6 for the weaker or stronger case, respectively. Further, size of the search set and number of draws are parameters of the model. In free recall the object is to recall as many items as possible; how can this be done? Suppose four draws are possible; all four can be from the four-item ensemble, there could be two from each state, or other possibilities as well. In this case the highest expected mean output occurs when the smaller search sets are examined, and Shiffrin says this conclusion is generally true.

This particular example illustrates a fairly general point about free recall. In effect, the instructions to the subject are to sample randomly without replacement. That is, from the designated ensemble (the list presented) the subject is to name each item once and only once. If the mind were like an urn and items of information were like marbles, then a simple solution would be to draw items, one by one, and discard each after every drawing. Then the number recalled would be the number of items available, and there would be no problem of accessibility. However, the mind is not like an urn, and the retrieval process seems unable to sample without replacement. So the appropriate characterization is that of sampling with replacement, and the repetition problem becomes ever more troublesome. That is, the closer you get toward the end, the more draws are needed to retrieve an acceptable item.

The basic incompatibility between the task demands and the normal mode of operation of the system is one of the most salient points about free recall. Since this point may not be generally appreciated, let me belabor it with a personal example. I once asked our youngest child, then six years old, simply to name all of the members of our immediate family without repeating names. There were six: herself, her mother and father, and three older siblings. She tried several times but, incredible as it might seem, she could not do it. That is, she could not recite all six names once and only once, without repeating any. There was clearly neither an availability nor an accessibility problem here. The point is that the retrieval mechanism of an individual is not designed to sample without replacement.

Another manifestation of this problem can be seen in latency measures. The simplest possible example would seem to the the category-naming example. The subject is simply instructed to report all the instances of a large category (e.g., U.S. cities) as quickly as he can. As reported by Bousfield and Sedgewick (1944) the rate of response is proportional to the number of instances yet to name. Such a result would be consistent with a mechanism that sampled perfectly with replacement. That of course is an ideal case; more realistic assumptions have been investigated by Indow and Togano (1970) and by Kaplan, Carvellas, and Metlay (1969, 1971).

In free recall, the analogous finding is that interresponse time increases in positively-accelerated fashion with output position, as illustrated in Fig. 8.4. The exact prediction depends upon the detailed assumptions one chooses to make about the processes involved. Here is a simple model which I have investigated (albeit in a rather desultory fashion). After list presentation there is a store of available items. To retrieve, the central processor samples randomly with replacement from this store. To avoid repetition, each recalled item is saved in an output pool, and every sampled item is compared against this output pool before recall. If a match is found, the item is not recalled; if not, it is. As recall proceeds, the number of unrecalled items in the store decreases while the size of the pool increases.

Assume that each comparison of a sampled item with an item in the pool takes a constant amount of time. This time is the same regardless of how many items have been recalled or how many items there are in the pool. Further, assume the comparison process is serial and self-terminating. That is, a sampled item is compared against all items in the pool until a match is found (if it is). Finally, assume that this comparison process accounts for most of the interresponse time in single-trial free recall. Other components (in particular, re-sampling) are assumed to be negligible and affect only the intercept of the interresponse time function.

It is not immediately obvious how interresponse time in this model would vary with output position as a function of the number of available items. On the one hand, the more items available, the easier sampling is with replacement; on the other hand, the more items in the pool, the more time required for scanning. To see if this model could generate anything like the interresponse times shown in Fig. 8.4, I ran several Monte Carlo simulations under various conditions. The most satisfactory is shown in Fig. 8.9. The number of available items was set at (M =) 4, 6, or 8, and an arbitrary stop rule was invoked to preclude responses in excess of 12 seconds. The scaling of the vertical axis is of course quite arbitrary; it was based on the scaling factor of one second per count. The general point is that the data of Figs. 8.4 and 8.9 look quite alike. Thus, a simple random-access model with provision for monitoring seems

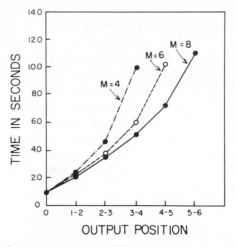

FIG. 8.9. Simulation of random-access model with monitoring process. Items were randomly sampled from set of (4, 6, or 8) available items and checked against each item in pool of recalled items. The scaling of the items on the vertical axis is arbitrary.

able in principle to account for the typical latency findings. However, as is generally recognized, the problem is that such a model has no provision for regularizing the output order, and such effects generally characterize data obtained from experimental studies.

A model appropriate for categorized word lists has been suggested by Patterson, Meltzer, and Mandler (1971). A description of the model is given by their flow chart, shown here in Fig. 8.10. The subject must decide whether to continue sampling within a category or to sample categories. The more items that have been sampled from a given category, the less productive the first alternative is likely to be. Changing categories will be beneficial if there are untapped categories, but since categories are sampled like words, the probability of finding a new category also decreases as recall continues. A monitoring process is included, and the method of computing P (Boxes C and G) is described in their article. A Monte Carlo simulation of the model gave data on interresponse times and cluster size that agreed well with data from an accompanying experiment.

A hierarchically-organized search model has been suggested by Rundus (1973). Assume at the time of presentation several items become attached to retrieval cues. For instance, to take a miniature example, suppose in a five-word list W_1, W_2, and W_5 get attached to RQ_1, while W_3 and W_4 get attached to RQ_2. In retrieval, the subject first samples a retrieval cue (randomly and with replacement) then, within that cue, samples words randomly until the stop-rule criterion is exceeded. The stop rule would be to quit once the number of unsuccessful draws exceeded k, where by unsuccessful is meant items previously recalled. After sampling within a category terminates, the subject resamples retrieval cues, and the process continues in this

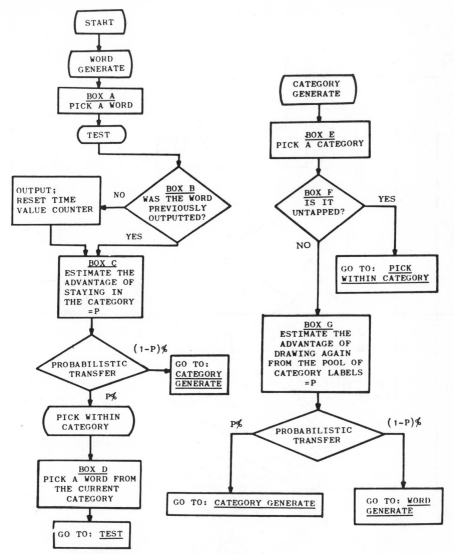

Fig. 8.10. Flow chart to describe the processes involved in the free recall of items from categorized lists. (Fig. 3 from Patterson, Meltzer, & Mandler, 1971.)

manner until the stop rule for retrieval cues is exceeded. A flow chart to describe these processes is shown in Fig. 8.11.

As in the Shiffrin model, items (and retrieval cues) are of different strengths, and a ratio rule is invoked to make probability of recall proportional to strength. Also, successful recalls increase the strength of the recalled item and, as a consequence, they lower (relatively) the strength of unrecalled items. The strength distributions

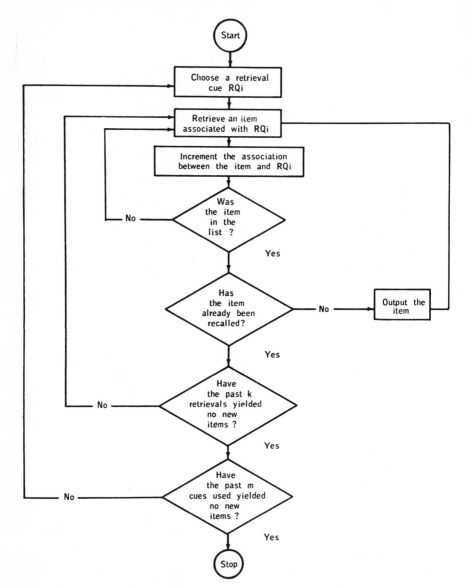

FIG. 8.11. Flow chart to describe the prcesses involved in the free recall of items from a hierarchically organized memory. (Fig. 2 from Rundus, 1973.)

and the criterion points for the stop rule would be parameters of the model. Monte Carlo's have been run on a computer to determine whether the expected outcomes from the model agree with experimental data.

One of the original inspirations for the model was the cuing effect reported by Slamecka (1968). Briefly, this effect (or, more accurately, noneffect) is that provid-ing a subject with some members of a category after the list has been presented, and then asking him to recall the rest, does not facilitate recall. In fact it may do the opposite—depress recall of the cued category. This effect is explicable in terms of the Rundus model, if one assumes that presenting items is equivalent to recalling them. Since strengthening of associations occurs as a consequence of recall, and since strengthening some items associated with a particular retrieval cue must (given the ratio rule) weaken the others, it follows that recall (or presentation) of specified items within a category will tend to inhibit the recall of others. Presentation of W_1 reduces the probability that W_2 or W_5 will be drawn if RQ_1 is sampled. And this, of course, is the essence of the Slamecka cuing effect.

Another phenemenon that would seem to follow from the model is the interresponse-time data for categorized lists reported by Patterson et al. (1971). They report data that suggest increases in interresponse times within categories and between categories, which is what the Rundus model would suggest. That is, if each sample takes a constant unit of time then, by the principles of sampling with replacement, the more recalled items from a category, the longer it will be until the next item is recalled; also, the same would apply at the category level. Comparable results with repeated presentation of noncategorized lists have been reported by Puff (1972).

Neither the Shiffrin nor the Rundus model makes explicit provision for the monitoring process. Although the random-access model I described above does that, it has no provision for organized lists like the models of Patterson et al. and Rundus. A combination of the best features of all four models might not be completely trivial. While urn-type models are not much in favor these days, they do seem to capture one key feature of the task requirements of single-trial free recall, namely, the sampling-with-replacement problem. Permitting variations in strength and letting strength determine sampling probabilities might even handle, in a crude fashion, some of the output-order effects so obvious by inspection (and so refractory for theoretical analysis). Further work along these lines might be promising, but we shall have to wait and see.

LEVELS OF ANALYSIS

The next topic in this chapter is the levels-of-analysis approach suggested by Craik and Lockhart (1972) and Craik (1973) (see also Cermak, 1972). It is more a conceptual framework than a developed theory. However, these authors suggest it may be a more heuristic approach than those based on temporally-partitioned stores.

Craik and Lockhart make three criticisms of temporal models. One is capacity. A defining characteristic of most temporal models is a fixed-capacity notion as, for instance, represented by r, the number of slots in the buffer model of Atkinson and Shiffrin. However, as they point out, empirical estimates of capacity vary widely, from 2–20. A second criticism is based on coding. The coding used by the subject appears to be quite flexible, and under various conditions it can be phonemic, semantic, orthographic, associative, or even iconic. Such flexibility seems inconsistent with the implications of temporal models. Finally, the retention characteristics seem quite variable as well. For instance, recency with paired associates spans two items; in single-trial free recall, eight items; and in item recognition, there probably is no asymptote. Forgetting rates seem to be a characteristic of the paradigm.

Basically, the view suggested is that stimuli may be processed to different levels, and this initial level of analysis determines the subsequent rate of forgetting. Perception involves the rapid analysis of stimuli, and an analysis to different stages. Some stimuli are barely analyzed, or not analyzed at all; memory for them is transient at best. Others are processed more extensively, to a deeper (really richer) level, and their memory traces are more permanent. The memory trace is a result of the perceptual analysis so, as many others have suggested, there is a basic continuity between perception and pattern recognition (early in the system) and memory (later in the system).

The order of processing may be from the physical characteristics of the stimulus (as in a feature-extraction model) progressively deeper to the semantic or abstract linguistic level. However, it need not be, and there is some recent evidence (e.g., Macnamara, 1972; Savin & Bever, 1970) to suggest when it is not. Studies of selective attention are clearly relevant here, and the leading-lagging studies of Treisman (1964) are interpreted as consistent with this view.

What generally goes under the name of primary memory is viewed as continued attention to an item. It is maintaining an item at a high level of accessibility but not necessarily leading to the formation of a more permanent trace. Thus, the recency effect in single-trial free recall occurs because the last few items in the list are still in this high-accessibility state and generally are recalled first when list presentation ends. Introducing an interpolated distraction diverts attention and so the recency effect drops out. This effect of course is that reported by Glanzer and Cunitz (1966) and Postman and Phillips (1965). A deeper level of processing is required for the more permanent memory evidenced by the secondary-memory component of the retention curve.

Evidence of Reitman (1971), who used a signal-detection task, would appear to contradict this view. If the subject is required to listen for and report a weak tone, his attention is surely distracted, but performance was not greatly affected. However, she did not use an immediate-retention test, so one cannot say that no forgetting occurred. Atkinson and Shiffrin (1971) used five-item strings with 1, 8, or 40 seconds of detection and found near-perfect performance throughout. However, Craik (1973) reports data with five-item strings and an interpolated nonverbal auditory shadowing task which do show the expected forgetting. Also, he reports an experiment with free recall followed by a pursuit-rotor task, and the recency effect falls off quite nicely. Thus, his conclusion is that diverting attention from recent items results in a loss of their initial high accessibility, and as a consequence the recency effect becomes attenuated or disappears.

Formation of more persistent memory traces is seen as requiring a deeper level of processing. Rote rehearsal is probably not sufficient. In this same paper Craik provides a test of this view by emphasizing the importance of the recall of the last few words of the list and, for the experimental condition, providing an interpolated period for overt rehearsals. While the last few words are indeed repeated in this interval, their subsequent recall (a measure of long-term strength) is no better than a control condition with immediate recall which does not afford the opportunity for these extra rehearsals.

The critical variable for durable memory is thus seen as the level of processing achieved during the initial encoding. What is important then is how the item is encoded. An implication of this view is that incidental learning could be as good as, perhaps even better than, intentional learning. Intent to learn *per se* is not the critical variable; it is how the item is processed. Further, Craik and Lockhart (1972) suggest that an incidental-learning paradigm (wherein the subject is given some orienting task but no information about a subsequent memory test) may be a better measure than an intentional-learning paradigm, as the processing activities of the subject are under better control. If the subject knows he will subsequently be tested, he may use various strategies which are both idiosyncratic and covert. As a consequence, experimental analysis may be difficult.

As these authors note, there is already some evidence for the efficacy of incidental learning. Eagle and Leiter (1964) reported that recognition (though not recall) was actually better under incidental- than intentional-learning instructions, where the orienting task required subjects to classify each word as a noun, verb, adverb, or adjective. Hyde and Jenkins (1969) found that using the word as a semantic unit (e.g., rating it on pleasantness) resulted in incidental recall equal to that of an intentional group, but orthographic analysis of the word (e.g., checking for a particular letter) resulted in worse performance (both recall and clustering). Johnston and Jenkins (1971) reported similar effects when the orienting task was to write rhymes or to write appropriate modifiers or nouns (depending on whether the word was a noun or an adjective). However, the special composition of the lists (e.g., Hyde, 1973) might be noted.

Two experiments along these lines are reported in Craik (1973). In one, tachistoscopic presentation was used and the subject had to decide as quickly as possible whether (a) there is a word present; (b) the word is in capital letters/lower case; (c) the word rhymes with _____; (d) the word is a member of the category _____; or (e) the word fits into the sentence _____. As depth of processing increased, so did decision latency. Also, a subsequent (unexpected) recognition test showed that recognition accuracy increased with the initial depth of processing required. The second experiment was similar except that the final test was recall rather than recognition, but the same results occurred.

It would seem then that this incidental task with varied orienting instructions may be a useful tool to control and study initial processing and subsequent retention. The results are quite compatible with a levels-of-analysis view. Instead of memory being partitioned into sensory, short-term, and long-term stores, stimuli at the time of presentation are processed in various ways and to various depths. The resulting memory trace is a consequence of this initial encoding, and the measured performance will reflect an interaction between the characteristics of the memory trace and the task demands of the test.

FRAN

The acronym FRAN stands for Free Recall by an Associative Network. It is a computer-simulation model developed and described by Anderson (1972), Anderson and Bower (1972a), and Bower (1972a). It was designed as an explicit associative-net model to see what data from laboratory studies of free recall could and could not be explained by such an approach. I shall describe the 1972 version of this model; it may be modified or revised in Anderson and Bower (1973).

Since FRAN is a computer-simulation model, it exists in the form of a computer program. This program has certain features and carries out certain operations. To describe FRAN is to describe these features and operations. One makes deductions from the model by running the program on the computer, generating data, then analyzing them. One test of the adequacy of the model is how accurately it mirrors experimental data obtained from human subjects. The comments about computer-simulation models made in the section on EPAM in Chapter 6 would also apply to FRAN.

FRAN is endowed with a memory structure. It consists of a vocabulary of 262 nouns which are interassociated. From dictionary definitions, links or associations were constructed, and each word in the vocabulary is associated with 3–19 other words in the vocabulary. In addition to dictionary associations, two random associations were given each word to reflect human idiosyncracies. These associations are bidirectional. One has a multiply-connected graph, and it is possible to trace a path from any one node (word) to any other node. The number of paths (associations) will vary depending upon the particular instances. (A discussion of the potential usefulness of graph theory in describing structural relationships among words may be found in Kiss, 1968.)

FRAN has a short-term store much like the buffer of Atkinson and Shiffrin. It can hold exactly five items. During list presentation in free recall each word as it arrives is placed in the buffer. FRAN then tags the item (its long-term memory representation) and tries to tag associative pathways from this item to other list items. This second process will continue as long as the item is in the buffer, so it is sensitive to presentation rate. Tagging the item also is rate sensitive; the probability that an item will be tagged as a list member increases (in negatively accelerated fashion) as a function of the length of time it is in the buffer.

In addition to the buffer there is an additional short-term store named ENTRYSET. This consists of three items which provide starters for associative retrieval. Initially it is the first three words in the list, but they are replaced when better ones come along. One criterion for "better" is perceptual distinctiveness. It could, in principle, handle a von Restorff effect, though this feature has not been implemented in the model. A second criterion is associative centrality; one word is better than another if it has more associative connections with other list items. As its name implies, ENTRYSET provides one means of access to list items. It would seem not unlike the address register in the Broadbent model.

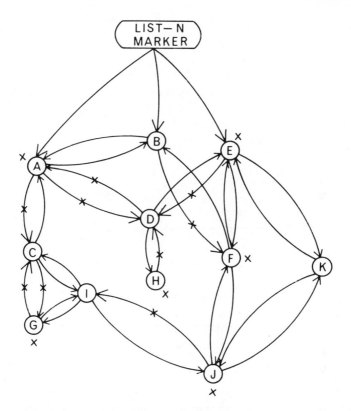

FIG. 8.12. A diagram of the hypothetical memory structure which might exist after list presentation in free recall. The nodes represent items and the arrows denote associations. Those marked x have been tagged. (Fig. 3 from Anderson, 1972.)

A hypothetical memory structure that might exist at the end of list presentation is shown in Fig. 8.12. Three points of entry to the list are items A, B, and E; these would be words in the short-term store or in ENTRYSET. The arrows denote preexisting associations, and those marked with an x have been tagged during list presentation. So too with the items; as noted above, tagging of items and tagging of associations are separate. While the pre-existing associations are bidirectional, tagging is independent, so 0, 1, or 2 of them may be tagged.

FRAN begins recall by reporting the contents of the short-term store (unless it has been cleared by an interpolated activity). Then items from the buffer and from ENTRYSET are randomly sampled as retrieval cues for other items. FRAN searches along tagged pathways to try to find tagged items. The search follows a depth-first pattern. FRAN could recognize all tagged items but could retrieve only those which could be reached by a marked path. Thus, words H and J in Fig. 8.12 could not be retrieved because, even though marked, there is no access route. On the other hand, a list item such as C could mediate the recall of G from A, even though it would not be recalled itself since it was not marked.

Recall continues until all marked pathways have been exhausted. That is, there are a certain number of items which can be reached from the items in the buffer and in ENTRYSET; once these have been traced down there is no more to recall. Learning in the multitrial situation occurs from a combination of three different factors. First, during recall itself each retrieved item is assumed to be placed briefly in the buffer where new associations can be established. Second, each additional study trial allows new items and associations to be tagged. Third, the composition of ENTRYSET gradually changes, with more effective items replacing less effective items.

What empirical results can FRAN explain? The list is long and impressive indeed. As a start, it seems capable of explaining the four basic free-recall phenomena enumerated at the beginning of this chapter. It generates an exponential acquisition curve (see Fig. 5, Anderson, 1972). It generates appropriate total-time effects (see Figs. 10–15), and it is even clever enough to favor Waugh (1967) over Murdock (1960b) (see Anderson, 1972, Fig. 12). It generates a very reasonable serial-position curve for first-trial performance (see Anderson, 1972, Fig. 7), though I have doubts about subsequent trials. Finally, though not explicitly stated in the model, it seems reasonable to assume that distant associations would take longer to trace out than adjacent associations and so, at least intuitively, the interresponse-time data fall out too.

For order of output, FRAN apparently does not mirror input order as closely as some subjects do. In the multitrial situation, it would not show the priority in recall of previously nonrecalled items reported by Battig, Allen, and Jensen (1965), but if this effect is simply a deliberate strategy used by the subject to maximize recall (Roberts, 1969) this defect could perhaps be remedied. FRAN would seem to predict that the recency effect would wash out with interpolation, as shown earlier in Fig. 8.7. It predicts an increase in subjective organization over trials (see Fig. 8, Anderson, 1972). It predicts clustering in categorized lists and, to some extent, the blocked-random effect (see Anderson's Fig. 20). It would predict the clustering in recall of associatively related words as reported by Jenkins and Russell (1952) and the effect of interitem associative strength as reported by Deese (1959a).

For cuing studies, it is consistent with the effect reported by Tulving and Osler (1968) that, to be effective, a retrieval cue must accompany the item at the time of presentation. In FRAN this effect results from the marking of pathways at the time of presentation. It would not predict the negative cuing effect reported by Slamecka (1968), wherein presenting list items as cues reduced recall. In fact, this effect is one of the more important problems, since it runs counter to the basic expectation of an associative model such as FRAN. On the other hand, it can apparently mimic the test-trials effect reported by Tulving (1967), wherein there is some variability in the content (but not the number) of words recalled in an RTTT paradigm. It does not predict a lag effect (Melton, 1970) which is probably another major failing. (Many of these empirical effects will be discussed more extensively in the next chapter.)

Finally, embedded within FRAN is a model for recognition memory. Free recall proceeds by following marked pathways, but in item recognition the response would be determined by whether or not the memory node corresponding to the probe was tagged. As described so far, the model would fail abysmally; there is no provision for forgetting and, since tags are all-or-none, any confidence-judgment data would immediately discredit the model. However, in Anderson and Bower (1972a) the assumptions have been appreciably enriched and a rather detailed model for recognition is presented. However, that aspect of FRAN is beyond the scope of the present coverage and so will not be described further.

What can be said by way of evaluating FRAN? On the positive side, it is clearly the most detailed, comprehensive, and elaborate model of free recall we have. Although not perfect, all the major and many of the derivative findings in the literature are consistent with it. Even its failures are instructive. (They seem primarily in the organization area.) In fact, Bower (1972a) suggests that one of the chief virtues of FRAN is to pinpoint exactly where and how it does break down. It sets a standard for other theories and models to surpass.

On the negative side, four points may be noted. First, it is not a model of free recall; it is a model of a particular strategy used in free recall. I suspect that many of the empirical effects reported will still obtain when subjects are instructed to (or do) use other strategies; if so, the model will lose much of its explanatory power. Second, it is a temporally-partitioned model of memory, with all the attendant defects. Third, it makes organization dependent upon simple pairwise associations, and there are many who will dislike this feature. Fourth, I think the simple notion of tagging and direct access for item recognition is wrong. Memory is more representational, and even in the simplest of situations there does not seem to be direct access.

SUMMARY

There are four basic findings which any theory of free recall must explain. The first is the negatively-accelerated (exponential) learning curve in multitrial free recall. The second is the trade-off (invariance) between list-length and item-presentation time when total presentation time is held constant. The third is serial-position effects with a primacy effect extending over the first three positions, a recency effect extending over the last eight positions, and a flat middle section or asymptote. The fourth is the interresponse-time data which increase in positively-accelerated fashion over output position.

Temporally-structured models partition memory into a sensory, short-term, and long-term store. Forgetting mechanisms are decay, displacement, and interference. Attention and rehearsal are processes associated with transfer of information from one store to another. The buffer model of Atkinson and Shiffrin is the most detailed and explicit of these models, and it emphasizes the importance of control processes in short-term memory. There seems to be little interest in testing these models; instead, they are viewed more as a convenient way of talking about empirical effects.

An alternate point of view is organization theory. In multitrial free recall it emphasizes the importance of clustering or organization, while in single-trial free recall it emphasizes the importance of retrieval cues in mediating performance. Though it has an affinity with the Gestalt concept of organization, the standard measures used (based on intertrial repetition ratios) do not. Organization theorists have uncovered a number of large, reliable, and impressive empirical effects; whether or not the suggested interpretations are correct is currently a matter of some dispute.

The address-register model of Broadbent is a revised and updated version of filter theory. For short-term memory, an additional storage system is suggested—an address register which can point to information either in short- or in long-term memory. It is like indirect addressing in computer programming. Two types of categorizing are envisaged, filtering and pigeonholing. The former is directed more towards the input of information; the latter, more towards the output of information. These processes are reflected by the d' and β measures of signal-detection theory. As with other temporally-partitioned models, it seems intended more as an expository device than a formal model.

Sampling models emphasize retrieval processes, while a levels-of-analysis view emphasizes encoding processes. In the former, trying to recall words in free recall is seen as similar to classic probability problems of drawing marbles from an urn, and output limitations are seen as reflecting the repetition problem inherent in a sampling-with-replacement mechanism. In the latter, various types of processing are envisaged, and the emphasis is on the initial memorial representation. As one moves from physical analysis to semantic analysis, the level of processing is viewed as "deeper." The data suggest that recall improves, particularly under conditions of incidental learning, the deeper the processing.

FRAN is a model of the associative strategy that may be used in free recall. Its semantic memory is organized in an associative network, and list presentation serves to tag items and pathways (associations). Items from a short-term store or from ENTRYSET serve to gain access to tagged items. This model can explain an impressive number of the empirical effects in the free-recall literature; the main exceptions seem to be organization effects. The main features of FRAN that can draw criticism are that it models strategy, it partitions memory temporally, it bases organization on simple pairwise associations, and it postulates direct access to tagged information in long-term memory.

9
DATA ON FREE RECALL

In this chapter we shall discuss five main topics which have been studied in free recall. These phenomena are forgetting functions, repetition effects, test-trial effects, cuing effects, and part-to-whole transfer.

FORGETTING FUNCTIONS

As is the case in serial ordering, the forgetting function for free recall is defined by the serial-position function. However, it should be kept in mind that the relationship between the forgetting function and the serial-position function is even less direct than in serial ordering. The problem is output interference. In serial ordering, one at least knows the number of intervening input and output items up to the point of the first error (assuming serial recall from the beginning). But in single-trial free recall the order of output is so variable that almost no two are alike, and in multitrial free recall both input and output order vary. Without an explicit theory of the retrieval process one simply cannot extrapolate from the serial-position function to the forgetting function. Consequently, the interest focuses on the serial-position function itself. We shall therefore of necessity restrict our discussion of forgetting functions to the question of how the serial-position function varies with experimental conditions, though in the last analysis we are really interested in the forgetting process.

The test for serial-position effects can either be by recall or by recognition, and it can either be immediate or delayed. Actually a 2×2 classification of this sort is too simple; the test delay can vary over a continuous range. However, three conditions have been studied most: immediate testing, testing after a brief period of interpolation, and testing after a number of other lists have been presented. Immediate testing gives serial-position curves like those shown in Fig. 8.2. In the intermediate case the exact period of interpolation seems not too important; for instance, Postman and Phillips (1965) found little difference between 15 and 30 seconds delay (see Fig. 8.7). The third case is often referred to as final free recall (after Craik, 1970). A final test is given at the end of the experimental session (or later), and the subject is asked to recall all the words from all of the lists.

The interesting result, first reported by Craik (1970), is that the serial-position curves for immediate and final free recall look quite different. Not only does the recency effect wash out, there is actually negative recency. That is, the serial-position curve for the last few items in the list actually drops below the level of the middle items. This characteristic has already been displayed in the theoretical curve shown in Fig. 8.5. So perhaps there are three types of recency curves in single-trial free recall: the typical S-shaped positive recency with immediate recall, zero recency with interpolation of neutral delay as in Postman and Phillips (1965) or Glanzer and Cunitz (1966), and negative recency with final recall after a number of lists have been presented and tested.

Such a possibility must be considered only tentative at this point. Experimentally, distinguishing between a zero and a negative recency is not easy when one considers problems of reliability of data and the floor effects involved. Also, from the point of view of temporally-structured models such a trichotomy does not make sense. They would say there is negative recency on an immediate test but it is masked by primary memory. That is, as one gets towards the end of the list there is a decreasing probability that items will be in secondary memory. This view assumes that rehearsal (and consequently the transfer process) stops when the list ends. However, it simply does not show up on an immediate recall test because primary memory items are recalled first. There is a suggestion (Thompson & Gardiner, 1972) that, with auditory and visual lists, negative recency occurs with a distractor task in the same mode, but zero recency occurs with a distractor task in the alternate mode. However, further confirmation is needed to be sure.

Why does the negative-recency effect occur? One possibility, investigated by Cohen (1970), is that it somehow reflects the fact that the last words in the list were recalled first. If this were the determining factor, then negative recency should disappear when ordered recall was required. However, Cohen found that recall in the order of presentation gave essentially the same pattern of negative recency as free recall. Consequently, the interpretation of negative recency as an output effect was rejected. An alternative explanation was in terms of availability and accessibility. Since Cohen found that a final recognition test gave positive recency while a final recall test gave negative recency, he concluded that somehow the final list items were less accessible though not less available on a final test than the earlier list items. Cohen also points out that an earlier experiment by Craik, Gardiner, and Watkins (1970) found negative recency on a final recognition test, but their data reported the results in terms of conditional probabilities. It was the probability of recognizing an old item on a final recognition test, given that the item had been recalled initially.

Cohen's interpretation was investigated further by Darley and Murdock (1971) who gave both final recall and final recognition on tested and untested lists

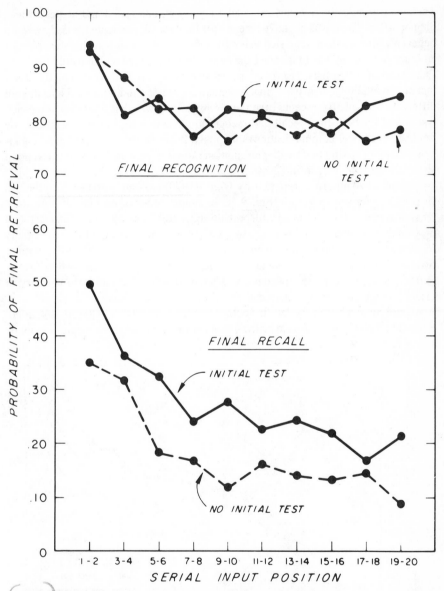

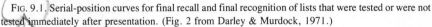

FIG. 9.1. Serial-position curves for final recall and final recognition of lists that were tested or were not tested immediately after presentation. (Fig. 2 from Darley & Murdock, 1971.)

(2 × 2). That is, half the lists were given an immediate recall while the other half were given a brief distractor task instead. Then at the end, the subjects were divided and half were given a final free recall while the other half were given a final three-alternative forced-choice recognition test. The main results are shown in Fig. 9.1.

There was no negative recency for final recognition, and tested and nontested lists did not differ. There was negative recency for final recall, and tested lists showed up better overall here than nontested lists. The conclusion drawn was that the effect of an immediate recall was to increase the accessibility of items which would facilitate final recall of tested lists. However, it was suggested that immediate recall did not increase availability, hence the final recognition of tested and nontested lists did not differ. As for negative recency, the point emphasized was that nonpositive recency was found for both final recall and recognition. Some recent unpublished data by Lockhart (personal communication) may make it necessary to modify this conclusion (the point having to do with presentation rate); for the time being, this last point should be held in abeyance.

Another striking effect reported by Craik (1970) was an output-order effect in final recall. As shown here in Fig. 9.2, the output order of an item in immediate recall was positively correlated with probability of correct recall on the final test. Not only do the data shown in this figure suggest a monotonic function, but it essentially seems to span the whole range, from near zero recall probability for the first item or two recalled to near unity for the last item recalled (in those few cases when it was). Further, it seems to be independent of whether presentation had been auditory or visual and whether immediate recall had been written or spoken.

According to a buffer model, this output function should be U-shaped, not monotonic. The first items out would be from primary memory, and they would be poor on

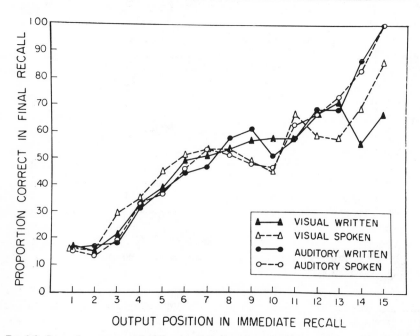

FIG. 9.2. Proportion correct on final free recall for those items initially recalled as a function of the position of the items in the immediate recall. (Fig. 3 from Craik, 1970.)

final recall because they had built up little strength in secondary memory. The secondary-memory recall should initially be ordered for strength (as, for instance, in the Shiffrin search model) so the very last items recalled on an immediate test should be weaker than those (secondary memory) items recalled earlier. Evidence for a nonmonotonic effect of this sort for Vincentized data (broken down by fifths of immediate recall) was reported in Rundus, Loftus, and Atkinson (1970). However, this U-shaped effect was not present in the data of Darley and Murdock (1971). Other data I have seen also fail to show the U-shaped function predicted by the model. However, the extent of the output-position effect shown in Fig. 9.2 may be a bit atypical. When one conditionalizes on the number of items recalled on the immediate test, the curve for final recall as a function of output position seems to level off at some value rather less than unity (Tulving, personal communication).

Up to this point the discussion has proceeded as if the serial-position curve for immediate recall was invariant. While in fact it is reasonably stable, it is certainly not independent of all possible experimental conditions. For one, as is common knowledge among experimenters, though not very well documented in the literature, the curve is different for naive subjects. On the very first trial, subjects typically show more primacy and less recency than practiced subjects. This effect is very transitory; by the second or third list, subjects have shifted over. Why this change from primacy to recency occurs is a moot point, though the reader should see the previous discussion of this point in Chapter 7. If conditions (e.g., list length) change from trial to trial one might continue to maintain subjects at this naive level, much as one gets release from proactive inhibition with change of material. This could explain why Bousfield, Whitmarsh, and Esterson (1958) found larger primacy than recency effects. Another factor operating in their experiment was that two minutes of an irrelevant task preceded each list. In an unpublished study, Donaldson (personal communication) has found an increase in primacy as the intertrial interval is increased.

The similarities between free-recall and proactive-inhibition effects seem to be more than fortuitous. In both, there is a change from primacy to recency with practice, and intertrial spacing seems to modify forgetting. The general implication, of course, is that interference is exerted by prior items (or lists) on subsequent items (or lists). This comparison is also supported by the results of Murdock and Carey (1972) who reported the counterpart of release from proactive inhibition in miniature serial-position curves within a single free-recall list. They blocked auditory and visual presentation of items within lists, and shifting modality of presentation in this way resulted in curves quite compatible with release effects from modality changes as reported by Hopkins, Edwards, and Gavelek (1971).

Other factors can affect the serial-position curve as well. The overt rehearsal procedure used by Rundus and Atkinson (1970) and Rundus (1971) employ both a slow presentation rate (typically five seconds per item) and a rehearsal procedure wherein the subject is to say aloud all items that he can rehearse. As is apparent from their data, such a procedure magnifies the primacy effect and reduces the recency effect. Also, modified free-recall instructions wherein subjects are instructed to start their recall either from the beginning or at the end result in accentuated primacy and recency effects, respectively (Craik, 1969; Murdock, 1968c). Insertion of a single high-priority item such as one's own name in a free-recall list seems to depress slightly the recall of the prior item (Tulving, 1969); both prior and subsequent items are recognized less well (Schulz, 1971). Finally, I have reanalyzed the data shown in Fig. 8.2 by conditionalizing upon the serial position of the first word recalled; each curve is distinctive and different from the others.

Further instances of departures could no doubt be found, but the above list perhaps includes some of the more notable effects. It illustrates that the serial-position effect can vary with experimental conditions, but there is really very little that cannot. What we need is a theory of parameters to explain both when invariance is to be expected and when not, but that goal is still some way off. We still do not have any completely satisfactory theoretical explanation of the serial-position function itself.

Finally, to return to the initial point, immediate tests may use either recall or recognition. A series of experiments comparing recall and recognition were reported by Schwartz and Rouse (1961), and some of them seemed to suggest clear differences between recall and recognition. On the other hand, Shiffrin (1970, Fig. 8, p. 408) has reported data where the serial-position curves for recognition and recall look much the same. Except for these two studies, I know of no other direct comparisons between recall and recognition for serial-position effects. However, studies of recognition memory generally take lag rather than serial position as their independent variable, and there is clearly no lack of information on recognition memory *per se* (see Chapter 3). Whether or not it even makes sense to compare serial-position curves for recall and recognition depends upon one's theoretical views of the processes operative in the two situations.

However, there is in the literature one other suggestive bit of evidence for the argument that the serial-position curve of single-trial free recall does mirror underlying processes quite independently of the recall process *per se*. Data reported by Buschke (1963b) and Buschke and Hinrichs (1968) who used a recognition-like procedure, show what is not unlike a typical free-recall serial-position curve with an eight-item recency effect. The procedure used was the missing-scan method previously reported by Buschke (1963a) wherein all but one element of a known set is presented to the subject who is then instructed merely to report the missing item. It is claimed that this method makes it possible to study immediate memory without retrieval, and what is interesting is that the serial-position curve so obtained is like that usually found with free recall.

REPETITION EFFECTS

Three main topics will be included here. The first is the total-time effect, where the joint effects of number of repetitions and presentation time are considered. The second is the lag effect (the interval between repetitions) and its possible explanations. The third is one of the cornerstones of organization theory, the relationship between two measures of performance under repetition, accuracy and organization.

Total-time Effect

As noted in the introduction to the last chapter, if a list of items is presented for a fixed amount of study time, then various combinations of list length and presentation time per item will not affect the number of items recalled. There is an invariance; the number of items recalled will be the same provided total study time is constant. This invariance should be distinguished from the possible linear relationship between number recalled and total study time when the latter is varied. It was also mentioned that within limits this relationship was linear as given by Eq. (8.1). However, some studies have shown that, over an extended range, the linearity may break down.

Murdock (1960b) reported data which showed that the same number of words were recalled for 20-3, 30-2, 40-1.5, and 60-1 lists. Postman and Warren (1972) found that, on both an immediate and a delayed test, approximately the same number of words were recalled for 20-3, 30-2, and 60-1 lists. As they point out, it is quite possible for this invariance to hold even if the effect of total presentation time on number of words recalled is not linear.

Waugh (1962) introduced another variable, that of intralist repetition. She found the probability of recall of an item to be a linear function of the number of times it was presented in a list, where critical items (one each) were presented two, three, four, or five times in a 50-item list. (That is, there were 50 slots for item presentation; in the control condition, each slot was filled by a different item, while in the experimental condition several slots could be taken by the same item. In fact only 40 different words appeared.) Also there was a trade-off; in the experimental condition fewer once-presented items were recalled. There was the same invariance reported by Postman and Warren (1972), namely, in the same total presentation time, the same number of items were recalled for the control and experimental conditions. These findings are actually rather surprising, as probabilities are generally not additive. That is, if each presentation laid down an independent trace, then by simple probability theory the probability that at least one of them would be recalled should increase in negatively accelerated, not linear, fashion, with repetition.

Waugh (1963) varied the number of repeated (twice presented) items from 1–8 within the framework of a 30-item list. (There were 30 slots for item presentation.) In general, repeated items had twice the recall probability of once-presented items; the exception was when there was only one repeated item in the list, and that gave somewhat better performance. There was no lag effect; the number of items separating repetitions was immaterial. We shall consider this point further in the next section. Though not as extensive a test as the previous study, this experiment also supported the total-time invariance principle.

Waugh (1967) considered both (a) invariance over repetition when total time was held constant and (b) number recalled when total presentation time was varied. As before, the invariance turned out quite nicely, here over a range of 1–5 presentations. When total presentation time varied, number recalled increased in logarithmic or exponential fashion, not the linear function of Murdock (1960b) given in Eq. (8.1). Repetition of a different sort was studied by Kolers (1966) who found that $n/2$ presentations of an item in two different languages was equivalent to n presentations of an item in one language. The same linearity effect was found as well, here spanning a range of 1–8 presentations (assuming that the translation of a word counts as a repetition). However, somewhat different results have been reported by Tulving and Colotla (1970).

Waugh and Anders (1972) used very slowly presented items and varied the number of presentations from 1–6. Again linearity resulted and, for the constant-time lists, essentially spanned the full probability range. Also, the slope reported for this function (.056) was essentially the same as that reported by Murdock (1960b) as the median value (.060) for experiments varying list length and time per item. Finally, Roberts (1972) reported an extensive parametric study of the linearity relationship where the total presentation time varied from a few seconds to more than 5 minutes. When number recalled was plotted as a function of total presentation time, the functions were negatively accelerated when the parameter was either list length or presentation time per item. These results agree with Waugh (1967) and data reported in Shiffrin (1970), not with the linear function given in Eq. (8.1). They are shown here in Figs. 9.3 and 9.4.

It would seem, then, that the invariance when total presentation time is constant holds up very consistently in all studies cited. The linearity is another matter; it holds for restricted ranges but not extended ranges. It may be, as Roberts (1972) suggests, that my early findings resulted from the use of cued recall. (The answer sheets used by subjects were arranged alphabetically.) The linear relationship does seem to occur in cued recall (paired associates); examples may be found in Murdock (1967a) or Tulving and Pearlstone (1966). Also, this interpretation would be consistent with a retrieval-factor explanation (Shiffrin, 1970; Waugh, 1967). However, it has not yet been subject to experimental testing.

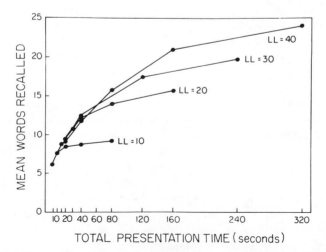

FIG. 9.3. Mean free recall as a function of total presentation time with list length as the parameter. (Fig. 1 from Roberts, 1972.)

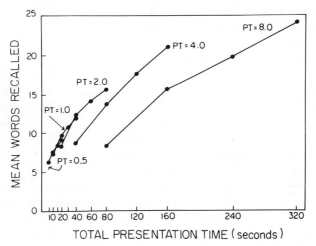

FIG. 9.4. Mean free recall as a function of total presentation time with presentation time per item as the parameter. (Fig. 2 from Roberts, 1972.)

Lag Effect

As discussed by Melton (1970), this effect deals with the spacing of repetition. Within the single presentation of a long list of items, the more widely separated the two presentations of a particular item the better the subsequent recall. The magnitude of this effect can really be very impressive. As shown here in Fig. 9.5, a replication of an early study of Melton (1967) by Madigan (1969) showed a monotonic effect over the range 0–40. Probability of recall at lag 40 was almost exactly twice the probability of recall at lag 0. In these studies, it is typically the case that a long list

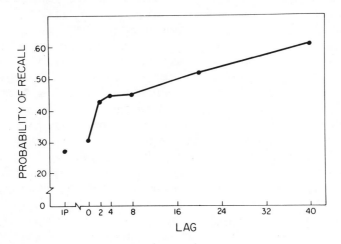

FIG. 9.5. Recall probability for an item presented once (1P) or twice at lag 0, 2, 4, 8, 20, or 40. (Fig. 1 from Madigan, 1969.)

of items is presented, some items are presented once and others twice, and a primacy and recency buffer is included to restrict attention to nonterminal items. Counter-balancing lag over serial position is a tricky matter, and the need for care in this regard has been pointed out by Shaughnessy, Zimmerman, and Underwood (1972).

One of the problems with lag effects is that they don't always occur, and the reasons for this are still slightly obscure. Waugh (1963, 1967) found no effect of lag, and in fact concluded that the critical variable influencing recall of an item was the number of seconds for which it had been presented, regardless of how the time is distributed within a list. Subsequently (Waugh, 1970b) she reported some data suggesting that presentation rate may be a critical variable, with no lag effect at either a fast or a slow rate but a difference between massed and spaced presentation at the slower rate. Melton (1970) did get a lag effect for rates of 1.3, 2.3, and 4.3 sec/item. More recently, Melton and Glenberg (1971) reported a parametric study of presentation rate with results suggesting that the faster the presentation rate the greater the spacing interval which did not differ from massed presentation. There is still the refractory data of Underwood (1969b) where degree of spacing had no effect, and there the presentation rate was very slow (5 seconds per item). However, both there and in a later paper (Underwood, 1970) there is a big difference favoring spaced repetition over massed repetition.

Following Melton (1970) in this regard, it does seem that there is enough positive evidence to accept the lag effect as genuine, the occasional misses notwithstanding. Why does it occur? The most popular explanation seems to be in terms of context. The greater the separation between the two presentations the greater the difference in context, where context is produced by the surrounding items. On the assumption that the more varied the context the better the recall (two retrieval cues are better than one), then recall should improve with spacing.

Early evidence for the importance of varied context comes from a study by Bevan, Dukes, and Avant (1966). They presented eight instances of generic stimuli with either one, two, three, or four different exemplars. Free recall improved with the number of different exemplars, so a varied context (or high type-token ratio) facil-itates recall. (Types refer to the number of unique instances, and tokens refer to the total number of instances. For a recent use of this distinction see Tulving & Hastie, 1972; for further examples see Miller, 1951). A later study by Dukes and Bevan (1967) found that, in paired associates, recall of a specific response was hampered by variation in context, at the same time that identifying members of a class was facilitated. The benefits of varied context can also be obtained with random shapes and nonsense syllables (Avant & Bevan, 1968a) but are considerably reduced under a recognition-memory procedure (Avant & Bevan, 1968b).

One way to test the varied context hypothesis is to see if one can make the lag effect disappear by experimentally controlling the context rather than letting it vary haphazardly in terms of whatever items happen to be presented. If one varies the context deliberately then, to the extent that context is under experimental control, short lags should be as effective as long lags. This approach was used by Madigan (1969) with retrieval cues accompanying the to-be-remembered items, as earlier studied by Tulving and Osler (1968). If the retrieval cue was different on the two presentations of an item, then that aspect of the context differed and the lag effect should be less than if the same retrieval cue was present both times. In fact, the lag effect nearly disappeared with cued recall, so the hypothesis was supported. Similar results were reported by Winograd and Raines (1972) for sentence context.

This conclusion was affirmed in a different manner by Bjork and Allen (1970). As they point out, an alternative explanation would be in terms of consolidation. The longer the lag between the two presentations, the more time the first trace would have to consolidate, so the better the subsequent memory should be. To separate the encoding and the consolidation interpretations they varied the difficulty of a task interpolated between the two presentations. Increasing the difficulty should interfere with the consolidation, but the results showed that performance was actually slightly better. Consequently, their results support the encoding interpretation. Still another approach to this problem is with bilinguals. Glanzer and Duarte (1971) found a greater lag effect (for noncued recall) within, rather than between, language repetition.

An explanation of the lag effect in terms of rehearsal processes was investigated by Rundus (1971). He repeated items at various lags and measured the number of overt rehearsals given. As one might expect, the total number of rehearsals an item received increased with lag. The second presentation of an item initializes its processing and so terminates whatever rehearsing is still in progress. Since recall has clearly been shown to vary with number of rehearsals (e.g., Rundus & Atkinson, 1970) one could plausibly argue that a differential amount of rehearsal underlies the lag effect. Reasonable as this may seem, it does not predict that change in context should attenuate or eliminate the lag effect (e.g., Glanzer & Duarte, 1971; Madigan, 1969). Thus, the context manipulation would seem to support an encoding-variability interpretation more than a rehearsal interpretation.

There is one small problem with a context interpretation of the lag effect. It is the assumption that a change in context benefits recall. In fact, there is reason to believe exactly the opposite. Murdock and Babick (1961) repeated a single word in a constantly changing context and found no benefits whatsoever from repetition. This work was extended by Tulving (1970) who spanned the entire range. At one extreme, no items were repeated in each successive list; at the other extreme, all items were repeated in each successive list. This latter procedure of course defines the standard multitrial free-recall procedure where we know that improvement occurs. In this paper Tulving reported that the larger the number of repeated items, the more items were recalled, so again the implication is that the more context that is the same, the better the memory for the items in question. These findings would seem to contradict the encoding-variability hypothesis.

To conclude this section, a different approach to measuring the lag effect should be mentioned. One can record latencies; for instance, one can vary the lag between the first and the second presentation and then record the latency of reaction to the third presentation at some specified retention interval(s). Unfortunately, two such studies give conflicting evidence. Hintzman (1969a) used lags of 1, 2, 4, 8, or 16 items and found that latencies on the third presentation (16 items after the second presentation) declined monotonically with lag. Okada (1971) varied orthogonally both the lag between the first and second and the lag between the second and third presentations. He found that there was no consistent difference in latency on the third presentation as a function of the first lag. Since the monotonic effect found by Hintzman was less than 25 msec overall, perhaps the appropriate conclusion to draw at this point is that, if there is an effect of lag on latencies, it is probably rather small in magnitude.

Accuracy and Organization

The other main topic to be considered is the relationship between two measures of performance—number of items recalled and stereotypy in output order. The latter is a measure of organization, and it is assumed by organization theorists to underlie the former. That is, the reason that the number of items recalled increases over trials (i.e., that learning occurs with repetition) is that organization takes place. This point was suggested by Tulving (1962) who proposed a measure of organization based on repeated sequences and suggested that the co-variation in the organization measure

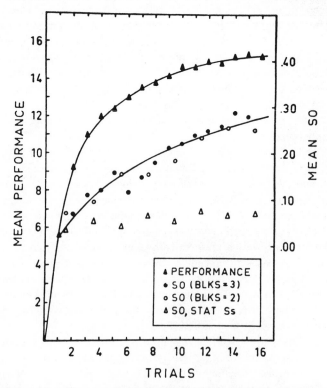

FIG. 9.6. Mean number of items recalled (top curve), subjective organization (bottom curve), and the organization measure for Monte Carlo data with no sequential order. (Fig. 1 from Tulving, 1962.)

and the recall measure was not coincidental. Some data from this paper are shown here in Fig. 9.6 where the upper curve shows the mean number of items recalled, the lower curve shows the measure of organization (mean SO), and the horizontal points show the same SO measure computed on Monte Carlo data to insure that the increase in the organization measure was not simply an artifact of the increasing number of items entering into the calculation over trials.

There are various measures of organization possible, and they are generally based on intertrial repetition ratios. A related but somewhat different viewpoint has been suggested by Ehrlich (1965, 1970) who measured organization not by stereotypy in order of recall but by a measure of structuration. The trial on which the subject recalls all items (hence the last trial) is taken as the reference point, and earlier trials are compared to it. Looking retrospectively, there is a progressive increase in the extent to which the two agree as trials increase. This measure of structuration may be closer to the Gestalt concept of organization than measures based on intertrial repetition ratios.

The view that organization underlies the improved performance over trials was reiterated by Tulving (1968). However, this relationship is correlational and, to date, no casual relationship has been demonstrated. Further, evidence is beginning to appear to demonstrate that organization and learning may be decoupled. Laurence (1966) showed that ten-year old children (Group IV) learned better than the elderly subjects but had clearly lower subjective organization scores. These relations held despite the fact that both groups separately showed reasonable increases over trials in both measures. An experiment with similar import is that of Puff (1970). In a categorized list he found no difference in recall between those subjects who showed high clustering and low clustering.

It would be unwise to take the opposite stance and say that organization is not involved in learning. Certainly the correlation has been demonstrated sufficiently often to lead us to have confidence that there is some relation between the two. But as everyone recognizes, there may be some additional factor which underlies both the increased stereotypy in recall and the improved retention over trials. To account for the above results it would be necessary to explain when there was covariation and when there was not. In any case, it would seem incumbent for organization theorists to document a bit more convincingly the exact principles involved. It is not enough simply to assume a basic casual relationship between organization and learning as an article of faith. This general problem has been discussed much more thoroughly by Postman (1972), who emphasizes the importance of anchoring organization both to antecedent conditions and to observable consequences, and by Wood (1972), who suggests that the problem may be primarily the inadequacies of the organizational measures themselves.

TEST-TRIAL EFFECTS

One of the views on free recall is that it reflects the operation of a limited-capacity retrieval system. As suggested by Tulving (1968), it might be the case that different retrieval cues were operating for items in different parts of the list, thus giving rise to recency effects because of temporally salient cues and an asymptote for items retrieved on other bases. (For comments on this view see Broadbent, 1970.) To test this idea, Tulving (1967) varied the usual RTRT paradigm and employed an RTTT paradigm. Each presentation trial was followed by three test trials. More specifically, the list was 36 items long and was presented at a rate of 1 item per second. Thirty-six seconds were allowed for recall. Thus, four 36-second periods could be occupied with two study-test cycles in the conventional RTRT arrangement, or such periods could be occupied with one study and three test cycles in the RTTT arrangement. For the latter, after 36 seconds had elapsed the subject was in effect simply told to recall again.

The main results from this experiment are shown in Fig. 9.7. Group S is the standard (RTRT), Group R the recall group (RTTT), and Group P is the presentation group (RRRT). The latter had three successive study trials before each test trial. As can be seen, on the second and third test trials Group R dropped down a bit, but overall there seemed to be no handicap. By and large, after comparable numbers of 36-second periods it seemed to make little difference whether the preceding periods had been filled primarily with study trials, test trials, or half of each. In examining the distribution of recall over items for the RTTT condition it was found that, of those words recalled at least once within a cycle, only about 50% were recalled on all three test trials. These results were taken as support for the limited-capacity retrieval hypothesis.

This initial finding has led to considerable subsequent experimentation in an attempt to clarify the phenomenon. Lachman and Tuttle (1965) suggested that both study and test trials contribute to free-recall learning though the contribution of each varies with the performance level of the subject at the time. Rosner (1970) looked at organization effects and concluded that, though study and test trials may contribute equally to the formation of such units, recall trials were more beneficial than study trials in their consolidation effects (though see also Hudson, Solomon, & Davis, 1972). Patterson (1972) demonstrated effects of category size and retrieval cues (category names) on both cued and noncued recall from categorized lists. Bregman and Wiener (1970) compared paired associates and free recall in this RTTT paradigm and found clear differences. Paired associates did not show the same benefits from repeated test trials; in fact, the RTTT group was at a considerable disadvantage compared to the RTRT group. On the other hand, the paired-associate group was more stable from trial to trial than was the free-recall group.

By and large, much of the experimental evidence suggests little or no difference between RTRT and RTTT groups. One exception has been reported by Birnbaum and Eichner (1971). They used categorized lists and had subjects return 48 hours later for a second test. Though performance of RTRT and RTTT groups did not differ in acquisition, on the delayed recall the RTRT group clearly outperformed the RTTT group regardless of whether this second recall was cued (category names) or noncued. It was suggested that perhaps the standard group had more items in store than the RTTT group but that, with weaker retrieval cues, the differences

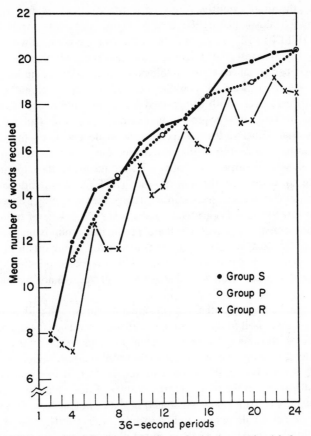

Fig. 9.7. Multitrial free-recall learning curves for Group S with three study trials for every test trial (RRRT), Group P with alternating study and test trial (RTRT), and Group R with three recall trials for every study trial (RTTT). (Fig. 2 from Tulving, 1967.)

would only show up with repeated searches of the memory store (the second phase of the delayed recall).

Hogan and Kintsch (1971) used recall and recognition comparisons on an immediate or delayed test to try to separate availability and accessibility factors. In general, the RTRT paradigm gave better results than the RTTT paradigm on recognition, but worse results on recall. Thus, it was suggested that study trials facilitate availability of storage of items, so that the group with more study trials (total time held constant) will recognize more. On the other hand, test trials facilitate accessibility, so that the group with more test trials will recall more. Of course, this conclusion is predicated on the two-process view of recall whilch is not universally accepted. However, as has been mentioned, there are other cases where the effects of a particular manipulation go one way with recall as the measure, but the other way with recognition as the measure.

Probably the most extensive study of test-trial effects in free recall has been reported by Donaldson (1971). He used as many as seven test trials between each study trial (RTTTTTTT). In general, his results were consistent with those reported above, namely, that test trials increase the accessibility of information in the store. By and large, performance at comparable points in the experiment were as good with up to seven test trials (and the consequent reduced number of study trials) as with the standard paradigm. With categorized lists, more items per category were recalled (after the first trial) the greater the number of test trials that occurred between each study trial. Finally, these effects seem to depend upon the time spent retrieving, not how the retrieval time is parceled out into recall trials.

In general, what is surprising about such findings is that the experimental groups (RTTT) are not worse than the control group (RTRT). In a traditional view, where presentation of list items is seen as reinforcing, then one might expect them to be at a severe disadvantage because they have, over the course of training, so many fewer reinforcements. The fact that the experimental group is not inferior (in fact, on some measures may excel) is taken as evidence for the importance of accessibility factors in single-trial free recall. It suggests that repeated practice spent recalling is as beneficial as study trials for subsequent recall (though not, as noted above, for recognition).

It might also be noted that these results are not inconsistent with sampling models such as those discussed in the last chapter. If one postulates that there is a store of available items immediately after list presentation, and recalling involves sampling from this store, then one would expect some variation from sample to sample in the case where successive recalls were required. In fact, if one considers sampling without replacement as the proper representation of this situation, then the accessibility problem is perhaps not as great as it might at first appear. Suppose the probability that any available item would be recalled was .80. Then the probability that an item would be recalled on all three output phases would be approximately .50, a figure that was cited by Tulving (1967). Thus, by this reasoning only 20% of the available items are inaccessible.

Of course, a simple urn model would have to explain not only why performance improves over trials but also why, at comparable points in time, the control group is not better than the experimental group. Presumably study trials would increase the store of available items, so if all test trials did was to provide three independent (but nonstrengthening) samples from this (ever-growing) pool then clearly this model would not suffice. There would have to be some mechanism whereby test trials had a facilitating effect like study trials. So, for the present at least, a simple random-sampling model, even with monitoring, would be embarrassed by these test-trial effects. However, there is no reason why such a model could not be elaborated to accommodate them.

Finally, despite the flurry of recent interest in test-trial effects, it might be noted that their existence is not without precedent. Brown (1923) reported a simple experiment in which he gave an immediate and a delayed recall after the single presentation of a list. The intervening time was filled with a classroom lecture. He found similar total recall on the two test trials but was surprised by the existence of a number of items recalled on the second test but not on the first test. Thus, this early study by Brown also showed that a single recall trial does not provide a complete enumeration of the set of available items.

CUING EFFECTS

Cuing effects are of two general types, positive and negative. In the former case, cuing facilitates recall; in the latter case, it inhibits recall. These are obviously two rather different matters and, as one might expect, different types of cues are involved in the two cases. In the former case the cues are ancillary; generally they represent information over and above that which the subject is to recall, and such cues are dubbed retrieval cues in the terminology of Tulving (1968). In the latter case the cues are not ancillary; they are in fact part of the to-be-recalled material itself. As independently reported by Brown (1968) and by Slamecka (1968), presentation or recall of a subset of the retrieval ensemble decreases the number recalled from the complementary subset.

Positive Cuing

To consider positive cuing effects first, perhaps the first deliberate study was that of Tulving and Pearlstone (1966). They had categories such as four-footed animals, weapons, substances flavoring food, and professions. They presented lists of 12, 24, or 48 words with one, two, or four items per category. There were two types of recall: cued (by the category name) and noncued (without the category name). The main finding was that, while the number of words recalled under cued recall was higher than the number of words recalled under noncued recall, the number of items recalled per category was the same. The implication was that, once access to a category had been achieved, all available items were recalled. The retrieval cues (category names) simply increased the number of categories accessed. A similar conclusion was implied by two earlier studies of Cohen (1963, 1966) who found that the number of chunks recalled varied with experimental conditions, but the number of words per chunk tended to stay fairly constant. Also, Bahrick (1969, 1970) has attempted to vary the effectiveness of retrieval cues by different associative prompts.

This work was extended to noncategorized lists by Tulving and Osler (1968). Pairs of words that (normatively) were weakly associated such as leg–MUTTON, dirty–CITY, and vigor–HEALTH were presented. The subjects were instructed to remember only the words in capitals, but the initial words were included because they might help. Two sets of cues were used (between subjects) which, in two cases, were the same at presentation and recall but, in two other cases, were not. Mean number of words recalled (out of 24) was approximately 15 in the former case but only 7.5 in the latter case. The strong conclusion was drawn that cues facilitate recall if and only if they are stored with the to-be-remembered item at the time of presentation.

There was no evidence from the Tulving and Osler study that two retrieval cues were any better than one. This finding was questioned by McLeod, Williams, and Broadbent (1971) who compared recall with one and two separate cues. After list presentation there was first noncued recall, then recall with one cue for each nonrecalled word, then recall with two cues (the original plus one additional) for each nonrecalled word. The second condition was better than the first, but the third condition was the best of the three. There was a guessing control group, and the analysis of the data suggested that the facilitation was greater than an independence model would predict.

Another variation was suggested by Dong and Kintsch (1968) who used the sorting technique of Mandler and Pearlstone (1966). After an initial sorting of words into categories, each subject was asked to label each category. Then free recall of the sorted items was requested. One group was given the category labels; another group was not. While the number of words recalled was appreciably larger for the cued than the noncued group, the number of words recalled per category was essentially the same. Thus, again the implication is that retrieval cues provide access to categories, but exhausting a category is indepedent of how it had been accessed.

As has been mentioned, retroactive inhibition in free recall can be reduced if not eliminated by use of retrieval cues (Tulving & Psotka, 1971). Retrieval cues are not restricted to recall measures; they seem to apply to recognition as well (Tulving & Thomson, 1971). Finally, at a more anecdotal level, many of us have probably experienced this effect ourselves. Is it not often the case that hastily scribbled lecture notes, memos, or whatever serve later to reinstate a more complete reconstruction of the target information? This phenomenon has long gone under the name of redintegration, and the positive effects of retrieval cues may be another example of the reinstatement of memory traces through the operation of redintegration.

Negative Cuing

For negative cuing, Brown (1968) suggested that strong associations block weak ones. An experimental group studied a list containing the names of 25 states of the Union, then was asked to recall all 50 states. The control group was not given the initial study on the subset. Not surprisingly, the experimental group recalled more of the studied subset. What was surprising, perhaps, was that the experimental group actually recalled less of the complementary subset (those 25 states not studied) than the control group. Cumulative recall was taken, and this effect held up throughout the ten-minute recall period.

More extensive documentation of this point was provided by Slamecka (1968) who used post-list cuing in free recall. After list presentation some of the list items were presented gratis, as it were, and subjects in the experimental condition were merely to recall as many of the remaining words as they could. Although the expectation was that this subset would facilitate recall of the remainder, in fact the results were generally the opposite. The experimental groups recalled significantly fewer words than the noncued control groups. This effect seemed quite general; it occurred for a variety of types of lists and was quite independent of what proportion of the list items were presented as cues to the experimental subjects. The results were interpreted as suggesting that memory traces are independent in storage, but that the interdependence (as might be manifest in organization or clustering methods) develops through a retrieval plan set up at input and executed at output.

Much of the subsequent research has focused on this interpretative issue. Allen (1969) concluded that cuing could facilitate recall and so disagreed with the independence interpretation, but his results were only marginally significant. Freund and Underwood (1969) used four different instructions (to form interitem associations, to organize by serial position, to organize alphabetically, and control) crossed with three different types of cues (serially organized, alphabetically organized, or randomized) and found essentially no benefits from cuing. They concluded that free recall empties the store. Slamecka (1969b), Wood (1969), and Hudson and Austin (1970) extended this work to the multitrial situation. Slamecka (1969b) again found a negative cuing effect, but the latter two studies did find some facilitation. Most recently Slamecka (1972) has suggested that positive cuing will be found only when the cues provide access to categories which the subject would not otherwise have retrieved. He is still reluctant to espouse an associative (interdependent) model for storage.

By now there seems to be sufficient evidence to conclude that positive, zero, or negative cuing effects can be obtained, depending upon the particular experimental conditions. Where does that leave us? There are really two issues here, the storage independence hypothesis and the negative cuing effect. The former may be a less fruitful issue to pursue. The model of Rundus (1973) shows that it is possible to have organized storage and yet still have negative cuing effects under certain free-recall conditions.

On the other hand, the fact that negative cuing effects can be obtained under certain conditions seems clearly established, and it seems to be a phenomenon of interest in its own right. Keppel (Lake Arrowhead Conference, June, 1972) reported that simple presentation of the names of half the states of the Union before recall was enough to depress recall of the remainder. Tulving and Hastie (1972) reported that, for token recall, words only presented once in an experimental list were at a disadvantage compared to a control condition in which all words were presented only once. (In the experimental condition, five words were presented once and five twice; in the control group, 15 words were each presented once.) The general principle would seem to be the inhibitory effects of reducing the size of the pool of to-be-recalled items. Regardless of whether the initial (inhibiting) items are recalled by the subject or presented by the experimenter, their existence seems to put the remainder in a disadvantageous position.

To go beyond the above statement to any deeper level of understanding probably requires a particular model of the free-recall process. That suggested by Rundus (1973) is particularly suited to handling the negative cuing effect. Since it is based on sampling with replacement, segregating (by whatever means) part of the items subsumed under a particular retrieval cue will make the remainder more inaccessible. On the other hand, providing retrieval cues which the subject does not access himself would be expected to have the opposite effect, namely, to facilitate recall. These of course are exactly the empirical effects reported. So in a general way this model could explain both positive and negative cuing effects.

Cuing to Forget

To conclude this section, one final topic will be considered. That is the cuing-to-forget experiments, where a cue inserted into a list instructs a subject that he need not remember certain designated items. This manipulation of course is instructional, so in a sense it is different from those effects previously considered. However, it is included here because it is clearly a cuing effect. Paired-associate studies were discussed in the section on Testing Effects in Chapter 5.

Bjork, LaBerge, and LeGrande (1968) presented one or two consonant quadragrams inserted in digit series with instructions to forget, sometimes, the first quadragram. In such cases recall (of the second quadragram) was better than in the absence of such a cue but worse than if the first item was not even presented. A subsequent study with paired associates (Bjork, 1970b) suggested that proactive-inhibition effects could be attenuated with instructions to forget. Three possible explanations of these cuing effects were tested, and the most promising was that subjects partition the items into two subsets (to-be-remembered and to-be-forgotten) and selectively rehearse only the former.

In a free-recall experiment, Woodward and Bjork (1971) presented either a "forget" cue or a "remember" cue after each word. In immediate recall, subjects were quite able to restrict themselves to those words with the "remember" cue. Final recall (in the Craik sense) showed similar results, even though the "forget" cue was countermanded but, when categorized lists were used, "forget" words were recalled from accessed categories. The inference was drawn that the "forget" instructions operate on retrieval rather than storage processes. On the other hand, Davis and Okada (1971) tested both recall and recognition and found that recognition as well as recall was depressed (for the "forget" items). From one point of view, such a result would not be expected if the "forget" cue operated solely on retrieval processes.

A study by Block (1971) attempted to determine whether instructions to forget affected only rehearsal or differentiation as well. Since a final recognition test showed that forget-cued words were recognized as well as noncued words, he concluded that both differential storage and retrieval were involved. However, Davis (1973) repeated this study and included a condition where some lists were not tested (recalled) after initial presentation. Particularly for this condition, forget-cued items were less well recognized on a final test than remember-cued items. More important, there was an interaction such that List-2 (Serial Position 7–12) items following the "forget" cue were better recognized than List-2 items following a "remember" cue. These results (and the general conclusion) was that "forget" cues allow a redistribution of rehearsal or processing capacity with a resulting effect on storage.

There have been a number of additional studies, and they are reviewed by Bjork (1972). In interpreting these results, it should be kept in mind that the term "forget cue" is really shorthand (or laboratory slang) for instructions of a particular kind. They really tell the subject simply that he need not remember the specified item or items. It is not that the subject dramatically expunges an item from memory (any more than testing items in paired associates remove them from a hypothetical memory store). Instead it sets up a selective discrimination so the subject presumably concentrates his rehearsal on the to-be-remembered items. The evidence would seem to suggest that there is some residual mnemonic information about the cued items, but they do not seem to be incorporated into any particular retrieval scheme.

It may be that the forget-cue manipulation is most useful as a technique for investigating other processes. For instance, Turvey and Wittlinger (1969) found less proactive inhibition with cuing-to-forget instructions. Already there have been two examples where this technique has been employed to study some of the underlying processes in free recall. Bruce and Papay (1970) were interested in the primacy effect in single-trial free recall. Since the primacy effect over the functional beginning of a list was not diminished by a forget cue, the possibility of intraserial proactive inhibition was ruled out. A von Restorff-type explanation for the forget cue was not likely, and tests on the final list (to recall all items) gave results more in accord with a rehearsal-buffer interpretation than a retrieval-cues explanation.

The other example is a study by Waugh (1972). She was interested in the question of why it is relatively more difficult to remember a long list than a short list. According to a restrictive-storage hypothesis, simply attending to the initial items in a list would be sufficient to depress retention of the subsequent items, and the longer the list the greater this depression. An alternative would be a restrictive-retention hypothesis when the deficit is produced by the concurrent retention requirement. If the subject is allowed to forget the initial items then, by the latter hypothesis, recall of the second half of the list should be better if there is a forget cue for the first half than if there is not. Recall was better, suggesting that active review and re-rehearsal is necessary for single-trial free recall, and that this is more efficient the smaller the number of items in the to-be-remembered set.

PART-TO-WHOLE TRANSFER

The part-to-whole transfer paradigm was introduced by Tulving (1966) to assess the effect of repetition in multitrial free recall. The paradigm is simplicity itself. The experimental group learns a second list twice as long as the first list, with the first list a subset of the second. For the control group, the two lists are unrelated. In the whole-list learning the standard procedures of free recall are observed. That is, presentation order is randomized which means that, for the experimental group, old and new items are randomly intermixed.

The main results of this first experiment are shown here in Fig. 9.8. On the second list (36 words long) the experimental group (open circles) starts out above the control group (closed circles) but there is a crossover at Trial 4. Thereafter the experimental group is at a disadvantage. Thus, there is negative part-to-whole transfer in this situation, as the slope of the learning curve for the control group is steeper than

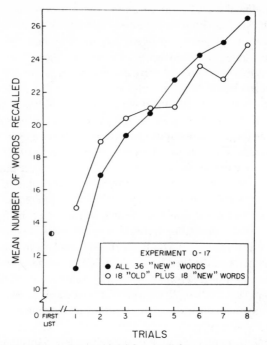

FIG. 9.8. Second-list performance in multitrial free recall for experimental group (open circles) and control group (closed circles) in part-to-whole transfer paradigm. (Fig. 2 from Tulving, 1966.)

that of the experimental group. That is, these curves plot number recalled as a function of amount of practice, and the slope (rate of change) of the function is a measure of learning.

This experimental paradigm and result was presented as one of several attempts to test differential predictions of organization theory as contrasted with an associative interference theory in multitrial free recall. According to an interference-theory view of learning, improvement in performance is due to some sort of strengthening of associative connections through repetition. Since the experimental group had the advantage of a first list that was part of the second list, they had already learned half the material and so should have had an easier time throughout. Such was clearly not the case. The organization view, by comparison, suggests that multitrial free recall involves the formation of appropriate subjective units and, for any given list of items, that some arrangements might be better than others. The experimental group might be handicapped by the prior organization of the subset, and they would either have to unlearn it or be forced into a suboptimal organization for the remainder. In either case they would be at a disadvantage. Consequently, the fact that the experimental group started higher but progressed more slowly seemed quite consistent with an organization view but quite inconsistent with an interference-theory view of learning.

Novinski (1969) replicated this result and suggested that the locus of the disadvantage was in the old words, at least through the first half of the second-list learning.

Bower and Lesgold (1969) showed that negative transfer was obtained in a replication condition but that positive transfer could be obtained if the structure was such as to make part-list organization compatible with whole-list learning. Birnbaum (1969) found a similar result, as did Ornstein (1970). Wood and Clark (1969) and Novinski (1972) have reported that informing subjects in the experimental group as to the part-whole list structure used is sufficient to eliminate the negative transfer effect. The effect also seems to depend upon the material used (Hicks & Young, 1972). Thus, in the few years since this paradigm has been introduced we know that the effect is very reliable, we know some of the necessary preconditions, and we know how we can make the effect go away.

However, a major problem of interpretation has been raised by Slamecka, Moore, and Carey (1972). They suggest that using unstructured lists does not provide a fair test of the two opposing theories, since no result (positive or negative transfer) can refute the organization view. One can always make a *post hoc* explanation in terms of compatibility or incompatibility of part-list organization for whole-list learning. They suggest using instead categorized lists where one can experimentally control the organization so on an *a priori* basis it should either hinder or facilitate second-list learning. When they did this experiment, using the appropriate control conditions they concluded that only positive transfer was found throughout, thus supporting a frequency interpretation rather than an organization interpretation.

Another point they raise is the criterion problem. Subjects in the experimental group presumably recognize the fact that some of the words in the whole list are old, but they may not be certain that all have been included. To avoid possible intrusions, they argue, the subjects in the experimental group may raise their emission criterion

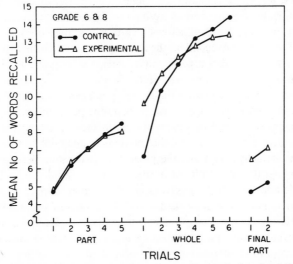

FIG. 9.9. Comparison of experimental and control groups with part-list learning followed by whole-list learning followed in turn by two relearning trials on the initial part list. (Data from Carey & Okada, 1973.)

thus lowering their observed performance. To counteract this tendency they instructed their subjects to adopt a lax criterion. With neutral instructions they obtained the crossover, but under the permissive condition they did not. This finding, they suggest, is also consistent with the previously-reported result that instructed subjects do not show the negative transfer effect. Presumably, when subjects are informed, there is no reason for them to raise their criterion.

The general conclusion, then, of Slamecka *et al.* is that the case for an organizational interpretation of the part-to-whole transfer effect is far from proved. On balance, they seem to feel that a simple frequency principle is perhaps more appropriate. A further test is provided by Carey and Okada (1973), who carry the part-to-whole design one step further. Following second-list learning, they test for retention of the first list. Thus, it is a retroactive-inhibition paradigm rather than a transfer paradigm. In learning the second list the experimental group should, by an organization view, have to reorganize its initial first-list organization. As a consequence, their memory for the first list should be impaired.

The combined results from their experiments are shown here in Fig. 9.9. As can be seen, the crossover effect was obtained in the second (whole) list learning. Subjects were then given two relearning trials on the first (part) list. As can be seen, the experimental group was clearly superior to the control group on both. Thus, contrary to an organization view, there does not seem to be more unlearning of the initial list for the experimental group when a retroactive-inhibition paradigm is used.

SUMMARY

The standard forgetting function for single-trial free recall is the serial-position curve with primacy, recency, and an asymptote. Immediate recall shows a positive recency effect, but delayed recall shows a zero or negative recency effect. An immediate recall test seems to facilitate the accessibility but not the availability of list items. On a delayed recall test performance seems to improve the later in output an item was recalled on an immediate test.

For a constant total presentation time, the number of items recalled will be the same regardless of how list length, presentation time per item, and number of repetitions are arranged. As total presentation time increases, so will number recalled, and, for times over a minute or two, the relationship may not be linear. For repetition, a critical variable is lag, and the greater the separation between two presentations, the greater the probability of recall. One explanation for the lag effect is in terms of varied context, but there is evidence from other types of recall studies that such variation is not necessarily facilitative. Measures of organization generally show an increase with repetitions in a multitrial situation, but the exact causal relationship between learning and organization is not yet a settled matter.

Test trials seem to be almost interchangeable with study trials in multitrial free-recall learning. Number of correct recalls after RTTT and RRRT sequences seem to be about the same, even when the number of tests is as large as seven. However, delayed tests, organization measures, and recognition may show some differences.

The general test-trial effect would be compatible with a sampling or search model for free recall.

Cuing effects in free recall are of two types: positive or negative. Positive cues are retrieval cues which facilitate recall. The critical variable seems to be that they are effective only if their cuing function is established at the time of presentation; stronger associative cues introduced only at the time of testing are less effective. Negative cuing refers to the fact that presentation or recall of some members of a set seems to depress recall of the remainder. A possible explanation for this effect can be found in the random-sampling model of Rundus (1973). Still another type of cuing effect is cuing to forget, and this instructional variable is quite effective. Probably the main reason that it works is that ''forget-cued'' items are not incorporated into the subject's rehearsal patterns, thus freeing processing capacity for noncued items.

In part-to-whole transfer the first list learned is a subset of the second. The control group has two unrelated lists and generally shows a steeper slope (faster learning) than the experimental group. It was originally used to demonstrate the importance of organizational factors in multitrial free recall, as the experimental group might be expected not to use the optimal grouping in second-list learning. However, when the grouping is controlled by the experimenter, positive transfer may be obtained instead; also, a retroactive-inhibition design shows better first-list recall for the experimental group than for the control group.

10
MODELS OF MEMORY

As noted in the Preface and documented in the intervening chapters, we now have empirical data of sufficient quantity and reliability to warrant the development of deductive models. Many such models have been discussed in the theory chapters of this book. In this last chapter I shall give my own views on item, associative, and serial-order information. I shall present or review a conveyor-belt model for item information, the fluctuation or cross-reference model for associative information, and a nesting model for serial-order information. In each case, the main features of the model will be described first. Then an evaluation will be given, including an attempt to show how well it can explain the main empirical effects described in the relevant data chapter. These models will be preceded by a section on memory and information processing. Here the role of memory in the broader scheme of things will be considered, and some analytic procedures for separating encoding, storage, and retrieval will be discussed. There will also be a section on free recall, but the theoretical suggestions will be somewhat vaguer there.

It goes without saying that all the theoretical suggestions in this chapter are provisional. We have not yet reached the point where we can make definite assertions about the mental mechanisms involved in human memory. However, the hope is that these models will do what any model attempts to do, namely, to integrate and organize current knowledge and suggest directions for future research. Even though some features of these models may seem counterintuitive, these models seem to me to be the best way we now can explain the experimental data. Finally, they are not hypothetico-deductive models in the sense, say, of Hull (1943), but hopefully they are specific enough so that deductions can be made and predictions tested.

One of the main features to be emphasized is that memory is continuous, not dichotomous. As I have said before, we have short-term, medium-term, and long-term memories, but the transitions are gradual, not abrupt. This view is not currently too well-accepted; many seem to favor the idea of discrete stores. Since the temporal partitioning of memory is so popular and well-accepted today, why try to suggest a redirection of current thinking? Can we not simply say that memory consists of a sensory information store, a short-term store, and a long-term store? We then have three systems, each with its own characteristics. Having agreed on that, we can settle our differences and get down to the business of discovering the characteristics and methods of functioning of each. The reason is that I think this view is wrong, and I am convinced that we will progress faster if we adopt an alternative view instead. At the risk of being unduly repetitious, let me try to summarize in a few words just why I think this view is wrong.

There are three main reasons. First, there is the language argument (Murdock, 1972). As envisaged by the modal model, short-term memory is specialized to retain perfect information about a limited number of items (typically about four). Yet to understand language requires that we retain partial information about a large number of items (words) for a relatively long period of time (e.g., the writing-righting example of Lashley, 1951, p. 120). It seems unlikely that language would have evolved into its present form if the short-term memory system really worked the way the modal model says it does.

Second, there is the matter of time constants (Craik & Lockhart, 1972). How long is short-term memory? If one looks at the animal literature and the work on consolidation and retrograde amnesia (McGaugh & Herz, 1972), the estimates of short-term memory are in terms of minutes or hours, perhaps even a day or so. In the types of studies reported in this book, short-term memory can span several hours, as in the picture-memory experiments of Haber (1970) for example, or the self-paced paired-associate procedure of Wallace, Turner, and Perkins (1957). Again, in item recognition short-term memory can easily cover a lag range of 100–200 items (e.g., Yntema & Trask, 1963) yet the recency effect spans 15 items in the probe-digit task of Waugh and Norman (1965), eight items in single-trial free recall (Murdock, 1962a), but no more than two or three pairs in a probe paired-associate task (Murdock, 1970). Surely variation this wide cannot all be encompassed in a single box labelled "short" term memory.

Third, there is the displacement or overwriting problem (Murdock, 1968c). If there were a discrete component of the memory system which only could hold a few items, then past that limit no trace of a displaced or overwritten item should be available. However, short-term memory seems to contain a limited amount of information about a large number of items, rather than perfect information about a few items. Failure to recall an item may indicate more an insensitive measure of memory than displacement from a limited-capacity buffer. If one gives a recognition test, then one gets a graded function which seems to be continuous over a range of lags of perhaps 100 or so intervening items. Both for a discrete-trials procedure and a continuous recognition-memory task a smooth continuous function seems to characterize forgetting.

Thus, in sympathy with sentiments expressed by others (e.g., Bernbach, 1969; Craik & Lockhart, 1972; Melton, 1963) I would prefer not to conceptualize memory in terms of discrete temporal partitions.

MEMORY AND INFORMATION PROCESSING

What is the place of memory in an information-processing analysis of human cognition? A simple illustration may suggest the general direction that any answer must take. Stop for a minute and perform the following task: Add the digits of your telephone number and "mentally register" (take note of) their sum. Then analyze the steps you went through to arrive at this answer. This simple task suggests a simple but fundamental point—one must distinguish between the contents of memory and the operations performed upon it. Let me try to elaborate this position and make it a bit more explicit.

The Role of Memory

At a very general level, the role I would assign to memory in an information-processing account of cognitive behavior is as follows. Information is entered directly into memory through sensory receptors, afferent pathways, cortical projection areas, and whatever additional neurophysiological systems are involved. (Recent work has suggested that information processing may occur far earlier in this system than was heretofore believed, but this topic cannot be pursued here.) Some "central processing mechanism" interacts with memory, using its information at certain times and selectively consolidating current features at other times. When I ask you to add the digits of your telephone number, "you" are the central processor and the information you are using is stored in and retrieved from the memory system. Any output is also from the central processor.

There are major differences between the human information-processing system and that of digital computers. First, in a computer the input generally goes through the central processing unit into memory; likewise, output from memory is again through the central processor. Thus, memory in a computer is a vast reservoir or repository of information which sits in splendid isolation from the vicissitudes of the environment, except when it is being operated upon by the central processor. In the human case, the contents of memory (or, more accurately, a very small subset of the contents of memory) are constantly changing, and there is no isolation or buffering from the external environment. (In fact, the situation is changing somewhat in this matter. Some computers now are able to make direct entry into memory and so bypass the central processor. However, in many cases this is still not possible.)

A second major difference is that information in human memory is temporally organized and, as a consequence, in a continual state of flux. Human memory is historical, but computer memory is ahistorical. Unless one interrupts the read-in process during execution there is no way, later, to infer which bits of information have resided longest in core or which bits are most recent. (The knowledgeable programmer could dispute this statement or at least come up with counter examples. Still, as a first approximation it is correct; or, if you wish, there are relative if not absolute differences between human and computer memories.) The fact that human memories are temporally organized—or, more correctly, how this organization is done—is one of the major unsolved mysteries of the human mind. We know little more than the Greeks did about this matter, but our ignorance should not lead us to overlook its importance.

A third major difference is that the relative speeds of operation seem to be opposite. In a computer, it is well known that input and output are slow, while processing is fast. In fact, very often large computers only talk to small computers, who in turn communicate with their users; in this way input and output can be speeded up somewhat. But it is still the internal processing which goes on at incredible speeds. In humans, the central processing seems to be relatively slow. As noted, for instance, by Welford (1960) the bottleneck in human information processing is in the middle.

There are other differences as well. Human memory is at least partly associative or content-addressable; computer memories generally are not (though they can be made so by programming). Human memory seems to be composed of unreliable elements, and the noise level is quite high; neither of these obtains in a computer. Other examples could be given; the interested reader might consult von Neumann (1958) or Wooldridge (1963). So while there are parallels between human information processing and that done by computers, there are differences as well. These differences are not trivial, and we want to make sure that we model the right system.

This overall viewpoint makes it possible to interpret many experiments quite simply and directly. Let me cite three examples. In a subsidiary task study Murdock (1965d) found that free recall deteriorated the more difficult a given secondary task was (it happened to be card sorting). Thus, compared to a control condition, performance decreased when subjects simply had to sort playing cards by color (red or black), and decreased still more when they were sorted by suit (diamonds, spades, clubs, and hearts, in that order). The interpretation would be that the more demanding the subsidiary task, the less processing capacity could be devoted to studying the items in the free-recall task. As a consequence, memory performance should be impaired, and it was, though more for the asymptote of the serial-position curve than for recency. Interpretation of this interaction depends upon what interpretation of serial-position effects one prefers.

A second example is a study by Burrows (1972) who attempted to determine if subjects could restrict their scanning to the relevant modality when auditory and visual presentations were mixed. Using a procedure similar to that of Sternberg (1966), a list of items was presented and each item was auditory or visual. From the data it seemed as if memory was not organized by mode of presentation, or, if it was, that subjects could not restrict their scanning to a single mode. The interpretation is probably obvious. The scanned material would represent the contents of memory and the central processor was doing the scanning. Actually, I am not too happy about this result; I would have expected some evidence for channel separation. Perhaps there are cases where temporal organization predominates and others where a modality organization predominates.

A third and final example is a psychological refractory-period study by Palef (1973b). She presented two sets of stimuli with different interstimulus intervals, and each set required a "same" or "different" judgment. The stimuli were either visual or auditory and either verbal (words from common categories) or nonverbal (tones or shapes). The results suggested that the basic processes were qualitatively the same (though varying in speed of execution) for the four cases (visual, auditory, verbal, and nonverbal). Here is a situation where the central processor is comparing items in memory and giving a same-different judgment for the two sets of material. The general implication is that the comparison process is the same regardless of the representation of the information in memory and whether the decision is based on the semantic characteristics of the material (category membership) or its physical features (intensity or form).

Analytic Separation

Given that human memory involves encoding, storage, and retrieval, how can we separate these three? What methods do we have to localize the effect of a particular experimental variable at one of these three stages? The answer is not easy or obvious, but perhaps the question deserves consideration.

Basically I think the analytic separation of these three processes is model dependent. What answers you get depend very much on what assumptions you care to entertain. Almost any model discussed in this book could illustrate this point. Thus, if you wish to assume that recognition by-passes the search problem then you can separate storage and retrieval by comparing recognition and recall. However, if you dislike this assumption, then this method may not be satisfactory. How you separate encoding, storage, and retrieval (if you can) depends upon what model you accept. It is becoming more and more difficult (and less and less fruitful) to study memory in a crassly empirical fashion.

This answer to the question is probably not too helpful. There are some who dislike models, or who are unwilling to entertain or accept the underlying assumptions they entail. Must they stop doing research? Clearly not; some compromise position may be necessary. Perhaps the following viewpoint might be generally acceptable both to the empiricist and the modeller.

Encoding, storage, and retrieval are sequential processes. For the time being, we had better consider them interdependent. So, any variable that affects encoding may also, perhaps, affect both storage and retrieval. Any variable that affects storage may also affect retrieval but not, by any reasonable view, affect encoding. (Backward action over time is not permissible.) Finally, retrieval follows encoding and storage, so retrieval variables *per se* cannot affect either of the other two. Thus, in a sense, retrieval is the easiest to study; by contrast, encoding requires the largest number of associated assumptions.

What variables do we have to effect such separation? The instructional variable of intentional versus incidental learning is one of the standard attempts to manipulate encoding. Some interesting variations on this theme have been developed by Jenkins and his colleagues (e.g., Hyde, 1973; Hyde & Jenkins, 1969; Johnston & Jenkins, 1971). Also, some very imaginative techniques have been reported by Craik (1973).

However, interpretation of results obtained with such techniques may be difficult. When subsequent performance is differentially affected is it because certain material was encoded better initially, retained better over time, or more accessible at the time of retrieval? The standard solution to such questions has been to employ appropriate control conditions and draw conclusions accordingly. But what control conditions are appropriate depends upon what processes are assumed to be involved, so again we are back to the underlying model. Conclusions require commitments, and we had all best accept this fact.

Storage has been studied by simply varying the length of the retention interval. For long-term memory we have no alternative; for short-term memory it is no longer very adequate. Too many confoundings are possible. In the human-memory area reviewed here we have such techniques as manipulating the information-processing demands (Posner & Rossman, 1965), the similarity of the material (Neimark, Greenhouse, Law, & Weinheimer, 1965), the rehearsal (Levy, 1971; Murray, 1967; Sanders, 1961) or rehearsal-prevention techniques (Glassman, 1972; Reitman, 1971), and, most generally, the amount of interpolated interference.

Finally, for retrieval there are several standard techniques. One is the recall-recognition comparison already mentioned; for an account and critique see Tulving and Thomson (1971). Another is to vary the number of alternatives in a forced-choice procedure (Davis, Sutherland, & Judd, 1961; Murdock, 1963). Yet another is the comparison of cued versus noncued recall, a procedure much used by Tulving and his colleagues (e.g., Tulving & Pearlstone, 1966; see also Bahrick, 1970). The recall-recognition comparison can no longer be used in an atheoretic way; however, within the framework of a particular model it may be a very useful procedure. The possibility of quantitative predictions from one to the other may also be a strong point in its favor. So too with the forced-choice variation. The cued versus noncued comparison is probably less model dependent, but there is a measurement problem. One is trying to compare recall of associative information with free recall, and that is not easy.

ITEM INFORMATION

The theories discussed in Chapter 2 were various versions of a threshold theory, strength theory, and two attribute models. The main difficulty with simple threshold theories is that they are discredited by the ROC curves and the *a posteriori* probability functions obtained from recognition-memory studies. Contrary to what these theories predict, the ROC curves are generally linear when plotted on double-normal probability scales and the *a posteriori* probability functions are graded (monotonic) over the confidence-judgment intervals used. Strength theory has two main problems, discriminability and retrieval. As detailed by Anderson and Bower (1972a) memory traces seem discriminable on a variety of different bases, none well-represented in the model itself. The retrieval processes are at best ill specified, and a direct-access process seems assumed. There are also problems with some aspects of the latency data (Murdock & Dufty, 1972).

Two attribute models were discussed, one proposed by Bower and one proposed by Lockhart. The former would seem to have trouble with representational memory; given that an item was remembered as old, there would seem to be no way one could identify a specific characteristic of its original presentation. As in strength theory, both models would seem to imply direct access. Given a probe, the central processor simply interrogates the appropriate location in memory and bases the response on what it finds. As I shall attempt to show, there is reason to doubt that direct access occurs.

According to the Lockhart attribute model, the underlying (old- and new-item) distributions should be Poisson. If this were the case, and if the subjects based their confidence judgments on an attribute count, then a direct test of the model is simple and straightforward. One can obtain an ROC curve based on Poisson distributions and see if a plot of log λ (the likelihood ratio) as a function of confidence judgment is linear for studies of recognition memory. (The procedure along with the necessary assumptions is described briefly in Murdock, 1970; to apply that reasoning to the present case substitute "attributes" for "copies.") I have made such Poisson ROC curves for various sets of recognition-memory data, and in general the fit is quite respectable. In fact one study (Murdock, 1968a) showed a nice experimental separation; modality of presentation (auditory or visual) affected the mean of the old-item distribution but not the mean of the new-item distribution, while the nature of the lure (novel, or from the prior list) affected the mean of the new-item distribution but not the mean of the old-item distribution.

However, detailed analyses of the distribution of confidence judgments were less favorable. As one example, I have analyzed the distribution of confidence judgments to new items for the subjects in Experiment I of Murdock and Dufty (1972) blocked by output sixths (Tests 1–5, 6–10, . . . , 26–30). In all cases (for each subject for each output block) the variance was about twice what it should have been. (The Poisson is a one-parameter distribution, and its variance should equal its mean.) Unfortunately, such a result is not unequivocal, since of necessity one has to pool over items. If items come from different populations, then it can be shown that pooling will have exactly this effect, namely, to inflate the variance. So the matter is simply not settled. Perhaps the main problem is, as noted, the direct-access issue.

If we are to understand memory for item information in any detail, we must be able to explain the data at three different levels of analysis. First and most basic are single-presentation effects: the distribution of confidence judgments, changes in these distributions as interference increases, *a posteriori* probability functions, changes in hit rates and false-alarm rates, ROC curves, the relationship between forced-choice and yes-no procedures, and judgments of recency. Second, we must be able to explain multiple-presentation effects. These include such things as changes in d' with repetition, lag effects, changes in latency, and judgments of frequency. Third, and most global, we must be able to explain the effects of various independent variables. These include such variables as list length, rate of presentation, meaningfulness, word frequency, study and test-trial comparisons, context effects, set-size effects, encoding specificity, and recall-recognition comparisons. We cannot claim to understand recognition memory until we can explain all three. My preference is to start with single-presentation effects; once we have an adequate model for them, then perhaps there is some hope that the more complex problems will fall out in a fairly simple and direct fashion. The opposite direction of theorizing strikes me as less promising.

Conveyor-belt Model

The most likely model I can suggest to portray the main features for the encoding, storage, and retrieval of item information is a simple conveyor-belt model. The initial encoding of an item is representational. This representational encoding of an item seems to contain information about its physical, associative, and semantic characteristics. Whether it should really be viewed as a literal copy or replica, or as a bundle of attributes, or as a structural description (e.g., Clowes, 1971) depends upon how the pattern-recognition system works. We don't know, and so we must be vague. What is important is that the information initially encoded in memory is sufficiently veridical so as to support identification of many of the physical characteristics of the stimulus, yet the initial encoding also has semantic or associative features as well. Perhaps the physical encoding comes first and the others are soon added, but there is little evidence in this matter.

There is a constant stream of incoming information. This stream is segmented into discrete items. As additional items are presented, earlier ones recede into the past. Somehow the brain must encode or represent temporal information in a spatial format and, as Milner (1961) has written, the question is how. Let me suggest a very simple physical analogy to illustrate how the process might work. My intention is to communicate, not impress, so it will not be an elaborate illustration.

Imagine a conveyor belt moving at a constant speed. Little packets or globs of material are dropped onto it, much as suitcases on a loading ramp at an airport. However, it is an endless conveyor belt, receding ever further into the distance. As a glob or packet gets further and further away it becomes more amorphous; it loses its attributes, the contents of the suitcase if you will. But the glob does not disappear; it simply becomes less distinctive. Retrieval of item information involves looking over this conveyor belt to find if a particular packet (or suitcase) is on the belt. If it was loaded it will be; but the further back it is, the less distinct it will be. Because of its age, the latency of the response will be longer, and because of the loss of distinctive features, the accuracy will suffer and confidence judgments will be lower. Judgments of recency, judgments of frequency, and list discrimination are all based on this same information (see Hintzman & Waters, 1970; Winograd, 1968; Yntema & Trask, 1963).

How does retrieval work? A broad overview is shown by means of a flowchart in Fig. 10.1. When the probe is presented it must be encoded. A memory comparison ensues, that is, the encoded version of the probe is compared against the contents of the memory store. The output from this stage is the input to the decision stage. Then one of two things happens. Either a response is given or a return loop reactivates the memory-comparison process. Some stop rule is necessary to prevent an endless loop, but that is not shown in the figure.

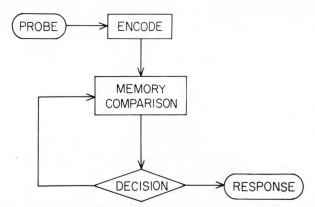

F IG. 10.1. A flow chart to indicate the memory-comparison process and decision.

The flow chart in Fig. 10.1 is only a slight elaboration and extension of that introduced as Fig. 1.1. Let me elaborate a bit more. The three stages are encoding, memory comparison, and decision. A fourth stage (response selection or preprogramming) might be necessary. Evidence for experimental separation may be found, e.g., in Palef (1973a). Criterion factors enter at the decision stage; whether to return or exit is clearly discretionary. Discriminability factors will affect the memory-comparison stage, as will the number of items required to undergo examination. The standard variable in this regard is set size (Sternberg, 1966); shortly we shall consider another (lag).

Representational features. It seems likely that human memory is organized first by mode of presentation and then, within that, by time of arrival. The view that modality organization is basic was stated by Wallach and Averbach (1955). A more restricted position is the two-store hypothesis which applies to auditory and visual modalities (Margrain, 1967; Murdock & Walker, 1969; Warrington & Shallice, 1972). Basically, all a two-store hypothesis says is that there are separate memory representations for auditorily-presented and visually-presented information.

No one would dispute that there are separate input systems for auditory and visual presentation; there are, after all, different sensory systems. There is also some evidence that early low-level processing may be conducted separately, even independently, in the two systems. Brown and Hopkins (1966) suggest there are separate auditory and visual signal-detection systems feeding into a "probabilistic response adder" which integrates the two (independent) inputs. There is some evidence (Chase & Calfee, 1969; Chi & Chase, 1972) that a translation process is necessary when the probe is presented in a different modality from the mode of presentation of the target item. However, once one starts using verbal material it seems to be immediately assumed that some common linguistic system comes into play and takes over. However, digits, letters, and words are still visual or auditory stimuli, as initially presented to the subject, and the problems that children have in learning to read would seem to be clear evidence for a two-store hypothesis.

There are seven main findings that seem relatively clear. First, the item information which is initially encoded in these modality-specific stores is representational.

Most if not all the information present in the stimulus is represented in the initial memory trace, so presentation of a word does not merely tag its long-term memory representation. Second, some of this representational information persists for an appreciable period of time. Third, the initial memory trace is prelinguistic, perhaps preperceptual. Fourth, with simultaneous encodings in separate modalities there is poor channel communication. Fifth, there is selective interference during any retention interval, so the mode of any interpolated activity will be more interfering if it is conducted in the representational mode of the format of storage. Sixth, loss of features (forgetting) occurs over time. Seventh, at least in a sense the auditory information store is specialized for sequential processing and the visual information store is specialized for simultaneous processing.

Some of the evidence for the above can be found in my four-channel paper (Murdock, 1971a) along with additional discussion elsewhere (Murdock, 1972). There is perhaps most evidence for the idea of modality-specific interference. Studies that demonstrate such an effect include Brooks (1968), Cohen and Grandstrom (1970), Deutsch (1970), Hopkins, Edwards, and Cook (1973), Kroll, Bee, and Gurski (1973), Morton and Holloway (1970), Ternes and Yuille (1972), and Wells (1972). The general superiority of auditory over visual short-term memory (e.g., Murdock, 1966d, 1967e) has even been reversed with auditory shadowing (Kroll, Parks, Parkinson, Bieber, & Johnson, 1970) and with counting backward in a distractor task (Scarborough, 1972).

Evidence for the persistence of the representational characteristics of short-term memory over reasonably long time periods has been found by Bray and Batchelder (1972), Craik and Kirsner (1974), Hintzman, Block, and Inskeep (1972), Kirsner (1973a, 1973b), Kolers (1973), Light, Stansbury, Rubin, and Linde, 1973, Madigan and Doherty (1972), Mann (1970, discussed in Murdock, 1972), Murdock (1971a), and Nilsson (1973). In general, it seems quite clear that a variety of characteristics of the stimulus (e.g., its mode of presentation, spatial location, lower- or upper-case type, or male- or female-speaker) persist with fair accuracy for retention intervals of a minute or two. The various time intervals studied make it quite clear that there is no such thing as a single unitary time constant for the decay of representational information.

The seventh of the above conclusions is probably the least well documented. Or perhaps one should say that it is only correct in certain special cases. For instance, in the Broadbent two-channel case, order of report tends to be ear-by-ear with dichotic presentation but pair-by-pair with dichoptic presentation (e.g., Corballis & Luthe, 1971). In an attempt to get further evidence on this point Penney (1974) presented alternating pairs of auditory (dichotic) and visual words, four pairs in all. Then she probed for recall of either the four auditory words or the four visual words. Though nothing was said to the subjects about order of report, recall of the auditory words tended to be successive (ABAB) while recall of the visual words tended to be simultaneous (AABB), where A and B denote the first and second set.

Perhaps it would be more nearly correct to say that when sequential information is involved auditory presentation will be superior but, if preservation of spatial information is required, visual presentation will be superior if it cannot be reconstructed from a temporal sequence. In the former case, Nazzaro and Nazzaro (1970) found that Morse-code patterns were learned more easily with auditory presentation than with visual presentation. By contrast, in a keeping-track situation where spatial separation was employed, visual presentation was as good as or perhaps slightly better than auditory presentation (Fisher & Karsh, 1971). The role of individual differences in modality effects is quite unclear. In one study (Laughery & Fell, 1969) it was found that auditory presentation was superior to visual presentation regardless of initial preferences, while in another study (Ingersoll & DiVesta, 1972) each type performed better according to preference.

The view that short-term memory is representational may not find favor in some quarters. A more cognitive or reconstructive position may be preferred instead. Let me close this section by describing a brief Gedanken experiment that bears on this issue, then comment briefly on some evidence apparently favoring the reconstructive view.

Imagine the following hypothetical experiment. A list of items is presented one by one, and the subject is instructed simply to rate each item on "wordness." At one extreme he would rate an item as "sure it is a word," and at the other extreme he would rate an item as "sure it is not a word." All items in fact would be words, but taken from the extremes of a word count such as Thorndike and Lorge (1944). For the low end, there would probably be some items which the subject rated in the nonword category. If this rating task were unexpectedly followed by a recognition test where the items were re-presented and the subject had now to judge them as old or new, from what we know of word-frequency effects in recognition memory the low-frequency words would probably be more accurately identified as old or new. My guess is that those items that were rated most surely as nonwords might be the most accurately remembered of all. Here would be a case where presentation of an item could not "tag its representation in semantic memory" because the subject himself is telling you that there is no representation there to tag. The more reasonable interpretation of this hypothetical outcome would be in terms of some representational persistence from the rating part of the experiment to the recognition test. Experimental evidence relevant to these speculations may be found in Walker (1973).

An experiment which would seem to support a reconstructive view is that of Bransford and Franks (1971). They presented various idea units and then tested with probes containing various numbers of these units. For new probes, the more idea units they contained the higher the false-alarm rate. The results (Franks & Bransford, 1972) have been said to demonstrate, ". . . that when presented with a set of sentences each expressing a partial meaning of an idea, subjects integrated the partial meanings and stored the complete idea in memory [p. 311]." However, the results are also consistent with quite a different interpretation. If the subject simply remembered each idea unit in an all-or-none fashion, did no integration of meaning at all, but simply responded to the probe on the basis of the number of idea units still available that it evoked, then exactly these results would be expected. This alternative explanation has been considered more extensively by Reitman and Bower (1973).

Temporal factors. What evidence do we have for temporal factors? Studies of short-term memory are replete with such evidence; this point has been noted elsewhere (Murdock, 1972). For item information, the data on judgments of recency and judgments of frequency discussed in Chapter 3 are particularly compelling. One study in particular that deserves mention is that of Lockhart (1969a). Forced-choice judgments of recency could be predicted from knowledge of the two lags taken separately. It is as though the subject determines the recency of each item separately, then, in the comparison, he chooses accordingly.

How does item information change over time? What is the nature of the forgetting? Clearly there is loss of item information over time; the features of the trace become less distinct. Perhaps the most analytic study in this regard is that of Bregman (1968) who traced out separate retention curves for semantic, phonetic, graphic, and contiguity cues by means of appropriate probes at different retention intervals. The curves, as it happened, seemed quite similar. Evidence on picture memory (e.g., Nickerson, 1968; Shepard, 1967) is also quite consistent with this view.

Whether the attributes or features of memory are lost independently is not quite so easy to answer. To the best of my knowledge, very little work has been done on this problem. An unpublished study conducted several years ago here at Toronto by Michael Gray was one such attempt. The stimuli were constructed from four binary attributes (shape, border, vertical, and horizontal location on the card) and recognition-memory tests on each attribute were given following interpolated distraction. The data did seem to be binomially distributed as predicted by an independence model, but unfortunately the performance level was so low it was hard to rule out the possibility that all one was measuring was guessing.

According to the conveyor-belt model, the older a trace, the further removed it is from the psychological present. The bag on the ramp is further away in whatever way the brain preserves a record of human experience. Changes over time can only be revealed by tapping into the system at different retention intervals, but this necessitates consideration of retrieval. Next, we shall present a progressively more detailed view of the possible retrieval processes, along with some relevant evidence.

Retrieval processes. An expanded view of Fig. 10.1 for the retrieval of item information is portrayed in Fig. 10.2. Here there is an inner loop and an outer loop. Imagine a discrete-trials recognition-memory procedure where a probe has been presented and the central processor is interrogating memory. In the inner loop the items are examined, one by one or in parallel, until the end is reached. There is either an acceptable outcome and the process terminates with a response, or there is not. In the latter case memory is again interrogated, perhaps with different criteria.

Evidence for the outer loop comes from studies of recognition memory which record confidence judgments and latency. As reported in Murdock and Dufty (1972) and detailed in Chapter 3 (see Fig. 3.4) longer latencies are associated with lower confidence judgments. Our data suggest that it might take an experienced subject per-

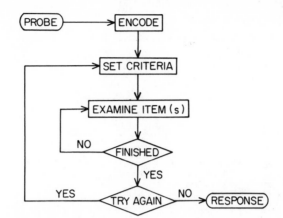

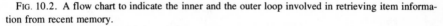

FIG. 10.2. A flow chart to indicate the inner and the outer loop involved in retrieving item information from recent memory.

haps 250 msec for each execution of the outer loop, if one can assume that each iteration decreases the confidence exactly one point on the three-point scale we use. No independent confirmation of this hypothesis is yet available, so this point must be regarded as inferential.

How does the inner loop work? Some relevant evidence comes from an experiment that we have just completed. It was a recognition-memory study along the lines of Murdock and Dufty (whose procedure is also described in the section on Model Tests in Chapter 2). In the present study four subjects were each tested for 24 sessions, 12 sessions with a yes-no procedure and 12 with a forced-choice procedure. In the former, each trial consisted of the presentation of 15 items followed by the test for 30 items, half old and half new. The subject responded with the same six-point confidence judgment scale, and latency (from onset of probe to execution of the response) was recorded. Lists were constructed by randomly sampling from the Toronto word pool, the one restriction being that two intervening lists had to be presented before any word could reappear. The experiment was run on an on-line laboratory computer which controlled stimulus presentation and response recording. (One practice session was given to familiarize subjects with the procedure and to make the oscilloscope display easier to read.)

Figure 10.3 shows the mean reaction time for high-confident "yes" responses to old items as a function of their lag (number of items intervening between presentation and test). The lag-latency function seems reasonably linear with a slope just under 5 milliseconds per item. Figure 10.4 shows the mean reaction time for high-confident "no" responses to new items as a function of their mean test position. Again the function seems reasonably linear, and it too has a slope of 5 milliseconds per item. The results seem to suggest that the inner loop of Fig. 10.2 involves a backward, serial self-terminating scan through the current list. For old items, the scan continues until the target item is found. For new items, it continues until the

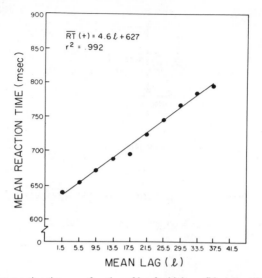

FIG. 10.3. Mean reaction time as a function of lag for high-confident "yes" responses to old items. The data have been pooled over subjects and presentation rate.

beginning of the list is reached. Study and test items are both examined, apparently at the same rate. The scanning process seems to require about 5 msec/item.

Several points require further comment. First, the independent variable for old items is lag, the number of items intervening between presentation and test. The lag range was 0–43, and here it was blocked into 0–3, 4–7, 8–11, . . . , 40–43. Thus, it is as though every presentation and every test of an item deposits a new suitcase on the conveyor belt. Each one must be examined, and the search proceeds through

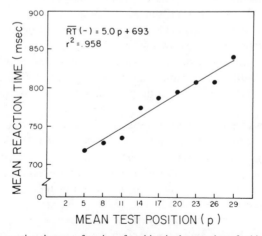

FIG. 10.4. Mean reaction time as a function of position in the test phase for high-confident "no" responses to new items. The data have been pooled over subjects and presentation rate.

memory backward in time, starting with the most recent arrival. In the case of new items, the independent variable is output position; the central processor must search through the entire list as well as all tested items, again from back to front.

Second, we have conditionalized on high-confident responses. In terms of Fig. 10.2, these illustrate those cases where the subject did not have to try again. There is always the possibility of criterion change, particularly over test position. However, analysis of the data of Murdock and Dufty showed that, while the distributions of confidence judgments to old and new items changed markedly over test positions (blocked into sixths), *a posteriori* probabilities for the most-confident "yes" and "no" responses did not change at all. By this measure one could rule out the possibility of criterion changes in this recognition-memory procedure.

Third, as is common in an additive model such as this, the intercept indicates the time for other processes to occur. In particular, here that would seem to be encoding time and response selection. The intercept difference between "yes" and "no" responses is 66 msec. On the average, an old item will be found in the middle of the list, so 35–40 msec of this difference will be absorbed by the fact that, for new items, the subject has more to examine. There remains then only 25–30 msec difference between old and new items to account for.

It might be mentioned that the data shown in Fig. 10.3 and 10.4 are based on a fairly large number of observations. Each trial required 30 responses, there were 32 trials per session, 12 sessions per subject on the confidence-judgment procedure, and four subjects in all. Since over 80% of all responses were in the high-confident category, nearly 40,000 observations enter into the data of these two graphs.

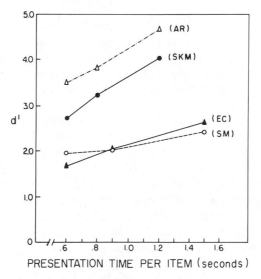

FIG. 10.5. The d' values for each subject as a function of the presentation time used during list presentation. The data for old items have been pooled over lag, and the data for new items have been pooled over test position.

TABLE 10.1

Scanning Rate (in msec/item)
for Each Subject at Each Presentation Rate

	Presentation rate		
Subject	Fast	Medium	Slow
EC	6.8	5.3	6.8
AR	4.5	2.0	4.8
SM	6.3	5.3	5.8
SKM	1.9	1.6	2.6

Does the scanning rate vary with presentation rate? In terms of the conveyor-belt analogy, the faster the presentation rate the more densely-packed the suitcases on the conveyor belt, so perhaps the less discriminable they might be. In the above experiment, the 12 sessions were divided into four sets of three presentation rates, tailor-made for each subject. Accuracy data in terms of d' values are shown for each of the four subjects in Fig. 10.5, and the positive slope of these functions shows that the experimental manipulation did have some effect on memory. The d' values were obtained from the EPCROC program of Ogilvie and Creelman (1968). The scanning rates for each subject for each presentation condition are shown in Table 10.1, and the answer seems quite clear. Scanning is not dependent upon rate of arrival, at least within the limits studied here.

Are older items more difficult to discriminate than younger items? Does it take longer to examine a suitcase on the conveyor-belt the further back it was loaded? Apparently not. Were such the case, then the mean reaction time should increase with lag, yet that does not happen. As lag increases there are in fact more and more misses. So, the number of correct detections clearly decreases with age, but the scan time does not.

Why are there more and more misses (or, if you wish, progressively fewer high-confident ''yes'' responses to old items) as lag increases? Perhaps suitcases fall off the conveyor belt. It would not be unreasonable to think that there might be a constant probability of loss per unit time, in which case the longer the retention interval the lower the probability that an item would still be available in memory. Preliminary results from a further experiment cast doubt on this possibility. In this further experiment two different word pools were used. The standard Toronto word pool was dichotomized on the basis of part-of-speech. One word pool consisted of nouns, and the other word pool consisted of non-nouns. On each session, each subject either had the noun or the non-noun word pool.

The non-noun word pool was more difficult than the noun word pool. Mean d' values were 2.06 and 2.70, respectively, and all 8 subjects showed a difference in this direction. One interpretation would be that there were more bags on the conveyor belt when the noun word pool was used than when the non-noun word pool was used. As such there would be more to examine and, when plotted in terms of mean lag or mean output position, the slope of the reaction-time function should be steeper. In fact it was not; the scanning rate was 2.6 msec/item for the noun word pool but 4.9 msec/item for the non-noun word pool.

The implication, then, is that the memory-comparison process works by comparing the encoded version of the probe to every single item which should be in memory, regardless of whether or not it is in memory. How does this comparison occur?

Perhaps when a probe is presented and encoded, some small number of features are abstracted. Then these same features are abstracted from the most recent item in memory, and the two are compared. If they match, the process terminates and a "yes" response occurs. If they do not, the same features of the next most recent memory item are abstracted and they are compared (to the probe features). Again, with a match the process stops. This process continues, item by item, until a match is found or until the subject comes to the end of the list (really the beginning in point of time). The process takes longer to describe than to occur.

Thus, the suggestion is that the feature-testing goes on at the time of retrieval (memory comparison). The complete probe is not literally compared in its entirety with the complete memory representation of each item. That would be impossibly complex. Instead, a few of its characteristics are compared, but at a rapid rate. As already stated, the original encoding of information at the time of presentation is representational, and the importance of the features enters at the time of the memory-comparison stage. A somewhat similar viewpoint has been suggested for pattern recognition by Norman (1968).

Perhaps there is a match register (e.g., Sternberg, 1969a) which contains a record of the comparison (number of feature matches). Its contents are not updated each time; instead, it records the closest match (largest number of identical features) found to date. As soon as its value exceeds a given cutoff point, the process stops and a sure-yes response occurs. If the criterion is not exceeded, the search continues until the beginning of the list is reached. Then the decision is made as to whether to respond or try again. If the decision is made to respond, then the confidence judgment is based on the contents of the match register.

A flow-chart for a computer program to simulate these processes is shown in Fig. 10.6. The box labelled COMPARE PROBE AND ITEM AT SPECIFIED LAG would have to be elaborated to portray the feature-testing process, but otherwise the flow-chart is reasonably comprehensive. I have not tried to simulate the model, but it should not be hard. The main point of this flow-chart is to suggest something about the nature of the retrieval processes that must be involved even in a simple recognition-memory discrete-trials procedure.

Evaluation

This conveyor-belt model may strike the reader as rather improbable. I would agree completely, so let me explain why I am suggesting it as a possible model for the encoding, storage, and retrieval of item information. There are three main reasons.

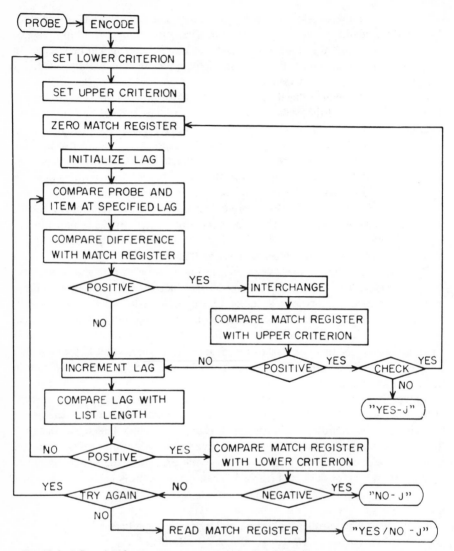

FIG. 10.6. A flow chart for a computer program to simulate the detailed processes involved in retrieving item information from short-term memory.

First, it represents the temporal format of storage in a natural and direct fashion, which I think is one of the first prerequisites for any model of item information. Second, the forgetting characteristics also seem quite reasonable, as there is little doubt that loss of information is gradual but pervasive. Third, I have learned to believe my data rather than my intuitions. The data of Figs. 10.3 and 10.4 were what convinced me that something like the processes envisaged must be occurring.

Explanatory ability. There were seven main topics discussed in Chapter 3. The first was the forgetting functions obtained with discrete- and continuous-trials procedures. In the former the decay is exponential; in the latter the decay is probably even more precipitous. I imagine that the conveyor-belt can describe these forgetting functions. To be sure, the model should be formalized, parameters estimated, and goodness-of-fits reported, but I have not done that yet. Any differences between discrete- and continuous-task procedures could reflect the effect of a discrete starting point, but the details remain to be worked out.

The supplementary measures of confidence judgments and latency are clearly reflected in the model. Latency is the sum of a number of additive processes, and two major components have been specified. Memory interrogation is relatively slow, requiring perhaps 250 milliseconds for practiced subjects. The comparison process is much faster, and 5 msec/item is a reasonable estimate. Confidence judgments reflect the number of excursions made along the outer loop. The fact that *a posteriori* probabilities for the high-confident responses do not change over test position is indicative of a constant criterion. Changes in the distribution of confidence judgments with test position (or lag) indicates the forgetting that is taking place. There is both input and output interference in recognition memory.

One may well ask why scanning here is on the order of 5 msec/item while in the Sternberg paradigm 35 msec/item is more typical. One answer to this question might be a naming-latency facilitation effect or, more generally, priming. As noted in Chapter 3, the Colotla experiment which by-passed this problem gave a scan rate of about 15 msec/item. Another possibility (different processing of subspan and supraspan lists) will be discussed shortly. It also should be mentioned that the data of Juola, Fischler, Wood, and Atkinson (1971) suggest a scanning rate of 3–6 msec/ item for a memorized list of 10–26 items. However, it is only fair to add that their values depend upon the assumption of a serial exhaustive search, and here I am suggesting a self-terminating process instead.

Different types of stimulus material are differentially remembered. One variation is stimulus meaningfulness; another is the variation among words, sentences, and pictures. When we have standard methods of calibrating such variation we shall understand it better, but the existence of variation is clearly compatible with the model. The evidence for attributes (phonemic, semantic, associative, physical, etc.) is also consistent with the model. However, we are a long way from sorting out the locus of these effects, i.e., whether they are in encoding, storage, or retrieval. If those features abstracted from the probe are under program control, then the model would say that retrieval factors were implicated in these effects.

The fact that performance goes down as the number of alternatives increases is explicable in several ways. One is to attribute this effect to increasing output interference, and the conveyor-belt model assumes such an effect. Another is to say that there is a single memory interrogation for each test alternative—so the more alternatives there are, the later (on the average) the target will enter into the comparison process. We plan to analyze the forced-choice data of this recent experiment to try to test these two possibilities.

The false-recognition effect, though well documented, is difficult to interpret. If one takes a feature-testing point of view, it could reflect little more than the fact that the distinguishing feature did not enter in to the comparison process. That is, by definition the lure that elicits the false-positive effect is similar in several ways to a target item but differs on one or two distinctive features. These latter features may not be included when the probe is encoded. So in fact the false-recognition effect may tell us more about the comparison process than it does about initial encoding or forgetting.

Of the recall-recognition comparisons, some go the same way and some do not. Of the former, number of presentations, presentation rate, and list length are probably the most notable. Of the latter, word-frequency, relative number of study and test trials, and organization have received some attention. Again, while the empirical results are quite clear, their interpretation is less so. As noted above, one is now comparing recognition memory and free recall. Not only are the two quite different, but we certainly do not understand free recall very well. Until we do, I think interpretation of these findings will be difficult.

Absolute judgments, however, are another matter. In particular, the conveyor-belt model is particularly applicable to judgments of recency. Elsewhere (Murdock, 1972) I suggested how this might take place. Given the probe, the subject looks back over the list searching for the memory trace of the probe. If he finds it, he counts the number of intervening available items and gives that as his judgment of recency. Otherwise he guesses, and his guess will be his best estimate. On the assumption that items are independent, then the distribution of available items at lag n is

$$f_{r,n} = \sum_{j=r}^{n} \left\{ (-1)^{j+r} \binom{j}{r} \Sigma \pi_j \right\} \tag{10.1}$$

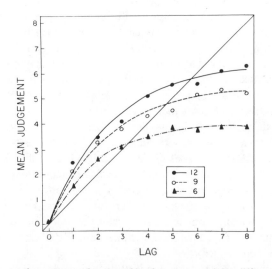

FIG. 10.7. Judgments of recency as a function of lag for groups receiving different instructions as to maximum possible lag. The smooth curves have been drawn through the values predicted by the conveyor-belt model. (Data from Hinrichs, 1970.)

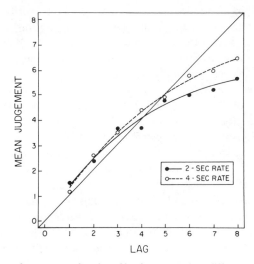

Fig. 10.8. Judgments of recency as a function of lag for groups given different presentation rates. The smooth curves have been drawn through the values predicted by the conveyor-belt model. (Data from Peterson, 1967.)

where $\Sigma\pi_j$ refers to the sum of all $\binom{n}{j}$ combinations of products of individual probabilities taken j at a time. (The interested reader is referred to Murdock, 1972, for further details but should be alerted to a small error; the coefficients of Equation 19 in that article should be 1, 2, and 3 not 3, 3, and 1.)

It is easy to fit this model to data, and two examples are shown in Figs. 10.7 and 10.8. The first is the data of Hinrichs (1970) discussed in Chapter 3 and shown in Fig. 3.11. In Fig. 10.7 the data points are repeated and the smooth curves are the fit of the conveyor-belt model to these data. The SIMPLEX program was used and there were four free parameters. One was forgetting probability, which was assumed constant for all three groups; the other was the value of the guessing parameter, which differed for each group. The resulting estimate was .794 for the probability value; this probability is actually the complement of α in the fluctuation model (see Equation 17, Murdock, 1972). The estimates for the guessing parameters were 3.82, 5.43, and 6.51 for groups with instructed maximum lag of 6, 9, and 12, respectively. (We have plotted the data and reported the parameter values in terms of lag, but the numbers denoting instructed maximum lag are actually relative ordinal position, not lag.) As can be seen, the fit was quite good; the standard error of estimate (square root of the sum of the squared deviations) was 0.15.

The data of Fig. 10.8 come from a study by Peterson (1967) and the data points were read off from Fig. 7.2 of that article (combining the single- and double-presentation conditions). There were four free parameters in the SIMPLEX program, a separate probability and guessing parameter for each group (they differed in presentation rate). The best probability estimates were .908 and .936 for the 2- and 4-sec groups respectively, and the guessing parameter values were 5.35 and 6.65 for the two groups. Again the fit was quite good; the standard error of estimate here was also 0.15. Thus, it seems fair to say that the conveyor-belt model does an adequate job of accounting for data from experiments on judgments of recency.

As for judgments of frequency, here one gets into the problem of repetition. While current data seem more consistent with a multiplex model than with a trace-strength view, there is still the problem of the lag effect, and this is not trivial. The prevalent feeling at Toronto is that the lag effect has something to do with retrieving the first presentation at the time of the second, but just what, no one is sure. So judgments of frequency are a problem yet to be solved.

The final topic discussed in Chapter 3 was retrieval processes, and that has been rather thoroughly elaborated here. What remains to be discussed is context effects; why, for instance, the subject does not recognize the JAM of STRAWBERRY JAM as the same JAM of TRAFFIC JAM. Or, why a subject cannot recognize a word generated on a word-association test, even though he can recall it in response to a weakly-associated retrieval cue. In both cases, the features abstracted from the probe are not appropriate for the target item sought in memory. That a type-token distinction exists is not surprising, but we need to understand better the conditions under which it occurs.

Alternative explanations. In an evaluation of the conveyor-belt model, it is probably best to settle first the issue of the retrieval processes. As noted earlier, that is most amenable to theoretical analysis. In this regard, there are two rather different questions one could ask. One question is why a serial scanning model is suggested rather than a parallel scanning model. The other question is why a search process is suggested rather than direct access. The latter is probably a more fruitful question to explore than the former, but let me comment on the first question briefly.

I have suggested a backward, serial self-terminating scan to account for the linear reaction-time functions of Figs. 10.3 and 10.4. Could not a parallel-processing model account equally well for such data? While a parallel model can mimic a serial ex-

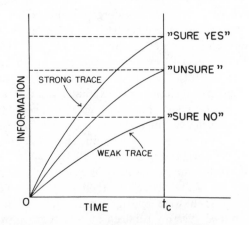

FIG. 10.9. A possible representation for the processing of item information. The memory trace is examined for a fixed length of time (t_c) and the amount of information which accumulates is fed into the decision system. The resulting confidence judgments are labelled accordingly.

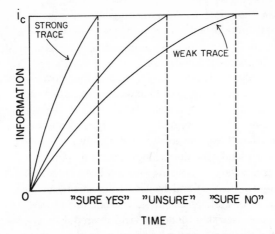

FIG. 10.10. Another possible representation for the processing of item information. The memory trace is examined until a fixed amount of information (i_c) has accumulated, and the time required is the basis on which the decision system responds. Again the resulting confidence judgments are labelled.

haustive model (Murdock, 1971b), it is not clear that it can mimic a serial self-terminating model. However, if past experience is any guide, it seems likely that such a parallel model could be found. Then the theoretical issues become very difficult to untangle, and progress slows accordingly. Perhaps the issue of direct access versus search is more amenable to experimental resolution.

To understand why a search model seems favored over a direct-access model, it is instructive to consider various direct-access models and see what troubles they encounter with the data we now have on recognition memory. One such model is shown in Fig. 10.9. It says that the information in memory is processed for some fixed amount of time, t_c. The rate constants differ as a function of the characteristics of the trace, so for strong traces more information accumulates in this time than for weak traces. The amount of information which accumulates is fed into the decision system, which then responds accordingly. This, then, is a possible explication of what goes on in the memory stage of Fig. 1.1. It is also essentially a classical signal-detection theory view of memory wherein energy integration occurs over a fixed observation interval.

At least in its simple version this view is surely wrong. It would suggest that reaction time should be independent of memory-trace strength. That is, differing amounts of information are fed into the decision system (and associated with confidence judgments as labelled in the graph) but the observation interval is independent of memory-trace strength. However, data show that there is a very strong and clear relationship between reaction times and confidence judgments in tests of item recognition (see Fig. 3.4).

A second possibility is shown in Fig. 10.10. Here the trace is examined until a fixed amount of information, i_c, has accumulated. (Presumably i_c could be moved up or down to accommodate criterion changes.) With different rate constants, strong traces reach criterion faster than weak traces. Then the input to the decision system is the amount of time which has been required for processing. The consequent confidence judgments are labelled accordingly. Such a model is not new; as noted by Kintsch (1970b, p. 274), as long as sixty years ago it was suggested that processing time might be the basis of familiarity.

Here too the same problem arises; the relationship between confidence judgments and latency is not what it should be. One would expect that sure-no judgments would be the slowest of all, since new items would have the weakest traces. Yet as this same Fig. 3.4 shows, high-confident "no" responses are executed almost as quickly as high-confident "yes" responses, and clearly much faster than low-confident responses of either kind. The discerning reader may point out that in neither case is the argument completely convincing. As has been noted, observed reaction times are a combination of memory and decision components, and here all that is modelled is the memory stage. Perhaps one could cascade one of these two memory models with an appropriate decision model to yield the requisite combination.

A variation of this second possibility might be appropriate for a strength-theory point of view. Suppose one has a decaying memory trace and interrogation of the memory system involves examining this trace to ascertain its age. (The age would then either be above or below a threshold, in order to lead to recognition judgments, or to map into judgments of recency as suggested, for instance, by Hinrichs, 1970.) One could detect the age by measuring the rate of change of the trace. But if the decay is exponential (as is often assumed) then more and more interrogation time would be required as the trace was older. But the evidence we have is negative; it seems to take no more time to decide about older items than to decide about younger items. So this variation is not promising either.

A more serious contender than these processing models is a direct-access strength theory. Could one not explain the data of Figs. 10.3 and 10.4 by saying simply that items at longer lags are weaker, and reaction time is therefore slower because it takes longer to read off a weaker trace? The fact that the function is linear just happens to be the way that it works out. There are two main problems with this interpretation; the first is perhaps obvious, but the second less so. The first is as follows: If the subject simply had direct access to items in memory (given the probe, he looked to see whether it had a tag), why is the reaction time to new items a linear function of output position? One might think that reaction time would be independent of output position, since a new item is new, regardless of its position in the test series. If the error rate were shifting systematically across the testing period that might account for it but, as noted above, the false-alarm rate stays reasonably constant over output position. And is it just coincidental that the two functions (Figs. 10.3 and 10.4) have the same slope? Remember, these are two separate estimates, each based on a different set of data.

The second point is a bit more subtle. For strength theory, to talk about latency functions requires that one specify the transfer function mapping strength into latency. Given the results of Murdock and Dufty (1972), the most reasonable one is exponential (see Fig. 3.3). So, assume that latency decreases exponentially on either side of the yes-no criterion. What happens to mean latency of "yes" responses to old items as lag increases? Contrary to what was claimed in that paper, an analytic solution is possible. (I would like to thank Michael Corballis for pointing out the solution to me.) According to strength theory, the mean latency (assuming an exponential transfer function) is

$$\mu = \frac{\Phi \ (a + b)}{\Phi \ (a)} \ \exp \left[(b^2/2) + ab \right] \tag{10.2}$$

where Φ denotes the integral of the unit normal curve from a to ∞, a is the yes-no cut-off on the strength continuum, and b is the slope of the exponential transfer function.

We know from strength theory that d' decreases exponentially with lag, with parameters α and ϕ as shown in Eq. (2.7). All we have to do, then, is let a in Eq. (10.2) so vary with lag, and introduce yes-no criterion as a free parameter. With these four parameters (α, ϕ, b, and the criterion) it is possible to fit strength theory to the lag-latency data shown in Fig. 10.3. I did so using SIMPLEX and, much to my amazement, the fit was very good. One can indeed generate a linear lag-latency function for old items assuming exponential decay in d' and an exponential transfer function mapping strength into latency.

However, as soon as one examines the parameter values of the solution, the picture changes. The best values found by SIMPLEX were 2.84, 0.95, 4.02, and 1.35 for the parameters α, ϕ, b, and the criterion. This would yield a hit rate of 93% at lag 0 and 16% at lag 40. Since the obtained hit rates were more like 99% and 80% at these two values, the problem is quite obvious. Strength theory can account for the accuracy data or it can account for the latency data, but it cannot account for both at the same time. Thus, latency and accuracy together show what the weakness is.

Parallel and serial scanning. Let me close this section on item information with a rather speculative suggestion. It has been placed last for that very reason, namely, it is the most speculative. The suggestion is that, for small amounts of information (subspan lists, or less than seven chunks) processing goes on in parallel, while for larger amounts of information (supraspan lists, or more than seven chunks) the processing is serial.

The data that suggest this possibility are some reaction-time data recently collected at Toronto by David Burrows and Ronald Okada, and they have given me permission to include their results here. Subjects were given lists of 2, 4, 6, 8, 10, 12, 16, or 20 words to memorize (by the method of whole presentation) to a criterion of two consecutive correct free recalls. Then they were shown the words, one by one, with an equal number of positive and negative probes and were required only to respond "yes" or "no" to indicate list membership. This procedure has been used extensively by Atkinson and his colleagues (e.g., Atkinson & Juola, 1973) following the original work of Sternberg (1966), but in the Burrows and Okada study the set-size variation went from clearly subspan to clearly supraspan lengths in small increments (see also Corballis & Miller, 1973). Small set sizes were tested more frequently than larger set sizes to try to equalize the reliability of the data. The items were all drawn from the Toronto word pool, and no items were repeated within Session 1–5 or within Session 6–10.

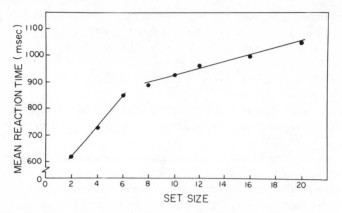

F<small>IG</small>. 10.11. Mean reaction time as a function of set size pooled over subjects and over positive and negative probes. The two straight lines have been fit to the data by eye. (Unpublished data of Burrows and Okada, 1973.)

The main results are shown in Fig. 10.11 where the mean reaction times for the five subjects are plotted as a function of set size. Two straight lines clearly fit the data; the lower limb has a slope of about 60 msec/item while the upper limb has a slope of about 15 msec/item. The discontinuity occurs at a set size of approximately seven items. The suggestion is that the lower limb indicates parallel processing, the upper limb indicates serial processing, and the break-point indicates the changeover.

The justification for interpretation of the subspan component in terms of parallel processing comes from a parallel-processing model I recently suggested (Murdock, 1971b) for scanning effects in the Sternberg paradigm. Essentially, it was suggested that, with small set sizes, presentation of a probe initiated processing of all items simultaneously. The rate at which each item was processed was assumed to vary with serial position. There was a primacy component which was linear and a recency component which was logarithmic, and the processing rate for each item was the sum of these two components. As shown in this article, this simple parallel-processing model can generate linear reaction-time functions, parallel curves for positive and negative probes, and serial-position effects. A slightly more general version may be found in Aubé and Murdock (1974) where nonlinear functions can also be handled by introducing assumptions about priming and forgetting. The expectancy effects noted by Klatzky and Smith (1972) and Theios, Smith, Haviland, Traupmann, and Moy (1973) may be related to priming and could occur in the encoding stage. A problem noted by Shiffrin and Schneider (1972) is that, contrary to the model, serial-position curves tend to peak at the second rather than the next-to-last serial position. However, where the peak occurs would depend upon the values of the two processing parameters for the particular experimental task under investigation, and they would have to be estimated for each set of data.

Why should the comparison process be parallel for subspan lists but serial for supraspan lists? The more material to be processed, the more difficult the task, so methods suitable for the former may not work well (or may not work at all) for the latter. If the time per item is less for long than for short lists, why not simply extrapolate the longer-term process into the short-term (subspan) range? Presumably there are other processes determining reaction time, and there must be a trade-off. For serial scanning it has been suggested that features of the probe must be abstracted before the comparison process can start. Perhaps this is a relatively slow operation and is by-passed or short-circuited in the subspan lists. It could be that the parallel processing of subspan lists is more like a template-matching operation than the feature testing assumed to occur in the search process. For another view of parallel scanning with subspan lists, see Burrows and Okada (1973).

It should be emphasized that I am not suggesting a partitioning of *memory* into subspan and supraspan lengths. The memory is continuous; the processes used to operate on it may differ. As has been noted, it is useful to distinguish between memory and a central processing mechanism, and here I am suggesting that the latter may differ with the nature of the material to be processed. In case it is not obvious, in a discrete-trials procedure the subject does not know the lag of a probe when it is presented, so he must use a serial scan even for subspan lags. In the unpublished Burrows and Okada study the subject obviously knew what set size was in use—he had just memorized the list—so he could choose his processing method accordingly.

Is it not inefficient to have two different mechanisms to process information in memory? From one point of view, perhaps it is; but from another, it is surely not. The information contained in memory varies from very recent to very old, in the same way that the energy variations which impinge on the eye or the ear span many log units. It does not seem unreasonable to have different mechanisms to span a vast range; one mechanism might not work well over all parts of the scale. Different mechanisms in vision and in audition seem to work this way, and perhaps memory processing is comparable. It is interesting that the break-point in Fig. 10.11 occurs so neatly at set size seven.

ASSOCIATIVE INFORMATION

Item information allows us to remember past objects and events; associative information allows us to remember associations. To use an association we must first recognize the probe, so item and associative information are not independent. It has long been known that associative processes do not stand alone; stimulus discriminability and response integration have often been suggested as additional determinants of behavior (e.g., Adams, 1967; Battig, 1968; Gibson, 1940; McGuire, 1961; Morikawa, 1959, Murdock, 1958). The distinction between item and associative information is similar to the distinction between stimulus discriminability and associations which has long been accepted in the paired-associate field.

Since item and associative information differ, encoding and storage must differ as well. Retrieval is the utilization of stored information, and the same definition applies both to item and associative information. The simple flow chart of Fig. 1.1 is applicable, but clearly it needs extensive elaboration and refinement to be of any use. Two different kinds of information are being retrieved in the two cases, however. For associative information the probe A must make contact with the stored trace a (the Höffding problem) which in turn must link up with its associated b in order to lead to the evoking of B as a response to the probe. Item information only involves the first part of the process (retrieving a as the response to A). This example should illustrate that associative and item information are not disjoint (or mutually exclusive). Just as a sensory system involves receptor activity, afferent pathways, and cortical projection areas, so item information must be involved in retrieving associative information. There is evidence (e.g., Bernbach, 1967b; Martin, 1967b) that associative information cannot be used (if it exists) when the requisite item information cannot be found. Conversely, Bower (1970c) found that imagery facilitated associative memory quite apart from stimulus-recognition effects.

The distinction between item and associative information may help to clarify the recall-recognition issue. This issue is the question of why recognition is generally better than recall. There are two parts to the answer to this question. The first part is that some of these comparisons have pitted recognition of item information against recall of associative information. They are probably not strictly commensurable, but to the extent that they are, recognition is better than recall because item information has a much slower decay rate than associative information. The second part applies when recognition and recall of associative information are directly compared. There too, recognition is generally better than recall, though it may depend upon the particular theoretical assumptions used in correcting for guessing (Freund, Brelsford, & Atkinson, 1969). If guessing is a negligible factor, then recognition may be better than recall because backward associations can help performance under recognition but not under recall. It has been said that recall involves a search process while recognition does not. It may be that the search or retrieval problem is more characteristic of item information than of associative information. At least in short-term memory, recall of associative information seems hindered more by loss of availability than by difficulties of accessibility. So it is not the case that recognition (of associative information) is better than recall because it bypasses the search process. Rather, recognition is better than recall because it can make use of available backward associations, either from the target to the probe or from the lures to other items.

One justification for separating out and identifying associative information when it seems to include item information is that quite different levels of accuracy are involved. That is, item information is so accurate and accessible in testing short-term associative information that we can generally afford to disregard it. In the same way, we can probably afford to disregard the retinal processes occurring in the eye of the subject as he is watching the memory drum. Not ultimately, perhaps, but for the time being.

Fluctuation Model

The fluctuation or cross-reference model was described rather extensively in Chapter 4. Here I would like to present some additional evidence, then an evaluation. First, however, a brief review is in order.

Review. To dispel any possible confusion, let me say that I use the term "association" as shorthand for associative information. What an association really is depends upon how the nervous system encodes and stores information. No one yet knows. But there must be something which leads from a to b or links them functionally, and whatever that is we call an association. So that is what I am talking about in this discussion of associations.

The basic principles are as follows: (*1*) Associations are all or none, not graded in strength. We can use the term availability to characterize these conditions, so an association in State A is available while an association in State N is not. (*2*) Associations are independent, so what happens to one association has no effect on what happens to any other associations. (*3*) Associations can be forgotten, and they can recover. When an association changes from State A to State N we can say it has been forgotten, but when it changes from State N to State A we can say it has recovered. (*4*) Forgetting and recovery occur through interference caused by presenting or testing other pairs, not through the passage of time *per se*. Probably the same effects can be achieved by thinking about other pairs, so the physical presence of interfering pairs may not be necessary. (*5*) Associations are bidirectional—there is one association from a to b and another association from b to a. It is like a divided highway with traffic only in one direction on each side of the road. Whether they are symmetric depends upon the material used. (*6*) These bidirectional associations (forward and backward) are also independent. Each can be forgotten and each can recover without being affected by the other. (*7*) Encoding of these associations occurs at the time of initial presentation and is probabilistic rather than certain. Encoding or formation of an association is not equivalent to perception, since the two words of a pair may both be perceived without an association being formed. Entering an association into memory probably requires more processing capacity than is required for perception.

What variables affect these processes? Modality of presentation affects the encoding probability, and the probability of an association being formed is greater if the pair is spoken or echoed rather than simply shown. Presentation time increases the probability of recovery in negatively-accelerated fashion. However, over small values it is approximately linear. Recovery probability seems to summate within and between trials; one presentation at a four-second rate adds about as much as four presentations at a one-second rate. Each successful utilization of an association (correct retrieval) decreases the probability that it will subsequently be forgotten. Learning in the conventional paired-associate procedure then is increased resistance to forgetting, and it occurs through two processes. The more times each pair is presented, the more likely is recovery from any forgetting during the intratrial retention interval; the more times the response to a probe has been correctly retrieved, the less likely it is that any recovery will be necessary. In terms of relative magnitudes, at least over 5–10 trials, the latter is probably appreciably more important than the former.

The same associations underlie recall and recognition. While they are the same, how they are used differs. In recall from short-term memory there seems to be no accessibility problem; if the association is intact the correct response will occur, otherwise the subject must guess. If the subject cannot recognize the probe—make contact with the stored trace—performance again will be at a guessing level. In a yes-no recognition test the subject can use the forward and backward associations to mediate performance. If confidence judgments are required, he may use the number of associations (i.e., 0, 1, or 2) as a basis for his confidence judgment, though this is not yet sure. In an m-alternative forced-choice procedure, he will be correct if either the forward or the backward association involving probe and target is intact. Otherwise, he will eliminate all alternatives whose backward associations are intact and then guess among the remainder. Performance will decrease with the number of alternatives, and quantitative predictions are possible.

Additional evidence. All of the above has been reported in Chapter 4 with appropriate documentation, so the above is just a quick review. Let me now mention several more lines of evidence which are at least qualitatively consistent with this view. The first finding has to do with latency. The general idea of this fluctuation model (and also that of Wolford, 1971) is that the same associative information is used in recall and recognition. Thus, the subject uses the association when it is intact to mediate recall, and in recognition he uses an implicit version of this response to mediate performance. An implication of this view is that response latency should be quickest for recall, next fastest for yes-no judgments, and progressively slower for an m-alternative forced-choice procedure as the value of m increases. The data of Norman and Wickelgren (1969) show exactly this ordering of response latencies.

The second line of evidence is mentioned here to indicate that an alternative explanation for associative information is not promising. In a very general way, one could apply the Brown-Conrad view and suggest that retrieving associations has features in common with detecting a weak signal against a noisy background. Were this the case, then recall or recognition should be related to d', and variables that increase one should increase the other. One such variable should be a speed-accuracy manipulation. In one case, instruct subjects to respond as rapidly as possible even at the risk of the occasional error; in the other case, instruct subjects to be as accurate as possible without worrying about the time required to decide.

As has been mentioned, since the standard signal-detection view involves energy integration over time, increasing the length of the observation interval (by accuracy instructions) should result in a greater signal strength (e.g., Hancock & Wintz, 1966). According to this view, it should result in greater accuracy as well. We have conducted two such experiments, one on recall and one on recognition. In both cases they were short-term probe paired-associate procedures much like those reported elsewhere (e.g., Murdock, 1970). In the recall experiment, for early serial positions the probability of a correct response was .27 and .35, but d' was 1.94 and 1.59 for speed and accuracy instructions, respectively. Thus, with increased time, accuracy did go up, but discriminability (as measured by Type II d') went down. In the recognition experiment, probability correct was .60 and .57 for speed and accuracy instructions, but d' values were 0.36 and 0.28 for the two conditions, respectively. Thus, in both experiments d' decreased as the observation interval increased. This finding is not very encouraging for one who would like to interpret retrieval of associative information as similar to the problem of detecting a weak signal against a noisy background.

Another explanation which might initially seem promising is to think of a pair as a unit. Rather than separate forward and backward associations, there is simply a unitary whole. Then the two members of the pair (i.e., A and B) could simply be different ways of accessing this unit. (This view might be a Gestalt interpretation as opposed to an associationistic interpretation; see Anderson & Bower, 1972b.) This view seems unlikely for the following reason. In a recognition test, the lures are incorrectly paired items from the list. If the correct pair is A–B, then the lure would be A–D. Were the wholistic interpretation correct then one might expect more accurate performance on A–D lures than on A–B targets, because the subject has two chances on the lures but only one chance on the targets. That is, if A taps into a–b and D taps into c–d, if either the a–b or the c–d association were intact then the subject could correctly respond "no" to an A–D probe. By contrast, A and B each tap into the same pair, so the subject has only one association to use in responding "yes" to an A–B probe. Since our data generally show that, if anything, it is the other way around (subjects are slightly more accurate on A–B probes than on A–D probes), this interpretation does not seem promising either. Of course, one could invoke the *ad hoc* rejoinder that two probes to one pair provide more reliable access than one probe to two pairs, and this effect offsets the 2:1 advantage mentioned above. However, such a view would have to be developed more explicitly to see how well it could account for the data.

Yet another possibility would be to consider a graded temporal basis for performance. Perhaps list presentation simply lays down a temporally-ordered string, and what seems descriptively to us like associations are really temporally-mediated reconstructions. It is possible to test this view with a recognition-memory procedure. Were such the case, temporal gradients based on the serial position of the lures should be found. Thus, if the list presented were A–B, C–D, E–F, G–H, I–J, and K–L, then lures A–D, A–F, and A–H should be progressively less attractive. We have recently completed an experiment to test this possibility; eight subjects were tested for 12 sessions, each with 60 lists per session. Computer-generated lists from the Toronto word pool were used, presentation was visual, correctly and incorrectly paired probes were equally probable, and subjects responded on a six-point confidence-judgment scale (from "sure-no" to "sure-yes"). The mean confidence judgment for each of the 36 possible combinations (6 A positions and 6 B positions) are shown in Table 2; numerically, the confidence-judgment scale was ordered

TABLE 10.2

Mean Confidence Judgment as a Function of the Serial Position
of the A and the B Member of the Probe

A member	B member					
	1	2	3	4	5	6
1	4.71	2.48	2.41	2.61	2.34	1.24
2	2.67	4.55	2.94	2.76	2.66	1.14
3	2.52	2.77	4.52	2.90	2.23	1.19
4	2.68	2.05	2.60	4.76	2.94	1.33
5	2.38	2.22	2.15	2.97	5.64	1.48
6	1.25	1.25	1.11	1.36	1.24	5.92

1–6 from "sure-no" to "sure-yes," respectively. Except for Serial Position 6, there seems little or no evidence for any temporal gradients. (For recall, the intrusions always show marked temporal gradients, which is yet another example of differences between recall and recognition.) Thus, going by the data of this experiment, there seems to be little support for the idea that recognition of associatively-based information is mediated by graded temporal reconstruction.

Evaluation

Explanatory ability. Let me review briefly some of the findings consistent with this model. It generates a forgetting function with recency, an asymptote, and no primacy, as is generally found in a probe paired-associate task. The asymptote increases with presentation time but only recency is affected by modality of presentation. Associative symmetry occurs in the single-trial situation but not in the multitrial situation. The number of pairs recalled after a single presentation is a linear function of list length, and the slope of this function is the asymptote of the short-term retention function. Imagery instructions increase the asymptote but have little or no effect on recency. Retrieval cues vary in effectiveness, but they change the slope of the regression function, not its nature. Quantitative estimates of recognition are quite accurate. The asymptote of the forgetting function is deduced as a consequence of more basic processes (forgetting and recovery), not simply labelled "secondary memory."

Given that this fluctuation model can account for a number of effects, what can it not explain? High on this list would probably be the effects of imagery and mediation. Imagery instructions or mediating associations certainly facilitate recall, and the effects can be quite large. This fluctuation model is not very useful in explaining such results. What could be said is that one could at least discover whether such memory aids produced their effect by decreasing forgetting or facilitating recovery. No such separation has yet been tried. Some mediators are probably more effective than others. However, just as there are individual differences among people so there must be individual differences among stimulus materials, and the problems are similar. We have no very profound way of understanding or conceptualizing variation in either, and we can do little more than describe them. So the problem may not be unique to imagery and mediators or the fluctuation model. Until we have a deeper conceptual framework for representing such variation, we are unlikely to progress very fast, theoretically.

What about the distinction between availability and accessibility? At least in the simple short-term case it is suggested that associations wax and wane in availability, but accessibility is not a problem. If an association is available at the time of the probe then the response will be recalled, but otherwise it will not. Please note: I am referring to associative information, not free recall. Clearly there is a real accessibility problem in free recall, but more of that later.

What about the tip-of-the-tongue effect? Perhaps this is a case where the association is intact but the features of the memory trace of the response are too illegible to support recall. It would be the converse of the Höffding problem, where the difficulty is to make contact with the memory trace a given the probe A. Here the problem is to make contact with the response B, given a degraded version of the memory trace b. There might be sufficient information in memory to permit identification of some of the attributes of B (Brown & McNeill, 1966) or feeling-of-knowing judgments (Blake, 1973). However, how the eventual recall might come about (if it does) is certainly not clear from this account.

Does this fluctuation model have anything useful to say about long-term memory? Can it apply to multitrial paired-associate learning paradigms, transfer, or retroactive- and proactive-interference designs? In principle it can, but the details remain to be worked out. By appropriate selection of parameters one could probably generate many of the predictions of the Bower one-element model, and by appropriate values of the recovery parameter one could have stationarity or not as one wished. Learning curves have already been fit by the model, but only for one set of data. An interpretation of the Postman and Stark (1969) and Postman, Stark, and Fraser (1968) results in terms of forward and backward associations has even been suggested by Merryman (1971), though criticized by Postman and Stark (1972).

Relation to other models. The concepts of the fluctuation model are not unlike those of interference theory, with forgetting similar to unlearning and recovery similar to spontaneous recovery. The time scales are quite different, as is the level of analysis. The fluctuation model takes the pair as the unit of analysis while interference theory works with the list as a whole. By its nature the fluctuation model should be able to make specific predictions about transfer and retroaction effects, but how they will turn out remains to be seen.

Is this fluctuation or cross-reference model a strength theory? No, not really. The association is either available or it is not available; no provision is made for intermediate states. However, probability of change is graded. The vulnerability of an association to forgetting through interference varies continuously as does the probability of recovery. So while an association may be all-or-none it is certainly not static. And such changes that do occur (in the probabilities of forgetting and recovery) are by no means academic; they are what characterize learning through practice. However, little has been done at a quantitative level in the multitrial situation, and along this line I am expressing expectations but not accomplishments.

The main difference between the fluctuation model and the Bower one-element model is that the one-element model views associations as starting in a null state and then, after some particular presentation, moving into a learned state which is absorbing. In the fluctuation model the emphasis is on encoding, forgetting, and recovery of associations. Both models view the association as all-or-none, but the learned state is not absorbing in the fluctuation model. Also, with repetition the parameters of the fluctuation model are assumed to change, so it is a nonhomogeneous Markov process.

One well-known problem with any all-or-none model is the second-guess data. At least for recognition tests, these data are not necessarily incompatible with the fluctuation model. Conditionalizing upon an incorrect first response indicates that the two a–b associations are not available. Since the subject is then assumed to use a cross-out rule based on backward associations (eliminate as incorrect all lures with intact backward associations and then choose randomly from the remainder) above-chance performance would be expected.

The data shown in Table 4.1 can be used to test this possibility. Recall probability for early list pairs was .236, so this can serve as an estimate of the probability of the a to b association. Under these conditions associative symmetry generally occurs, so one can assume the probability of the backward b to a and d to c associations was also .236. According to the model, then, the predicted value on the recognition test would be .708. Since the obtained value (for Serial Positions 1–4) was actually .635, for these data the second-guess performance was not quite as good as it should have been.

The relation of the fluctuation model to various multistate models (e.g., Atkinson, 1972b; Greeno, James, & DaPolito, 1971) is probably obvious. The fluctuation model is restricted to two states, and neither is absorbing. These other models postulate three or more states, and the learned state generally is considered to be absorbing. As I have noted, this latter feature strikes me as unrealistic; a technical report by Bouwhuis (1969) bears out my suspicion. Also, these models seem to adhere to the traditional view that associations are gradually (or suddenly) built up through repetition. The progression is from the initial or unlearned state through an intermediate state to a terminal or learned state. Again, it seems to me better to start with a model that can explain the immediate-memory effects so characteristic of short-term probe experiments, then extend the model to account for the gradual benefits of repetition. The benefits of repetition are to make associative information more resistant to forgetting.

SERIAL-ORDER INFORMATION

What mechanisms underlie serial-order effects; how does seriation occur? In the simplest possible case, you read a short list of items to your subject and ask him to repeat them back in order. With short lists he can, but with increasing list length the probability of error grows. If the list is five items or less he will probably be perfect; if the list is ten items or more he will almost surely be wrong, and in going from 7 minus 2 to 7 plus 2 items, performance will go from one extreme to the other.

The fact that one can parrot back effortless 7 ± 2 items after a single presentation does not necessarily mean that a simple and direct storage-and-read-out takes place. Instead, it may mean that whatever mechanisms are involved operate effortlessly and without error under these conditions, but these mechanisms are not themselves necessarily simple and direct. To say that memory span is simply reading off a trace is merely describing the data. We need to understand how it is possible and when it breaks down.

The basic explanation of serial-order effects by interference theory has been in terms of a linear chaining model. If the list is represented as ABCDE then there is an association from A to B, an association from B to C, and so on, up to an association from D to E. The advantage of this description is that one is able to encompass associative and serial-order effects within the same conceptual framework. The disadvantage is that it is wrong. Linear chains mediated by linked associations just won't do. The problem is very simple. As shown by many studies of serial to paired-associate transfer, the test for these associations fails. Subjects generally do not learn a paired-associate list derived from adjacent items from the serial list in fewer trials than a jumbled paired-associate list (Young, 1968).

To focus specifically on one of the very basic questions, why is the serial-position curve bowed? It is obvious that a bowed or U-shaped function could result from a combination of two underlying monotonic gradients. One such possibility is interference effects operating on each particular item and stemming from two sources, number of prior items and number of subsequent items. These two sources separately are monotonic, so a model based on intraunit interference has the necessary ingredients to explain the phenomenon. However, as was detailed in Chapter 6, the model of Foucault (1928) was unsuccessful in explaining the data at a quantitative level, and the model of Melton (1963) was not developed sufficiently to generate quantitative predictions.

In a different vein, the distinctiveness model of Murdock (1960a) again suggested two underlying monotonic gradients. Here they resulted from the distance of any particular item from the beginning and from the end of a unidimensional scale. At best this model is descriptive and not explanatory; it does not say much about the processes involved in storing and retrieving short strings of items. What is needed is a process model; or perhaps, a two-process model. The item-and-order models in general and the structural model of Estes (1972) in particular are clearly attempts along these lines. However, none of these models has been developed to the point where it can be claimed to be very comprehensive. There are many serial-order effects, and these item-and-order models explain just a few.

Let me now suggest an alternative. It can be described as a nesting model because depth of nesting will be one of its key features. It is perhaps of somewhat greater generality than these other models; in principle it is relevant not only to accuracy and latency data, but to order errors, chunking, and motor skills as well. It has developed in the course of writing this book, so it is not only quite recent but largely untested to boot. I am offering it, then, in a provisional spirit; if nothing else, it may help to rekindle interest in serial-order effects, a topic that, despite its importance, has perhaps declined slightly in popularity in the last few years.

Nesting Model

Assume that the basic mechanism for seriation is a nesting process. Two items can be associated with each other, but three are too many. So one needs a coding element to link them. The encoding process for a five-item list is illustrated in Fig. 10.12. First S_1 is presented, then S_2. These two items can be associated, here indicated by a + sign. Presentation of S_3 necessitates the coding element A_1 to code the S_2–S_1 pair. Then presentation of S_4 requires A_2 to code S_3 and A_1, and A_1 in turn codes S_2 and S_1. Finally, presentation of the last item requires yet a third coding element A_3 to code S_4 and A_2. If interpolation preceded recall then it might even require a fourth element to code the string, but that is not shown here.

To utilize encoded information and generate an ordered recall, this string of nested associations must be unpacked. But when it is unpacked it is in a back-to-front order,

$$S_1$$
$$S_2 + S_1$$
$$S_3 + A_1 (S_2 + S_1)$$
$$S_4 + A_2 (S_3 + A_1 (S_2 + S_1))$$
$$S_5 + A_3 (S_4 + A_2 (S_3 + A_1 (S_2 + S_1)))$$

FIG. 10.12. Encoding of a serial string. The list items or stimuli are denoted by the letter S and the coding elements by the letter A. The subscripts run in temporal order.

and recall must go in the other direction. So assume that the string is unpacked into a response buffer which holds the items during the unpacking until they are ready for output. Another description of this process might be setting up a program of motor instructions, but here we are concerned with the short-term storage of these instructions. Loading the response buffer is illustrated in Fig. 10.13.

First item S_5 is entered into the buffer. Then the control element A_3 is stripped off and S_4 is unpacked. So now there are two items in the buffer, S_4 and S_5. Then A_2 is stripped off and S_3 is unpacked. Finally A_1 is stripped off and S_2 and S_1 are unpacked. Then (and only then) can the response occur; after execution the buffer is cleared. This process can then repeat, as it surely does in short-term memory experiments, as well as in the performance of many skills (e.g., typing, playing a musical instrument, reading aloud).

What exactly is this response buffer? Just as a tape recorder has two distinct modes, record and reproduce, so in a sense we do too. We can take in or absorb information, or we can put out or generate information. When the latter requires overt responding then the actual responses need to be preprogrammed or organized. Organization or integration of responses over time requires storage, and the response buffer is a metaphorical way of characterizing this storage. So, this response buffer comes into play when we change from the record to the reproduce mode. Crowder and Morton (1969) and Morton (1970) use the same term, but I think with a somewhat different view in mind. As I think of it, it seems designed for holding the necessary information to execute a short burst of responses (verbal, motor, or whatever) and is used and re-used over and over again; see, e.g., Keele (1968) or Schmidt (1968).

There are two main sources of error. One is unpacking. The deeper the nesting, the more likely something goes wrong in loading the response buffer. What it is (for instance, doing things in the wrong order or going off the track altogether) is not clear. The other source of error is decay in the response buffer. The longer an item has to wait in the buffer, the more likely that it (or some of its features) will be lost. These are two monotonic effects, and they combine to produce the ubiquitous serial-position effects one always finds in these serial-order tasks. Depth of nesting affects primacy, decay in the buffer affects recency, and together they produce the U-shaped function.

In order to derive quantitative predictions it is necessary to specify not only the

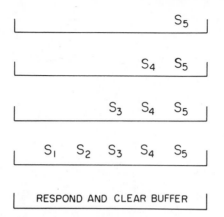

FIG. 10.13. Loading of the response buffer prior to the execution of the response. The temporal sequence is indicated by reading from top to bottom.

nature of these two monotonic functions but how they combine. I have investigated several possibilities, but none to my complete satisfaction. One of them is to assume that there must be errors both in unpacking and in the response buffer for an incorrect response to occur. That way one has a simple multiplicative relationship, and it is not hard to obtain reasonable serial-position curves. For instance, assume that the probability of decay increases as a linear function of time in the buffer and that the probability of an unpacking error increases in linear fashion as a function of depth of nesting. The probability of an incorrect recall would then be the product of these two independent probabilities, and it is easy to work out some of the predictions. For reasonable parameter values (i.e., slopes and intercepts of these linear functions) one can generate quite presentable bowed serial positions. Also, a nice result is that the point of maximum difficulty can bear a direct relation to n, the number of items in the string. While qualitatively these linear functions work quite nicely, quantitatively they do not. In absolute terms, the predicted percent-correct values are much too high. As an aside, it might be mentioned that this example illustrates one of the dangers in working at a qualitative level. Until one starts actually making quantitative predictions, you may think you have explained something, whereas in fact you have not.

Since linear gradients do not work, the next obvious possibility is to try exponential gradients. In particular, assume that the probability of decay is a negatively accelerated function of time in the buffer and that it is given by the expression $1 - (1 - \alpha)^i$. Here i is serial position and α is the decay parameter. Assume that the probability of an error in unpacking is also a negatively accelerated function of the order of unpacking which is given by the expression $1 - (1 - \beta)^{r(n + 1 - i)}$ where β is the unpacking parameter and r is a parameter which can absorb the effects of repetition. Then with α and β set to the same value of .1 and $r = 5$, the resulting error probability is shown in Fig. 10.14. All things considered, the curve seems quite good.

As a further example, a modified version of this model was fit to the data of Conrad and Hull (1968). They compared recall of visually-presented 7-item strings of digits

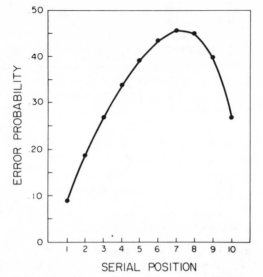

FIG. 10.14. Theoretical serial-position curve for a 10-item list resulting from the joint effects of unpacking and decay in the response buffer. Details of the assumptions are given in the text.

which were either read aloud (auditory) or simply shown (visual) at the time of presentation. The results of the parameter estimation are shown in Fig. 10.15 where the circles indicate the data points and the smooth curves are the model. While the fit is little short of spectacular (the standard error of estimate was .021), it was necessary to resort to SIMPLEX and nine free parameters to achieve it. For those who are interested, decay in the response buffer was assumed to increase exponentially with time, with the same rate constant for auditory and visual presentation, but different intercepts and asymptotes. Unpacking was assumed to be a stochastic process with a low probability of error if the prior step was correct, but a higher probability of error if it was not. The transition parameters were the same for auditory and visual presentation, but the start values differed in the two cases. Nine free parameters is a bit much to fit 14 points, so I urge the interested reader to do better.

There was no particular rationale for the selection of these exponential functions; it was quite arbitrary. Also, while the primacy function for decay is not unreasonable, the recency function for unpacking borders on the outrageous. In Fig. 10.14 there is a moderate probability (.410) that the first item will be wrongly unpacked and a near-certain probability (.995) that the last item will be wrongly unpacked. (In these computations the fact that the first two items in the list go as a unit was disregarded.) Thus, this particular realization must be wrong, but perhaps it will suggest better alternatives.

For the present then we must content ourselves with qualitative predictions, risky though that may be. It turns out that there are many empirical effects reported in the literature which seem, at this level, to be consistent with the model. That, after all, is what motivated it in the first place. So without further delay let me proceed to enumerate the empirical data that appears to be consistent with this seriation mechanism.

Supporting Evidence

1. There is no positive transfer in a serial to paired-associate transfer paradigm. The reason is that, except for the first two items in the list, stimuli are not associated to each other but to coding elements.

2. Performance deteriorates as the number of items in the string increases. This result is well-known and has been described by Melton (1963) as intraunit interference (see Fig. 7.2). It would occur because, as list length increases, opportunities for unpacking errors and decay in the buffer would both increase. With serial lists, there is also a marked proactive-retroactive interaction (see Fig. 6.3) which again would occur as the joint result of two processes.

3. The serial-position curve of memory span is bowed. When subjects are instructed to recall a list in order, error probability rises to a maximum at some value past the middle and then drops. There is a primacy effect and a recency effect but no asymptote; e.g., the Conrad and Hull (1968) data shown in Fig. 10.15.

4. The drop in this curve is much more pronounced if the presentation is vocalized or auditory than if it is visual (see also Crowder, 1972). If the decay in the response buffer were greater for visual than auditory presentation, then such an effect could occur, localized in the recency part of the serial-position curve. There is also some evidence (Cheng, 1972) that acoustic similarity effects are also localized in the recency part of the curve.

5. Backward memory span is more difficult than forward memory span. Since this seriation process only works in the forward direction, the information would have to be recoded somehow to yield a backward order of recall. Because of the necessary re-coding, accuracy should decrease. See point 10 for more on backward recall.

6. There is the Ranschburg (non) Effect. By and large, there is little effect of

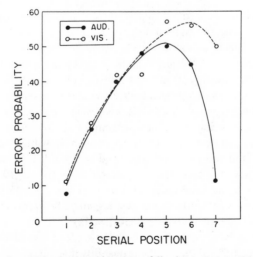

FIG. 10.15. Data and model for serial-position curves following spoken (auditory) and silent (visual) presentation of 7-item digit strings. (Data from Conrad & Hull, 1968.)

repeating an item in the list (e.g., Jahnke, 1972; Wickelgren, 1965b). Unless it were a massed repetition, a repeated element would have to be encoded as a new item, and so no effect would be expected.

7. Presentation rate should not affect memory span. As long as presentation is not too fast there is sufficient time to encode items at the time of presentation. Errors occur during the unpacking of the response buffer, so they should not be dependent upon the rate at which the material had been presented. The fact that a slower rate does seem to help visual memory span may reflect auditory elaboration and, as such, should be localized in the recency effect. The same conclusion about insensitivity to rate would apply to the probe-digit experiment of Waugh and Norman (1965).

8. Serial-position curves for memory span and probe tests should look somewhat different. In a sequential probe test, the unpacking occurs until the probe is encountered, then the previously unpacked item is read out. There is little or no chance for decay, so the only errors should come from unpacking. Consequently, there should be recency effects only, and over a more extensive range than with ordered recall. There is; see Waugh and Norman (1965). For a detailed comparison of probing versus recalling, see Dong (1972); also see Moss and Sharac (1970).

9. Positional and reverse-probe tests should yield much the same retention functions. Whether one probes for an item with its position, or for the position with the item, should (and does) not matter much; see Murdock (1968c). Why sequential and positional probes are so similar is not as clear (Woodward & Murdock, 1968).

10. Serial-position curves should be different for forward and backward recall. In backward recall, you unpack small parts of the list into the response buffer and read them off in reverse order. It is possible, but difficult. So unpacking should be of more importance, and there should be less opportunity for decay. Therefore, the recency effect should be more extensive, and there should be a smaller difference in recency as a function of mode of presentation. Such effects have been reported by Madigan (1971).

11. Since items are encoded and stored sequentially, reporting items back in numerical order rather than in temporal order (e.g., 31892 = 12389) should be slower and less accurate. It is (Colotla, 1969, discussed in Murdock, 1972).

12. Memory span for well-learned units (e.g., binary digits, letters, or words) should not vary very much with type of material (Miller, 1956; Crannell & Parrish, 1957). If all factors except vocabulary size could be equated, then no difference at all would be expected, but I do not know of any such study.

13. Serial-order intrusions tend to come from the appropriate position in the prior list (Conrad, 1959) and decrease with intertrial interval without affecting accuracy (Conrad, 1960b). If there were overwriting and decay in the response buffer, this is exactly what you would expect. There is also evidence (Noyd, 1965) that, with trigrams of varying length, serial-order intrusions tend to come from the appropriate subset. More generally, any prior list intrusions would be expected to show a strong recency gradient, which they do (Murdock, 1961a).

14. If unpacking is a stochastic process, then conditional-probability effects should occur in recall. For instance, the probability that the second item in the string

will be correctly recalled should be higher if the first item was correct than if it was not. In general, interdependencies of this sort do seem to characterize short-term serial recall. Since this effect may not be generally appreciated, an example is shown in Fig. 10.16. These data are from a study by Murdock (1961a) which used the distractor technique of Peterson and Peterson (1959). Shown here are conditional-probability analyses for the three-item strings, where A, B, and C symbolize the first, second, and third item in the string. The purpose of this figure is to demonstrate that it is manifestly incorrect to consider the three items in the string as independent. The top curve shows the probability that the third item will be recalled given recall of the first two, the next curve shows the probability the second item will be recalled given recall of the first, while the third curve from the top is the unconditional probability of recall of the first item. The product of these three gives the obtained result (shown in the fourth curve), while the bottom curve is the predicted value on the assumption of independence. Clearly the predicted curve is well below the obtained curve at each retention interval. Although not shown in this figure, recall of the second and third items was much less frequent when the prior item or two had not been recalled.

15. Some word pairs similar in spelling (e.g., MOWN–DOWN or HOME–SOME) are difficult to pronounce successively. The difference apparently lies in the initiation time, not the execution time (Bradshaw & Nettleton, 1974). Thus, the

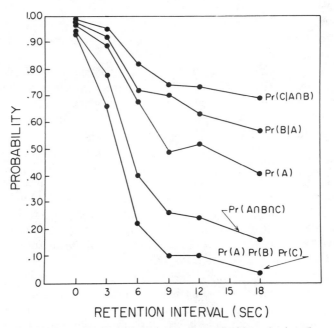

FIG. 10.16. Conditional-probability retention functions for recall of 3-word strings (here symbolized as A, B, and C) using the distractor technique of Peterson and Peterson (1959). (Data from Murdock, 1961a.)

1-12	$A_{11}(S_{12}+A_{10}(S_{11}+A_9(S_{10}+A_8(S_9+A_7(S_8+A_6(S_7+A_5(S_6+A_4(S_5+A_3(S_4+A_2$
(11)	$(S_3+A_1(S_2+S_1))))))))))$

2-6	$B_5(S_{12}+B_4(S_{11}+B_3(S_{10}+B_2(S_9+B_1(S_8+S_7)))))$
(5)	$A_5(S_6+A_4(S_5+A_3(S_4+A_2(S_3+A_1(S_2+S_1)))))$
	$C_1(B_5+A_5)$

3-4	$C_3(S_{12}+C_2(S_{11}+C_1(S_{10}+S_9)))$ $B_3(S_8+B_2(S_7+B_1(S_6+S_5)))$ $A_3(S_4+A_2(S_3+A_1(S_2+S_1)))$
(3)	$D_2(C_3+D_1(B_3+A_3))$

4-3	$D_2(S_{12}+D_1(S_{11}+S_{10}))$ $C_2(S_9+C_1(S_8+S_7))$ $B_2(S_6+B_1(S_5+S_4))$ $A_2(S_3+A_1(S_2+S_1))$
(3)	$E_3(D_2+E_2(C_2+E_1(B_2+A_2)))$

6-2	$F_1(S_{12}+S_{11})$ $E_1(S_{10}+S_9)$ $D_1(S_8+S_7)$ $C_1(S_6+S_5)$ $B_1(S_4+S_3)$ $A_1(S_2+S_1)$
(4)	$G_5(F_1+G_4(E_1+G_3(D_1+G_2(C_1+G_1(B_1+A_1)))))$

FIG. 10.17. Different groupings for a 12-item string. The boxes at the left indicate the number of groups and the number of items per group. The maximum depth of nesting is indicated below each box. As before, S denotes stimulus elements and the letters A–G denote coding elements. The subscripts run in temporal order.

time to set up a program of motor instructions (load the response buffer) is responsible for the effect; it is more difficult to preprogram heterophone pairs, but the interresponse time does not differ from control pairs.

16. Finally, this nesting model would not be vulnerable to the serial-integration criticism of Lashley (1951). Response organization precedes response execution, so there is no necessary limit on speed of response as measured, say, by interresponse time. The assumption, of course, is that the same seriation mechanism is involved both in short-term recall and the execution of skilled acts.

Higher-order Coding

All this is fine for short lists, but what happens as list length increases? Perhaps some sort of hierarchical structure can come into play. One could pyramid lower-order coding elements to form higher-order coding elements, and in this way a longer string could be handled. The same rules apply, but now a coding element can represent or be associated with two other coding elements. An illustrative example is shown in Fig. 10.17. It represents five different ways that a 12-item string could be coded. The five different groupings are indicated in the box at the left of each row, and below that in parentheses is the maximum depth of nesting for that arrangement.

As can be seen, a simple 1-12 grouping with no pyramiding is a bit ungainly, and the deepest nesting is 11. With two groups of six the deepest nesting is reduced to 5, but an additional coding element C_1 is needed to code the order of the two groups. With either a 3-4 or a 4-3 grouping the deepest nesting is 3, but more varied coding elements are needed to preserve order. Finally, if the list is coded as paired associates (6-2) then the deepest nesting rises to 4, but it is for the coding elements not the list items.

It would seem that grouping is desirable, but there is a trade-off. The smaller the group size, the less deeply each list item will be nested, but the more deeply embedded will be the coding elements in the higher-order string. With a 12-item string the minimum nesting depth occurs with either a 3-4 or a 4-3 grouping. If the subject were encouraged to rehearse or organize so as to form groups of three or four, or if the material lent itself to this grouping arrangement, then performance might be expected to be optimal. At least for shorter lists there is some data supporting this prediction (Severin & Rigby, 1963; Wickelgren, 1964).

It does not take much imagination to extend this analysis to account for some of the grouping effects reported in the literature (e.g., Bower & Winzenz, 1969; Johnson, 1970, 1972). Transition-error probabilities (TEPs) would be different between and within groups. (In general they would be higher across groups, because in addition to the things that can go wrong in unpacking a single group, there is also the possibility of going to the incorrect next grouping.) One could get interference or regrouping effects within a cluster without affecting the arrangement in other clusters. One might even expect some transpositions within clusters (groups) but serial-order intrusions (Conrad, 1959) across clusters. In a 4-3 grouping, one might find S_5 substituted for S_8. That should be more common than either S_4 or S_6 substituted for S_8.

Considerations of grouping suggest a possible clarification of the item and order problem. As noted in Chapter 6, some models separate the forgetting of item and the forgetting of order information and suggest what the interrelationships might be. Here there is at least a clear specification of what the item and order information is. The item information would be represented by the stimulus items themselves $(S_1, S_2, \ldots)$ while the order information would be represented by the coding elements $(A_1, B_1, C_1, \ldots)$. Conceptually it is quite possible to separate the forgetting of item and order information. In principle one could be faster than the other, so it is not a logical necessity that order information be forgotten more rapidly than item information.

However, while the conceptual separation of item and order information is clear, the mechanism for transpositions is not. If they only occur during unpacking or during the stay in the buffer one would expect a monotonic gradient over serial position, which does not happen. As reported by Estes (1972) and clearly confirmed in some of my own unpublished data, there is a U-shaped gradient for transpositions just as there is for item errors. I am a bit uneasy about the Conrad approach of explaining transpositions in terms of the loss of acoustic features, since the data I have with words as list items show many transpositions but no more acoustic similarity for pairs of words that transpose than for pairs that do not. One possibility is to make retention of order information basic and let item errors result from (or be contingent on) the loss of order information. This was the conclusion of Murdock and vom Saal (1967) and is the basis of the Estes (1972) model. (A contrary point of view is suggested in Fozard, Myers, & Waugh, 1971.) Although such a possibility is not necessarily inconsistent with the seriation mechanism discussed here, exactly how it might work is far from clear.

However, whatever the mechanism for transpositions is, it should be the same for short-term tasks and long-term skills (see point 16 above). One should expect the same pattern of transpositions in skilled acts such as typing or keypunching. Clearly the contents of long-term memory do not exist in garbled form, so the existence of order errors must characterize the utilization more than the representation of information. This view is one of the reasons I doubt the Estes model, since it would seem to require quite separate mechanisms for the two cases.

Once one allows for the grouping effects represented in Fig. 10.17, the mechanisms become somewhat more complicated. Some parallel processing is needed for this scheme to work. Consider the case where there are four groups of three. After the first string has been coded, then A_2 must be held in memory while S_4–S_6 are being encoded. Then, while S_7–S_9 are being encoded A_2 and B_2 are being encoded by E_1. That in turn will combine with C_2 to form E_2 which must be held while the last group of items (S_{10}–S_{12}) is being read in. Easy and effortless though this may seem with short lists, there suddenly comes a point where the difficulty rises sharply and performance deteriorates accordingly.

Also, complications arise during output. The response buffer surely cannot hold all 12 items, so several passes through the coding elements might be needed. That is, in a grouping like 4-3 the first element codes the last three list items, but in serial recall they must wait. Perhaps E_3 is unpacked three times, first to get items 1–6, then 7–9, and finally 10–12. Considering encoding and decoding problems, it is no wonder people cannot cope very well with strings this long.

Clearly, sequential redundancies must be considered. If the list items were common abbreviations (e.g., IBM, SOS, TWA) they could be handled more like single items, so depth of nesting would be much reduced. Conceivably, one could even code sentences in this way for verbatim recall, and there memory span is more like 20 words (Craik, 1971).

With long lists, segmentation or grouping of this kind may occur. One could imagine nesting up to depth 3 or 4, then a break to start again, and so on. A particularly appropriate task here would be running memory-span (Nixon, 1946; Pollack, Johnson, & Knaff, 1959), where the subject is required to recall as many of the last items as he can. Known list lengths are beneficial, as they should be, for then the subject can pick the most efficient point to start his last grouping.

To speculate still further, one could incorporate some rules about repetition to attempt to explain grouping effects in repetition. There is apparently some memorial residue after a single presentation (Hebb, 1961), so whether repetition would benefit performance should depend upon whether or not the group structure is preserved (Bower & Winzenz, 1969). Reordering within a group should not matter if the group has not been learned and if the overall list structure is unaltered (Jensen, 1963; Johnson, 1970). Why performance improves with practice (i.e., how serial learning occurs) is surely not clear from this description, but at least this analysis suggests some possibilities one might explore.

FREE RECALL

The basic issue in multitrial free recall is the nature of the organization that takes place with repetition. The basic issue in single-trial free recall is the retrieval process: how it works and what information it uses. I shall consider only the latter here.

Alternative Retrieval Mechanisms

Let me use the conveyor-belt analogy and the distinction between item and associative information to discuss the retrieval of information in single-trial free recall. Basically, there are two somewhat different views that are currently popular. One would be the random sampling models (e.g., Rundus, 1973; Shiffrin, 1970a), which would say that list presentation deposits a number of globs of information on the conveyor belt and, at the time of retrieval, a sampling-with-replacement process comes into play. Thus, only item information is used in the retrieval; associative information plays no role. The organization on the conveyor belt may be simply by order of arrival, and the sampling mechanism chugs along somehow to generate the sequential effects one finds in output order. Or, regrouping by category may take place to generate the clustering one finds on a taxonomic basis. But whatever the means, the structuring is represented either in the format of storage or in the rules governing the sampling mechanism, not in the interitem associations.

The other point of view, as suggested by Kintsch (1970a, 1972b) or in FRAN (Anderson & Bower, 1972a) is somewhat different. Take the FRAN model. There is an ENTRYSET consisting of a few list items. They will provide access to the list, and associative pathways will be followed to see if further tagged items will turn up. Thus, the general idea is that associative information is used to gain access to items, while item information is used to decide on list membership. Retrieval of information in single-trial free recall is basically a search and decision process, with associative information used to guide the search and item information used to make the decision.

What solid evidence do we have to evaluate these two views? We certainly know that there is an accessibility problem in single-trial free recall. On the one hand, recognition performance is far better than recall performance; on the other hand, retrieval cues can be most effective in eliciting responses, and these effects can be quite powerful indeed (Tulving & Pearlstone, 1966; Tulving & Osler, 1968; Tulving & Thomson, 1973). However, it should be noted that, in manipulating retrieval cues, one is essentially using associative information to study how we gain access to item information. As pointed out by Underwood (1972), studies with retrieval cues may tell us about accessibility of information in memory, but it is not at all clear that they tell us anything about the retrieval processes of single-trial free recall. Such associative links may or may not be used by the subject in free recall.

To return to FRAN for a minute, it might be noted in passing that this model uses exactly the same assumptions that I have suggested for the fluctuation or cross-reference model for paired associates. Associations are all-or-none, bidirectional, independent, and probably symmetrical. Also, there is a clear separation between associative and item information. So perhaps there is coming to be some agreement on the characteristics of associative information in short-term memory. What is less clear is whether this associative information underlies the retrieval process of free recall.

Broadly, then, the question is whether the packets of information on the conveyor belt are independent or related. If the latter, they may be related either one to another or (as some prefer) to self-generated retrieval cues which are not themselves list items. This question, of course, is the issue investigated in the cuing studies originated by Slamecka (1969b). These cuing studies have been the inspiration for the Rundus (1973) model and a distinct embarrassment to FRAN (e.g., Anderson, 1972). However, as noted in the previous chapter, the interpretive difficulty with the cuing effects is the recall-inhibition effect as reported by Brown (1968). There may, then, be a balance of inhibitory and facilitative factors operating here; this point is discussed in Tulving and Hastie (1972).

The issues, then, are very far from settled. On the one hand, one could take an associative point of view and say that, as in FRAN, pathways are tagged and serve as access routes to stored information. On the other hand, one could say that grouping or organization of the items during list presentation is crucial, and it is the clustering or organization internally, not externally, which is critical. Evidence that could be cited in favor of the former would be the incidental-learning studies, which seem to show that generating semantically-relevant extralist associations results in recall that is as good as the intentional-learning condition. (These studies are discussed in Craik & Lockhart, 1972.) Alternatively, one could cite the overt-rehearsl data which suggest that the critical factor is structuring or organizing the list. These are the results of Rundus (1971) and Rundus and Atkinson (1970), and this view seems favored by Underwood (1972).

Fluctuation Model

Elsewhere (Murdock, 1972) I have suggested an extension of the fluctuation model to single-trial free recall. The model assumed that item availability could be represented in the same way as associations, and that a pool of available items was gradually built up over the period of list presentation. Retrieval was characterized by a sampling process; it was assumed that the last chunk was reported first, then random sampling was used for the remainder. The last chunk was considered to be an unbroken terminal string of available items. The recovery parameter was attenuated by the number of currently available items, to reflect the strain on the rehearsal mechanism as list presentation built up a larger and larger storage load. The forgetting probability was constant over list presentation, and the encoding parameter p_0 was another of the free parameters. By and large, the model did a reasonable job of fitting the group serial-position curves of single-trial free recall (Fig. 8.2), but little else was attempted.

As promised in that paper, further work was done to fit the model to the data of individual subjects. (The group data is that shown in Fig. 8.2 and is also given in

Norman, 1970b.) The results were a bit disappointing. In most cases, the estimations for individual subjects were quite reasonable, and for the six groups the most succinct characterization of the overall results was to say that the main change was a reduction in the value of the retrieval parameter θ as list length increased. This much was fine; analyses of variance came out quite nicely, and we could even say with considerable accuracy that $\theta = 2 - \log L$, where L is list length. However, a moment's reflection shows that once $L > 100$ than θ becomes negative. Or, to make a long story short, the model would have to predict that the number of words recalled would actually decrease as list length increased. That did not strike me as a very desirable feature of the model.

Consequently, the particular version of this model described in Murdock (1972) has simply not worked out very well. Perhaps it could be patched up; perhaps it was ill-conceived in the first place. However, it does make a few general points that are still valid, and they might be noted briefly. (a) Experimental separation of recency effects and the asymptote (as in Glanzer & Cunitz, 1966) does not necessitate postulating a two-store model. One-store models can do exactly the same thing; all it takes is one parameter for the recency effect and another for the asymptote. (b) This fluctuation model could at least explain how a variable such as mode of presentation could affect recency and not the asymptote, a continuing source of embarrassment to two-store models. (c) The chunk-size manipulation makes it quite clear that an S-shaped recency effect is not inconsistent with exponential forgetting. If one considers the terminal string of available items, even though the items taken singly undergo exponential forgetting, it is quite possible to produce a Gompertz-type recency effect with the particular assumptions of the model. (d) The model attributed the primacy effect to the progressive attenuation of the recovery parameter β. This effect was due to the fact that, as list presentation continued, the limited processing capacity had to be spread further and further to rehearse the ever-growing number of available items. Such a mechanism would generate a monotonic serial-position effect extending over the whole range of the list. Although serial-position curves of immediate recall do not look like this, in fact final free-recall curves show exactly this effect (e.g., Craik, 1970).

The problem with the fluctuation model in free recall may be in the retrieval process. Perhaps what happens in retrieval is as follows. The first chunk is recalled, and then an item from the chunk is used as the probe to interrogate memory. When the probe is found, then a related item can be identified. In noncategorized lists, a related item can be phonemically, associatively, semantically, or temporally similar. In a categorized list, category membership is a further cue. Perhaps whatever feature or features are used to locate the recalled item (probe) are also used to locate a related item. But whatever the process, it is recursive. The extracted item is itself recalled, then used as a new probe for a further memory comparison. This process continues, item by item, until a stop rule is invoked and the recall period terminates. (A similar process has been suggested by Norman, 1968, but it seems more directed towards the retrieval of associative information from memory.)

Why is recall often so limited, and why do interresponse times increase as dramatically as they do (Fig. 8.4)? For one thing, with noncategorized lists the similarity relationships are generally minimal, and the temporal features may become progressively less efficacious as the probe item becomes older. For another, recalling items is an on-going process and adds additional information to the store. To think of recall as depleting a store is probably misleading; in terms of the conveyor-belt model, during the output the recalled items are additional bags placed on the ramp, and the longer output proceeds, the more blurred the exact demarcation point between presentation and recall.

Thus, there are at least two factors involved in answering these questions. One is that the more items that have been recalled, the fewer the number of remaining items that share the attribute or attributes of the current probe. The second factor is that, as recall proceeds, there is more and more to examine, and a monitoring process is necessary to guard against repetition. Given these two factors it is not hard at all to see how interresponse time could increase considerably with output position. It also happens in categorized lists (Patterson, Meltzer, & Mandler, 1971).

The total-time effects would be consistent with this general viewpoint. The longer the list, the more items there would be that would share common attributes (assuming, that is, that the useful attributes are small in number compared to list length), so more items should be recalled with longer lists. Increasing presentation time would have a similar effect for one of two possible reasons: More attributes would be encoded initially, or those encoded would persist longer. The former is consistent with the Lockhart attribute model, while either is consistent with the data shown in Fig. 10.5.

Other aspects of free recall could be discussed in these terms, but it would be very *ad hoc*. All I am really suggesting is that the temporal format of the store be represented in any model of free recall. So let me draw to a close with some evidence that temporal dependencies exist in so-called ''free'' recall. Here are six bits of evidence, the first four culled from unpublished analyses of the data shown in Fig. 8.2 and the last two from unpublished studies conducted here at Toronto.

1. If two items which had been adjacent in list presentation are recalled consecutively, the odds are at least 2:1 that they will be recalled in a forward rather than a backward order. Almost all subjects individually show this effect, and it is highly significant statistically by any test you care to make. (The same tendency is clear in trigrams as well as digrams, though there are far fewer cases to analyze.) For the first two words recalled, the odds exceed 10:1.

2. If the first word recalled is the fourth from the end (e.g., position 17 in a 20-word list), and if the next three words recalled are the last three words in the list, the probability that they will be recalled in the forward order (i.e., 18, 19, 20) is .873. The chance level (with six permutations) is .167. In fact, one can even do a transposition analysis on the remaining cases, and adjacent transpositions (e.g., 17, 19, 18, 20) outnumber remote transpositions (e.g., 17, 20, 18, 19) by 2:1 even though the chance level is 2:3.

3. If an extra-list intrusion came from one of the two prior lists, the odds are 4:1 that it came from the list one back rather than the list two back.

4. There is a monotonic intrusion gradient extending over the past 20 lists. That is, the more remote the list, the less likely it was to contribute an intrusion. (This

effect was not corrected for opportunity per session, which it should be given that there were 20 lists per session over four sessions. However, my guess is that any such correction would flatten, but not eliminate, the gradient.)

5. In an unpublished study using the final free-recall procedure of Craik (1970), after five lists had been presented and recalled the subjects were requested to recall as many words as they could remember from the entire experiment. The earlier the list, the fewer were the number of words recalled on the final recall; this point is discussed elsewhere (Murdock, 1972, p. 79).

6. In an unpublished study by Wayne Donaldson, a two-minute blank intertrial interval was either used or omitted in a conventional single-trial paradigm. The serial-position curves showed appreciably more primacy when the preceding two minutes were empty than when they were not. Perhaps the beginning of the list is easier to find when it is uncluttered by previous activity.

Future Directions

Since we do not fully understand free recall, what should we do next? There would seem to be no need to document further the availability-accessibility distinction. This point seems quite clear and does not need further support. Nor will the study of retrieval cues necessarily tell us much about free recall. They will tell us about associative information, which may or may not be used in single-trial free recall.

Experimentally, to test the models, we must start to make free recall a bit less free. We could control the encoding in the manner of Craik (1973) or Hyde (1973). We might start requiring certain types of output: to start from the beginning, to start from the end, or to start with a particular word. Such manipulations have already been tried, and as a first step (e.g., Craik, 1969; Murdock, 1968c) some large differences have been obtained. In the multitrial situation one could investigate interactive presentation. List presentation on Trial $n + 1$ then depends upon recall performance on Trial n. A study by Murdock, Penney, and Aamiry (1970) used the following manipulation. All words recalled on Trial n were presented either first or last on Trial $n + 1$. Compared to a control group with noncontingent presentation, the serial-position curves were very different and the performance level of both experimental groups was superior, though not by much. Conditional probability analyses also showed some differences. To understand organization, we shall have to start setting up clusters, breaking them down, and seeing what makes them cohere. Postexperimental statistical manipulations are simply not strong enough. We must provide some experimental demonstrations of the reality of clusters.

Finally, why should we try to understand free recall? While it is the simplest paradigm experimentally, it may be the most difficult conceptually. And surely it is not a common everyday aspect of memory. Is it not usually the case that item, serial-order, or associative information is sufficient? Perhaps the main reason why free recall has been and will continue to be an experimental paradigm of some interest is the challenge it poses. Simpler aspects of memory come into play here. What they are and how they work is certainly not clear. But it is a touchstone. If we can come to understand what is going on in free recall, then we can have some confidence that we understand the more basic processes and how they come together in one particular situation.

REVIEW

Human memory involves the encoding, storage, and retrieval of information. The initial encoding is representational. It is like a movie camera or a tape recorder, but with a difference. The record is selective; the camera has different focal-length lenses, or the tape recorder has different band-pass filters. Perhaps a better analogy would be that the initial encoding is like a computer program that could be written in machine language, assembly language, or a problem-oriented programming language. If the subject is asked to observe whether the picture has an inverted triangle or the word was spoken in a female voice, then the initial encoding is directed towards the physical aspects of the stimuli (machine language, in a sense). If the subject is instructed to attend to certain alphabetic characters on a slide or the sequence of phonemes in a particular utterance, and to remember the *words,* then the initial encoding is directed towards the lexical aspects of the stimuli (assembly language, as it were). If the subject is presented strings of items which we call sentences and asked to remember the meaning, then the initial encoding is directed towards the syntactic-semantic aspects of the stimuli (problem-oriented programming language).

This initial encoding is embedded in a temporal format which changes constantly over time. As described by Sherrington (1953), we may think of ". . . an enchanted loom where millions of flashing shuttles weave a dissolving pattern, always a meaningful pattern though never an abiding one . . . [p. 184]." Features slowly are lost or decay, so the older the event, the less distinct is its memory. Retrieval is the utilization of this stored information. It involves memory and decision. The memory component involves some sort of memory comparison or search process, where the characteristics of the probe are compared to the features of the memory traces. The decision component determines whether an observable response will be forthcoming.

At least three types of information are stored in memory. These are item, associative, and serial-order information. Item information is rich, complex, graded, and relatively permanent. Associative information (at least initially) is simple, dichotomous, and labile. Item information results in the sense of familiarity we experience when we encounter something a second time. Associative information provides a cross-referencing mechanism so as to facilitate retrieval. Retrieval of item information seems to reflect the temporal properties of the memory store, while retrieval of associative information may not.

Serial strings are remembered and learned, but not on the basis of direct associative chains. We do not remember the days of the week, the months of the year, or the letters of the alphabet in terms of simple a–b, b–c, and c–d associations. A possibility is that abstract coding elements represent pairwise contingencies, so that the string ABC is represented in memory by an association between c and s where s codes b and a (the memorial representation of the stimuli B and A). Depth of nesting increases with the length of the string, and higher-order coding elements might permit the formation of hierarchical encodings.

Free-recall experiments require the subject to sample without replacement from his recent memory. There seems to be a mismatch here; the human information-processing system was not designed with this in mind. Some sort of modified random-sampling process seems to be involved, and it may be recursive. A monitoring process is necessary to prevent resampling old items, and the recall itself adds new information rather than depleting the contents of the memory store.

A conveyor-belt analogy is useful to portray the temporal-to-spatial conversion of human short-term memory. The suitcases on the ramp characterize the contents of the store. They are distributed on the ramp by time of arrival, in backward order. The youngest is nearest, the oldest most distant. What is inside the suitcase (patterns, features, or blueprints) is still not clear but, by using assembly-language programming, we can avoid the issue for the time being.

Retrieving item information from this ramp involves some sort of memory comparison. It could be a backward, serial self-terminating scan in which features of the probe are compared with features of each of the items in memory until a match is found. Whether or not this is the particular comparison process, the memory comparison phase of retrieval is a high-speed operation, perhaps in the range of a few milliseconds per item. The decision stage of retrieval determines whether adequate information has been obtained from the comparison process; in other words, the output from the memory stage is the input to the decision stage. If the memory system is re-examined, the reaction latency will be longer as a consequence. For practiced subjects, an estimate of 250 milliseconds per examination is not unreasonable. Small amounts of information may be processed in parallel, larger amounts serially, but in either case direct access to information stored in recent memory seems unlikely.

Confidence judgments in a recognition-memory experiment will reflect both the number of interrogations of the memory store and the feature-match between the probe and the old items. The hit rate will decrease with lag because of the gradual loss of features. At least in some cases (unrelated words) recognition of item information can be quite good over long periods of time. Latency of response will reflect both the memory-comparison and the decision stage, as well as the encoding and response-selection processes. Shorter latencies are associated with high-confident responses, and their frequency decreases over lag as well.

Associations are independent, all-or-none, and bidirectional. They undergo both forgetting and recovery, and in the short-term case stability is rapidly achieved. While the associations themselves are dichotomous, the transition probabilities are graded. Their fluctuation can be characterized by a simple Markov process, and these parameters seem to reflect encoding and learning effects. In particular, increased presentation time makes recovery more probable, each successful recall decreases the probability of subsequent forgetting, and modality of presentation (auditory or visual) affects the initial probability of information being encoded. An association is more likely to be formed with auditory presentation than with visual presentation.

The same associations underlie recall and recognition and, for recognition, underlie confidence-judgment and forced-choice procedures. Recognition is better than recall because, in recognition, the subject can make use of backward associations. In a confidence-judgment procedure the subject can respond "yes" to an old pairing if the a–b or the b–a association is intact. In a forced-choice procedure the subject can also eliminate all lures with backward associations, and then guess at random from the remainder.

Throughout this book I have considered human memory as a topic in its own right. It is, after all, what I have been primarily interested in. But clearly it also operates in many of the cognitive activities of our daily life. We use it in conversation, reading and writing, solving problems, making decisions, and much more. In closing it might be fitting to comment a bit on this broader aspect.

My conviction is that the understanding of human memory will be an important step forward to the ultimate understanding of these more complex processes. To give two examples, let me comment briefly first on sentence comprehension and then on reading. For sentence comprehension, we must operate in the problem-oriented programming language. We are interested neither in the physical characteristics of the utterance nor in the lexical items *per se*. We are interested in the meaning. However, it is quite possible that simple item and associative information still play a role in this more cognitive processing. For item information, it would be hard to interpret the writing-righting example of Lashley without assuming some persistence of representational memory over time. As for associative information, some of the current semantic-memory models are predicated on very simple relational models, and data in Anderson and Bower (1972b) yield considerable evidence for the existence of simple associative relationships in memory for sentences.

As for reading, let me make the following very speculative suggestions. We have reason to believe that, for skilled subjects, decision processes in item recognition require approximately 250 milliseconds. We also know that, in reading, the duration of each fixation is approximately 250 milliseconds. It could be coincidental, or it could not be. Perhaps during the process of reading one indeed does make decisions, and does so at this very fast rate. What could these decisions be about?

It has been suggested (e.g., F. Smith, 1972) that the comprehension involved in reading comes about by using the sense of the passage to interpret the printed word, rather than the other way around. Suppose we change this slightly to say that one uses the sense of the passage to interpret the memory trace of the printed word. In reading for comprehension the experienced reader gradually builds up a picture or thematic construction embodying the sense of the passage. Now this is progressive, and every now and then one must check back to see whether new bits and pieces fit into the established framework. In other words, one must check for comprehension. Now reading is an accomplished skill that runs off at a high rate of speed, so we must continually be checking for understanding. Perhaps we do it frequently; perhaps we do it at four times a second.

To be less oblique, what I am suggesting, at least as a possibility, is that the decision process identified in recognition memory also operates in the course of reading for comprehension. Each saccadic movement brings in a new block or segment of information. We must assimilate it and go on, or go back and check. Going back and checking can be identified by the regressive eye movements which are well known (e.g., Morton, 1964). But we also know about the eye-voice span, so the decision process is not checking the most recent block of information. The central processor is checking through recent memory to make sense out of the block one back, while the current field of view is being processed into this short-term memory. And the checking of the central processor is the high-speed internal comparison process also identified in the experiments on item recognition reported earlier in this chapter.

Thus, reading is an on-going cognitive activity which involves information processing at several levels. Information is being encoded in memory, new segments come in every 250 msec, previous segments are being analyzed for meaning, and four times per second the decision must be made whether to continue or to go back. All the while, a high-speed comparison process is in operation to insure that the assimilation of information over time is interpreted correctly. As discussed by Conrad (1972b), this example might serve to illustrate the contribution of short-term memory to more complex cognitive activities.

Finally, how do the conveyor-belt model, the fluctuation model, and the nesting model fit together to provide an integrated picture of human memory? The conveyor-belt model may adequately characterize the short-term retention of item information, but a backward, serial self-terminating scan does not seem like a very efficient method of retrieving information from long-term memory. The fluctuation model may characterize the encoding, storage, and retrieval of associations, but the evidence argues against strings of pairwise associations providing the basis for seriation. The nesting model may explain short-term serial-order effects, but no forgetting mechanism was suggested and long-term serial-order memory is surely not perfect.

Perhaps it fits together as follows. The coding elements enter into associations with lower-order units, and basically these associations may be no different from those envisaged by the fluctuation model. Thus, forgetting does occur but repetition makes these associations more resistant to forgetting. A serial string is a chunk of information, but it needs a retrieval cue. One such cue is the name of the string; to write down the alphabet is to write down A, B, C, . . . , Z. So the encoded or encapsulated string has some name or label associated with it which provides the means of access. However, as has been noted several times, before one can generate the string (or answer a question) the location of the probe must be found in memory; here is where item information comes in. The conveyor-belt model characterizes the way in which we access a probe, the fluctuation model characterizes the association or associations between question and answer, and the answer can be a string of information rather than a single item.

It is often said that a temporally-organized storage system is a poor way to construct a memory. However, temporal organization embellished with an elaborate cross-reference system may not be quite so unwieldy or inefficient. Presumably mechanisms exist to allow us to update the contents of our long-term store. By adding the appropriate linking associations one can have a rich and elaborate information network. Whether this is the basis for long-term memory and the broader aspects of memory storage and retrieval remains to be seen, but it is not unreasonable given the data we now have on short-term memory.

In the past 15 years we have made considerable progress. We have developed standard and accepted methodologies, found large and stable effects, and have a number of differing theoretical interpretations. Fifteen years ago we did not even know how to study forgetting over short periods of time. Now we almost know too much. But we should realize how fortunate we are. Not only are our empirical effects large and reliable, but also they are relatively independent of many minor procedural details. Some of our colleagues must envy us.

Some may be bothered by the proliferation of theoretical views. Indeed, half of this book has been devoted to an exposition of different approaches. Certainly we would all like to know the truth. But it is far better to have too many different theoretical ideas than not enough. I can remember when the field was barren and lacking in interesting ideas. Others may be bothered by the large amount of experimentation and research effort, some more inspired than others. But in science as in other endeavors, a fair amount of trial-and-error is often necessary before the proper avenues of approach become clear. And even if we do not have all the answers, we have ruled out many unpromising avenues of approach.

Finally, what is the larger purpose of this whole research enterprise? It has been suggested that, after the discovery of particles by the physicists and the breaking of the genetic code by the molecular biologists, the next major scientific problem of our time is how the brain encodes, stores, and retrieves information. Ultimately we will know only when there has been a convergence of behavioral data, quantitative models, and neurophysiological or biochemical findings. The solution will require all three. As psychologists we can contribute to the first two. To the extent that our research on human memory has illuminated some of the important problems and suggested some of the possible answers, we may be participating in this larger scientific enterprise.

HUMAN MEMORY:
THEORY AND DATA

REFERENCES

Aaronson, D., & Markowitz, N. The temporal course of retrieval from short-term memory. Paper presented at the meeting of the Eastern Psychological Association, Washington, D. C., April, 1968.

Aaronson, D., Markowitz, N., & Shapiro, H. Perception and immediate recall of normal and "compressed" auditory sequences. *Perception & Psychophysics,* 1971, **9,** 338–344.

Abramson, N. *Information theory and coding.* New York: McGraw–Hill, 1963.

Adams, J. A. *Human memory.* New York: McGraw–Hill, 1967.

Adams, J. A., & Montague, W. E. Retroactive inhibition and natural language mediation. *Journal of Verbal Learning and Verbal Behavior,* 1967, **6,** 528–535.

Albert, D., Freies Reproduzieren von Wortreihen als stochastische Entleerung eines Speichers. *Zeitschrift für Experimentelle und Angewandte Psychologie,* 1968, **15,** 564–581.

Allen, G. A., Mahler, W. A., & Estes, W. K. Effects of recall tests on long-term retention of paired associates. *Journal of Verbal Learning and Verbal Behavior,* 1969, **8,** 463–470.

Allen, M. M. Cuing and retrieval in free recall. *Journal of Experimental Psychology,* 1969, **81,** 29–35.

Anderson, J. R. FRAN, a simulation model of free recall. In G. H. Bower (Ed.), *The psychology of learning and motivation: Advances in research and theory.* Vol. 5. New York: Academic Press, 1972. Pp. 315–378.

Anderson, J. R., & Bower, G. H. Recognition and retrieval processes in free recall. *Psychological Review,* 1972, **79,** 97–123. (a)

Anderson, J. R., & Bower, G. H. Configural properties in sentence memory. *Journal of Verbal Learning and Verbal Behavior,* 1972, **11,** 594–605. (b)

Anderson, J. R., & Bower, G. H. *Human associative memory.* Washington, D.C.: Winston, 1973.

Anderson, N. S. Poststimulus cuing in immediate memory. *Journal of Experimental Psychology,* 1960, **60,** 216–221.

Anisfeld, M. False recognition of adjective-noun phrases. *Journal of Experimental Psychology,* 1970, **86,** 120–122.

Anisfeld, M., & Knapp, M. Association, synonymity, and directionality in false recognition. *Journal of Experimental Psychology,* 1968, **77,** 171–179.

Ansbacher, H. L. On the history of Adlerian interpretation of early recollections. *Journal of Individual Psychology,* 1973, **29,** 135–145.

Arbak, C. Latency and probability of recall in a continuous paired associate task. Unpublished master's thesis, University of Toronto, 1972.

Arbuckle, T. Y. Intratrial interference in "immediate" memory. Unpublished doctoral dissertation, University of Toronto, 1964.

Asch, S. E. A problem in the theory of associations. *Psychologische Beiträge*, 1962, **6**, 553–563.

Asch, S. E. The doctrinal tyranny of associationism: Or what is wrong with rote learning. In T. R. Dixon & D. L. Horton (Eds.), *Verbal learning and general behavior theory*. Englewood Cliffs: Prentice-Hall, 1968. Pp. 214–228.

Asch, S. E. A reformulation of the problem of associations. *American Psychologist*, 1969, **24**, 92–102.

Asch, S. E. & Ebenholtz, S. M. The principle of associative symmetry. *Proceedings of the American Philosophical Society*, 1962, **106**, 135–163.

Asch, S. E., & Lindner, M. A note on "strength of association." *Journal of Psychology*, 1963, **55**, 199–209.

Atkinson, R. C. A stochastic model for rote serial learning. *Psychometrika*, 1957, **22**, 87–95.

Atkinson, R. C. Ingredients for a theory of instruction. *American Psychologist*, 1972, **27**, 921–931. (a)

Atkinson, R. C. Optimizing the learning of a second-language vocabulary. *Journal of Experimental Psychology*, 1972, **96**, 124–129. (b)

Atkinson, R. C., Bower, G. H., & Crothers, E. J. *An introduction to mathematical learning theory*. New York: Wiley, 1965.

Atkinson, R. C., Brelsford, J. W., & Shiffrin, R. M. Multiprocess models for memory with applications to a continuous presentation task. *Journal of Mathematical Psychology*, 1967, **4**, 277–300.

Atkinson, R. C., & Crothers, E. J. A comparison of paired-associate learning models having different acquisition and retention axioms. *Journal of Mathematical Psychology*, 1964, **1**, 285–315.

Atkinson, R. C., Holmgren, J. E., & Juola, J. F. Processing time as influenced by the number of elements in a visual display. *Perception & Psychophysics*, 1969, **6**, 321–326.

Atkinson, R. C., & Juola, J. F. Factors influencing speed and accuracy of word recognition. In S. Kornblum (Ed.), *Attention and performance IV*. New York: Academic Press, 1973. Pp. 583–612.

Atkinson, R. C., & Paulson, J. A. An approach to the psychology of instruction. *Psychological Bulletin*, 1972, **78**, 49–61.

Atkinson, R. C., & Shiffrin, R. M. Mathematical models for memory and learning. Technical Report Number 79, Institute for Mathematical Studies in the Social Sciences, Stanford University, 1965.

Atkinson, R. C., & Shiffrin, R. M. Human memory: A proposed system and its control processes. In K. W. Spence & J. T. Spence (Eds.), *The psychology of learning and motivation: Advances in research and theory*. Vol. 2, New York: Academic Press, 1968. Pp. 89–195.

Atkinson, R. C., & Shiffrin, R. M. The control of short-term memory. *Scientific American*, August, 1971, 82–90.

Aubé, M., & Murdock, B. B., Jr. Sensory stores and high-speed scanning. *Memory & Cognition*, 1974, in press.

Avant, L. L., & Bevan, W. Acquisition of class responses when the number of cases per stimulus class was varied. *Journal of General Psychology*, 1968, **78**, 229–240. (a)

Avant, L. L., & Bevan, W. Recognition of a stimulus class member after training with varied numbers of cases per class. *Journal of General Psychology*, 1968, **78**, 241–246. (b)

Averbach, E., & Coriell, A. S. Short-term memory in vision. *Bell System Technical Journal*, 1961, **40**, 309–328.

Baddeley, A. D. Short-term memory for word sequences as a function of acoustic, semantic, and formal similarity. *Quarterly Journal of Experimental Psychology*, 1966, **18**, 362–365. (a)

Baddeley, A. D. The influence of acoustic and semantic similarity on long-term memory for word sequences. *Quarterly Journal of Experimental Psychology*, 1966, **18**, 302–309. (b)

Baddeley, A. D. How does acoustic similarity influence short-term memory? *Quarterly Journal of Experimental Psychology*, 1968, **20**, 249–264.

Baddeley, A. D. Human memory. In P. C Dodwell (Ed.), *New horizons in psychology 2*. Harmondsworth, England: Penguin, 1972. Pp. 36–61. (a)

Baddeley, A. D. Retrieval rules and semantic coding in short-term memory. *Psychological Bulletin*, 1972, **78**, 379–385. (b)

Baddeley, A. D., & Dale, H. C. The effect of semantic similarity on retroactive interference in long- and short-term memory. *Journal of Verbal Learning and Verbal Behavior*, 1966, **5**, 417–420.

Baddeley, A. D., & Ecob, J. R. Reaction time and short-term memory: A trace strength alternative to the high-speed scanning hypothesis. Technical Report Number 13, Center for Human Information Processing, University of California, San Diego, 1970.

Baddeley, A. D., & Levy, B. A. Semantic coding and short-term memory. *Journal of Experimental Psychology*, 1971, **89**, 132–136.

Baddeley, A. D., & Patterson, K. E. The relation between long-term and short-term memory. *British Medical Bulletin*, 1971, **27**, 237–242.

Baddeley, A. D., Scott, D., Drynan, R., & Smith, J. C. Short-term memory and the limited capacity hypothesis. *British Journal of Psychology*, 1969, **60**, 51–55.

Baddeley, A. D., & Warrington, E. K. Amnesia and the distinction between long- and short-term memory. *Journal of Verbal Learning and Verbal Behavior*, 1970, **9**, 176–189.

Bahrick, H. P. Measurement of memory by prompted recall. *Journal of Experimental Psychology*, 1969, **79**, 213–219.

Bahrick, H. P. Two-phase model for prompted recall. *Psychological Review*, 1970, **77**, 215–222.

Baker, J. D., & Organist, W. E. Short-term memory: Non-equivalence of query and message items. Technical Report Number ESD-TDR-64-254, Decision Sciences Laboratory, L. G. Hanscom Field, Bedford, Massachusetts, February, 1964.

Banks, W. P. Criterion change and response competition in unlearning. *Journal of Experimental Psychology*, 1969, **82**, 216–223.

Banks, W. P. Signal detection theory and human memory. *Psychological Bulletin*, 1970, **74**, 81–99.

Banks, W. P. Confidence-rated recall, d_r, and tests of Bernbach's finite-state theory in recall. *Psychological Bulletin*, 1971, **76**, 151–152.

Barnes, J. M., & Underwood, B. J. "Fate" of first-list associations in transfer theory. *Journal of Experimental Psychology*, 1959, **58**, 97–105.

Bartlett, F. C. *Remembering: A study in experimental and social psychology*. Cambridge: Cambridge University Press, 1932.

Bartz, W. H. Repetition and the memory stores. *Journal of Experimental Psychology*, 1969, **80**, 33–38.

Bartz, W. H. Repetition effects in dichotic presentation. *Journal of Experimental Psychology*, 1972, **92**, 220–224.

Battig, W. F. Paired-associate learning. In T. R. Dixon & D. L. Horton (Eds.), *Verbal behavior and general behavior theory*. Englewood Cliffs: Prentice-Hall, 1968. Pp. 146–171.

Battig, W. F., Allen, M. M., & Jensen, A. R. Priority of free recall of newly learned items. *Journal of Verbal Learning and Verbal Behavior*, 1965, **4**, 175–179.

Bergson, H. L. *Matter and memory*. Authorized translation by Nancy Margaret Paul and W. Scott Palmer. London: G. Allen, 1913.

Bernbach, H. A. A forgetting model for paired-associate learning. *Journal of Mathematical Psychology*, 1965, **2**, 128–144.

Bernbach, H. A. Decision processes in memory. *Psychological Review*, 1967, **74**, 462–480. (a)

Bernbach, H. A. Stimulus learning and recognition in paired-associate learning. *Journal of Experimental Psychology*, 1967, **75**, 513–519. (b)

Bernbach, H. A. Replication processes in human memory and learning. In G. H. Bower & J. T. Spence (Eds.), *The psychology of learning and motivation: Advances in research and theory*. Vol. 3. New York: Academic Press, 1969. Pp. 201–239.

Bernbach, H. A. A multiple-copy model for postperceptual memory. In D. A. Norman (Ed.), *Models of human memory*. New York: Academic Press, 1970. Pp. 103–116.

Bernbach, H. A. Strength theory and confidence ratings in recall. *Psychological Review*, 1971, **78**, 338–340. (a)

Bernbach, H. A. Invariance of d^* in memory: Response to Banks. *Psychological Bulletin*, 1971, **76**, 149–150. (b)

Bernbach, H. A. Confidence ratings for individual items in recall. *Psychological Review*, 1972, **79**, 536–537.

Bernbach, H. A., & Bower, G. H. Confidence ratings in continuous paired-associate learning. *Psycho-*

nomic Science, 1970, **21**, 252–253.

Bertelson, P. S–R relationships and reaction times to new versus repeated signals in a serial task. *Journal of Experimental Psychology,* 1963, **65**, 478–484.

Bertelson, P. Central intermittency twenty years later. *Quarterly Journal of Experimental Psychology,* 1966, **18**, 153–163.

Bevan, W., Dukes, W. F., & Avant, L. L. The effect of variation in specific stimuli on memory for their superordinates. *American Journal of Psychology,* 1966, **79**, 250–257.

Biederman, I., & Kaplan, R. Stimulus discriminability and S–R compatability: Evidence for independent effects in choice reaction time. *Journal of Experimental Psychology,* 1970, **86**, 434–439.

Birnbaum, I. M. Prior-list organization in part-whole free-recall learning. *Journal of Verbal Learning and Verbal Behavior,* 1969, **8**, 836–841.

Birnbaum, I. M., & Eichner, J. T. Study versus test trials and long-term retention in free-recall learning. *Journal of Verbal Learning and Verbal Behavior,* 1971, **10**, 516–521.

Bjork, R. A. Learning and short-term retention of paired associates in relation to specific sequences of interpresentation intervals. Technical Report Number 106, Institute for Mathematical Studies in the Social Sciences, Stanford University, 1966.

Bjork, R. A. Repetition and rehearsal mechanisms in models for short-term memory. In D. A. Norman (Ed.), *Models of human memory.* New York: Academic Press, 1970. Pp. 307–330. (a)

Bjork, R. A. Positive forgetting: The noninterference of items intentionally forgotten. *Journal of Verbal Learning and Verbal Behavior,* 1970, **9**, 255–268. (b)

Bjork, R. A. Theoretical implications of directed forgetting. In A. W. Melton & E. Martin (Eds.), *Coding processes in human memory.* Washington, D.C.: Winston, 1972. Pp. 217–235.

Bjork, R. A., & Allen, T. W. The spacing effect: Consolidation or differential encoding? *Journal of Verbal Learning and Verbal Behavior,* 1970, **9**, 567–572.

Bjork, R. A., LaBerge, D., & LeGrande, R. The modification of short-term memory through instructions to forget. *Psychonomic Science,* 1968, **10**, 55–56.

Blake, M. Prediction of recognition when recall fails: Exploring the feeling-of-knowing phenomenon. *Journal of Verbal Learning and Verbal Behavior,* 1973, **12**, 311–319.

Block, R. A. Effect of instructions to forget in short-term memory. *Journal of Experimental Psychology,* 1971, **89**, 1–9.

Bobrow, D. G. Natural language input for a computer problem-solving system. In M. Minsky (Ed.), *Semantic information processing.* Cambridge, Mass.: MIT Press, 1968. Pp. 146–226.

Bogartz, W. A small error in Thurstone's length-difficulty function. *Psychological Review,* 1968, **75**, 442–445.

Bousfield, A. K., & Bousfield, W. A. Measurement of clustering and of sequential constancies in repeated free recall. *Psychological Reports,* 1966, **19**, 935–942.

Bousfield, W. A. The occurrence of clustering in the recall of randomly arranged associates. *Journal of General Psychology,* 1953, **49**, 229–240.

Bousfield, W. A., & Cohen, B. H. The effects of reinforcement on the occurrence of clustering in the recall of randomly arranged associates. *Journal of Psychology,* 1953, **36**, 67–81.

Bousfield, W. A., & Cohen, B. H. The occurrence of clustering in the recall of randomly arranged words of different frequencies-of-usage. *Journal of General Psychology,* 1955, **52**, 83–95.

Bousfield, W. A., & Cohen, B. H. Clustering in recall as a function of the number of word-categories in stimulus word lists. *Journal of General Psychology,* 1956, **54**, 95–106.

Bousfield, W. A., & Sedgewick, C. H. An analysis of sequences of restricted associative responses. *Journal of General Psychology,* 1944, **30**, 149–165.

Bousfield, W. A., Whitmarsh, G. A., & Esterson, J. Serial position effects and the "Marbe effect" in the free recall of meaningful words. *Journal of General Psychology,* 1958, **59**, 255–262.

Bouwhuis, D. All-or-none learning and forgetting. *IPO Annual Progress Report,* No. 4. Eindhoven, Holland, 1969. Pp. 119–122.

Bower, G. H. Application of a model to paired-associated learning. *Psychometrika,* 1961, **26**, 255–280.

Bower, G. H. An association model for response and training variables in paired-associate learning. *Psychological Review,* 1962, **69**, 34–53.

Bower, G. H. A descriptive theory of memory. In D. P. Kimble (Ed.), *Learning, remembering, and forgetting*. Vol. 2. New York: New York Academy of Sciences, 1967. Pp. 112–185. (a)

Bower, G. H. A multicomponent theory of the memory trace. In K. W. Spence & J. T. Spence (Eds.), *The psychology of learning and motivation: Advances in research and theory*. Vol. 1. New York: Academic Press, 1967. Pp. 229–325. (b)

Bower, G. H. Analysis of a mnemonic device. *American Scientist*, 1970, **58**, 496–510. (a)

Bower, G. H. Organizational factors in memory. *Cognitive Psychology*, 1970, **1**, 18–46. (b)

Bower, G. H. Imagery as a relational organizer in associative learning. *Journal of Verbal Learning and Verbal Behavior*, 1970, **9**, 529–533. (c)

Bower, G. H. Adaptation-level coding of stimuli and serial position effects. In M. H. Appley (Ed.), *Adaptation-level theory*. New York: Academic Press, 1971. Pp. 175–201.

Bower, G. H. A selective review of organizational factors in memory. In E. Tulving & W. Donaldson (Eds.), *Organization of memory*. New York: Academic Press, 1972. Pp. 93–137. (a)

Bower, G. H. Stimulus-sampling theory of encoding variability. In A. W. Melton & E. Martin (Eds.), *Coding processes in human memory*. Washington, D.C.: Winston, 1972. Pp. 85–123. (b)

Bower, G. H. Mental imagery and associative learning. In L. W. Gregg (Ed.), *Cognition in learning and memory*. New York: Wiley, 1972. Pp. 51–88. (c)

Bower, G. H., Clark, M. C., Lesgold, A. M., & Winzenz, D. Hierarchical retrieval schemes in recall of categorized word lists. *Journal of Verbal Learning and Verbal Behavior*, 1969, **8**, 323–343.

Bower, G. H., & Lesgold, A. M. Organization as a determinant of part-to-whole transfer in free recall. *Journal of Verbal Learning and Verbal Behavior*, 1969, **8**, 501–506.

Bower, G. H., & Theios, J. A learning model for discrete performance levels. In R. C. Atkinson (Ed.), *Studies in mathematical psychology*. Stanford: Stanford University Press, 1964. Pp. 1–31.

Bower, G. H., & Winzenz, D. Group structure, coding, and memory for digit series. *Journal of Experimental Psychology Monograph Supplement*, 1969, **80**, (Pt. 2.), 1–17.

Bradshaw, J. L., & Nettleton, N. C. Articulatory interference and the MOWN-DOWN heterophone effect. *Journal of Experimental Psychology*, 1974, in press.

Bransford, J. D., & Franks, J. J. The abstraction of linguistic ideas. *Cognitive Psychology*, 1971, **2**, 331–350.

Bray, N. W., & Batchelder, W. H. Effects of instructions and retention interval on memory of presentation mode. *Journal of Verbal Learning and Verbal Behavior*, 1972, **11**, 367–374.

Bregman, A. S. Forgetting curves with semantic, phonetic, graphic, and contiguity cues. *Journal of Experimental Psychology*, 1968, **78**, 539–546.

Bregman, A. S., & Chambers, D. W. All-or-none learning of attributes. *Journal of Experimental Psychology*, 1966, **71**, 785–793.

Bregman, A. S., & Wiener, J. R. Effects of test trials in paired-associate and free-recall learning. *Journal of Verbal Learning and Verbal Behavior*, 1970, **9**, 689–698.

Brelsford, J. W., & Atkinson, R. C. Recall of paired-associates as a function of overt and covert rehearsal procedures. *Journal of Verbal Learning and Verbal Behavior*, 1968, **7**, 730–736.

Briggs, G. E., Acquisition, extinction, and recovery functions in retroactive inhibition. *Journal of Experimental Psychology*, 1954, **47**, 285–293.

Briggs, G. E., & Blaha, J. Memory retrieval and central comparison times in information processing. *Journal of Experimental Psychology*, 1969, **79**, 395–402.

Broadbent, D. E. The role of auditory localization in attention and memory span. *Journal of Experimental Psychology*, 1954, **47**, 191–196.

Broadbent, D. E. Successive responses to simultaneous stimuli. *Quarterly Journal of Experimental Psychology*, 1956, **8**, 145–152.

Broadbent, D. E. Immediate memory and simultaneous stimuli. *Quarterly Journal of Experimental Psychology*, 1957, **9**, 1–11. (a)

Broadbent, D. E. A mechanical model for human attention and immediate memory. *Psychological Review*, 1957, **64**, 205–215. (b)

Broadbent, D. E. *Perception and communication*. New York: Pergamon Press, 1958.

Broadbent, D. E. Flow of information within the organism. *Journal of Verbal Learning and Verbal Behavior,* 1963, **2**, 34–39.

Broadbent, D. E. Two-state threshold model and rating scale experiments. *Journal of the Acoustical Society of America,* 1966, **40**, 244–245. (a)

Broadbent, D. E. The well ordered mind. *American Educational Research Journal,* 1966, **3**, 281–295. (b)

Broadbent, D. E. Communication models for memory. In G. A. Talland & N. C. Waugh (Eds.), *The pathology of memory.* New York: Academic Press, 1969. Pp. 167–171.

Broadbent, D. E. Psychological aspects of short-term and long-term memory. *Proceedings of the Royal Society, Series B,* 1970, **175**, 333–350.

Broadbent, D. E. *Decision and stress.* New York: Academic Press, 1971.

Broadbent, D. E., & Gregory, M. Division of attention and the decision theory of signal detection. *Proceedings of the Royal Society, Series B,* 1963, **158**, 222–231.

Broadbent, D. E., & Gregory, M. On the interaction of S–R compatability with other variables affecting reaction time. *British Journal of Psychology,* 1965, **56**, 61–67.

Broadbent, D. E., & Heron, A. Effects of a subsidiary task on performance involving immediate memory by younger and older men. *British Journal of Psychology,* 1962, **53**, 189–198.

Brooks, L. R. The suppression of visualization by reading. *Quarterly Journal of Experimental Psychology,* 1967, **19**, 289–299.

Brooks, L. R. Spatial and verbal components of the act of recall. *Canadian Journal of Psychology,* 1968, **22**, 349–368.

Brown, A. E., & Hopkins, H. K. Interaction of the auditory and visual sensory modalities. *Journal of the Acoustical Society of America,* 1967, **41**, 1–7.

Brown, J. The nature of set-to-learn and of intramaterial interference in immediate memory. *Quarterly Journal of Experimental Psychology,* 1954, **6**, 141–148.

Brown, J. Some tests of the decay theory of immediate memory. *Quarterly Journal of Experimental Psychology,* 1958, **10**, 12–21.

Brown, J. Information, redundancy and decay of the memory trace. In *The mechanization of thought processes.* National Physical Laboratory Symposium No. 10. London: H.M.S.O., 1959.

Brown, J. Multiple response evaluation of discrimination. *British Journal of Mathematical and Statistical Psychology,* 1965, **18**, 125–137.

Brown, J. Reciprocal facilitation and impairment of free recall. *Psychonomic Science,* 1968, **10**, 41–42.

Brown, R., & McNeill, D. The "tip of the tongue" phenomenon. *Journal of Verbal Learning and Verbal Behavior,* 1966, **5**, 325–337.

Brown, W. To what extent is memory measured by a single recall? *Journal of Experimental Psychology,* 1923, **6**, 377–382.

Bruce, D., & Crowley, J. J. Acoustic similarity effects on retrieval from secondary memory. *Journal of Verbal Learning and Verbal Behavior,* 1970, **9**, 190–196.

Bruce, D., & Fagan, R. L. More on the recognition and free recall of organized lists. *Journal of Experimental Psychology,* 1970, **85**, 153–154.

Bruce, D., & Murdock, B. B., Jr. Acoustic similarity effects on memory for paired associates. *Journal of Verbal Learning and Verbal Behavior,* 1968, **7**, 627–631.

Bruce, D., & Papay, J. P. Primacy effects in single-trial free recall. *Journal of Verbal Learning and Verbal Behavior,* 1970, **9**, 473–486.

Bryden, M. P. Order of report in dichotic listening. *Canadian Journal of Psychology,* 1962, **16**, 291–299.

Bryden, M. P. A model for the sequential organization of behavior. *Canadian Journal of Psychology,* 1967, **21**, 37–56.

Bryden, M. P. Attentional strategies and short-term memory in dichotic listening. *Cognitive Psychology,* 1971, **2**, 99–116.

Bugelski, B. R. A remote association explanation of the relative difficulty of learning nonsense syllables in a serial list. *Journal of Experimental Psychology,* 1950, **40**, 336–348.

Bugelski, B. R. Images as mediators in one-trial paired-associate learning. II: Self-timing in successive lists. *Journal of Experimental Psychology*, 1968, **77**, 328–334.

Bugelski, B. R. Words and things and images. *American Psychologist*, 1970, **25**, 1002–1012.

Bugelski, B. R., Kidd, E., & Segman, J. Image as a mediator in one-trial paired-associate learning. *Journal of Experimental Psychology*, 1968, **76**, 69–73.

Burrows, D. Modality effects in retrieval of information from short-term memory. *Perception & Psychophysics*, 1972, **11**, 365–372.

Burrows, D., & Murdock, B. B., Jr. Effects of extended practices on high-speed scanning. *Journal of Experimental Psychology*, 1969, **82**, 231–237.

Burrows, D., & Okada, R. Serial position effects in high-speed memory search. *Perception & Psychophysics*, 1971, **10**, 305–308.

Burrows, D., & Okada, R. Parallel scanning of semantic and formal information. *Journal of Experimental Psychology*, 1973, **97**, 254–257.

Buschke, H. Retention in immediate memory estimated without retrieval. *Science*, 1963, **140**, 56–57. (a)

Buschke, H. Relative retention in immediate memory determined by the missing scan method. *Nature (London)*, 1963, **200**, 1129–1130. (b)

Buschke, H. Types of immediate memory. *Journal of Verbal Learning and Verbal Behavior*, 1966, **5**, 275–278.

Buschke, H., & Hinrichs, J. V. Relative vulnerability of item-information in short-term storage for the missing scan. *Journal of Verbal Learning and Verbal Behavior*, 1968, **7**, 1043–1048.

Bush, R. R. Estimation and evaluation. In R. D. Luce, R. R. Bush, & E. Galanter (Eds.), *Handbook of mathematical psychology*. Vol. 1. New York: Wiley, 1963. Pp. 429–469.

Bush, R. R., & Mosteller, F. *Stochastic models for learning*. New York: Wiley, 1955.

Calfee, R. C. Interpresentation effects in paired-associate learning. *Journal of Verbal Learning and Verbal Behavior*, 1968, **7**, 1030–1036.

Campos, L., & Siojo, L. The recall of single paired associates with an A–B, A–Br sequential paradigm. *Philippine Journal of Psychology*, 1969, **2**, 39–42.

Carey, S. T. Delayed recognition testing, incidental learning and proactive-inhibition release. *Journal of Experimental Psychology*, 1973, **100**, 361–367.

Carey, S. T., & Okada, R. Part-list recall following part-whole learning. *Memory & Cognition*, 1973, **1**, 172–176.

Carr, H. A. The laws of association. *Psychological Review*, 1931, **38**, 212–228.

Carroll, J. B., & Burke, M. L. Parameters of paired-associate verbal learning. *Journal of Experimental Psychology*, 1965, **69**, 543–553.

Cavanagh, J. P. Relation between the immediate memory span and the memory search rate. *Psychological Review*, 1972, **79**, 525–530.

Ceraso, J. The interference theory of forgetting. *Scientific American*, October, 1967, 117–124.

Cermak, L. S. *Human memory: Research and theory*. New York: Ronald, 1972.

Chase, W. G., & Calfee, R. C. Modality and similarity effects in short-term recognition memory. *Journal of Experimental Psychology*, 1969, **81**, 510–514.

Cheng, Chao-Ming. Acoustic and articulatory coding functions in immediate memory. Unpublished doctoral dissertation, Yale University, 1972.

Cherry, E. C. Some experiments on the recognition of speech, with one and with two ears. *Journal of the Acoustical Society of America*, 1953, **25**, 975–979.

Chi, M. T. H., & Chase, W. G. Effects of modality and similarity on context recall. *Journal of Experimental Psychology*, 1972, **96**, 219–222.

Christie, L. S., & Luce, R. D. Decision structure and time relations in simple choice behavior. *Bulletin of Mathematical Biophysics*, 1956, **18**, 89–112.

Clifton, C., Jr., & Birenbaum, S. Effects of serial position and delay of probe in a memory scan task. *Journal of Experimental Psychology*, 1970, **86**, 69–76.

Clowes, M. B. On seeing things. *Artificial Intelligence*, 1971, **2**, 79–116.

Cofer, C. N. On some factors in the organizational characteristics of free recall. *American Psychologist*,

1965, **20**, 261–272.

Cofer, C. N. Does conceptual organization influence the amount retained in immediate free recall? In B. Kleinmuntz (Ed.), *Concepts and the structure of memory.* New York: Wiley, 1967. Pp. 181–214.

Cofer, C. N., Bruce, D., & Reicher, G. M. Clustering in free recall as a function of certain methodological variations. *Journal of Experimental Psychology,* 1966, **71**, 858–866.

Cofer, C. N., Faile, N. F., & Horton, D. L. Retroactive inhibition following reinstatement or maintenance of first-list responses by means of free recall. *Journal of Experimental Psychology,* 1971, **90**, 197–205.

Cohen, B. H. Recall of categorized word lists. *Journal of Experimental Psychology,* 1963, **66**, 227–234.

Cohen, B. H. Some-or-none characteristics of coding behavior. *Journal of Verbal Learning and Verbal Behavior,* 1966, **5**, 182–187.

Cohen, B. H., Bousfield, W. A., & Whitmarsh, G. A. *Cultural norms for verbal items in 43 categories.* Technical Report No. 22, University of Connecticut, 1957.

Cohen, R. L. Recency effects in long-term recall and recognition. *Journal of Verbal Learning and Verbal Behavior,* 1970, **9**, 672–678.

Cohen, R. L., & Grandstrom, K. Reproduction and recognition in short-term visual memory. *Quarterly Journal of Experimental Psychology,* 1970, **22**, 450–457.

Colle, H. A. The reification of clustering. *Journal of Verbal Learning and Verbal Behavior,* 1972, **11**, 624–633.

Collins, A. M., & Quillian, M. R. Retrieval time from semantic memory. *Journal of Verbal Learning and Verbal Behavior,* 1969, **8**, 240–247.

Collins, A. M., & Quillian, M. R. Does category size affect categorization time? *Journal of Verbal Learning and Verbal Behavior,* 1970, **9**, 432–438.

Collins, A. M., & Quillian, M. R. How to make a language user. In E. Tulving & W. Donaldson (Eds.), *Organization of memory.* New York: Academic Press, 1972. Pp. 309–351.

Colotla, X. G. Scanning processes in numerical recall. Unpublished master's thesis, University of Toronto, 1969.

Conrad, C. Cognitive economy in semantic memory. *Journal of Experimental Psychology,* 1972, **92**, 149–154.

Conrad, R. Accuracy of recall using keyset and telephone dial, and the effect of a prefix digit. *Journal of Applied Psychology,* 1958, **42**, 285–288.

Conrad, R. Errors of immediate memory. *British Journal of Psychology,* 1959, **50**, 349–359.

Conrad, R. Very brief delay of immediate recall. *Quarterly Journal of Experimental Psychology,* 1960, **12**, 45–47. (a)

Conrad, R. Serial order intrusions in immediate memory. *British Journal of Psychology,* 1960, **51**, 45–48. (b)

Conrad, R. Acoustic confusions in immediate memory. *British Journal of Psychology,* 1964, **55**, 75–84.

Conrad, R. Order error in immediate recall of sequences. *Journal of Verbal Learning and Verbal Behavior,* 1965, **4**, 161–169.

Conrad, R. Interference or decay over short retention intervals? *Journal of Verbal Learning and Verbal Behavior,* 1967, **6**, 49–54.

Conrad, R. Short-term memory processes in the deaf. *British Journal of Psychology,* 1970, **61**, 179–195.

Conrad, R. The effect of vocalization on comprehension in the profoundly deaf. *British Journal of Psychology,* 1971, **62**, 147–150.

Conrad, R. The developmental role of vocalizing in short-term memory. *Journal of Verbal Learning and Verbal Behavior,* 1972, **11**, 521–533. (a)

Conrad, R. Speech and reading. In J. F. Kavanagh & I. G. Mattingly (Eds.), *The relationships between speech and reading.* Cambridge, Mass.: MIT Press, 1972. Pp. 205–240. (b)

Conrad, R., & Hille, B. A. The decay theory of immediate memory and paced recall. *Canadian Journal of Psychology,* 1958, **12**, 1–6.

Conrad, R., & Hull, A. J. Input modality and the serial position curve in short-term memory. *Psychonomic Science,* 1968, **10**, 135–136.

Conrad, R., & Rush, M. L. On the nature of short-term memory encoding by the deaf. *Journal of Speech and Hearing Disorders,* 1965, **30**, 336–343.

Cooper, E. H., & Pantle, A. J. The total-time hypothesis in verbal learning. *Psychological Bulletin,* 1967, **68**, 221–234.

Corballis, M. C. Immediate recall of spoken digits presented three at a time. *Canadian Journal of Psychology,* 1967, **21**, 416–424. (a)

Corballis, M. C. Serial order in recognition and recall. *Journal of Experimental Psychology,* 1967, **74**, 99–105. (b)

Corballis, M. C., Kirby, J., & Miller, A. Access to elements of a memorized list. *Journal of Experimental Psychology,* 1972, **94**, 185–190.

Corballis, M. C., & Luthe, L. Two-channel visual memory. *Perception & Psychophysics,* 1971, **9**, 361–367.

Corballis, M. C., & Miller, A. Scanning and decision processes in recognition memory. *Journal of Experimental Psychology,* 1973, **98**, 379–386.

Corballis, M. C., & Philipp, R. Channel by channel report of visually presented "Stroop" items. *Psychonomic Science,* 1966, **5**, 465–466.

Craik, F. I. M. Modality effects in short-term storage, *Journal of Verbal Learning and Verbal Behavior,* 1969, **8**, 658–664.

Craik, F. I. M. The fate of primary memory items in free recall. *Journal of Verbal Learning and Verbal Behavior,* 1970, **9**, 143–148.

Craik, F. I. M. Primary memory. *British Medical Bulletin,* 1971, **27**, 232–236.

Craik, F. I. M. A "Levels of Analysis" view of memory. In P. Pliner, L. Krames, & T. M. Alloway (Eds.), *Communication and affect: Language and thought.* New York: Academic Press, 1973, in press.

Craik, F. I. M., Gardiner, J. M., & Watkins, M. J. Further evidence for a negative recency effect in free recall. *Journal of Verbal Learning and Verbal Behavior,* 1970, **9**, 554–560.

Craik, F. I. M., & Kirsner, K. The effect of speaker's voice on word recognition. *Quarterly Journal of Experimental Psychology,* 1974, in press.

Craik, F. I. M., & Levy, B. A. Semantic and acoustic information in primary memory. *Journal of Experimental Psychology,* 1970, **86**, 77–82.

Craik, F. I. M., & Lockhart, R. S. Levels of processing: A framework for memory research. *Journal of Verbal Learning and Verbal Behavior,* 1972, **11**, 671–684.

Crannell, C. W., & Parrish, J. M. A comparison of immediate memory span for digits, letters, and words. *Journal of Psychology,* 1957, **44**, 319–327.

Crossman, E. R. F. W. Information and serial order in human immediate memory. In C. Cherry (Ed.), *Information theory.* London: Butterworths, 1961. Pp. 147–159.

Crowder, R. G. The relation between interpolated-task performance and proactive inhibition in short-term retention. *Journal of Verbal Learning and Verbal Behavior,* 1968, **7**, 577–583.

Crowder, R. G. The sound of vowels and consonants in immediate memory. *Journal of Verbal Learning and Verbal Behavior,* 1971, **10**, 587–596.

Crowder, R. G. Visual and auditory memory. In J. F. Kavanagh & I. G. Mattingly (Eds.), *The relationships between speech and reading.* Cambridge, Mass.: MIT Press, 1972. Pp. 251–275.

Crowder, R. G. Representation of speech sounds in precategorical acoustic storage (PAS). *Journal of Experimental Psychology,* 1973, **98**, 14–24.

Crowder, R. G., & Melton, A. W. The Ranschburg phenomenon: Failures of immediate recall correlated with repetition of elements within a stimulus. *Psychonomic Science,* 1965, **2**, 295–296.

Crowder, R. G., & Morton, J. Precategorical acoustic storage (PAS). *Perception & Psychophysics,* 1969, **5**, 365–373.

Dale, H. C. A. Familiarity and free recall. *Quarterly Journal of Experimental Psychology,* 1967, **19**, 103–108.

Dale, H. C. A., & Baddeley, A. D. Alternatives in testing recognition memory. *Nature (London),* 1962, **196**, 93–94.

Dale, H. C. A., & Baddeley, A. D. Remembering a list of two-digit numbers. *Quarterly Journal of*

Experimental Psychology, 1966, **18**, 212–219.

Dale, H. C. A., & McGlaughlin, A. Evidence of acoustic coding in long-term memory. *Quarterly Journal of Experimental Psychology,* 1971, **23**, 1–7.

Dallett, K., Wilcox, S. G., & D'Andrea, L. Picture memory experiments. *Journal of Experimental Psychology,* 1968, **76**, 312–320.

Dalrymple-Alford, E. C. Measurement of clustering in free recall. *Psychological Bulletin,* 1970, **74**, 32–34.

Dalrymple-Alford, E. C., & Aamiry, A. Language and category clustering in bilingual free recall. *Journal of Verbal Learning and Verbal Behavior,* 1969, **8**, 762–768.

Darley, C. F., & Murdock, B. B., Jr. Effects of prior free-recall testing on final recall and recognition. *Journal of Experimental Psychology,* 1971, **91**, 66–73.

Darwin, C. J., Turvey, M. T., & Crowder, R. G. An auditory analogue of the Sperling partial report procedure: Evidence for brief auditory storage. *Cognitive Psychology,* 1972, **3**, 255–267.

Davis, J. C. Instructed-forgetting procedures: What do they reveal about memory? Unpublished doctoral dissertation, University of Toronto, 1973.

Davis, J. C., & Okada, R. Recognition and recall of positively forgotten items. *Journal of Experimental Psychology,* 1971, **89**, 181–186.

Davis, J. C., & Smith, M. C. Memory for unattended input. *Journal of Experimental Psychology,* 1972, **96**, 380–388.

Davis, R., Sutherland, N. S., & Judd, B. R. Information content in recognition and recall. *Journal of Experimental Psychology,* 1961, **61**, 422–429.

Deese, J. Influence of inter-item associative strength upon immediate free recall. *Psychological Reports,* 1959, **5**, 305–312. (a)

Deese, J. On the prediction of occurrence of particular verbal intrusions in immediate recall. *Journal of Experimental Psychology,* 1959, **58**, 17–22. (b)

Deese, J. From the isolated verbal unit to connected discourse. In C. N. Cofer (Ed.), *Verbal learning and verbal behavior.* New York: McGraw-Hill, 1961. Pp. 11–31.

Deese, J. *The structure of associations in language and thought.* Baltimore: The Johns Hopkins Press, 1965.

Deese, J., & Kaufman, R. A. Serial effects in recall of unorganized and sequentially organized verbal material. *Journal of Experimental Psychology,* 1957, **54**, 180–187.

Detterman, D. K., & Ellis, N. R. Distinctiveness in short-term memory. *Psychonomic Science,* 1971, **22**, 239–241.

Deutsch, D. Tones and numbers: Specificity of interference in immediate memory. *Science,* 1970, **168**, 1604–1605.

Dillon, R. F., & Reid, L. S. Short-term memory as a function of information processing during the retention interval. *Journal of Experimental Psychology,* 1969, **81**, 261–269.

Dollard, J., & Miller, N. E. *Personality and psychotherapy.* New York: McGraw-Hill, 1950.

Donaldson, W. An examination of false positives in short-term recognition memory. Unpublished doctoral dissertation, University of Toronto, 1967.

Donaldson, W. Retention of item and order information. *Journal of Experimental Psychology,* 1971, **90**, 293–296. (a)

Donaldson, W. Output effects in multitrial free recall. *Journal of Verbal Learning and Verbal Behavior,* 1971, **10**, 577–585. (b)

Donaldson, W., & Glathe, H. Recognition memory for item and order information. *Journal of Experimental Psychology,* 1969, **82**, 557–560.

Donaldson, W., & Glathe, H. Signal-detection analysis of recall and recognition memory. *Canadian Journal of Psychology,* 1970, **24**, 42–56.

Donaldson, W., & Murdock, B. B., Jr. Criterion change in continuous recognition memory. *Journal of Experimental Psychology,* 1968, **76**, 325–330.

Dong, T. Probe versus free recall. *Journal of Verbal Learning and Verbal Behavior,* 1972, **11**, 654–661.

Dong, T., & Kintsch, W. Subjective retrieval cues in free recall. *Journal of Verbal Learning and Verbal Behavior*, 1968, **7**, 813–816.

Dornbush, R. L. Input variables in bisensory memory. *Perception & Psychophysics*, 1968, **4**, 41–44.

Drachman, D. A., & Leavitt, J. Memory impairment in the aged: Storage versus retrieval deficit. *Journal of Experimental Psychology*, 1972, **93**, 302–308.

Dukes, W. F., & Bevan, W. Stimulus variation and repetition in the acquisition of naming responses. *Journal of Experimental Psychology*, 1967, **74**, 178–181.

Eagle, M., & Leiter, E. Recall and recognition in intentional and incidental learning. *Journal of Experimental Psychology*, 1964, **68**, 58–63.

Ebbinghaus, H. *Memory: A contribution to experimental psychology*. New York: Teachers College, Columbia University, 1913. (Reprinted by Dover, 1964.)

Ebenholtz, S. M. Position mediated transfer between serial learning and a spatial discrimination task. *Journal of Experimental Psychology*, 1963, **65**, 603–608.

Ebenholtz, S. M. Serial learning and dimensional organization. In G. H. Bower (Ed.), *The psychology of learning and motivation: Advances in research and theory*. Vol. 5. New York: Academic Press, 1972. Pp. 267–314.

Egan, J. P. Recognition memory and the operating characteristic. Technical Note AFCRC-TN-58-51, Hearing and Communication Laboratory, Indiana University, 1958.

Ehrlich, S. Le rôle de la structuration dans l'apprentissage verbal. *Psychologie Française*, 1965, **10**, 119–146.

Ehrlich, S. Structuration and destructuration of responses in free-recall learning. *Journal of Verbal Learning and Verbal Behavior*, 1970, **9**, 282–286.

Eichelman, W. H. Stimulus and response repetition effects for naming letters at two response-stimulus intervals. *Perception & Psychophysics*, 1970, **7**, 94–96.

Eimas, P. D., & Zeaman, D. Response speed change in an Estes' paired-associate "miniature" experiment. *Journal of Verbal Learning and Verbal Behavior*, 1963, **1**, 384–388.

Ekstrand, B. R. Backward associations. *Psychological Bulletin*, 1966, **65**, 50–64.

Ekstrand, B. R., Wallace, W. P., & Underwood, B. J. A frequency theory of verbal discrimination learning. *Psychological Review*, 1966, **73**, 566–578.

Elmes, D. G. Short-term memory as a function of storage load. *Journal of Experimental Psychology*, 1969, **80**, 203–204. (a)

Elmes, D. G. Role of prior recalls and storage load in short-term memory. *Journal of Experimental Psychology*, 1969, **79**, 468–472. (b)

Epstein, W. Mechanisms of directed forgetting. In G. H. Bower (Ed.), *The psychology of learning and motivation: Advances in research and theory*. Vol. 6. New York: Academic Press, 1972. Pp. 147–191.

Epstein, W., Massaro, D. W., & Wilder, L. Selective search in directed forgetting. *Journal of Experimental Psychology*, 1972, **94**, 1, 18–24.

Estes, W. K. Statistical theory of spontaneous recovery and regression. *Psychological Review*, 1955, **62**, 145–154. (a)

Estes, W. K. Statistical theory of distributional phenomena in learning. *Psychological Review*, 1955, **62**, 369–377. (b)

Estes, W. K. Learning theory and the new "mental chemistry." *Psychological Review*, 1960, **67**, 207–223.

Estes, W. K. All-or-none processes in learning and retention. *American Psychologist*, 1964, **19**, 16–25.

Estes, W. K. An associative basis for coding and organization in memory. In A. W. Melton & E. Martin (Eds.), *Coding processes in human memory*. Washington, D.C.: Winston, 1972. Pp. 161–190.

Estes, W. K., & DaPolito, F. J. Independent variation of information storage and retrieval processes in paired-associate learning. *Journal of Experimental Psychology*, 1967, **75**, 18–26.

Evans, R. B., & Dallenbach, K. M. Single-trial learning: A stochastic model for the recall of individual words. *American Journal of Psychology*, 1965, **78**, 545–556.

Feigenbaum, E. A. The simulation of verbal learning behavior. In E. A. Feigenbaum & J. Feldman (Eds.), *Computers and thought*. New York: McGraw-Hill, 1963. Pp. 297–309.

Feigenbaum, E. A. Information processing and memory. In D. A. Norman (Ed.), *Models of human memory*. New York: Academic Press, 1970. Pp. 451–468.

Feigenbaum, E. A., & Simon, H. A. Comment: The distinctiveness of stimuli. *Psychological Review*, 1961, **68**, 285–288.

Feigenbaum, E. A., & Simon, H. A. A theory of the serial position effect. *British Journal of Psychology*, 1962, **53**, 307–320.

Feigenbaum, E. A., & Simon, H. A. Brief notes on the EPAM theory of verbal learning. In C. N. Cofer & B. S. Musgrave (Eds.), *Verbal behavior and learning*. New York: McGraw-Hill, 1963. Pp. 333–335.

Feller, W. *An introduction to probability theory and its applications*. Vol. I. (3rd ed.) New York: Wiley, 1968.

Field, W. H., & Lachman, R. Information transmission (*I*) in recognition and recall as a function of alternatives (*k*). *Journal of Experimental Psychology*, 1966, **72**, 785–791.

Fillenbaum, S. Words as feature complexes: False recognition of antonyms and synonyms. *Journal of Experimental Psychology*, 1969, **82**, 400–402.

Fisher, D. F., & Karsh, R. Modality effects and storage in sequential short-term memory. *Journal of Experimental Psychology*, 1971, **87**, 410–414.

Fitts, P. M., & Posner, M. I. *Human performance*. Belmont, Cal.: Wadsworth, 1967.

Forrin, B., & Cunningham, K. Recognition time and serial position of probed item in short-term memory. *Journal of Experimental Psychology*, 1973, **99**, 272–279.

Foucault, M. Les inhibitions internes de fixation. *Année Psychologique*, 1928, **29**, 92–112.

Fozard, J. L. Proactive inhibition of prompted items. *Psychonomic Science*, 1969, **17**, 67–68.

Fozard, J. L. Apparent recency of unrelated pictures and nouns presented in the same sequence. *Journal of Experimental Psychology*, 1970, **86**, 137–143.

Fozard, J. L., Myers, J. R., & Waugh, N. C. Recalling recent exemplars of a category. *Journal of Experimental Psychology*, 1971, **90**, 262–267.

Fozard, J. L., & Weinert, J. R. Absolute judgments of recency for pictures and nouns after various numbers of intervening items. *Journal of Experimental Psychology*, 1972, **95**, 472–474.

Frankel, F., & Cole, M. Measures of category clustering in free recall. *Psychological Bulletin*, 1971, **76**, 39–44.

Franks, J. J., & Bransford, J. D. The acquisition of abstract ideas. *Journal of Verbal Learning and Verbal Behavior*, 1972, **11**, 311–315.

Fraser, D. C. Decay of immediate memory with age. *Nature (London)*, 1958, **182**, 1163.

Freund, J. S., & Underwood, B. J. Storage and retrieval cues in free recall learning. *Journal of Experimental Psychology*, 1969, **81**, 49–53.

Freund, R. D., Brelsford, J. W., & Atkinson, R. C. Recognition vs. recall: Storage or retrieval differences? *Quarterly Journal of Experimental Psychology*, 1969, **21**, 214–224.

Frijda, N. H. Simulation of human long-term memory. *Psychological Bulletin*, 1972, **77**, 1–31.

Frost, R. R., & Jahnke, J. C. Proactive effects in short-term memory. *Journal of Verbal Learning and Verbal Behavior*, 1968, **7**, 785–789.

Gardiner, J. M., Craik, F. I. M., & Birtwistle, J. Retrieval cues and release from proactive inhibition. *Journal of Verbal Learning and Verbal Behavior*, 1972, **11**, 778–783.

Garner, W. R. *Uncertainty and structure as psychological concepts*. New York: Wiley, 1962.

Gazzaniga, M. S. One brain—two minds? *American Scientist*, 1972, **60**, 311–317.

Gianutsos, R. Free recall of grouped words. *Journal of Experimental Psychology*, 1972, **95**, 419–428.

Gibson, E. J. A systematic application of the concepts of generalization and differentiation to verbal learning. *Psychological Review*, 1940, **47**, 196–229.

Gibson, E. J. Learning to read. *Science*, 1965, **148**, 1066–1072.

Gibson, E. J. *Principles of perceptual learning and development*. New York: Appleton-Century-Crofts, 1969.

Gibson, E. J., Bishop, C. H., Schiff, W., & Smith, J. Comparison of meaningfulness and pronunciability as grouping principles in the perception and retention of verbal material. *Journal of Experimental Psychology*, 1964, **67**, 173–182.

Gibson, J. J., & Gibson, E. J. Perceptual learning: Differentiation or enrichment? *Psychological Review*, 1955, **62**, 32–41.

Glanzer, M. Grammatical category: A rote learning and word association analysis. *Journal of Verbal Learning and Verbal Behavior*, 1962, **1**, 31–41.

Glanzer, M. Storage mechanisms in recall. In G. H. Bower (Ed.), *The psychology of learning and motivation: Advances in research and theory*. Vol. 5. New York: Academic Press, 1972. Pp. 129–193.

Glanzer, M., & Cunitz, A. R. Two storage mechanisms in free recall. *Journal of Verbal Learning and Verbal Behavior*, 1966, **5**, 351–360.

Glanzer, M., & Dolinsky, R. The anchor for the serial position curve. *Journal of Verbal Learning and Verbal Behavior*, 1965, **4**, 267–273.

Glanzer, M., & Duarte, A. Repetition between and within languages in free recall. *Journal of Verbal Learning and Verbal Behavior*, 1971, **10**, 625–630.

Glanzer, M., Koppenaal, L., & Nelson, R. Effects of relations between words on short-term storage and long-term storage. *Journal of Verbal Learning and Verbal Behavior*, 1972, **11**, 403–416.

Glassman, W. E. Subvocal activity and acoustic confusions in short-term memory. *Journal of Experimental Psychology*, 1972, **96**, 164–169.

Glucksberg, S., & Cowan, G. N. Memory for nonattended auditory material. *Cognitive Psychology*, 1970, **1**, 149–156.

Goldberg, S. *Difference equations*. New York: Wiley, 1961.

Gorfein, D. S., & Jacobson, D. E. Proactive effects in short-term recognition memory. *Journal of Experimental Psychology*, 1972, **95**, 211–214.

Gorman, A. M. Recognition memory for nouns as a function of abstractness and frequency. *Journal of Experimental Psychology*, 1961, **61**, 23–29.

Grams, W., & van Belle, G. Departures from binomial assumptions in short-term memory models. *Psychometrika*, 1972, **37**, 137–141.

Grasha, A. F. Detection theory and memory processes: Are they compatible? *Perceptual and Motor Skills*, 1970, **30**, 123–135.

Green, D. M., & Moses, F. L. On the equivalence of two recognition measures of short-term memory. *Psychological Bulletin*, 1966, **66**, 228–234.

Green, D. M., & Swets, J. A. *Signal detection theory and psychophysics*. New York: Wiley, 1966.

Greeno, J. G. Paired-associate learning with massed and distributed repetitions of items. *Journal of Experimental Psychology*, 1964, **67**, 286–295.

Greeno, J. G. Paired-associate learning with short-term retention: Mathematical analysis and data regarding identification of parameters. *Journal of Mathematical Psychology*, 1967, **4**, 430–472.

Greeno, J. G. How associations are memorized. In D. A. Norman (Ed.), *Models of human memory*. New York: Academic Press, 1970. Pp. 257–284.

Greeno, J. G., James, C. T., & DaPolito, F. J. A cognitive interpretation of negative transfer and forgetting of paired associates. *Journal of Verbal Learning and Verbal Behavior*, 1971, **10**, 331–345.

Gregg, L. W., & Simon, H. A. An information-processing explanation of one-trial and incremental learning. *Journal of Verbal Learning and Verbal Behavior*, 1967, **6**, 780–787. (a)

Gregg, L. W., & Simon, H. A. Process models and stochastic theories of simple concept formation. *Journal of Mathematical Psychology*, 1967, **4**, 246–276. (b)

Grossman, L., & Eagle, M. Synonymity, antonymity, and association in false recognition responses. *Journal of Experimental Psychology*, 1970, **83**, 244–248.

Haber, R. N. Effects of coding strategy on perceptual memory. *Journal of Experimental Psychology*, 1964, **68**, 357–362.

Haber, R. N. Eidetic images. *Scientific American*, April, 1969, 36–44.

Haber, R. N. How we remember what we see. *Scientific American*, May, 1970, 104–112.

Hall, J. F. Learning as a function of word-frequency. *American Journal of Psychology*, 1954, **67**, 138–140.

Hall, J. F. *Verbal learning and retention*. Philadelphia: Lippincott, 1971.

Halwes, T., & Jenkins, J. J. Problem of serial order in behavior is not resolved by context-sensitive associative memory models. *Psychological Review,* 1971, **78**, 122–129.

Hancock, J. C., & Wintz, P. A. *Signal detection theory.* New York: McGraw-Hill, 1966.

Harcum, E. R. Parallel functions of serial learning and tachistoscopic pattern perception. *Psychological Review,* 1967, **74**, 51–62.

Harris, C. S., & Haber, R. N. Selective attention and coding in visual perception. *Journal of Experimental Psychology,* 1963, **65**, 328–333.

Healy, A. F., & Jones, C. Criterion shifts in recall. *Psychological Bulletin,* 1973, **79**, 335–340.

Hebb, D. O. *Organization of behavior.* New York: Wiley, 1949.

Hebb, D. O. Distinctive features of learning in the higher animal. In J. F. Delafresnaye (Ed.), *Brain mechanisms and learning.* New York: Oxford University Press, 1961. Pp. 37–46.

Hebb, D. O. Concerning imagery. *Psychological Review,* 1968, **75**, 466–477.

Hellyer, S. Frequency of stimulus presentation and short-term decrement in recall. *Journal of Experimental Psychology,* 1962, **64**, 650.

Helson, H. *Adaptation-level theory.* New York: Harper & Row, 1964.

Henley, N. M., Noyes, H. L., & Deese, J. Semantic structure in short-term memory. *Journal of Experimental Psychology,* 1968, **77**, 587–592.

Hermelin, B., & O'Connor, N. Ordering in recognition memory after ambiguous initial or recognition displays. *Canadian Journal of Psychology,* 1973, **27**, 191–199.

Heslip, J. R. Temporal contiguity and spatial separation of items in input as sources of serial order information. *Journal of Experimental Psychology,* 1969, **81**, 593–595.

Hicks, R. E., & Young, R. K. Part-whole transfer in free recall: A reappraisal. *Journal of Experimental Psychology,* 1972, **96**, 328–333.

Hilgard, E. R., & Bower, G. H. *Theories of learning* (3rd ed.). New York: Appleton-Century-Crofts, 1966.

Hillier, F. S., & Lieberman, G. J. *Introduction to operations research.* San Francisco: Holden-Day, 1967.

Hinrichs, J. V. A two-process memory-strength theory for judgment of recency. *Psychological Review,* 1970, **77**, 223–233.

Hintzman, D. L. Classification and aural coding in short-term memory. *Psychonomic Science,* 1965, **3**, 161–162.

Hintzman, D. L. Articulatory coding in short-term memory. *Journal of Verbal Learning and Verbal Behavior,* 1967, **6**, 312–316.

Hintzman, D. L. Explorations with a discrimination net model for paired-associate learning. *Journal of Mathematical Psychology,* 1968, **5**, 123–162.

Hintzman, D. L. Recognition time: Effects of recency, frequency, and the spacing of repetitions. *Journal of Experimental Psychology,* 1969, **79**, 192–194. (a)

Hintzman, D. L. Apparent frequency as a function of frequency and the spacing of repetitions. *Journal of Experimental Psychology,* 1969, **80**, 139–145. (b)

Hintzman, D. L. Effects of repetition and exposure duration on memory. *Journal of Experimental Psychology,* 1970, **83**, 435–444.

Hintzman, D. L. On testing the independence of associations. *Psychological Review,* 1972, **79**, 261–264. (a)

Hintzman, D. L. Confidence ratings in recall: A reanalysis. *Psychological Review,* 1972, **79**, 531–535. (b)

Hintzman, D. L., & Block, R. A. Memory judgments and the effects of spacing. *Journal of Verbal Learning and Verbal Behavior,* 1970, **9**, 561–566.

Hintzman, D. L., & Block, R. A. Repetition and memory: Evidence for a multiple-trace hypothesis. *Journal of Experimental Psychology,* 1971, **88**, 297–306.

Hintzman, D. L., Block, R. A., & Inskeep, N. R. Memory for mode of input. *Journal of Verbal Learning and Verbal Behavior,* 1972, **11**, 741–749.

Hintzman, D. L., & Waters, R. M. Recency and frequency as factors in list discrimination. *Journal of Verbal Learning and Verbal Behavior,* 1970, **9**, 218–221.

Höffding, H. *Outlines of psychology*. (Translated by M. E. Lowndes.) London: Macmillan, 1891.

Hogan, R. M., & Kintsch, W. Differential effects of study and test trials on long-term recognition and recall. *Journal of Verbal Learning and Verbal Behavior*, 1971, **10**, 562–567.

Hohle, R. H. Inferred components of reaction times as functions of foreperiod duration. *Journal of Experimental Psychology*, 1965, **69**, 382–386.

Hopkins, R. H., Edwards, R. E., & Cook, C. L. Presentation modality, distractor modality, and proactive interference in short-term memory. *Journal of Experimental Psychology*, 1973, **98**, 362–367.

Hopkins, R. H., Edwards, R. E., & Gavelek, J. R. Presentation modality as an encoding variable in short-term memory. *Journal of Experimental Psychology*, 1971, **90**, 319–325.

Horowitz, L. M., Norman, S. A., & Day, R. S. Availability and associative symmetry. *Psychological Review*, 1966, **73**, 1–15.

Horowitz, L. M., & Prytulak, L. S. Redintegrative memory. *Psychological Review*, 1969, **76**, 519–531.

Hovland, C. I. Human learning and retention. In S. S. Stevens (Ed.), *Handbook of experimental psychology*, New York: Wiley, 1951. Pp. 613–689.

Howe, M. J. A. *Introduction to human memory*. New York: Harper & Row, 1970.

Hudson, R. L., & Austin, J. B. Effect of context and category name on the recall of categorized word lists. *Journal of Experimental Psychology*, 1970, **86**, 43–47.

Hudson, R. L., Solomon, M. L., & Davis, J. L. Effects of presentation and recall trials on clustering and recall. *Journal of Verbal Learning and Verbal Behavior*, 1972, **11**, 356–361.

Hull, C. L. Knowledge and purpose as habit mechanisms. *Psychological Review*, 1930, **37**, 511–525.

Hull, C. L. *Principles of behavior*. New York: Appleton-Century-Crofts, 1943.

Hull, C. L., Hovland, C. I., Ross, R. T., Hall, M., Perkins, D. T., & Fitch, F. B. *Mathematico-deductive theory of rote learning*. New Haven: Yale University Press, 1940.

Humphreys, M., & Greeno, J. G. Interpretation of the two-stage analysis of paired-associate memorizing. *Journal of Mathematical Psychology*, 1970, **7**, 275–292.

Hyde, T. S. Differential effects of effort and type of orienting task on recall and organization of highly associated words. *Journal of Experimental Psychology*, 1973, **79**, 111–113.

Hyde, T. S., & Jenkins, J. J. Differential effects of incidental tasks on the organization of recall of a list of highly associated words. *Journal of Experimental Psychology*, 1969, **82**, 472–481.

Indow, T., & Togano, K. On retrieving sequence from long-term memory. *Psychological Review*, 1970, **77**, 317–331.

Ingersoll, G. M., & DiVesta, F. J. Effects of modality preferences on performance on a bisensory missing-units task. *Journal of Experimental Psychology*, 1972, **93**, 386–391.

Izawa, C. Function of test trials in paired-associate learning. *Journal of Experimental Psychology*, 1967, **75**, 194–209.

Izawa, C. Comparison of reinforcement and test trials in paired-associate learning. *Journal of Experimental Psychology*, 1969, **81**, 600–603.

Izawa, C. Optimal potentiating effects and forgetting-prevention effects of tests in paired-associate learning. *Journal of Experimental Psychology*, 1970, **83**, 340–344.

Izawa, C. The test trial potentiating model. *Journal of Mathematical Psychology*, 1971, **8**, 200–224.

Jahnke, J. C. Serial position effects in immediate serial recall. *Journal of Verbal Learning and Verbal Behavior*, 1963, **2**, 284–287.

Jahnke, J. C. The Ranschburg effect. *Psychological Review*, 1969, **76**, 592–605.

Jahnke, J. C. Probed recall of strings that contain repeated elements. *Journal of Verbal Learning and Verbal Behavior*, 1970, **9**, 450–455.

Jahnke, J. C. The effects of intraserial and interserial repetition on recall. *Journal of Verbal Learning and Verbal Behavior*, 1972, **11**, 706–716.

Jakobson, R., & Halle, M. *Fundamentals of language*. The Hague: Mouton, 1956.

Jenkins, J. J., & Russell, W. A. Associative clustering during recall. *Journal of Abnormal and Social Psychology*, 1952, **47**, 818–821.

Jensen, A. R. Temporal and spatial effects of serial position. *American Journal of Psychology*, 1962,

75, 390–400. (a)

Jensen, A. R. Spelling errors and the serial-position effect. *Journal of Educational Psychology,* 1962, **53**, 105–109. (b)

Jensen, A. R. An empirical theory of the serial-position effect. *Journal of Psychology,* 1962, **53**, 127–142. (c)

Jensen, A. R. Serial rote-learning: Incremental or all-or-none? *Quarterly Journal of Experimental Psychology,* 1963, **15**, 27–35.

Jensen, A. R., & Roden, A. Memory span and the skewness of the serial-position curve. *British Journal of Psychology,* 1963, **54**, 337–349.

Johnson, N. F. Sequential verbal behavior. In T. R. Dixon & D. L. Horton (Eds.), *Verbal behavior and general behavior theory.* Englewood Cliffs: Prentice-Hall, 1968. Pp. 421–450.

Johnson, N. F. The role of chunking and organization in the process of recall. In G. H. Bower (Ed.), *The psychology of learning and motivation: Advances in research and theory.* Vol. 4. New York: Academic Press, 1970. Pp. 171–247.

Johnson, N. F. Organization and the concept of a memory code. In A. W. Melton & E. Martin (Eds.), *Coding processes in human memory.* Washington, D.C.: Winston, 1972. Pp. 125–159.

Johnston, C. D. & Jenkins, J. J. Two more incidental tasks that differentially affect associative clustering in recall. *Journal of Experimental Psychology,* 1971, **89**, 92–95.

Jones, J. E. All-or-none versus incremental learning. *Psychological Review,* 1962, **69**, 156–160.

Jung, J. *Verbal learning.* New York: Holt, Rinehart, and Winston, 1968.

Juola, J. F., Fischler, I., Wood, C. T., & Atkinson, R. C. Recognition time for information stored in long-term memory. *Perception & Psychophysics,* 1971, **10**, 8–14.

Kaplan, I. T., Carvellas, T., & Metlay, W. Searching for words in letter sets of varying size. *Journal of Experimental Psychology,* 1969, **82**, 377–380.

Kaplan, I. T., Carvellas, T., & Metlay, W. Effects of context on verbal recall. *Journal of Verbal Learning and Verbal Behavior,* 1971, **10**, 207–212.

Katz, J. J., & Fodor, J. A. The structure of a semantic theory. *Language,* 1963, **39**, 170–210.

Keele, S. W. Movement control in skilled motor performance. *Psychological Bulletin,* 1968, **70**, 387–403.

Keppel, G., & Underwood, B. J. Proactive inhibition in short-term retention of single items. *Journal of Verbal Learning and Verbal Behavior,* 1962, **1**, 153–161.

Kimura, D. Functional asymmetry of the brain in dichotic listening. *Cortex,* 1967, **3**, 163–178.

Kintsch, W. The effects of repetition on the short-term memory function. *Psychonomic Science,* 1965, **2**, 149–150. (a)

Kintsch, W. Habituation of the GSR component of the orienting reflex during paired-associate learning before and after learning has taken place. *Journal of Mathematical Psychology,* 1965, **2**, 330–341. (b)

Kintsch, W. Recognition learning as a function of the length of the retention interval and changes in the retention interval. *Journal of Mathematical Psychology,* 1966, **3**, 412–433.

Kintsch, W. Memory and decision aspects of recognition learning. *Psychological Review,* 1967, **74**, 496–504.

Kintsch, W. An experimental analysis of single stimulus tests and multiple-choice tests of recognition memory. *Journal of Experimental Psychology,* 1968, **76**, 1–6. (a)

Kintsch, W. Recognition and free recall of organized lists. *Journal of Experimental Psychology,* 1968, **78**, 481–487. (b)

Kintsch, W. Models for free recall and recognition. In D. A. Norman (Ed.), *Models of human memory.* New York: Academic Press, 1970. Pp. 333–374. (a)

Kintsch, W. *Learning, memory, and conceptual processes.* New York: Wiley, 1970. (b)

Kintsch, W. Abstract nouns: Imagery versus lexical complexity. *Journal of Verbal Learning and Verbal Behavior,* 1972, **11**, 59–65. (a)

Kintsch, W. Notes on the structure of semantic memory. In E. Tulving & W. Donaldson (Eds.), *Organization of memory.* New York: Academic Press, 1972. Pp. 247–308. (b)

Kintsch, W., & Buschke, H. Homophones and synonyms in short-term memory. *Journal of Experimental Psychology*, 1969, **80**, 403–407.

Kintsch, W., & Morris, C. J. Application of a Markov model to free recall and recognition. *Journal of Experimental Psychology*, 1965, **69**, 200–206.

Kirsner, K. Naming latency facilitation: An analysis of the encoding component in recognition reaction time. *Journal of Experimental Psychology*, 1972, **95**, 171–176.

Kirsner, K. An analysis of the visual component in recognition memory for verbal stimuli. *Memory & Cognition*, 1973, **1**, 449–453. (a)

Kirsner, K. Modality differences in recognition memory for words and their attributes. *Journal of Experimental Psychology*, 1973, in press. (b)

Kirsner, K., & Craik, F. I. M. Naming and decision processes in short-term recognition memory. *Journal of Experimental Psychology*, 1971, **88**, 149–157.

Kiss, G. R. Words, associations, and networks. *Journal of Verbal Learning and Verbal Behavior*, 1968, **7**, 707–713.

Klatzky, R. L., & Smith, E. E. Stimulus expectancy and retrieval from short-term memory. *Journal of Experimental Psychology*, 1972, **94**, 101–107.

Kolers, P. A. Interlingual facilitation of short-term memory. *Journal of Verbal Learning and Verbal Behavior*, 1966, **5**, 314–319.

Kolers, P. A. Some psychological aspects of pattern recognition. In P. A. Kolers & M. Eden (Eds.), *Recognizing patterns: Studies in living and automatic systems.* Cambridge, Mass.: The MIT Press, 1968. Pp. 4–61.

Kolers, P. A. Remembering operations. *Memory & Cognition*, 1973, **1**, 347–355.

Krantz, D. H. Threshold theories of signal detection. *Psychological Review*, 1969, **76**, 308–324.

Kroll, N. E. A., Bee, J., & Gurski, G. Release of proactive interference as a result of changing presentation modality. *Journal of Experimental Psychology*, 1973, **98**, 131–137.

Kroll, N. E. A., Parks, T. E., Parkinson, S. R., Bieber, S. L., & Johnson, A. L. Short-term memory while shadowing: Recall of visually and of aurally presented letters. *Journal of Experimental Psychology*, 1970, **85**, 220–224.

Krueger, W. C. F. The effect of overlearning on retention. *Journal of Experimental Psychology*, 1929, **12**, 71–78.

Kurtz, K. H., & Hovland, C. I. The effect of verbalization during observation of stimulus-objects upon accuracy of recognition and recall. *Journal of Experimental Psychology*, 1953, **45**, 157–163.

Kusyszyn, I., & Paivio, A. Transition probability, word order, and noun abstractness in the learning of adjective-noun paired associates. *Journal of Experimental Psychology*, 1966, **71**, 800–805.

Lachman, R., & Laughery, K. R. Is a test trial a training trial in free-recall learning? *Journal of Experimental Psychology*, 1968, **76**, 40–50.

Lachman, R., & Tuttle, A. V. Approximations to English (AE) and short-term memory: Construction or storage? *Journal of Experimental Psychology*, 1965, **70**, 386–393.

Lambert, W. E., Ignatow, M., & Krauthamer, M. Bilingual organization in free recall. *Journal of Verbal Learning and Verbal Behavior*, 1968, **7**, 207–214.

Laming, D. R. J. *Information theory of choice-reaction times.* New York: Academic Press, 1968.

Landauer, T. K., & Freedman, J. L. Information retrieval from long-term memory: Category size and recognition time. *Journal of Verbal Learning and Verbal Behavior*, 1968, **7**, 291–295.

Larkin, W. D. Rating scales in detection experiments. *Journal of the Acoustical Society of America*, 1965, **37**, 748–749.

Lashley, K. S. The problem of serial order in behavior. In L. A. Jeffress (Ed.), *Cerebral mechanisms in behavior.* New York: Wiley, 1951. Pp. 112–136.

Laughery, K. R. Computer simulation of short-term memory: A component-decay model. In J. T. Spence & G. H. Bower (Eds.), *The psychology of learning and motivation: Advances in research and theory.* Vol. 3. New York: Academic Press, 1969. Pp. 135–200.

Laughery, K. R., & Fell, J. C. Subject preferences and the nature of information stored in short-term memory. *Journal of Experimental Psychology*, 1969, **82**, 193–197.

Laughery, K. R., & Pinkus, A. L. Recoding and presentation rate in short-term memory. *Journal of Experimental Psychology*, 1968, **76**, 636–641.

Laurence, M. W. Age differences in performance and subjective organization in the free-recall learning of pictorial material. *Canadian Journal of Psychology*, 1966, **20**, 388–399.

Lawrence, D. H. The nature of a stimulus: Some relationships between learning and perception. In S. Koch (Ed.), *Psychology: A study of a science*. Vol. 5. New York: McGraw-Hill, 1963. Pp. 179–212.

Levine, G., & Burke, C. J. *Mathematical model techniques for learning theories*. New York: Academic Press, 1972.

Levy, B. A. Role of articulation in auditory and visual short-term memory. *Journal of Verbal Learning and Verbal Behavior*, 1971, **10**, 123–132.

Levy, B. A., & Murdock, B. B., Jr. The effects of delayed auditory feedback and intralist similarity in short-term memory. *Journal of Verbal Learning and Verbal Behavior*, 1968, **7**, 887–894.

Lewis, J. L. Semantic processing of unattended messages using dichotic listening. *Journal of Experimental Psychology*, 1970, **85**, 225–228.

Lewis, J. L. Semantic processing with bisensory stimulation. *Journal of Experimental Psychology*, 1972, **96**, 455–457.

Light, L. L., & Carter-Sobell, L. Effects of changed semantic context on recognition memory. *Journal of Verbal Learning and Verbal Behavior*, 1970, **9**, 1–11.

Light, L. L., Stansbury, C., Rubin, C., & Linde, S. Memory for modality of presentation: Within-modality discrimination. *Memory & Cognition*, 1973, **1**, 395–400.

Lindgren, N. Machine recognition of human language. Part I: Automatic speech recognition. *IEEE Spectrum*, 1965, **2**, 114–136. (a)

Lindgren, N. Machine recognition of human language. Part II: Theoretical models of speech perception and language. *IEEE Spectrum*, 1965, **2**, 45–59. (b)

Lindgren, N. Machine recognition of human language. Part III: Cursive script recognition. *IEEE Spectrum*, 1965, **2**, 105–116. (c)

Lindley, R. H. Effects of controlled coding cues in short-term memory. *Journal of Experimental Psychology*, 1963, **66**, 580–587.

Lindley, R. H. Effects of trigram-recoding cue complexity on short-term memory. *Journal of Verbal Learning and Verbal Behavior*, 1965, **4**, 274–279.

Lindley, R. H., & Nedler, S. E. Further effects of subject-generated recoding cues on short-term memory. *Journal of Experimental Psychology*, 1965, **69**, 324–325.

Lively, B. L. The von Restorff effect in short-term memory. *Journal of Experimental Psychology*, 1972, **93**, 361–366.

Lloyd, K. E., Reid, L. S., & Feallock, J. B. Short-term retention as a function of the average number of items presented. *Journal of Experimental Psychology*, 1960, **60**, 201–207.

Lockhart, R. S. Recency discrimination predicted from absolute lag judgments. *Perception and Psychophysics*, 1969, **6**, 42–44. (a)

Lockhart, R. S. Retrieval asymmetry in the recall of adjectives and nouns. *Journal of Experimental Psychology*, 1969, **79**, 12–17. (b)

Lockhart, R. S. Retrieval asymmetry and the criterion problem in cued recall. *Journal of Experimental Psychology*, 1969, **81**, 192–194. (c)

Lockhart, R. S., & Martin, J. E. Adjective order and the recall of adjective-noun triples. *Journal of Verbal Learning and Verbal Behavior*, 1969, **8**, 272–275.

Lockhart, R. S., & Murdock, B. B., Jr. Memory and the theory of signal detection. *Psychological Bulletin*, 1970, **74**, 100–109.

Loess, H. Proactive inhibition in short-term memory. *Journal of Verbal Learning and Verbal Behavior*, 1964, **3**, 362–368.

Loess, H., & Waugh, N. C. Short-term memory and intertrial interval. *Journal of Verbal Learning and Verbal Behavior*, 1967, **6**, 455–460.

Loftus, G. R. A comparison of recognition and recall in a continuous memory task. *Journal of Experimental Psychology*, 1971, **91**, 220–226.

Loftus, G. R. Eye fixations and recognition memory for pictures. *Cognitive Psychology*, 1972, **3**, 525–551.

Luce, R. D. *Individual choice behavior*. New York: Wiley, 1959.

Luce, R. D. A threshold theory for simple detection experiments. *Psychological Review*, 1963, **70**, 61–79.

Luce, R. D., & Green, D. M. A neural timing theory for response times and the psychophysics of intensity. *Psychological Review*, 1972, **79**, 14–57.

McCabe, L., & Madigan, S. Negative effects of recency in recall and recognition. *Journal of Verbal Learning and Verbal Behavior*, 1971, **10**, 307–310.

McConkie, G. W. Effects that a massed repetition of one pair has on other pairs in a list. *Journal of Experimental Psychology*, 1969, **82**, 187–189.

McCormack, P. D. Recognition memory: How complex a retrieval system? *Canadian Journal of Psychology*, 1972, **26**, 19–41.

McCormack, P. D., & Swenson, A. L. Recognition memory for common and rare words. *Journal of Experimental Psychology*, 1972, **95**, 72–77.

McCreary, J. W., & Hunter, W. S. Serial position curves in verbal learning. *Science*, 1953, **117**, 131–134.

McGaugh, J. L., & Herz, M. J. *Memory consolidation*. San Francisco: Albion, 1972.

McGeoch, J. A. Forgetting and the law of disuse. *Psychological Review*, 1932, **39**, 352–370.

McGeoch, J. A. *The psychology of human learning*. New York: Longmans, Green, 1942.

McGeoch, J. A., & Irion, A. L. *The psychology of human learning*. New York: Longmans, Green, 1952.

McGlaughlin, A., & Dale, H. C. A. Stimulus similarity and transfer in long-term paired-associate learning. *British Journal of Psychology*, 1971, **62**, 37–40.

McGovern, J. B. Extinction of associations in four transfer paradigms. *Psychological Monographs*, 1964, **78** (16, Whole No. 593).

McGuire, W. J. A multiprocess model for paired-associate learning. *Journal of Experimental Psychology*, 1961, **62**, 335–347.

Mackworth, J. F. Presentation rate and immediate memory. *Canadian Journal of Psychology*, 1962, **16**, 42–47. (a)

Mackworth, J. F. The effect of display time upon the recall of digits. *Canadian Journal of Psychology*, 1962, **16**, 48–54. (b)

Mackworth, J. F. The effect of the response upon the immediate memory span. *Canadian Journal of Psychology*, 1962, **16**, 120–127. (c)

McLean, R. S., & Gregg, L. W. Effects of induced chunking on temporal aspects of serial recitation. *Journal of Experimental Psychology*, 1967, **74**, 455–459.

McLeod, P. D., Williams, C. E., & Broadbent, D. E. Free recall with assistance from one and from two retrieval cues. *British Journal of Psychology*, 1971, **62**, 59–65.

Macnamara, J. Cognitive basis of language learning in infants. *Psychological Review*, 1972, **79**, 1–13.

McNulty, J. A. A partial learning model of recognition memory. *Canadian Journal of Psychology*, 1966, **20**, 302–315.

Madigan, S. A. Intraserial repetition and coding processes in free recall. *Journal of Verbal Learning and Verbal Behavior*, 1969, **8**, 828–835.

Madigan, S. A. Modality and recall order interactions in short-term memory for serial order. *Journal of Experimental Psychology*, 1971, **87**, 294–296.

Madigan, S. A., & Doherty, L. Retention of item attributes in free recall. *Psychonomic Science*, 1972, **27**, 233–235.

Madigan, S. A., & McCabe, L. Perfect recall and total forgetting: A problem for models of short-term memory. *Journal of Verbal Learning and Verbal Behavior*, 1971, **10**, 101–106.

Madsen, M. C., Rollins, H. A., & Senf, G. M. Variables affecting immediate memory for bisensory stimuli: Eye-ear analogue studies of dichotic listening. *Journal of Experimental Psychology Monograph Supplement*, 1970, **83**, (Pt. 2) Pp. 1–16.

Mandler, G. Organization and memory. In K. W. Spence & J. T. Spence (Eds.), *The psychology of learning and motivation: Advances in research and theory.* Vol. 1, New York: Academic Press, 1967. Pp. 327–372.

Mandler, G, Association and organization: Fact, fancies, and theories. In T. R. Dixon & D. L. Horton (Eds.), *Verbal behavior and general behavior theory.* Englewood Cliffs: Prentice-Hall, 1968. Pp. 109–119.

Mandler, G. Words, lists, and categories: An experimental view of organized memory. In J. L. Cowan (Ed.), *Studies in thought and language.* Tucson, University of Arizona Press, 1970. Pp. 99–131.

Mandler, G. Organization and recognition. In E. Tulving & W. Donaldson (Eds.), *Organization of memory.* New York: Academic Press, 1972. Pp. 139–166.

Mandler, G., & Anderson, R. A. Temporal and spatial cues in seriation. *Journal of Experimental Psychology,* 1971, **90**, 128–135.

Mandler, G., & Pearlstone, Z. Free and constrained concept learning and subsequent recall. *Journal of Verbal Learning and Verbal Behavior,* 1966, **5**, 126–131.

Mandler G., Pearlstone, Z., & Koopmans, H. S. Effects of organization and semantic similarity on recall and recognition. *Journal of Verbal Learning and Verbal Behavior,* 1969, **8**, 410–423.

Mann, J. E. Modality effects in free recall ordered by presentation mode. Unpublished bachelor's thesis, University of Toronto, 1970.

Margrain, S. A. Short-term memory as a function of input modality. *Quarterly Journal of Experimental Psychology,* 1967, **19**, 109–114.

Martin, E. Stimulus recognition in aural paired-associate learning. *Journal of Verbal Learning and Verbal Behavior,* 1967, **6**, 272–276. (a)

Martin, E. Relation between stimulus recognition and paired-associate learning. *Journal of Experimental Psychology,* 1967, **74**, 500–505. (b)

Martin, E. Stimulus meaningfulness and paired-associate transfer: An encoding variability hypothesis. *Psychological Review,* 1968, **75**, 421–441.

Martin, E. Verbal learning theory and independent retrieval phenomena. *Psychological Review,* 1971, **78**, 314–332.

Martin, E., & Greeno, J. G. Independence of associations tested: A reply to D. L. Hintzman. *Psychological Review,* 1972, **79**, 265–267.

Martin, E., & Melton, A. W. Meaningfulness and trigram recognition. *Journal of Verbal Learning and Verbal Behavior,* 1970, **9**, 126–135.

Martin, F. F. *Computer modeling and simulation.* New York: Wiley, 1968.

Massaro, D. W. Preperceptual auditory images. *Journal of Experimental Psychology,* 1970, **85**, 411–417.

Mayzner, M. S., Tresselt, M. E., & Helfer, M. S. A provisional model of visual information processing with sequential inputs. *Psychonomic Monograph Supplements,* 1967, **2**, 91–108.

Melton, A. W. Implications of short-term memory for a general theory of memory. *Journal of Verbal Learning and Verbal Behavior,* 1963, **2**, 1–21.

Melton, A. W. Repetition and retrieval from memory. *Science,* 1967, **158**, 532.

Melton, A. W. The situation with respect to the spacing of repetitions and memory. *Journal of Verbal Learning and Verbal Behavior,* 1970, **9**, 596–606.

Melton, A. W., & Glenberg, A. M. Interaction of presentation rate and lag effects in free recall. Paper presented at the Psychonomic Society Meeting, St. Louis, Missouri, November, 1971.

Melton, A. W., & Irwin, J. M. The influence of degree of interpolated learning on retroactive inhibition and the overt transfer of specific responses. *American Journal of Psychology,* 1940, **53**, 173–203.

Melton, A. W., Sameroff, A., & Schubot, E. D. Short-term recognition memory. Human Performance Center Memorandum Report Number 2, University of Michigan, 1967.

Merryman, C. T. Retroactive inhibition in the A–B, A–D paradigm as measured by a multiple-choice test. *Journal of Experimental Psychology,* 1971, **91**, 212–214.

Meyer, D. E. On the representation and retrieval of stored semantic information. *Cognitive Psychology,* 1970, **1**, 242–300.

Miller, G. A. *Language and communication.* New York: McGraw-Hill, 1951.

Miller, G. A. Finite Markov processes in psychology. *Psychometrika,* 1952, **17**, 149–167.

Miller, G. A. The magical number seven, plus or minus two: Some limits on our capacity for processing information. *Psychological Review,* 1956, **63**, 81–96.

Miller, G. A., Galanter, E., & Pribram, K. H. *Plans and the structure of behavior.* New York: Holt, Rinehart and Winston, 1960.

Miller, G. A., & Nicely, P. E. An analysis of perceptual confusions among some English consonants. *Journal of Acoustical Society of America,* 1955, **27**, 338–352.

Millward, R. B. Latency in a modified paired-associate learning experiment. *Journal of Verbal Learning and Verbal Behavior,* 1964, **3**, 309–316.

Millward, R. B. Theoretical and experimental approaches to human learning. In J. W. Kling & L. A. Riggs (Eds.), *Experimental psychology.* (3rd ed.) New York: Holt, Rinehart and Winston, 1971. Pp. 905–1017.

Milner, B. Interhemispheric differences in the localization of psychological processes in man. *British Medical Bulletin,* 1971, **27**, 272–277.

Milner, P. M. A neural mechanism for the immediate recall of sequences. *Kybernetik,* 1961, **1**, 76–81.

Montague, W. E., Adams, J. A., & Kiess, H. O. Forgetting and natural language mediation. *Journal of Experimental Psychology,* 1966, **72**, 829–833.

Moray, N. Attention in dichotic listening: Affective cues and the influence of instructions. *Quarterly Journal of Experimental Psychology,* 1959, **11**, 56–60.

Moray, N. *Attention: Selective processes in vision and hearing.* London: Hutchinson, 1969.

Moray, N., Bates, A., & Barnett, T. Experiments on the four-eared man. *Journal of the Acoustical Society of America,* 1965, **38**, 196–201.

Moray, N., & Jordan, A. Practice and compatability in 2-channel short-term memory. *Psychonomic Science,* 1966, **4**, 427–428.

Morikawa, Y. Functions of stimulus and response in paired-associate verbal learning. *Psychologia,* 1959, **2**, 41–56.

Morton, J. The effect of context upon speed of reading, eye movements and eye-voice span. *Quarterly Journal of Experimental Psychology,* 1964, **16**, 340–354.

Morton, J. Repeated items and decay in memory. *Psychonomic Science,* 1968, **10**, 219–220.

Morton, J. A functional model for memory. In D. A. Norman (Ed.), *Models of human memory.* New York: Academic Press, 1970. Pp. 203–260.

Morton, J., & Holloway, C. M. Absence of a cross-modal "suffix effect" in short-term memory. *Quarterly Journal of Experimental Psychology,* 1970, **22**, 167–176.

Moss, S. M., & Sharac, J. Accuracy and latency in short-term memory: Evidence for a dual retrieval process. *Journal of Experimental Psychology,* 1970, **84**, 40–46.

Mowbray, G. H. Perception and retention of verbal information presented during auditory shadowing. *Journal of the Acoustical Society of America,* 1964, **36**, 1459–1464.

Murdock, B. B., Jr. Intralist generalization in paired-associate learning. *Psychological Review,* 1958, **65**, 306–314.

Murdock, B. B., Jr. The distinctiveness of stimuli. *Psychological Review,* 1960, **67**, 16–31. (a)

Murdock, B. B., Jr. The immediate retention of unrelated words. *Journal of Experimental Psychology,* 1960, **60**, 222–234. (b)

Murdock, B. B., Jr. The retention of individual items. *Journal of Experimental Psychology,* 1961, **62**, 618–625. (a)

Murdock, B. B., Jr. Short-term retention of single paired associates. *Psychological Reports,* 1961, **8**, 280. (b)

Murdock, B. B., Jr. The serial position effect of free recall. *Journal of Experimental Psychology,* 1962, **64**, 482–488. (a)

Murdock, B. B., Jr. Direction of recall in short-term memory. *Journal of Verbal Learning and Verbal Behavior,* 1962, **1**, 119–124. (b)

Murdock, B. B., Jr. Short-term memory and paired-associate learning. *Journal of Verbal Learning and Verbal Behavior,* 1963, **2**, 320–328. (a)

Murdock, B. B., Jr. An analysis of the recognition process. In C. N. Cofer & B. S. Musgrave (Eds.), *Verbal behavior and learning.* New York: McGraw-Hill, 1963. Pp. 10–22. (b)

Murdock, B. B., Jr. Interpolated recall in short-term memory. *Journal of Experimental Psychology,* 1963, **66**, 525–532. (c)

Murdock, B. B., Jr. Short-term retention of single paired associates. *Journal of Experimental Psychology,* 1963, **65**, 433–443. (d)

Murdock, B. B., Jr. Proactive inhibition in short-term memory. *Journal of Experimental Psychology,* 1964, **68**, 184–189.

Murdock, B. B., Jr. Signal-detection theory and short-term memory. *Journal of Experimental Psychology,* 1965, **70**, 443–447. (a)

Murdock, B. B., Jr. A test of the "limited capacity" hypothesis. *Journal of Experimental Psychology,* 1965, **69**, 237–240. (b)

Murdock, B. B., Jr. Associative symmetry and dichotic presentation. *Journal of Verbal Learning and Verbal Behavior,* 1965, **4**, 222–226. (c)

Murdock, B. B., Jr. Effects of a subsidiary task on short-term memory. *British Journal of Psychology,* 1965, **56**, 413–419. (d)

Murdock, B. B., Jr. The criterion problem in short-term memory. *Journal of Experimental Psychology,* 1966, **72**, 317–324. (a)

Murdock, B. B., Jr. Forward and backward associations in paired associates. *Journal of Experimental Psychology,* 1966, **71**, 732–737. (b)

Murdock, B. B., Jr. Measurement of retention of interpolated activity in short-term memory. *Journal of Verbal Learning and Verbal Behavior,* 1966, **5**, 469–472. (c)

Murdock, B. B., Jr. Visual and auditory stores in short-term memory. *Quarterly Journal of Experimental Psychology,* 1966, **18**, 206–211. (d)

Murdock, B. B., Jr. Recent developments in short-term memory. *British Journal of Psychology,* 1967, **58**, 421–433. (a)

Murdock, B. B., Jr. A fixed-point model for short-term memory. *Journal of Mathematical Psychology,* 1967, **4**, 501–506. (b)

Murdock, B. B., Jr. Distractor and probe techniques in short-term memory. *Canadian Journal of Psychology,* 1967, **21**, 25–36. (c)

Murdock, B. B., Jr. The effects of noise and delayed auditory feedback on short-term memory. *Journal of Verbal Learning and Verbal Behavior,* 1967, **6**, 737–743. (d)

Murdock, B. B., Jr. Auditory and visual stores in short-term memory. *Acta Psychologica,* 1967, **27**, 316–324. (e)

Murdock, B. B., Jr. Modality effects in short-term memory: Storage or retrieval? *Journal of Experimental Psychology,* 1968, **77**, 79–86. (a)

Murdock, B. B., Jr. Response latencies in short-term memory. *Quarterly Journal of Experimental Psychology,* 1968, **20**, 79–82. (b)

Murdock, B. B., Jr. Serial order effects in short-term memory. *Journal of Experimental Psychology Monograph Supplement,* 1968, **76**, (Pt. 2) Pp. 1–15. (c)

Murdock, B. B., Jr. Decoding as a function of the number of bits per chunk. *Journal of Experimental Psychology,* 1968, **78**, 1–7. (d)

Murdock, B. B., Jr. Where or when: Modality effects as a function of temporal and spatial distribution of information. *Journal of Verbal Learning and Verbal Behavior,* 1969, **8**, 378–383.

Murdock, B. B., Jr. Short-term memory for associations. In D. A. Norman (Ed.), *Models of human memory.* New York: Academic Press, 1970. Pp. 285–304.

Murdock, B. B., Jr. Four-channel effects in short-term memory. *Psychonomic Science,* 1971, **24**, 197–198. (a)

Murdock, B. B., Jr. A parallel-processing model for scanning. *Perception & Psychophysics,* 1971, **10**, 289–291. (b)

Murdock, B. B., Jr. *Human memory.* New York: General Learning Press, 1971. Pp. 1–20. (c)

Murdock, B. B., Jr. Short-term memory. In G. H. Bower (Ed.), *The psychology of learning and motivation: Advances in research and theory.* Vol. 5. New York: Academic Press, 1972, Pp. 67–127.

Murdock, B. B., Jr., & Babick, A. J. The effect of repetition on the retention of individual words. *American Journal of Psychology,* 1961, **74**, 596–601.

Murdock, B. B., Jr., & Carey, S. T. Release from interference in single-trial free recall. *Journal of Verbal Learning and Verbal Behavior,* 1972, **11**, 398–402.

Murdock, B. B., Jr., & Cook, C. D. On fitting the exponential. *Psychological Reports,* 1960, **6**, 63–69.

Murdock, B. B., Jr., & Dufty, P. O. Strength theory and recognition memory. *Journal of Experimental Psychology,* 1972, **94**, 284–290.

Murdock, B. B., Jr., Dufty, P. O., & Okada, R. Using the PDP-12 in verbal learning and short-term memory research. *Behavior Research Methods and Instrumentation,* 1972, **4**, 70–71.

Murdock, B. B., Jr., & Ogilvie, J. C. Binomial variability in short-term memory. *Psychological Bulletin,* 1968, **70**, 256–260.

Murdock, B. B., Jr., & Okada, R. Interresponse times in single-trial free recall. *Journal of Experimental Psychology,* 1970, **86**, 263–267.

Murdock, B. B., Jr., Penney, C. G., & Aamiry, A. Interactive presentation in multi-trial free recall. *Journal of Verbal Learning and Verbal Behavior,* 1970, **9**, 679–683.

Murdock, B. B., Jr., & vom Saal, W. Transpositions in short-term memory. *Journal of Experimental Psychology,* 1967, **74**, 137–143.

Murdock, B. B., Jr., & Walker, K. D. Modality effects in free recall. *Journal of Verbal Learning and Verbal Behavior,* 1969, **8**, 665–676.

Murray, D. J. Vocalization-at-presentation and immediate recall, with varying presentation-rates. *Quarterly Journal of Experimental Psychology,* 1965, **17**, 47–56.

Murray, D. J. Vocalization-at-presentation and immediate recall, with varying recall methods. *Quarterly Journal of Experimental Psychology,* 1966, **18**, 9–18.

Murray, D. J. The role of speech responses in short-term memory. *Canadian Journal of Psychology,* 1967, **21**, 263–276.

Murray, D. J. Articulation and acoustic confusability in short-term memory. *Journal of Experimental Psychology,* 1968, **78**, 679–684.

Naylor, T. H., Balintfy, J. L., Burdick, D. S., & Chu, K. *Computer simulation techniques.* New York: Wiley, 1966.

Nazzaro, J. R., & Nazzaro, J. N. Auditory versus visual learning of temporal patterns. *Journal of Experimental Psychology,* 1970, **84**, 477–478.

Neimark, E. D., & Estes, W. K. (Eds.), *Stimulus sampling theory.* San Francisco: Holden-Day, 1967.

Neimark, E. D., Greenhouse, P., Law, S., & Weinheimer, S. The effect of rehearsal-preventing task upon retention of CVC syllables. *Journal of Verbal Learning and Verbal Behavior,* 1965, **4**, 280–285.

Neisser, U. *Cognitive psychology.* New York: Appleton-Century-Crofts, 1967.

Nelder, J. A., & Mead, R. A simplex method for function minimization. *Computer Journal,* 1965, **7**, 308–313.

Nelson, D. L., & Borden, R. C. Interference produced by phonetic similarities: Stimulus recognition, associative retrieval, or both? *Journal of Experimental Psychology,* 1973, **97**, 167–169.

Nelson, T. O., & Rothbart, R. Acoustic savings for items forgotten from long-term memory. *Journal of Experimental Psychology,* 1972, **93**, 357–360.

Newton, J. M., & Wickens, D. D. Retroactive inhibition as a function of the temporal position of the interpolated learning. *Journal of Experimental Psychology,* 1956, **51**, 149–154.

Nickerson, R. S. A note on long-term recognition memory for pictorial material. *Psychonomic Science,* 1968, **11**, 58.

Nilsson, L.-G. Organization by modality in short-term memory. *Journal of Experimental Psychology,* 1973, **100**, 246–253.

Nixon, S. R. Some experiments on immediate memory. A.P.U. Report 39, Applied Psychology Research Unit, 1946.

Norman, D. A. Acquisition and retention in short-term memory. *Journal of Experimental Psychology,* 1966, **72**, 369–381.

Norman, D. A. Toward a theory of memory and attention. *Psychological Review,* 1968, **75**, 522–536.

Norman, D. A. *Memory and attention: An introduction to human information processing.* New York: Wiley, 1969. (a)

Norman, D. A. Memory while shadowing. *Quarterly Journal of Experimental Psychology,* 1969, **21**, 85–93. (b)

Norman, D. A. (Ed.), *Models of human memory.* New York: Academic Press, 1970. (a)

Norman, D. A. Appendix: Serial position curves. In D. A. Norman (Ed.), *Models of human memory.* New York: Academic Press, 1970. Pp. 511–518. (b)

Norman, D. A., & Rumelhart, D. E. A system for perception and memory. In D. A. Norman (Ed.), *Models of human memory.* New York: Academic Press, 1970. Pp. 19–64.

Norman, D. A., & Waugh, N. C. Stimulus and response interference in recognition-memory experiments. *Journal of Experimental Psychology,* 1968, **78**, 551–559.

Norman, D. A., & Wickelgren, W. A. Short-term recognition memory for single digits and pairs of digits. *Journal of Experimental Psychology,* 1965, **70**, 479–489.

Norman, D. A., & Wickelgren, W. A. Strength theory of decision rules and latency in short-term memory. *Journal of Mathematical Psychology,* 1969, **6**, 192–208.

Norman, M. F. Incremental learning on random trials. *Journal of Mathematical Psychology,* 1964, **1**, 336–350.

Novinski, L. S. Part-whole and whole-part free recall learning. *Journal of Verbal Learning and Verbal Behavior,* 1969, **8**, 152–154.

Novinski, L. S. A reexamination of the part/whole effect in free recall. *Journal of Verbal Learning and Verbal Behavior,* 1972, **11**, 228–233.

Noyd, D. E. Proactive and intrastimulus interference in short-term memory for two-, three-, and five-word stimuli. Paper presented at the meeting of the Western Psychological Association, Honolulu, Hawaii, 1965.

Ogilvie, J. C., & Creelman, C. D. Maximum likelihood estimations of receiver operating characteristic curve parameters. *Journal of Mathematical Psychology,* 1968, **5**, 377–391.

Okada, R. Decision latencies in short-term recognition memory. *Journal of Experimental Psychology,* 1971, **90**, 27–32.

Olson, G. M. Learning and retention in a continuous recognition task. *Journal of Experimental Psychology,* 1969, **81**, 381–384.

Ornstein, P. A. Role of prior-list organization in a free recall transfer task. *Journal of Experimental Psychology,* 1970, **86**, 32–37.

Osgood, C. E. *Method and theory in experimental psychology.* New York: Oxford University Press, 1953.

Paivio, A. Mental imagery in associative learning and memory. *Psychological Review,* 1969, **76**, 241–263.

Paivio, A. *Imagery and verbal processes.* New York: Holt, Rinehart and Winston, 1971.

Paivio, A., & Csapo, K. Concrete image and verbal memory codes. *Journal of Experimental Psychology,* 1969, **80**, 279–285.

Paivio, A., Yuille, J. C., & Madigan, S. A. Concreteness, imagery, and meaningfulness values for 925 nouns. *Journal of Experimental Psychology,* 1968, **76** (1, Pt. 2).

Palef, S. R. Some stages of information processing in a choice reaction-time task. *Perception & Psychophysics,* 1973, **13**, 41–44. (a)

Palef, S. R. On seeing and hearing simultaneously: Divided attention within and between modalities. Unpublished doctoral dissertation, University of Toronto, 1973. (b)

Palmer, S. E., & Ornstein, P. A. Role of rehearsal strategy in serial probed recall. *Journal of Experimental Psychology,* 1971, **88**, 60–66.

Parkinson, S. R. Short-term memory while shadowing: Multiple-item recall of visually and of aurally presented letters. *Journal of Experimental Psychology,* 1972, **92**, 256–265.

Parkinson, S. R., Parks, T. E., & Kroll, N. E. A. Visual and auditory short-term memory: Effects of phonemically similar auditory shadow material during the retention interval. *Journal of Experimental Psychology*, 1971, **87**, 274–280.

Parks, T. E. Signal-detectability theory of recognition memory performance. *Psychological Review*, 1966, **73**, 44–58.

Patterson, K. E. Some characteristics of retrieval limitation in long-term memory. *Journal of Verbal Learning and Verbal Behavior*, 1972, **11**, 685–691.

Patterson, K. E., Meltzer, R. H., & Mandler, G. Inter-response times in categorized free recall. *Journal of Verbal Learning and Verbal Behavior*, 1971, **10**, 417–426.

Penfield, W., & Perot, P. The brain's record of auditory and visual experience: A final summary and discussion. *Brain*, 1963, **86**, 595–696.

Penney, C. G. Dichotic listening and sequential associations in auditory short-term memory. *Journal of Experimental Psychology*, 1974, in press.

Peterson, L. R. Search and judgment in memory. In B. Kleinmuntz (Ed.), *Concepts and the structure of memory*, New York: Wiley, 1967. Pp. 153–180.

Peterson, L. R., & Gentile, A. Proactive interference as a function of time between tests. *Journal of Experimental Psychology*, 1965, **70**, 473–478.

Peterson, L. R., Hillner, K., & Saltzman, D. Time between pairings and short-term retention. *Journal of Experimental Psychology*, 1962, **64**, 550–551.

Peterson, L. R., & Johnson, S. T. Some effects of minimizing articulation on short-term retention. *Journal of Verbal Learning and Verbal Behavior*, 1971, **10**, 346–354.

Peterson, L. R., Johnson, S. T., & Coatney, R. The effect of repeated occurrences on judgments of recency. *Journal of Verbal Learning and Verbal Behavior*, 1969, **8**, 591–596.

Peterson, L. R., & Kroener, S. Dichotic stimulation and retention. *Journal of Experimental Psychology*, 1964, **68**, 125–130.

Peterson, L. R., & Peterson, M. J. Short-term retention of individual verbal items. *Journal of Experimental Psychology*, 1959, **58**, 193–198.

Peterson, L. R., & Peterson, M. J. Minimal paired-associate learning. *Journal of Experimental Psychology*, 1962, **63**, 521–527.

Peterson, L. R., Saltzman, D., Hillner, K., & Land V. Recency and frequency in paired-associate learning. *Journal of Experimental Psychology*, 1962, **63**, 396–403.

Peterson, L. R., Wampler, R., Kirkpatrick, M., & Saltzman, D. Effect of spacing presentations on retention of a paired associate over short intervals. *Journal of Experimental Psychology*, 1963, **66**, 206–209.

Petrusic, W. M., & Dillon, R. F. Proactive interference in short-term recognition and recall memory. *Journal of Experimental Psychology*, 1972, **95**, 412–418.

Phillips, J. L., Shiffrin, R. M., & Atkinson, R. C. The effects of list length on short-term memory. *Journal of Verbal Learning and Verbal Behavior*, 1967, **6**, 303–311.

Phillips, W. A., & Baddeley, A. D. Reaction time and short-term visual memory. *Psychonomic Science*, 1971, **22**, 73–74.

Pollack, I., Johnson, L. B., & Knaff, P. R. Running memory span. *Journal of Experimental Psychology*, 1959, **57**, 137–146.

Pollio, H. R., Kasschau, R. A., & DeNise, H. E. Associative structure and the temporal characteristics of free recall. *Journal of Experimental Psychology*, 1968, **76**, 190–197.

Posner, M. I. Immediate memory in sequential tasks. *Psychological Bulletin*, 1963, **60**, 333–349.

Posner, M. I. Rate of presentation and order of recall in immediate memory. *British Journal of Psychology*, 1964, **55**, 303–306. (a)

Posner, M. I. Information reduction in the analysis of sequential tasks. *Psychological Review*, 1964, **71**, 491–504. (b)

Posner, M. I. Short-term memory systems in human information processing. *Acta Psychologica*, 1967, **27**, 267–284.

Posner, M. I. Abstraction and the process of recognition. In G. H. Bower & J. T. Spence (Eds.), *The psychology of learning and motivation: Advances in research and theory*. Vol. 3. New York: Academic Press, 1969. Pp. 43–100.

Posner, M. I., Boies, S. J., Eichelman, W. H., & Taylor, R. L. Retention of visual and name codes of single letters. *Journal of Experimental Psychology Monograph Supplement*, 1969, **79**, Part 2. Pp. 1–16.

Posner, M. I., & Konick, A. F. On the role of interference in short-term retention. *Journal of Experimental Psychology*, 1966, **72**, 221–231.

Posner, M. I., & Rossman, E. Effect of size and location of informational transforms upon short-term retention. *Journal of Experimental Psychology*, 1965, **70**, 496–505.

Postman, L. The present status of interference theory. In C. N. Cofer (Ed.), *Verbal learning and verbal behavior*. New York: McGraw-Hill, 1961. Pp. 152–179.

Postman, L. One-trial learning. In C. N. Cofer & B. S. Musgrave (Eds.), *Verbal behavior and learning*. New York: McGraw-Hill, 1963, Pp. 295–321.

Postman, L. Organization and interference. *Psychological Review*, 1971, **78**, 290–302.

Postman, L. A pragmatic view of organization theory. In E. Tulving & W. Donaldson (Eds.), *Organization of memory*. New York: Academic Press, 1972. Pp. 3–48.

Postman, L., & Kaplan, H. L. Reaction time as a measure of retroactive inhibition. *Journal of Experimental Psychology*, 1947, **37**, 136–145.

Postman, L., & Phillips, L. W. Short-term temporal changes in free recall. *Quarterly Journal of Experimental Psychology*, 1965, **17**, 132–138.

Postman, L., & Stark, K. Role of response availability in transfer and interference. *Journal of Experimental Psychology*, 1969, **79**, 168–177.

Postman, L., & Stark, K. On the measurement of retroactive inhibition in the A–B, A–D paradigm by the multiple-choice method: Reply to Merryman. *Journal of Verbal Learning and Verbal Behavior*, 1972, **11**, 465–473.

Postman, L., Stark, K., & Fraser, J. Temporal changes in interference. *Journal of Verbal Learning and Verbal Behavior*, 1968, **7**, 672–694.

Postman, L., & Underwood, B. J. Critical issues in interference theory. *Memory & Cognition*, 1973, **1**, 19–40.

Postman, L., & Warren, L. Test of the total-time hypothesis in free-recall learning. *Journal of Experimental Psychology*, 1972, **96**, 176–183.

Potter, M. C., & Levy, E. I. Recognition memory for a rapid sequence of pictures. *Journal of Experimental Psychology*, 1969, **81**, 10–15.

Potts, G. R. Distance from a massed double-presentation or blank trial as a factor in paired-associate list learning. *Journal of Verbal Learning and Verbal Behavior*, 1972, **11**, 375–386.

Puff, C. R. Role of clustering in free recall. *Journal of Experimental Psychology*, 1970, **86**, 384–386.

Puff, C. R. Temporal properties of organization in recall of unrelated words. *Journal of Experimental Psychology*, 1972, **92**, 225–231.

Purcell, D. G., Stewart, A. L., & Dember, W. N. Backward masking: Facilitation through increased target-field luminance and duration. *Psychonomic Science*, 1969, **15**, 87–88.

Pylyshyn, Z. W. What the mind's eye tells the mind's brain: A critique of mental imagery. *Psychological Bulletin*, 1973, **80**, 1–24.

Raphael, B. SIR: A computer program for semantic information retrieval. In M. Minsky (Ed.), *Semantic Information Processing*. Cambridge, Mass.: MIT Press, 1968. Pp. 33–145.

Raser, G. A. False recognition as a function of encoding dimension and lag. *Journal of Experimental Psychology*, 1972, **93**, 333–337. (a)

Raser, G. A. Recoding of semantic and acoustic information in short-term memory. *Journal of Verbal Learning and Verbal Behavior*, 1972, **11**, 692–697. (b)

Raymond, B. Short-term storage and long-term storage in free recall. *Journal of Verbal Learning and Verbal Behavior*, 1969, **8**, 567–574.

Reid, L. S., Lloyd, K. E., Brackett, H. R., & Hawkins, W. F. Short-term retention as a function of average storage load and average load reduction. *Journal of Experimental Psychology*, 1961, **62**, 518–522.

Reitman, J. S. Mechanisms of forgetting in short-term memory. *Cognitive Psychology*, 1971, **2**, 185–195.

Reitman, J. S., & Bower, G. H. Storage and later recognition of exemplars of concepts. *Cognitive Psychology*, 1973, **4**, 194–206.

Restle, F. Significance of all-or-none learning. *Psychological Bulletin,* 1965, **64**, 313–325.

Restle, F., & Greeno, J. G. *Introduction to mathematical psychology.* Reading: Addison-Wesley, 1970.

Rips, L. R., Shoben, E. J., & Smith, E. E. Semantic distance and the verification of semantic relations. *Journal of Verbal Learning and Verbal Behavior,* 1973, **12**, 1–20.

Roberts, W. A. The priority of recall of new items in transfer from part-list learning to whole-list learning. *Journal of Verbal Learning and Verbal Behavior,* 1969, **8**, 645–652.

Roberts, W. A. Free recall of word lists varying in length and rate of presentation: A test of total-time hypotheses. *Journal of Experimental Psychology,* 1972, **92**, 365–372.

Robinson, E. S. *Association theory to-day.* New York: Century, 1932. (Reprinted by Hafner Publishing Company, 1964.)

Rock, I. The role of repetition in associative learning. *American Journal of Psychology,* 1957, **70**, 186–193.

Rock, I. A neglected aspect of the problem of recall: The Höffding function. In J. Scher (Ed.), *Theories of the mind.* New York: Free Press, 1962. Pp. 645–659.

Roenker, D. L., Thompson, C. P., & Brown, S. C. Comparison of measures for the estimation of clustering in free recall. *Psychological Bulletin,* 1971, **76**, 45–48.

Rosner, S. R. The effects of presentation and recall trials on organization in multitrial free recall. *Journal of Verbal Learning and Verbal Behavior,* 1970, **9**, 69–74.

Rumelhart, D. E. The effects of interpresentation intervals on performance in a continuous paired-associate task. Technical Report Number 116, Mathematical Studies in the Social Sciences, Stanford University, 1967.

Rumelhart, D. E., Lindsay, P. H., & Norman, D. A. A process model for long-term memory. In E. Tulving & W. Donaldson (Eds.), *Organization of memory.* New York: Academic Press, 1972. Pp. 197–245.

Rundus, D. Analysis of rehearsal processes in free recall. *Journal of Experimental Psychology,* 1971, **89**, 63–77.

Rundus, D. Negative effects of using list items as recall cues. *Journal of Verbal Learning and Verbal Behavior,* 1973, **12**, 43–50.

Rundus, D., & Atkinson, R. C. Rehearsal processes in free recall: A procedure for direct observation. *Journal of Verbal Learning and Verbal Behavior,* 1970, **9**, 99–105.

Rundus, D., Loftus, G. R., & Atkinson, R. C. Immediate free recall and three-week delayed recognition. *Journal of Verbal Learning and Verbal Behavior,* 1970, **9**, 684–688.

Saltz, E. *The cognitive bases of human learning.* Homewood, Ill.: Dorsey, 1971.

Sampson, H. Immediate memory and simultaneous visual stimulation. *Quarterly Journal of Experimental Psychology,* 1964, **16**, 1–10.

Sampson, H., & Spong, P. Handedness, eye dominance and immediate memory. *Quarterly Journal of Experimental Psychology,* 1961, **13**, 173–180. (a)

Sampson, H., & Spong, P. Binocular fixation and immediate memory. *British Journal of Psychology,* 1961, **52**, 239–248. (b)

Sanders, A. F. Rehearsal and recall in immediate memory. *Ergonomics,* 1961, **4**, 25–34.

Savin, H. B. On the successive perception of simultaneous stimuli. *Perception & Psychophysics,* 1967, **2**, 479–482.

Savin, H. B., & Bever, T. G. The nonperceptual reality of the phoneme. *Journal of Verbal Learning and Verbal Behavior,* 1970, **9**, 295–302.

Scarborough, D. L. Stimulus modality effects on forgetting in short-term memory. *Journal of Experimental Psychology,* 1972, **95**, 285–289.

Schaub, G. R., & Lindley, R. H. Effects of subject-generated recoding cues on short-term memory. *Journal of Experimental Psychology,* 1964, **68**, 171–175.

Schmidt, R. A. Anticipation and timing in human motor performance. *Psychological Bulletin,* 1968, **70**, 631–646.

Schulz, L. S. Effects of high-priority events on recall and recognition of other events. *Journal of Verbal Learning and Verbal Behavior,* 1971, **10**, 322–330.

Schwartz, F., & Rouse, R. O. The activation and recovery of associations. *Psychological Issues,* 1961,

3 (1) (Monogr. 9).

Severin, F. T., & Rigby, M. K. Influence of digit grouping on memory for telephone numbers. *Journal of Applied Psychology*, 1963, **47**, 117–119.

Shaffer, W. O., & Shiffrin, R. M. Rehearsal and storage of visual information. *Journal of Experimental Psychology*, 1972, **92**, 292–296.

Shaughnessy, J. J., Zimmerman, J., & Underwood, B. J. Further evidence on the MP–DP effect in free-recall learning. *Journal of Verbal Learning and Verbal Behavior*, 1972, **11**, 1–12.

Shepard, R. N. Recognition memory for words, sentences, and pictures. *Journal of Verbal Learning and Verbal Behavior*, 1967, **6**, 156–163.

Shepard, R. M., & Chang, J. Forced-choice tests of recognition memory under steady-state conditions. *Journal of Verbal Learning and Verbal Behavior*, 1963, **2**, 93–101.

Shepard, R. N., & Teghtsoonian, M. Retention of information under conditions approaching a steady state. *Journal of Experimental Psychology*, 1961, **62**, 302–309.

Sherrington, C. *Man on his nature.* Garden City, N.Y.: Doubleday, 1953.

Shiffrin, R. M. Memory search. In D. A. Norman (Ed.), *Models of human memory.* New York: Academic Press, 1970. Pp. 375–447. (a)

Shiffrin, R. M. Forgetting: Trace erosion or retrieval failure? *Science*, 1970, **168**, 1601–1603. (b)

Shiffrin, R. M., & Schneider, W. An expectancy model for memory scanning. Technical Report No. 72-9, Department of Psychology, Indiana University, 1972.

Shuell, T. J. Clustering and organization in free recall. *Psychological Bulletin*, 1969, **72**, 353–374.

Shulman, H. G. Encoding and retention of semantic and phonemic information in short-term memory. *Journal of Verbal Learning and Verbal Behavior*, 1970, **9**, 499–508.

Shulman, H. G. Similarity effects in short-term memory. *Psychological Bulletin*, 1971, **75**, 399–415.

Shulman, H. G. Semantic confusion errors in short-term memory. *Journal of Verbal Learning and Verbal Behavior*, 1972, **11**, 221–227.

Siegel, J. A., & Siegel, W. Absolute judgment and paired-associate learning: Kissing cousins or identical twins? *Psychological Review*, 1972, **79**, 300–316.

Simon, H. A., & Feigenbaum, E. A. An information-processing theory of some effects of similarity, familiarization, and meaningfulness in verbal learning. *Journal of Verbal Learning and Verbal Behavior*, 1964, **3**, 385–396.

Simpson, P. J. High-speed memory-scanning: Stability and generality. *Journal of Experimental Psychology*, 1972, **96**, 239–246.

Slak, S. Phonemic recoding of digital information. *Journal of Experimental Psychology*, 1970, **86**, 398–406.

Slamecka, N. J. Differentiation versus unlearning of verbal associations. *Journal of Experimental Psychology*, 1966, **71**, 822–828.

Slamecka, N. J. Recall and recognition in list-discrimination tasks as a function of the number of alternatives. *Journal of Experimental Psychology*, 1967, **74**, 187–192. (a)

Slamecka, N. J. Serial learning and order information. *Journal of Experimental Psychology*, 1967, **74**, 62–66. (b)

Slamecka, N. J. An examination of trace storage in free recall. *Journal of Experimental Psychology*, 1968, **76**, 504–513.

Slamecka, N. J. A temporal interpretation of some recall phenomena. *Psychological Review*, 1969, **76**, 492–503. (a)

Slamecka, N. J. Testing for associative storage in multitrial free recall. *Journal of Experimental Psychology*, 1969, **81**, 557–560. (b)

Slamecka, N. J. The question of associative growth in the learning of categorized material. *Journal of Verbal Learning and Verbal Behavior*, 1972, **11**, 324–332.

Slamecka, N. J., Moore, T., & Carey, S. Part-to-whole transfer and its relation to organization theory. *Journal of Verbal Learning and Verbal Behavior*, 1972, **11**, 73–82.

Smith, A. D. Output interference and organized recall from long-term memory. *Journal of Verbal Learning and Verbal Behavior*, 1971, **10**, 400–408.

Smith, E. E., Barresi, J., & Gross, A. E. Imaginal versus verbal coding and the primary-secondary memory distinction. *Journal of Verbal Learning and Verbal Behavior*, 1971, **10**, 597–603.

Smith, F. *Understanding reading*. New York: Holt, Rinehart and Winston, 1971.

Smith, M. C. Theories of the psychological refractory period. *Psychological Bulletin*, 1967, **67**, 202–213.

Sperling, G. The information available in brief visual presentations. *Psychological Monographs*, 1960, **74** (11, Whole No. 498).

Sperling, G. A model for visual memory tasks. *Human Factors*, 1963, **5**, 19–31.

Sperling, G. Successive approximations to a model for short term memory. *Acta Psychologica*, 1967, **27**, 285–292.

Sperling, G., & Speelman, R. G. Acoustic similarity and auditory short-term memory: Experiments and a model. In D. A. Norman (Ed.), *Models of human memory*. New York: Academic Press, 1970. Pp. 151–202.

Sperry, R. W. Hemisphere deconnection and unity in conscious awareness. *American Psychologist*, 1968, **23**, 723–733.

Sternberg, S. High-speed scanning in human memory. *Science*, 1966, **153**, 652–654.

Sternberg, S. Memory-scanning: Mental processes revealed by reaction-time experiments. *American Scientist*, 1969, **57**, 421–457. (a)

Sternberg, S. The discovery of processing stages: Extensions of Donders' method. *Acta Psychologica*, 1969, **30**, 276–315. (b)

Stowe, A. N., Harris, W. P., & Hampton, D. B. Signal and context components of word-recognition behavior. *Journal of the Acoustical Society*, 1963, **35**, 639–644.

Strong, E. K. The effect of length of series upon recognition memory. *Psychological Review*, 1912, **19**, 447–462.

Stroop, J. R. Studies of interference in serial verbal reactions. *Journal of Experimental Psychology*, 1935, **18**, 643–662.

Suboski, M. D., Pappas, B. A., & Murray, D. J. Confidence ratings in recall paired-associates learning. *Psychonomic Science*, 1966, **5**, 147–148. (a)

Suboski, M. D., Pappas, B. A., & Murray, D. J. Confidence ratings in recall paired associates: The RTT paradigm. *Psychonomic Science*, 1966, **5**, 315–316. (b)

Sumby, W. H. Word frequency and serial position effects. *Journal of Verbal Learning and Verbal Behavior*, 1963, **1**, 443–450.

Suppes, P., & Ginsberg, R. A fundamental property of all-or-none models, binomial distribution of responses prior to conditioning, with application to concept formation in children. *Psychological Review*, 1963, **70**, 139–161.

Suppes, P., Groen, G., & Schlag-Rey, M. A model for response latency in paired-associate learning. *Journal of Mathematical Psychology*, 1966, **3**, 99–128.

Swets, J. A. (Ed.) *Signal detection and recognition by human observers: Contemporary readings*. New York: Wiley, 1964.

Taylor, D. H. Latency components in two-choice responding. *Journal of Experimental Psychology*, 1966, **72**, 481–487.

Teghtsoonian, M., & Teghtsoonian, R. Transitory effect of number of alternatives on performance in a recognition task. *Journal of Experimental Psychology*, 1970, **86**, 467–468.

Tell, P. M. The role of certain acoustic and semantic factors at short and long retention intervals. *Journal of Verbal Learning and Verbal Behavior*, 1972, **11**, 455–464.

Ternes, W., & Yuille, J. C. Words and pictures in an STM task. *Journal of Experimental Psychology*, 1972, **96**, 78–86.

Theios, J., Smith, P. G., Haviland, S. E., Traupmann, J., & Moy, M. C. Memory scanning as a serial, self-terminating process. *Journal of Experimental Psychology*, 1973, **97**, 323–336.

Thomas, E. A. C., & Legge, D. Probability matching as a basis for detection and recognition decisions. *Psychological Review*, 1970, **77**, 65–72.

Thompson, C. P., & Gardiner, J. M. Negative recency in initial filled-delay free recall. Paper presented at the Psychonomic Society Meeting, St. Louis, Missouri, November, 1972.

Thomson, D. M. Context effects in recognition memory. *Journal of Verbal Learning and Verbal Behavior,* 1972, **11**, 497–511.

Thorndike, E. L., & Lorge, I. *The teacher's word book of 30,000 words.* New York: Teachers College, Columbia University, Bureau of Publications, 1944.

Thurstone, L. L. The relation between learning time and length of task. *Psychological Review,* 1930, **37**, 44–58. (a)

Thurstone, L. L. The learning function. *Journal of General Psychology,* 1930, **3**, 469–493. (b)

Townsend, J. T. A note on the identifiability of parallel and serial processes. *Perception & Psychophysics,* 1971, **10**, 161–163.

Treisman, A. M. Monitoring and storage of irrelevant messages in selective attention. *Journal of Verbal Learning and Verbal Behavior,* 1964, **3**, 449–459.

Treisman, A. M. Strategies and models of selective attention. *Psychological Review,* 1969, **76**, 282–299.

Tulving, E. Subjective organization in free recall of "unrelated" words. *Psychological Review,* 1962, **69**, 344–354.

Tulving, E. Intratrial and intertrial retention: Notes towards a theory of free recall verbal learning. *Psychological Review,* 1964, **71**, 219–237.

Tulving, E. Subjective organization and effects of repetition in multi-trial free-recall learning. *Journal of Verbal Learning and Verbal Behavior,* 1966, **5**, 193–197.

Tulving, E. The effects of presentation and recall of material in free-recall learning. *Journal of Verbal Learning and Verbal Behavior,* 1967, **6**, 175–184.

Tulving, E. Theoretical issues in free recall. In T. R. Dixon & D. L. Horton (Eds.), *Verbal behavior and general behavior theory.* Englewood Cliffs: Prentice-Hall, 1968. Pp. 2–36.

Tulving, E. Retrograde amnesia in free recall. *Science,* 1969, **164**, 88–90.

Tulving, E. Free-recall learning of words in variable intratrial context. Paper presented at the Psychonomic Society Meeting, San Antonio, Texas, November, 1970.

Tulving, E. Episodic and semantic memory. In E. Tulving & W. Donaldson (Eds.), *Organization of memory.* New York: Academic Press, 1972. Pp. 381–403.

Tulving, E., & Arbuckle, T. Y. Sources of intratrial interference in immediate recall of paired associates. *Journal of Verbal Learning and Verbal Behavior,* 1963, **1**, 321–334.

Tulving, E., & Arbuckle, T. Y. Input and output interference in short-term associative memory. *Journal of Experimental Psychology,* 1966, **72**, 145–150.

Tulving, E., & Colotla, V. A. Free recall of trilingual lists. *Cognitive Psychology,* 1970, **1**, 86–98.

Tulving, E., & Hastie, R. Inhibition effects of intralist repetition in free recall. *Journal of Experimental Psychology,* 1972, **92**, 297–304.

Tulving, E., & Osler, S. Transfer effects in whole-part free recall learning. *Canadian Journal of Psychology,* 1967, **21**, 253–262.

Tulving, E., & Osler, S. Effectiveness of retrieval cues in memory for words. *Journal of Experimental Psychology,* 1968, **77**, 593–601.

Tulving, E., & Patkau, J. E. Concurrent effects of contextual constraint and word frequency on immediate recall and learning of verbal material. *Canadian Journal of Psychology,* 1962, **16**, 83–95.

Tulving, E., & Patterson, R. D. Functional units and retrieval processes in free recall. *Journal of Experimental Psychology,* 1968, **77**, 239–248.

Tulving, E., & Pearlstone, Z. Availability versus accessibility of information in memory for words. *Journal of Verbal Learning and Verbal Behavior,* 1966, **5**, 381–391.

Tulving, E., & Psotka, J. Retroactive inhibition in free recall: Inaccessibility of information available in the memory store. *Journal of Experimental Psychology,* 1971, **87**, 1–8.

Tulving, E., & Thomson, D. M. Retrieval processes in recognition memory: Effects of associative context. *Journal of Experimental Psychology,* 1971, **87**, 116–124.

Tulving, E., & Thomson, D. M. Encoding specificity and retrieval processes in episodic memory. *Psychological Review,* 1973, **80**, 352–373.

Turvey, M. T., & Wittlinger, R. P. Attenuation of proactive interference in short-term memory as a function of cueing to forget. *Journal of Experimental Psychology,* 1969, **80,** 295–298.

Tversky, B. Pictorial and verbal encoding in a short-term memory task. *Perception & Psychophysics,* 1969, **6,** 225–233.

Underwood, B. J. Retroactive and proactive inhibition after five and forty-eight hours. *Journal of Experimental Psychology,* 1948, **38,** 29–38.

Underwood, B. J. Interference and forgetting. *Psychological Review,* 1957, **64,** 49–60.

Underwood, B. J. Stimulus selection in verbal learning. In C. N. Cofer & B. S. Musgrave (Eds.), *Verbal behavior and learning.* New York: McGraw-Hill, 1963. Pp. 33–48.

Underwood, B. J. False recognition produced by implicit verbal responses. *Journal of Experimental Psychology,* 1965, **70,** 122–129.

Underwood, B. J. *Experimental psychology.* (2nd ed.) New York: Appleton-Century-Crofts, 1966.

Underwood, B. J. Attributes of memory. *Psychological Review,* 1969, **76,** 559–573. (a)

Underwood, B. J. Some correlates of item repetition in free-recall learning. *Journal of Verbal Learning and Verbal Behavior,* 1969, **8,** 83–94. (b)

Underwood, B. J. A breakdown of the total-time law in free-recall learning. *Journal of Verbal Learning and Verbal Behavior,* 1970, **9,** 573–580.

Underwood, B. J. Are we overloading memory? In A. W. Melton & E. Martin (Eds.), *Coding processes in human memory.* Washington, D.C.: Winston, 1972. Pp. 1–23.

Underwood, B. J., & Ekstrand, B. R. An analysis of some shortcomings in the interference theory of forgetting. *Psychological Review,* 1966, **73,** 540–549.

Underwood, B. J., & Erlebacher, A. H. Studies of coding in verbal learning. *Psychological Monographs,* 1965, **79** (13, Whole No. 606).

Underwood, B. J., & Freund, J. S. Relative frequency judgments and verbal discrimination learning. *Journal of Experimental Psychology,* 1970, **83,** 279–285. (a)

Underwood, B. J., & Freund, J. S. Word frequency and short-term recognition memory. *American Journal of Psychology,* 1970, **83,** 343–351. (b)

Underwood, B. J., & Keppel, G. One-trial learning? *Journal of Verbal Learning and Verbal Behavior,* 1962, **1,** 1–13.

Underwood, B. J., & Postman, L. Extraexperimental sources of interference in forgetting. *Psychological Review,* 1960, **67,** 73–95.

Underwood, B. J., & Schulz, R. W. *Meaningfulness and verbal learning.* Philadelphia: Lippincott, 1960.

Underwood, B. J., & Zimmerman, J. Serial retention as a function of hierarchical structure. *Journal of Experimental Psychology,* 1973, **99,** 236–242.

Underwood, B. J., Zimmerman, J., & Freund, J. S. Retention of frequency information with observations on recognition and recall. *Journal of Experimental Psychology,* 1971, **87,** 149–162.

von Neumann, J. *The computer and the brain.* New Haven: Yale University Press, 1958.

Voss, J. F. Serial acquisition as a function of stage of learning. *Journal of Experimental Psychology,* 1969, **79,** 220–225.

Voss, J. F. On the relationship of associative and organization processes. In E. Tulving & W. Donaldson (Eds.), *Organization of memory.* New York: Academic Press, 1972. Pp. 167–194.

Walker, J. H. Pronounceability effects on word-nonword encoding in categorization and recognition tasks. *Journal of Experimental Psychology,* 1973, **99,** 318–322.

Walker, K. D. Some tests of the two-store hypothesis. Unpublished master's thesis, University of Toronto, 1967.

Wallace, W. H., Turner, S. H., & Perkins, C. C. Preliminary studies of human information storage. Signal Corps Project 132C, Institute for Cooperative Research, University of Pennsylvania, Philadelphia, Pennsylvania, 1957.

Wallach, H., & Averbach, E. On memory modalities. *American Journal of Psychology,* 1955, **68,** 249–257.

Ward, L. B. Reminiscence and rote learning. *Psychological Monographs,* 1937, **49** (4, Whole No. 220).

Warrington, E. K. Neurological disorders of memory. *British Medical Bulletin*, 1971, **27**, 243–247.

Warrington, E. K., & Shallice, T. The selective impairment of auditory verbal short-term memory. *Brain*, 1969, **92**, 885–896.

Warrington, E. K., & Shallice, T. Neuropsychological evidence of visual storage in short-term memory tasks. *Quarterly Journal of Experimental Psychology*, 1972, **24**, 30–40.

Watkins, M. J. Locus of the modality effect in free recall. *Journal of Verbal Learning and Verbal Behavior*, 1972, **11**, 644–648.

Waugh, N. C. The effect of intralist repetition on free recall. *Journal of Verbal Learning and Verbal Behavior*, 1962, **1**, 95–99.

Waugh, N. C. Immediate memory as a function of repetition. *Journal of Verbal Learning and Verbal Behavior*, 1963, **2**, 107–112.

Waugh, N. C. Presentation time and free recall. *Journal of Experimental Psychology*, 1967, **73**, 39–44.

Waugh, N. C. The effect of recency and repetition on recall latencies. *Acta Psychologica*, 1969, **30**, 115–125.

Waugh, N. C. Associative symmetry and recall latencies: A distinction between learning and performance. *Acta Psychologica*, 1970, **33**, 326–337. (a)

Waugh, N. C. On the effective duration of a repeated word. *Journal of Verbal Learning and Verbal Behavior*, 1970, **9**, 587–595. (b)

Waugh, N. C. Retention as an active process. *Journal of Verbal Learning and Verbal Behavior*, 1972, **11**, 129–140.

Waugh, N. C., & Anders, T. R. Free recall of very slowly presented items. *Journal of Verbal Learning and Verbal Behavior*, 1969, **8**, 838–841.

Waugh, N. C., & Norman, D. A. Primary memory. *Psychological Review*, 1965, **72**, 89–104.

Welford, A. T. The measurement of sensory-motor performance: Survey and reappraisal of twelve years' progress. *Ergonomics*, 1960, **3**, 189–230.

Wells, J. E. Encoding and memory for verbal and pictorial stimuli. *Quarterly Journal of Experimental Psychology*, 1972, **24**, 242–252.

Wells, J. E. Words and pictures as distinct encoding categories in short-term memory. *Journal of Experimental Psychology*, 1973, **97**, 394–396.

Wichawut, C., & Martin, E. Independence of A–B and A–C associations in retroaction. *Journal of Verbal Learning and Verbal Behavior*, 1971, **10**, 316–321.

Wickelgren, W. A. Size of rehearsal group and short-term memory. *Journal of Experimental Psychology*, 1964, **68**, 413–419.

Wickelgren, W. A. Acoustic similarity and intrusion errors in short-term memory. *Journal of Experimental Psychology*, 1965, **70**, 102–108. (a)

Wickelgren, W. A. Short-term memory for repeated and non-repeated items. *Quarterly Journal of Experimental Psychology*, 1965, **17**, 14–25. (b)

Wickelgren, W. A. Distinctive features and errors in short-term memory for English vowels. *Journal of Acoustical Society of America*, 1965, **38**, 583–588. (c)

Wickelgren, W. A. Acoustic similarity and retroactive interference in short-term memory. *Journal of Verbal Learning and Verbal Behavior*, 1965, **4**, 53–61. (d)

Wickelgren, W. A. Short-term memory for phonemically similar lists. *American Journal of Psychology*, 1965, **78**, 567–574. (e)

Wickelgren, W. A. Associative intrusions in short-term recall. *Journal of Experimental Psychology*, 1966, **72**, 853–858. (a)

Wickelgren, W. A. Distinctive features and errors in short-term memory for English consonants. *Journal of the Acoustical Society of America*, 1966, **39**, 388–398. (b)

Wickelgren, W. A. Phonemic similarity and interference in short-term memory for single letters. *Journal of Experimental Psychology*, 1966, **71**, 396–404. (c)

Wickelgren, W. A. Rehearsal grouping and hierarchical organization of serial position cues in short-term memory. *Quarterly Journal of Experimental Psychology*, 1967, **19**, 97–102.

Wickelgren, W. A. Sparing of short-term memory in an amnesia patient: Implications for strength theory of memory. *Neuropsychologia*, 1968, **6**, 235–244.

Wickelgren, W. A. Context-sensitive coding, associative memory, and serial order in (speech) behavior. *Psychological Review*, 1969, **76**, 1–15. (a)

Wickelgren, W. A. Auditory or articulatory coding in verbal short-term memory. *Psychological Review*, 1969, **76**, 232–235. (b)

Wickelgren, W. A. Multitrace strength theory. In D. A. Norman (Ed.), *Models of human memory*. New York: Academic Press, 1970. (a)

Wickelgren, W. A. Time, interference, and rate of presentation in short-term recognition memory for items. *Journal of Mathematical Psychology*, 1970, **7**, 219–235. (b)

Wickelgren, W. A., & Norman, D. A. Strength models and serial position in short-term recognition memory. *Journal of Mathematical Psychology*, 1966, **3**, 316–347.

Wickens, D. D. Encoding categories of words: An empirical approach to meaning. *Psychological Review*, 1970, **77**, 1–15.

Wickens, D. D. Characteristics of word encoding. In A. W. Melton & E. Martin (Eds.), *Coding processes in human memory*. Washington, D.C.: Winston, 1972. Pp. 191–215.

Wickens, D. D., Born, D. G., & Allen, C. K. Proactive inhibition and item similarity in short-term memory. *Journal of Verbal Learning and Verbal Behavior*, 1963, **2**, 440–445.

Wicker, F. W. On the locus of picture-word differences in paired-associate learning. *Journal of Verbal Learning and Verbal Behavior*, 1970, **9**, 52–57.

Wilson, E. O. The prospects for a unified sociobiology. *American Scientist*, 1971, **59**, 400–403.

Wingfield, A. Effects of serial position and set size in auditory recognition memory. *Memory & Cognition*, 1973, **1**, 53–55.

Winograd, E. List differentiation as a function of frequency and retention interval. *Journal of Experimental Psychology Monograph Supplement*, 1968, **76** (February, Pt. 2). Pp. 1–18.

Winograd, E., & Conn, C. P. Evidence from recognition memory for specific encoding of unmodified homographs. *Journal of Verbal Learning and Verbal Behavior*, 1971, **10**, 702–706.

Winograd, E., & Raines, S. R. Semantic and temporal variation in recognition memory. *Journal of Verbal Learning and Verbal Behavior*, 1972, **11**, 114–119.

Winograd, T. Procedures as a representation for data in a computer program for understanding natural language. Massachusetts Institute of Technology Artificial Intelligence Laboratory Project MAC TR-84, 1971.

Wishner, J., Shipley, T. E., & Hurvich, M. S. The serial position curve as a function of organization. *American Journal of Psychology*, 1957, **70**, 258–262.

Wolff, P. Trace quality in the temporal ordering of events. *Perceptual and Motor Skills*, 1966, **22**, 283–286.

Wolford, G. Function of distinct associations for paired-associate performance. *Psychological Review*, 1971, **78**, 303–313.

Wood, G. Retrieval cues and the accessibility of higher-order memory units in multitrial free recall. *Journal of Verbal Learning and Verbal Behavior*, 1969, **8**, 782–789.

Wood, G. Organizational processes and free recall. In E. Tulving & W. Donaldson (Eds.), *Organization of memory*. New York: Academic Press, 1972. Pp. 49–91.

Wood, G., & Clark, D. Instructions, ordering, and previous practice in free-recall learning. *Psychonomic Science*, 1969, **14**, 187–188.

Woodward, A. E., Jr. Continuity between serial memory and serial learning. *Journal of Experimental Psychology*, 1970, **85**, 90–94.

Woodward, A. E., Jr., & Bjork, R. A. Forgetting and remembering in free recall: Intentional and unintentional. *Journal of Experimental Psychology*, 1971, **89**, 109–116.

Woodward, A. E., Jr., & Murdock, B. B., Jr. Positional and sequential probes in serial learning. *Canadian Journal of Psychology*, 1968, **22**, 131–138.

Wooldridge, D. E. *The machinery of the brain*. New York: McGraw-Hill, 1963.

Yntema, D. B. Keeping track of several things at once. *Human Factors*, 1963, **5**, 7–17.

Yntema, D. B., & Mueser, G. A. Remembering the present state of a number of variables. *Journal of Experimental Psychology*, 1960, **60**, 18–22.

Yntema, D. B., & Schulman, G. M. Response selection in keeping track of several things at once. *Acta*

Psychologica, 1967, **27**, 316–324.

Yntema, D. B., & Trask, F. P. Recall as a search process. *Journal of Verbal Learning and Verbal Behavior,* 1963, **2**, 65–74.

Young, R. K. Serial learning. In T. R. Dixon & D. L. Horton (Eds.), *Verbal behavior and general behavior theory.* Englewood Cliffs: Prentice-Hall, 1968. Pp. 122–148.

INDEXES

AUTHOR INDEX

Numbers in italics refer to the pages on which the complete references are listed.

M

McCabe, L., 100, 113, 114, 115, *331*
McConkie, G. W., 113, *331*
McCormack, P. D., 64, 65, 66, *331*
McCreary, J. W., 145, *331*
McGaugh, J. L., 260, *331*
McGeoch, J. A., 6, 7, 82, 173, *331*
McGlaughlin, A., 185, *322, 331*
McGovern, J. B., 85, 111, *331*
McGuire, W. J., 285, *331*
Mackworth, J. F., 168, *331*
McLean, R. S., 178, *331*
McLeod, P. D., 250, *331*
Macnamara, J., 226, *331*
McNeill, D., 185, 291, *318*
McNulty, J. A., 61, *331*
Madigan, S. A., 59, 100, 113, 114, 115, 133, 241, 242, 243, 268, 298, *331, 336*
Madsen, M. C., 194, *331*
Mahler, W. A., 122, *313*
Mandler, G., 68, 69, 194, 199, 214, 215, 222, 223, 225, 250, 306, *331, 332, 337*
Mann, J. E., 59, 268, *332*
Margrain, S. A., 267, *332*
Markowitz, N., 184, *313*
Martin, E., 54, 55, 62, 87, 115, 286, *332, 344*
Martin, F. F., 150, *332*
Martin, J. E., 128, *330*
Massaro, D. W., 126, 203, *323, 332*
Mayzner, M. S., 194, *332*
Mead, R., 110, 211, *335*
Melton, A. W., 7, 12, 54, 55, 62, 67, 82, 144, 161, 164, 169, 172, 178, 230, 241, 242, 261, 293, 297, *321, 332*
Meltzer, R. H.,68, 222, 223, 225, 306, *337*
Merryman, C. T., 291, *332*
Metlay, W., 221, *328*
Meyer, D. E., 214, *332*
Miller, A., 76, 283, *321*
Miller, G. A., x, 37, 56, 91, 130, 145, 158, 159, 178, 183, 212, 242, 298, *332, 333*
Miller, N. E., 54, *322*
Millward, R. B., 121, 151, *333*
Milner, B., 266, *333*
Milner, P. M., 133, 195, *333*
Montague, W. E., 130, *313, 333*
Moore, T., 216, 255, *340*
Moray, N., 152, 156, 195, *333*
Morikawa, Y., 285, *333*

Morris, C. J., 102, *329*
Morton, J., 59, 70, 177, 268, 294, 311, *321, 333*
Moses, F. L., 36, 60, 61, *325*
Moss, S. M., 298, *333*
Mosteller, F., 93, 135, *319*
Mowbray, G. H., 156, 191, *333*
Moy, M. C., 76, 284, *341*
Mueser, G. A., 116, *345*
Murdock, B. B., Jr., 13, 27, 32, 34, 36, 42, 44, 45, 48, 49, 51, 52, 53, 56, 57, 58, 59, 60, 62, 65, 66, 71, 76, 77, 81, 91, 95, 97, 98, 99, 100, 101, 102, 105, 106, 107, 108, 109, 110, 111, 114, 117, 118, 119, 120, 121, 123, 125, 126, 127, 128, 133, 141, 143, 145, 146, 148, 157, 161, 162, 169, 171, 176, 178, 181, 184, 186, 189, 190, 194, 195, 200, 201, 202, 203, 205, 206, 207, 211, 218, 230, 234, 235, 237, 238, 239, 240, 243, 260, 262, 264, 265, 267, 268, 270, 278, 279, 281, 282, 284, 285, 288, 293, 298, 299, 301, 304, 305, 307, *314, 318, 319, 322, 330, 333, 334, 335, 345*
Murray, D. J., 120, 184, 264, *335, 341*
Myers, J. R., 301, *324*

N

Naylor, T. H., 150, *335*
Nazzaro, J. N., 269, *335*
Nazzaro, J. R., 269, *335*
Nedler, S. E., 179, *330*
Neimark, E. D., 38, 168, 264, *335*
Neisser, U., 2, 11, 38, *335*
Nelder, J. A., 110, 211, *335*
Nelson, D. L., 114, *335*
Nelson, R., 218, *325*
Nelson, T. O., 185, *335*
Nettleton, N. C., 299, *317*
Newton, J. M., 85, *335*
Nicely, P. E., 37, 56, 183, *333*
Nickerson, R. S., 270, *335*
Nilsson, L.- G., 268, *335*
Nixon, S. R., 302, *335*
Norman, D. A., x, 2, 10, 28, 30, 31, 36, 38, 44, 48, 49, 51, 52, 141, 156, 157, 167, 170, 191, 204, 205, 207, 214, 218, 260, 275, 288, 298, 305, *336, 339, 344, 345*
Norman, M. F., 93, 135, *336*

SUBJECT INDEX

HUMAN MEMORY: THEORY AND DATA